# Robert Altman's Subliminal Reality

**Commerce and Mass Culture Series**
Edited by Justin Wyatt

Robert Altman's Subliminal Reality
Robert T. Self

Sex and Money: Feminism and Political Economy in the Media
Eileen R. Meehan and Ellen Riordan, Editors

Directed by Allen Smithee
Jeremy Braddock and Stephen Hock, Editors

Sure Seaters: The Emergence of Art House Cinema
Barbara Wilinsky

Walter Wanger, Hollywood Independent
Matthew Bernstein

Hollywood Goes Shopping
David Desser and Garth S. Jowett, Editors

Screen Style: Fashion and Femininity in 1930s Hollywood
Sarah Berry

Active Radio: Pacifica's Brash Experiment
Jeff Land

# Robert Altman's Subliminal Reality

ROBERT T. SELF

MIN NE SO TA

Commerce and Mass Culture Series
University of Minnesota Press
Minneapolis • London

**For Losey and SB**



See pages 317–18 for copyright and publication information about material in this book that has been previously published.



Published by the University of Minnesota Press
111 Third Avenue South, Suite 290
Minneapolis, MN 55401-2520
http://www.upress.umn.edu

Library of Congress Cataloging-in-Publication Data

Self, Robert T., 1941–
Robert Altman's subliminal reality / Robert T. Self.
p. cm. — (Commerce and mass culture series)
Includes bibliographical references and index.
ISBN 0-8166-3789-X (HC : alk. paper) — ISBN 0-8166-3790-3 (PB : alk. paper)
1. Altman, Robert, 1925– .—Criticism and interpretation. I. Title.
II. Series.
PN1998.3.A48 S45 2002
791.43'0233'092—dc21

2001005280

Printed in the United States of America on acid-free paper



12 11 10 09 08 07 06 05 04 03 02 10 9 8 7 6 5 4 3 2 1

# Contents

Robert Altman in sunflower fields at Arles. The Museum of Modern Art/Film Stills Archive.

# Introduction: Authorial Voices

Classical narrative cinema assumes the inevitability of certain functions—the authority of causal order and explanation, the efficacy of human agency, and the unself-conscious power of the storytelling machines of popular culture. Robert Altman asserts, however, that the goal of his movies is to capture "subliminal reality," which recognizes the unspoken, and unspeakable, dimensions in human interactions. Subliminal reality resides in lyrical fictions, in metaphoric discourse, and in inexplicable human associations. It arises from anxiety and doubt about ultimate meanings and values. It posits behavior as a gamble with random consequences and defines relationships in curious patterns of repetition. It glimpses the efforts of marginal men and women caught in irresistible systems that shape desire and action. It engages an active audience awareness as necessary and complicit in the construction of consequence. Subliminal reality paints myriad surfaces of the human enterprise to suggest rhizomes of subterranean tales. It tells meandering and unclosed stories, it depicts insecure and vulnerable social identity, and it critiques the assured simplicities of the entertainment business as false and destructive visions of social reality.

Subliminal reality in the films of Robert Altman displays the continuing vitality of an American art cinema. This cinematic practice means many different things in film history: a disparate film production derivative of European directors after World War II, a short-lived aspect of the counterculture resistance to mainstream values during the Vietnam War, the personal and anti-Hollywood movies of a handful of experimental auteurs in the late 1960s, the energetic renewal of Hollywood after its decline in the face of the antitrust decrees of the U.S. Supreme Court and the success of television, and the institutionalized aesthetic of a developing audience of postwar baby boomers. Within a critical context that occasionally dismisses the concept of art cinema in American film as insolvent, incoherent, inaccurate, and impossible, I describe in this book the ways Altman's movies illustrate a dynamic and consistent art-cinema discourse. I understand this cinema to include an open and lyrical mode of storytelling; a persistent perception of social identity as fragile, fractured, and fragmentary; and a critical reflexivity about the nature of narrative communication itself. Altman's films systematically challenge the mainstream discourse of the movie industry in their play with story form, their idea of character, and their self-conscious distance from the industry. In this volume I examine Altman's films in terms of three particular aspects of art-cinema narration: its interrogation of classical Hollywood storytelling and popular genres, its representation of debilitated and ineffectual social individuality, and its reflexive analysis of the entertainment industry as complicit in cultural alienation.

Critical responses to Altman's films have consistently registered their challenging, innovative, enigmatic, and idiosyncratic quality. In 1975, Robin Wood described

> the centrality of Altman's work to the development of the modern American cinema . . . : the growing sense of disorientation and confusion of values, with the consequent sapping of any possibilities for affirmation; attitudes to the Hollywood of the past and its traditional genres; awareness of the modern European cinema and the desire to assimilate its techniques; the change . . . in the role and status of the director from studio employee to . . . all-determining artist. (2)

Virginia Wright Wexman in 1984 characterized the vision of Altman's films as "fragmented" and "alienating," as "puzzles" and "self-parody" ("Critical" 17). In 1988, Robert Kolker pointed out that "Altman, more than any other American director, has insisted upon positioning the viewer within the *process* of narrative, requesting that he or she observe and comprehend the interacting details that cohere in sometimes non-directed ways" (355). In 1991, Helene Keyssar asserted that Altman's films

> rarely leave us with a conceptual conclusion or with the satisfaction that the world projected is complete and distinct from the world in which we live. Either the attention of the film is dispersed, . . . or motivations for characters' behavior remain emphatically unknown and unknowable, . . . or our conventional engagement with the plot of the film carries the ambiance of a joke, and we sense that the center of the film exists elsewhere than in the obvious narrative. (16)

Edward O'Neill in 1996 wrote:

> Altman repeatedly examines communities through the fragmentation of the disparate and irreconcilable lives of their individuals, giving a prismatic portrait of an individualistic society. He has refused to create heroes and has consistently poked holes in the way such heroes are manufactured, whether by politics, the press, or cinema itself. Altman's portraits of particular places thus turn back on themselves and become self-portraits of the culture industry, documentary films about themselves as fiction. (471)

In this book I consider Altman's feature films from 1968 to 2000 and examine in detail twenty-one movies that most clearly delineate the relationships among the story form of the art film, the social subject of contemporary culture, and the system of popular culture entertainment. I seek less to describe Robert Altman as the cinematic auteur of personal movies than to provide a detailed analysis of how these films both adhere to and embody the characteristics of art-cinema narration. I do not attempt to evaluate these films as works of art; rather, I describe their formal structures and reading strategies, their reconstitution of traditional genres, their depiction of antiheroic men and women living at the margins of patriarchy, and their reflexive self-consciousness regarding entertainment's reaction to and responsibility for the malaise of modern culture.

Key aspects of art-cinema narration recall the innovative features of modernist discourse in the first half of the twentieth century. The approach of that discourse to form was experimental, iconoclastic, and disturbing in its rejection of nineteenth-century values and in its disruptive vision of the contemporary world. Modernist discourse depicted individuals as alienated from society, from other people, and from the self. It reflexively meditated on the necessity and efficacy of aesthetic communication. Modernism edited together fragmentary voices and images from Eastern and Western history, mythology, and art as it gazed at the wreckage of modernity from the burial grounds of Flanders Field and the sepulchral cities of Europe. It asserted the necessity of these images as defense against cultural ruin in the traditional arts of poetry, theater, fiction, music, and painting after the social dislocations of World War I. Its legacy emerged again from the nightmare of even larger killing fields in Europe and Asia after World War II.

The cinema of the late 1940s and the 1950s in Scandinavia, Japan, Italy, France, Poland, and Spain generated a large body of films characterized by experiments in form, by pessimism and irony in social vision, and by reflexivity in theme and method. Defined in distinction to the canonical forms of the classical Hollywood cinema, this international art cinema continued the modernist "rehearsals of discomposure"—its themes of alienation and despair; its disruptive modes of storytelling that foreground the difficulties of continuity, connection, and communication; its self-conscious exploration of art as an inefficacious mode of social or personal expression and reconciliation. Films such as *Last Year at Marienbad* (1961), *Through a Glass Darkly* (1961), *Ugetsu* (1953), *Ashes and Diamonds* (1958), *8½* (1963), *Viridiana* (1961), *L'Avventura* (1960), *Breathless* (1959), and *Shoot the Piano Player* (1960) reflected a cinematic energy of innovation, despair, and dark humor that flowed aggressively into American cinema at the end of the 1960s amid the social upheaval of the civil rights movement, the war in Vietnam, and the assassinations of John F. Kennedy and Martin Luther King Jr.

In this book I examine the continuation of the international art cinema in the films of Robert Altman. These films demonstrate the open-ended form of modernist storytelling. They tell fractured stories of fragmented social subjects from broken positions of audience intelligibility. They reflexively examine the current social milieu in terms of its mediation by the entertainment industry. Altman's films appropriate the modernist force of the art cinema to convey in inventive form the radical complexities of the modern world. Between a modernist point of view of alienation and the postmodern celebration of being lost in the fun house, these films locate marginal characters working stoically and ineffectively to succeed in a world beyond their knowledge or comprehension. The reflexivity of these films condemns the facile fiscal motivation of the entertainment industry as well as the power of the show business to capture, convey, and construct debilitating roles of social subjectivity.

## Art-Cinema Auteurs

Closely related to the development of the art cinema is the notion of the director as artist of the film, and Robert Altman embodies a number of the critical paradigms ascribed to the art-cinema auteur. The concept of cinematic authorship over the decades of Altman's career has diversely posited the director as author of the movie, artist of the work, effect of the film, and agency of the show business. From a perspective of aesthetic romanticism, the director is the artist who possesses the power of a higher imagination, whose personal vision and genius drive the ultimate craft and art of the film. In the 1960s, Andrew Sarris popularized the French *politique des auteurs* in American film criticism, and by the end of the decade under the aegis of the new Hollywood cinema and academic auteurism, the director signified the creative presence behind the work, the source of expressive power that served indeed as the guarantor of its art. Auteur criticism then sought the organic wholes produced by the director as author and evaluated films according to coherence of artistic vision and craft. By the end of the 1970s, however, Hollywood exchanged its interest in the director as rebellious experimenter for the polished film-school productivity of young directors. The Lucas-Spielberg invention of the blockbuster with *Jaws* (1975) and *Star Wars* (1977) ushered "postclassical" Hollywood into its late-century success of big budgets, big-name stars and directors, and big box-office receipts. Film criticism then calibrated its vision between the romantic conceptualization of the director as artist and the industrial conceptualization of the director as an entrepreneur of big-ticket entertainment. The auteur critic came to recognize the director as the dominant signifier—among others such as the cinematographer, production designer, editor, and screenwriter—for the consistencies of narration, theme, and style discernible as an effect of a particular collection of films having the same director. Later, as the interests of poststructuralism developed during the 1980s, film criticism also recognized the "fiction of the author" or the "death of the author" and began to read films symptomatically, less for order than for disorder, to discover the textual other, the shadow, the unspeakable referenced there. Auteur criticism thus came to recognize, as Silvio Gaggi observes, "a radical intertextuality to all art that, when acknowledged, forces us to recognize that cultures create works as much as individuals. There is a social unconscious in any work that may or may not be adequately acknowledged by the artist who created it or by its audience" (*From Text* 29).

The success of the "high-concept" film in Hollywood in the 1990s reestablished the director as a figure of importance both in the industry and in film scholarship. Economic criticism located the director as a function of production in the cultural circulation of contracts, budgets, production processes, distribution, and ticket sales that constituted the business of moviemaking. An agent in the pitches and deals, the buying and selling of cinematic commerce, the director represented a new focus on capital investments and merchandising rather than on aesthetic investments in the cinematic work. The director emerged as an industrial worker within a system of production and a collaborative function of interpretation within the cognitive system of popular consumption. As Timothy Corrigan argues, the "auteurist marketing of films aims to guarantee a relationship between audience and movie whereby an intentional and authorial agency governs, as a kind of brand name vision whose aesthetic meanings and values have already been determined" ("Auteurs" 40). The success of high-concept films such as *Superman* (1978), *Raiders of the Lost Ark* (1981), *E.T. the Extra-Terrestrial* (1982), *Back to the Future* (1985), *Jurassic Park* (1993), and *Titanic* (1997) established a new pantheon of commercially successful authorial names: a Spielberg movie, a Lucas film, a Zemeckis movie.

Each of these perspectives on the director characterizes a different Robert Altman. The introductions that have routinely accompanied the numerous published interviews with Altman over his four-decade career illustrate his shifting identities within the Hollywood system and its mass-media support systems, both popular and professional. In 1976, for instance, a *Playboy* interviewer located the star value of artistic rebellion: "No director since Sam Peckinpah has provoked such passionate disputes; perhaps no director has ever taken such undisguised delight in watching himself become a cult figure and quasi legend under the very noses of the incumbent Hollywood moguls, who still consider him a freewheeling maverick with an erratic track record" (Williamson 53). A *Rolling Stone* interview in 1992 documented the exile's return:

> Just when we thought we wouldn't have Altman to kick around anymore, he came back with three impressive pieces: *Tanner '88,* in which he and Garry Trudeau ran a fictional character for president, was a clever, compelling mix of fact and fiction made for HBO. *Vincent and Theo,* in 1990, emerged as a slashing portrayal of a punkish Van Gogh and his brother and resurrected Altman's high-art credentials. And now, improbably, back to Hollywood waltzes this aging, acid dumpling of a man, where he turns out a killer—*The Player*—masquerading as a sheepish fluffy comedy. (Breskin 74)

Such conceptualizations of the author establish a wide range of schemata that aid us in hearing the voices that constitute the films of Robert Altman: mainstream industrial relations, audiences at the cinematic fringe, cultural success and rebellion, comebacks, generic patterns, mass-media criticism. The apparatus of film, with its mix of many crafts, its plurality of producers, its range of spectators, quite literally models the idea of the polyphonic text with many authorial hands. Within this apparatus the name "Robert Altman," as Foucault suggests about the name of the author, "characterizes a particular manner of existence of discourse. . . . It points to the existence of certain groups of discourse and refers to the status of this discourse within a society and culture" (284). "Robert Altman" is a name that consistently represents cinematic heterogeneity and plurality against the mainstream of the blockbuster approach to Hollywood moviemaking that has developed over the last quarter century. At the same time, that name designates, in opposition, the set of stabilities characteristic of the high-concept film: "films with strong marketing hooks which could act as 'tent poles' for the studio's distribution schedule." Altman's films, by contrast, "usually lacking stars, an exploitable premise, and an obvious marketing approach deviated significantly from this overall change in the industry" (Wyatt, "Economic Constraints" 59). An "Altman movie" signals uneasy relations of production, complex and chaotic stories, and failure at the box office.

The classical narrative cinema, despite the desire of its discourse to speak only unauthored stories, seeks to establish a wholeness and clarity of meaning, a totality that posits an origin, an authority, an author as guarantor of meaning. Unlike this classical cinema, which aims at a harmony of meaning and form, the signature "Robert Altman" constantly restates the heterogeneous, the contradictory, the plurality—qualities that threaten, delimit, and define the apparent unity sought by dominant strains of auteur criticism. Rather than the singular author of the thirty-some films that bear his name, "Robert Altman" is a subject position that, in the words of Stephen Heath, "allows at once the articulation of contradictions in the film text . . . and the recognition of a heterogeneity of structures, codes, languages at work in film" (*Questions* 217). The name of this author is contiguous with the variety of productive forces that intersect, cohere, assemble, and disperse across some three dozen American films during the late 1960s, the 1970s, the 1980s, and the 1990s. And at least half a dozen modes of narrative discourse are signified as a function of the name of the author Robert Altman. Each of these perspectives—technological, industrial, societal, formal, psychological, and academic—authorizes "a notional coherence" that "provides the means for us to grasp the text in the moment of its production before us" (Nowell-Smith, "Note" 232).

Two of Altman's films represent the plurality of authorial voices that constitutes any film, but modernist narration in particular. *Buffalo Bill and the Indians* (1976) depicts the complex interrelationship of self, text, and authorship. Not only the Wild West Show but its star as well are constructs crisscrossed by a number of conflicting egos. The hero "Buffalo Bill" is a fiction authored by history and legend, by the show business and its press agents, by producers and writers, by William F. Cody the individual and the character, and reflexively even by the star who plays him—a "combination of Custer, Gable, Redford, and me," as Paul Newman has described him (quoted in McGilligan 443). The film amounts to an analysis of the artistic self seen as a variety of evolving constraints within the entertainment industry and, as such, develops a theory of authorship like the one described here. The self in the fiction, the film itself, and the critical viewing self are all the products of competing authors.

*Popeye* (1980), on the other hand, demonstrates authorial complexity externally in the terms of its production. Robert Evans, of *Chinatown* (1974) fame, produced the film for Paramount and Walt Disney. Jules Feiffer, successful playwright and *Playboy* cartoonist, adapted the script from the E. C. Segar cartoon strip of the 1930s. Grammy Award winner Harry Nilsson wrote the music and lyrics. Ray Walston, Shelley Duvall, and Robin Williams (in his first film role) starred. Giuseppe Rotunno, of Fellini's *Satyricon* (1969) and *City of Women* (1980) and Bob Fosse's *All That Jazz* (1979), was director of photography. And Robert Altman directed—a strong mixture of accomplished, talented authors and strong, independent, conflicting egos, "the weirdest possible combination," Altman has said (quoted in McGilligan 491)—all with different interpretations of the meaning they intended in the film.

When the credits roll at the end of Altman's movies, they remind us that the signature "Robert Altman" always includes the names of other artists. The flexibility and freedom accorded other craftspeople by the director are well-known features of those films—whether the craftsperson is Richard Portman, sound mixer on Altman films through much of the 1970s and head of Lion's Gate 8 Sound, or Wolf Kroeger, the major author/craftsman/technician of the look in *Quintet* (1979), *Popeye,* and *Streamers* (1983) as art director or set designer in these films. Rick Altman points out that James E. Webb Jr., "in charge of sound recording for all Altman films from 1974–1978," was centrally responsible for the multitrack richness of sound in those films ("24-Track" 5). The compelling lyricism in the palette of blues and greens splashed, illuminated, scoriated by gold and red in *That Cold Day in the Park* (1969), *MASH* (1970), *McCabe & Mrs. Miller* (1971), *Images* (1972), *California Split* (1974), and *Quintet* may derive from their common production designer, Leon Ericksen, or variously from the cinematography of Paul Lohmann, Lászlό Kovács, and Vilmos Zsigmond. Patrick McGilligan claims that art directors "Chet Allen, Leon Ericksen, and in the late

1970s and early 1980s, Wolf Kroeger—for three decades . . . advanced the 'look' that Altman is famous for: the clutter of hidden meaning, the smoke, the nets, the gauze, the glass and mirrors, the symbolically charged color schemes, the hermetic interiors and the one-world exterior" (285–86). Both Altman and biographer McGilligan describe Scott Bushnell, who has produced all of Altman's films since *Thieves Like Us* (1974), as an authorial force in those films (50). The particular rhythm that characterizes the rich narrative tapestries of the more recent films *Vincent & Theo* (1990), *The Player* (1992), *Short Cuts* (1993), *Prêt-à-Porter* (1994), and *Kansas City* (1996) is largely due to the craft and authority of editor Geraldine Peroni. The look of every Altman film from *Streamers* in 1983 to *Dr. T & the Women* in 2000 represents the aesthetic vision of the director's son, Stephen Altman. "All these contributions compound one another, grow out of one another," says Altman (in Kaplan and Dorr). "These film are collaborations," in which the director figures as an electrician—"somebody has to be there to turn on the light switch and to turn it off"—or a "benevolent monarch. . . . I make them do what it is that they got into this business to do in the first place, which is to create" (quoted in Maltin 28). Helene Keyssar argues: "The constant in Altman's function as director is not only the presence of his own point of view but also the intersection of that perspective with others' points of view. . . . [He] appears to see his role as coordinator of many readings of several texts that become one film" (12). Altman describes his role this way:

> None of it certainly comes all from my brain or point of view. The script sets up an arena that we're dealing with; then I have to people that arena, and if I told every person how they should behave or act, it would be a very lopsided, onesided, arrogant kind of film. . . . The writer, the originator, the blueprint makers, the artist in these cases can sometimes be the actor, the producer, the director, the collaborative team that's making the film. *(The Player)*

This is so even, indeed, when Altman scripts the film himself, as he did after some tension with John Grisham in the adaptation of *The Gingerbread Man* (1998); in the film's credits, "Robert Altman" dissolves into the pseudonym "Al Hayes."

Altman constantly designates actors as the "main artists" of his films, and Maurice Yacowar has chronicled their authoritative energy: Shelley Duvall, for instance, with major or minor roles in seven Altman films, brings the anorexic body image and quirky roles of Millie in *3 Women*

(1977) and Keechie in *Thieves Like Us* to her performance of Olive Oyl in the role she was "born to play" (14). The force of his career—"a constellation of intertextual cues" (Simon and Spence 72)—grounds Paul Newman's address to the audience about Buffalo Bill's image as a star in that film. *Prêt-à-Porter* contrasts two different acting authorities in the relationship between Julia Roberts and Tim Robbins on one hand and Sophia Loren and Marcello Mastroianni on the other. When Jack Lemmon appears in the middle of *Short Cuts,* the narration asks the audience to construct his character in terms of a long and successful set of antecedent films, even as Andie MacDowell authors a new role in the early stages of her acting career. In a most telling rhetorical figure, *Cookie's Fortune* (1999) concludes with the director Camille (Glenn Close) lying in a jail cell contemplating suicide and the actress Cora (Julianne Moore) savoring a new self-concept discovered in portraying Salomé.

The well-known freedom for actors to develop their roles and to improvise their own lines—and in *Nashville* (1975) and *Kansas City* the music they perform—equally shapes the experience of an Altman film. The schizophrenia of *Images* is reflected in the duality of Susannah York's character, one side of which reads aloud a fantasy tale titled *In Search of Unicorns,* written and published by Susannah York. The low-angle slow zoom in on Barbara Jean as she sings "My Idaho Home" before her assassination is not just characterization in the fiction of *Nashville,* but a documentary as well of a musical performance by actress-musician-songwriter Ronee Blakley. Perhaps the most dramatic example of this aspect of Altman's films is Sam Shepard in the role of Eddie in the film *Fool for Love* (1985), giving substance to the role written by Shepard in his own play and adapted by him for the screen. *The Player* aggressively foregrounds the voice of the actor as some sixty different actors perform what Altman calls the toughest roles of their lives because they must enact themselves. In directing, he told them, "you're representing yourself, so you're fully responsible for your selves, and it's probably the hardest acting job they've ever done, because the one person they never do play is themselves very much" *(The Player).*

The productive freedom of an Altman project has also been widely recognized within the industrial pressures of the box office, the Hollywood production system, the Academy of Motion Picture Arts and Sciences—all the relations of production, distribution, consumption, and recognition. Within the industry, Altman's constant manipulation of various genres during the transitional 1970s amounted to an ongoing research and development effort on behalf of one of Hollywood's most successful commodities. Most of his earlier films are readable both against the long historical genre tradition and against more financially successful films released during the same period in the same genres: *McCabe & Mrs. Miller* against *Little Big Man* (1970), *Brewster McCloud* (1970) against *Bullitt* (1968), *Thieves Like Us* against *Bonnie and Clyde* (1967), *Quintet* against *Star Wars, Popeye* against *Superman,* and so on.

Altman's films constitute a subcode of the Hollywood fringe. They register a rebellious voice in the system of deals, egos, production values, and stars of the film industry that, nevertheless, extracts its dues. At the beginning of his Hollywood career with *Countdown* (1968), Altman later recollected, "Jack Warner hated it with a passion" (quoted in McGilligan 275). The dramatic failure of *Buffalo Bill and the Indians* to work as another film about heroes like Rocky Balboa led producer Dino De Laurentiis to drop Altman as the director of *Ragtime* (1981). The failure of *Quintet* at the box office and with the critics influenced the dismal performance of an entirely different film in the same year, *A Perfect Couple* (1979), and led Twentieth Century Fox not to release *Health* (1979) at all. After the big-name extravaganza and box-office failure of *Popeye,* Altman sold Lion's Gate Films and left Hollywood to stage off-Broadway plays and shoot film in super 16mm. The public fight over final-cut authority between Altman and PolyGram in 1997 doomed *The Gingerbread Man* to ongoing litigation between director and producer and to an initial release in only two theaters, one in New York and one in Los Angeles.

All of Altman's films were independently produced in the 1980s, and the production of his films since the 1990s by companies like Spelling Entertainment, Fine Line, Miramax, and October reflect the developing role of independent production in face of the blockbuster commitments of the major studios. These studios in the late stages of Altman's career have continued to identify him as a rebel and an outsider. Tellingly, *Cookie's Fortune* premiered in 1999 at the Sundance Film Festival, the national festival putatively for independent filmmakers. From *MASH* to *Popeye* in the 1970s, from *Come Back to the 5 & Dime, Jimmy Dean, Jimmy Dean* (1982) to *Vincent & Theo* in the 1980s, from *The Player* to *Dr. T & the Women* in the 1990s and 2000, Altman's films ask to be read in a constant tension with the dominant process of American film-making across the last three decades of the twentieth century. Justin Wyatt shows persuasively that "Altman's career can be conceptualized according to economic, industrial and institutional components which have, in turn, aided and aggravated his filmmaking" ("Economic Constraints" 52).

Perhaps the clearest models of the high-concept style dominant in Hollywood during this period derive from titles associated with such names as Sydney Pollack and Steven Spielberg. These films promote star images such as Jane Fonda, Robert Redford, Dustin Hoffman, Meryl Streep, and Tom Cruise. They reconstruct, without confusion, traditional and easily sold romance and adventure in *They Shoot Horses, Don't They?* (1969), *Three Days of the Condor* (1975), *The Electric Horseman* (1979), and the Indiana Jones adventure movies. They take experimental steps and win Academy Awards, like *Tootsie* (1982) and *Schindler's List* (1993). They make lots of money at the box office, like *Out of Africa* (1985), *Jaws, Raiders of the Lost Ark, E.T.,* and *Jurassic Park.* J. Hoberman compares Altman and Spielberg in the seventies:

> Altman—who worked in (and disassembled) every genre from sci-fi and war films through musicals and *noir* to the western and the gangster film—may have been . . . "The director of the seventies," but he didn't have a single solid commercial hit between *MASH* (1970) and *Popeye* (1980). Spielberg—who specialized in putting genres back together—became the most bankable director who ever lived. ("Ten Years" 35)

While Altman's films are radar echoes bouncing off the hulls of Hollywood tonnage, the social voices of the 1970s and 1980s provide further contextual paradigms for authorizing meaning in these films. *MASH* emerges from anguish and hostility over the Vietnam War and its managers. *McCabe & Mrs. Miller* laments the John Waynes who sold out to the power of those managers and the empty rhetoric of politicians. The cynicism and despair of the Watergate era authorizes the alienation and bleakness of *The Long Goodbye* (1973) and *Thieves Like Us.* In 1976, the American culture celebrated its two hundredth birthday with pride, disillusionment, exhaustion, and extravaganza. It made souvenir plates, staged big parades and historical pageants, elected Jimmy Carter president, and performed *Nashville* and *Buffalo Bill and the Indians* as indictments of American history and popular values. In the late 1970s, the oil crisis, the Iranian hostage situation, and economic recession produced both what the president ministerially called "a national crisis of spirit" and the apocalyptic imagination in *Quintet.* The time was right for a new hero, and in 1980 America got Ronald Reagan, *Superman,* and *Popeye.*

But the particular mental, emotional, personal, and social disaffection that traced across American life from the counterculture movement of the late 1960s to the dissolution of the fifty-year-old progressive Democratic coalition in the 1980s yielded to the economic high times at the end of the century. The negative understanding of American society gradually running down from an entropy of means and faith slowly transformed into the developing mood of optimism that surrounded the end of the Cold War and the international threat of communism. Even as the Reagan years gave way to the greater social optimism of George Bush's "thousand points of light" and the political youthfulness of the Clinton administration, Altman's films continued to chronicle disease in the American political and social community. Meanings emerge in many of these films from the backdrop of the American presidential elections. *Nashville* references the 1976 elections that brought Carter to the White House, and *Health* parodies the campaigns of Reagan and Carter in 1980. Altman claims that "*Health* could only have been made when it was made, and that was the end of the Carter era. I did want that film out during the conventions" (quoted in Braudy and Kolker, "Part I" 7). *Secret Honor* (1984) plays Nixon's defeat at the hands of invisible powermongers against Reagan's reelection campaign of 1984. *Kansas City* sets its story during the city elections of 1934 and its negative vision of gendered and racial American politics amid the presidential campaigns of Dole and Clinton in 1996. Perhaps *Tanner '88* (1988) most clearly epitomizes this string of films that may be read as critiques of American power and values. The eleven-hour HBO series ran the fictional Jack Tanner against the "real" candidates of the 1988 presidential campaign in which George Bush ultimately defeated Michael Dukakis, and like all those candidates, the production promoted its own platform for reform. Contemporary social, political, and cultural issues authorize central meanings in the films of Robert Altman.

Aesthetic and biographical auteurism examines the effective and intentional language of art primarily as it is reflected by the story and as it constitutes familiar thematic and structural components of the director's narrative vision. Certainly Altman's movies tell stories and constantly reveal what Jean-Pierre Baudry calls "the visible imprint and the all too noticeable dominance of the cinematographic signifier by an analyzable subject" (70, 75). Indeed, from a perspective of aesthetic formalism, part of the "Altman style" and "vision" is just the open-endedness of the creative process that foregrounds expressive discourse at the expense of story. Altman has encouraged the traditional artistic approach to his work through his many interviews and in his self-conscious descriptions of himself as "an artist, possibly, of popular culture" (quoted in Kloman et al. 24). He evokes the sense of the procreative auteur when he compares his films to his children: "None of your children is alike; none has the same success in the world, but you love them all for themselves and equally, and I love all my films" (quoted in Braudy and Kolker, "Part II" 13). And he has repeatedly urged the image of Robert Altman, auteur, as a painter and not a storyteller: "I try to show what I see, the way I see things" (quoted in Braudy and Kolker, "Part I" 3). In reaction to the communal viewing by the entire crew of the daily rushes on the typical Altman shoot, Giuseppe Rotunno has observed that "with Visconti, no one should talk. Everything was silent. . . . With Bob, everything is free. It is the difference between one painter and another" (quoted in Terry 143). Altman asserts, "I'm in the looking business" (quoted in Phipps).

Different narrative reading strategies also shape an awareness of multiple voices in Altman's films. Audiences conditioned by the terms of intelligibility and optimism of classical narrative cinema find the polyphonic quality of Altman's films difficult to comprehend. On the other hand, audiences familiar with the symbolic voices and the pessimism of modernist art read the films' discursive cues of realist and expressive representation for authorial ambiguity. They find coherence then between the restless zoom shots and the themes of the films, between the elaborate overlapping of sound and a vision of reality. Such readings find Leonard Cohen's music either highly appropriate to the situations in the story world of *McCabe & Mrs. Miller* or appropriate to the stylistic rhythms of editing rather than story. The eerie, cacophonous sounds created by Stomu Yamashta, Gerald Busby, Tom Pierson, and Gabriel Yared for *Images, 3 Women, Quintet,* and *Vincent & Theo,* respectively, reflect the musical intrusion of a desire beyond narrative. *Nashville* and *A Wedding* (1978), *Short Cuts,* and *Prêt-à-Porter* explode characterization into so many fragments as to disengage narrative continuity and to force reader reliance on intertextual codes for the construction of meanings that forever then reside outside the films. Indeed, as the spatial and temporal systems of these films constantly outrun the logical systems, Altman's films attract interest as much for the terms of their discursive construction as for the significance of their stories.

This formalistic play with the codes of classical realistic cinema suggests the inadequacy of the unitary function of the author in Altman's films, whether located in the director, the narratives, or the audience. Destruction of textual coherence and unity amounts to a renunciation of the symbolic order, a retreat from the wholeness of ego under the laws of the sentence and the narrative, with their subject positions of "I" in language and "eye" in cinema. The specular image afforded the viewer is refracted, splintered, an empty place, and the subject position of the spectator, unable to locate the ideal ego in the imaginary, is simultaneously destabilized. This psychological paradigm for the multivalent discourse of author and film emerges aggressively in films like *Images, 3 Women, Jimmy Dean,* and *Cookie's Fortune,* where the central narrative figures are those of women constantly depicted in mirrored images and broken relationships. The apparent dominant character in each of these stories is literally reflected in the mirror of artistry that achieves its shapes, that authors its fictions as an act of self-renunciation. In *Images,* Cathryn's double, her alter ego, recasts her fears into a child's fairy tale of monsters and unicorns and retreats into silence. In *3 Women,* Willie authorizes the triangles of the story in murals that temporally precede it and similarly retreats into silence. In *Cookie's Fortune,* Camille's production of *Salomé* reflects her anxious and unstable relationship with authority even as it depicts her desire to outwit the law and silence male prophecy.

These films stand against the dominant practice of "neoclassical Hollywood" in their stories, their sense of social identification, and their attitude toward entertainment itself. A major move of the international art cinema is to foreground the role of the director, both as an artistic persona that distinguishes art-cinema production from the industrial factories of Hollywood and as a position of interpretation within the film. Certainly the biographical Robert Altman performs the fascinating role of late-century cinematic auteur, the renegade artist battling and alienating crass Hollywood producers, assaulting the story sense of mainstream audiences, and courting the academic and art-house connoisseur of film. The story is a fascinating one: subversive success in the 1970s, industrial and critical exile to Paris in the 1980s, and dramatic return to contradictory acclaim in the 1990s. But another author emerges from the work of the films. Auteur criticism and modernist cinema both posit personal expressivity as a central tenet of interpretation, but that personality is constructed a posteriori as an effect of the text. David Bordwell argues that the interpreter resolves the contradiction between realism and expressionism in the art cinema as authorial subjectivity ("Art Cinema" 56). Consequently, the signifier "Robert Altman" is both a moviemaker from Kansas City and a subject position within a series of films that variously demonstrate the open-ended form of art-cinema narration, that tell fractured stories of fractured social individuals with fractured positions of audience comprehension, that reflexively examine the contemporary social milieu in terms of its mediation by show business.

The signature of Robert Altman has never been very popular with the general audience, perhaps because the range of authorial voices described here charts the vicissitudes of the divided self. Much of the energy of modernist art rests in the tensions between the historical and the metaphorical author and in those among impersonal, assertive, and decentered selves. The recognition and even acceptance of divergent egos and excess selves is not merely linguistic or psychological or postmodern, but personal. Altman's films record not in anguish but in excitement a plethora of narrative and cultural and personal voices. A central problem in the popular appreciation of Altman's movies has been the perceived bleakness of a vision that seldom has formally closed down the eruptions of plot conflict or resolved the conflicts of personal abilities and commitments, that has depicted the multiplicity of individual characters or multiplied the "central" character into many individuals leading contingent and disconnected lives.

A power of these films, however, resides in just those ways they evoke, both textually and intertextually, the competing discourses and subjectivities of modern life. There is no self in these texts, but there are many selves—creative, fictional, and interpretative. *Citizen Kane* (1941) is instructive in this regard. The "authentic" Charles Foster Kane is a fiction variously read and interpreted by the narrative voices of the plot. There are many Kanes; it just depends on who is talking about him, the selves who write him. Unified authors, unified stories, and unified selves are to be found in such works only after serious reduction of the films.

## Structure of the Book

Like Stanley Kubrick (born in 1928), Robert Altman (born in 1925) represents an older alternative voice in Hollywood, and thus as its shadow provides a clarifying focus on the industrial model. In this volume, I undertake an examination of Altman's movies with an interest less in what artist Robert Altman intended, and in how his art succeeds or fails, than in what the form and structure, style, and stance of his films, from *Countdown* in 1968 to *Dr. T & the Women* in 2000 document about the possibilities of narrative film. In this examination, I understand the author not as the creative artist outside the film but as a figure in the film, a position of both experimental construction and industrial deconstruction. I attempt specifically to define elements of a Hollywood art cinema by examining the films of one of its major practitioners. I employ the paradigms of both classical and art-cinema narration to situate the particular formal work of Altman's films. I employ the syntactic and semantic model of popular genre films to examine Altman's rewriting of the traditional generic forms. I employ knowledge about the social construction of individual identity to examine gendered subjectivity in Altman's films. I employ notions of reflexive self-consciousness to examine Altman's various refusals of classical narrative order as a critique of the entertainment industry. I view Altman's films as frequently reflexive sites of social contestation, divergence, and dispersal at the levels of the story, the narration, and the production.

I will argue that Altman's complex narrative practice can best be understood through three paradigms of the international art cinema—a mercurial story form that employs popular genres in innovative ways, depicts social identity in pessimistic terms, and comments self-consciously on the discursive effects of entertainment. These three dimensions of the art cinema shape the three major sections of the book. In the first chapter I posit the terms of reading demanded by the approach to cinematic representation that Altman calls subliminal reality, and in the last chapter I summarize the hypertextual effects of subliminal reality as the way Altman's films challenge dominant reading strategies and critical interpretation. In between appear three sections titled "Narrative Formations," "Living in Patriarchy," and "Putting on the Show." In the first of these, chapter 2 uses *MASH* to characterize the mode and style of the new American cinema at the end of the 1960s. Chapter 3 defines the formal properties of art-cinema narration in Altman's films, and chapter 4 examines how Altman's art cinema deploys traditional genre forms to develop interrogative films. In the second section, chapters 5 and 6 describe the broken ego of art-cinema modernism in the representation of masculine and feminine identities. In the third section, chapters 7 and 8 examine the self-conscious preoccupations of art cinema as a reflexive interrogation of the entertainment industry.

In chapter 1, I demonstrate, with a close analysis of *Kansas City*, the specific terms of reading required by Altman's movies, and I define the three cognitive categories that organize this book: the fluidity and instability of modernist narrative structure, the debilitating complexities of social identity, and the cultural impact of the entertainment industry. The 1930s story world of *Kansas City*'s working-class blacks and whites, innovative African American jazz, and big-city machine politics illustrates how heterogeneous narration shapes interpretation; how race, class, and gender shape social subjectivity; how entertainment reflects, reifies, and resists marginality.

Chapter 2 locates Altman's films within a particular historical setting. The counterculture, antiwar politics of the late 1960s and early 1970s opened a social door of dramatic change throughout American life, a door through which a number of directors like Robert Altman, with experience working in the conventions of classical Hollywood and television, walked into a new cinematic dispensation. In this chapter I trace Altman's evolution as a major director in the new American cinema in the late 1960s with three films: *Countdown*'s race toward the moon is classical Hollywood narration; offbeat style and story and insecure women in *That Cold Day in the Park* begin to suggest divergence from the mainstream; and then, in 1970, comes *MASH.* Close analysis of sound in this antiwar combat film illustrates the renaissance's experimental reconstruction of classical Hollywood practice. *MASH* reveals the complex way in which Altman's narrative form elicits viewer comprehension. It demonstrates the splintered construction of social identity in these films. It illuminates the reflexivity whereby these films frequently signal their own existence and distance the viewer from the transparent evocation of fictional reality practiced by classical cinema.

The next two chapters specifically delineate how Altman's films reflect the formal characteristics of an "Americanized art cinema" (Thompson and Bordwell 710). In chapter 3, I map the films and their cultural landscapes with the surveyor tools of art-cinema narration developed by David Bordwell and others. I examine how this practice employs the spatial and temporal aspects of film coequally and metaphorically with the cause-effect logic of narrative, how it submits to social criticism the faults of contemporary cultural experience and challenges its underlying ideology, and how it assumes a self-consciously expressionistic stance toward narrative voice in an effort to renew as well as critique the humanistic perspective of the classical narrative cinema. I closely analyze *3 Women* as an illustration of the reading strategies requisite for the art cinema: a comprehension of the play among divergent signifying systems as the dialectic between fictive characterization and artistic expressivity that ultimately renders more ironic, more complex, and more ambiguous the realism portrayed in the narrative.

A major aspect of the French New Wave films of Chabrol, Truffaut, and Godard was their appropriation of American narrative genres to forge a link between the modernist aversion and the postmodern embrace of popular mass culture. Chapter 4 looks at ways the American art cinema has interrogated and reconstituted the name-brand products of the classical Hollywood, the popular narrative genres. Where the classical genres once provided audiences with a conventional, familiar syntax and semantics that allowed an easy reading of the story, the genres provide auteurs in the American art cinema structural frames within which to arouse and then challenge, rather than satisfy, audience expectations. As Thomas Schatz writes, "The effect is to distance the viewer from the immediate narrative and consequently from the genre's traditional interpretation of American history, thus encouraging the viewer to renegotiate the values and belief systems underpinning that standard interpretation" (*Old Hollywood* 240). Altman's films interrogate the forms and themes of westerns, musicals, films noir, detective stories, gangster films, science fiction films, screwball comedies, and fantasy films. In chapter 4, I consider first the vicissitudes of romantic love in *A Perfect Couple* and *Popeye* and examine how preoccupations with biological reproduction and with insecurity, loneliness, and death regularly recur in the socially constructed drive toward heterosexual romance. I also look at the adventure genre in Altman's films, in particular *Quintet*'s depressing science fiction vision of a heat-dead future and *McCabe & Mrs. Miller*'s painted canvas of the ineffectuality of individual endeavor in mythic western narrative. These films favor the poetic as much as the plotted dimensions of narrative discourse, but the popular conventions of the romance, western, and science fiction provide the store of images from which they construct their verses and stanzas and by which these films communicate the continuing art-cinema image of alienation and despair.

The chapters in Part II examine the terms of contemporary social identity reflected in Altman's films—in particular the way in which conceptions of the self, individuality, and identity are functions of socially constructed gender roles. These films reveal the contradictory, powerless, isolated, and fragmented modern ego. Their stories seldom provide the context for significant, heroic action; rather, they reveal spaces that enclose and forces that act upon a multiplicity of selves. Nearly all of Altman's films challenge the primacy of the male image in American culture, whether in the unusual manipulation of iconic presences like Paul Newman, Warren Beatty, or Richard Gere or in the reconstruction of generic formulations to assert the inefficacy of male action. Nixon succumbs to elite treachery in *Secret Honor.* Van Gogh dies by his own hand in *Vincent & Theo.* Jack Lemmon's character dies emotionally from his infidelity in *Short Cuts.* Marcello Mastroianni's character sleeps in sexual incapacity in *Prêt-à-Porter.* Johnny dies from racist incompetence in

*Kansas City.* Griffin Mill falls into success by murder and greed in *The Player.* Sully Travis is swept out of his successful medical practice by the whirlwind of deconstructing gender roles and is literally blown away by a tornado in *Dr. T & the Women.* Films like *Brewster McCloud, Come Back to the 5 & Dime, Jimmy Dean, Jimmy Dean,* and *Short Cuts* display a culture where the masculine principle is psychologically and socially dehumanizing. Through detailed analysis of *Secret Honor, Tanner '88,* and *The Gingerbread Man* in chapter 5, I chart the debilitations of masculinity within the contexts of patriarchal authority. Together with the exploration of the displacement of women from roles of social power and control, Altman's films develop a subjectivity of the guilty male, insecure and defensive, in retreat from the self-determining pressure of the phallocentric culture.

Chapter 6 examines the converse of this image in the films about women that are the most systematically ambiguous and psychologically subjective of Altman's films. They represent the female image under patriarchy described by Judith Fetterley: "Bereft, disinherited, cast out, woman is the Other, the Outsider . . . never really child because never allowed to be fully self-indulgent; never really adult because never permitted to be fully responsible" (iv). *Images, 3 Women, Come Back to the 5 & Dime, Jimmy Dean, Jimmy Dean,* and *Cookie's Fortune* graphically convey crises in verbal, sexual, and economic production and exchange that constitute the female subject in all of Altman's films. The fictional, metaphoric, and actual destruction of the male and the related construction of divergent, pathological, interdependent femininity comes to its most forceful expression in *Jimmy Dean,* where Joe's self-renunciative castration gives birth to his feminine identity, Joanne. When his fatherhood of the bastard, mentally deficient son Jimmy Dean is displaced by Mona onto an imaginary relationship with the movie star James Dean, Joe renounces the power of fatherhood. The films about women in particular reveal the construction of the self as an action of retreat from phallic authority. Self-knowledge, self-confidence, self-certainty, and self-assessment are all casualties of the art-cinema modernism in Altman's films.

Modernist discourse frequently looks at itself in the act of creation, and the chapters in the last section of this book describe the third major paradigm that characterizes Altman's art cinema: industrial awareness and reflexivity. The antitheses of modernist art—the chasms between history and value, between belief and action, between reality and perception, between perception and communication, between artist and medium—have forged a tradition of reflexivity as a "process by which texts, both literary and cinematic, foreground their own production, their authorship, their intertextual influences, their reception, or their enunciation" (Stam xiii). These chapters describe how the reflexive mode in Altman's films employs "various counter-techniques to undermine the authority of the omniscient author, of the closure of the 'final' ending, of the definitive interpretation" (Waugh 13), how it urges an awareness of the plurality and multiplicity of meaning and describes for the viewer or reader an active, analytic, engaged rather than a passive, distanced position before the film. At the same time, rather than a self-consciousness that reflects the movieness of the films themselves, Altman's films develop a reflexivity that explores the world of mass media, that questions the motives of production, that critiques the effects of "the show business."

Chapter 7 explores the range of debilitations precipitated by the contemporary country music scene in *Nashville* and the confusions of historical and fictional identity perpetrated by the "stage picture show" in *Buffalo Bill and the Indians.* Chapter 8 details the condemnation of Hollywood producers who get away with murder in *The Player* and the contradictions of sexual identity and fashion in *Prêt-à-Porter.* This hostility toward the relationship between entertainment and illusion motivated Altman's first film, a 1957 documentary on the image of James Dean, and thematically structures his latest work—because, in Altman's words, "I don't like the idea of superstars—they're an excuse for the masses not to think about their own problems" (quoted in Allen 28). The fictions of these films comment on the entertainment-making business, the system of mass-media fantasy and storytelling, their constructions of reality, and the effects of those constructions on social subjectivity.

Finally, in the last chapter I return, after considering this evidence of form, identity, and industry, to the critical impulse of the first chapter—an effort to restate the terms of reading generated by the modernist narrative form, by the representation of marginal subjectivity, and by the reflexivity of Altman's films, with reference to *Short Cuts* in particular. Altman's adaptation of Raymond Carver's short stories in *Short Cuts* activates certain strategies not only of reading but of understanding the effect of cultural discourse at large. The cinematic adaptation of fiction models Altman's sense of subliminal reality. Adaptations focus the possibilities of reading beyond the construction simply of explicit meanings within the film to the awareness that meaning always derives from a multiplicity of cultural and generic codes. *Short Cuts* constantly refers

Movies about the movies *(The Player).*

readers outside its frames to those other texts—that range of social schemata necessary to the comprehension of the present film. Here, too, is the modernist predilection for the poetic, for the fragmentary, rather than the Aristotelian process of narration that opens, compounds, and then closes enigmas. Meanings constantly derive from systems external to the film. Subliminal reality forces us into the intertext.

*Short Cuts* thus summarizes the narrative drive of Altman's films as a condition of hypertext—that is, both the "organization of segments of text electronically linked in a network in such a way that the reader has the freedom of movement within that network" and the "more utopian notion of such a network expanded outward to access other systems and even a large, indeterminate portion of the textuality of the world" (Gaggi, *From Text* 102–3). While adaptation reminds us that the signs and symbols of the film have leaves and roots in air and soil elsewhere, subliminal reality models a way of traversing diversely linked narrative moments. As Madeleine Sorapure writes about Italo Calvino's fiction, readers "find themselves immersed in fragments of stories, clues that seem to lead nowhere, tangled complexities, and must extract their own meaning, make their own connections between fragments, trace their own paths through the labyrinth of the text" (705).

In the final chapter, I recapitulate the effect of subliminal reality in the art cinema of Robert Altman. The open-ended, fragmentary discourse that tells multiple stories in *Short Cuts* reiterates the difficulty of following a dominant story from a beginning through some middle to an inevitable end. The ambiguous intermingling and overlapping of the film's divergent stories are centered by the story, original to the film, of mother and daughter musicians, one a jazz vocalist, the other a classical cellist. Performance emerges out of the pain of their lonely and marginal lives and the pain caused by the film's array of absent, self-absorbed, dishonest, unfaithful, and ineffectual fathers. Like jazz, the narrative plays variations on the fiction of Carver; it riffs on the splintered sites of society and subject. In this last chapter I demonstrate how once again entertainment reflects, constitutes, and resists the broken sense of self and teleology in modern culture. We love the performance of art as it seeks to redeem life through play, but art's potentially redemptive ordering of the chaos of life breaks down in the art-cinema discourse of Altman's movies and returns the viewer to the discordant worlds from which it emerges. The trajectory of the nine chapters here traces Altman's subliminal reality as a specific form of Hollywood narration that diverges from dominant ways of cinematic discourse, as a particular recapitulation and interrogation of complacent norms of social identity, and as a self-conscious articulation against the glamorous valorization of the entertainment industry across the last three decades of the American twentieth century. Moving between the possibilities of continuing classicism and postclassical Hollywood at century's end, Altman's movies define the rich marginality of the art cinema in American film.

# Part I. Narrative Formations

# 1. Reading Strategies: Constructing *Kansas City*

Altman describes the "perfect movie" as a nonlinear, atmospheric, rationally baffling evocation of "subliminal reality." He states:

> I'm not so much interested with a good yarn as I am [with] atmosphere, of people's behavior and having a feeling out of this. My idea of what a great movie will be someday—and I don't believe one has been made yet—will be something . . . the audience will watch—and it will be very nonlinear—and they will walk away with it not being able to articulate what they think about it. I'm more interested in the subliminal reality. I'm more interested in touching people on an unconscious basis to where they sense something rather than intellectually know or agree to something. *(The Player)*

Altman has routinely expressed his distrust of straightforward stories with distinct beginnings, middles, and ends, with transparent causal connections and carefully delineated character psychology. His concept of subliminal reality assumes that communication exists on many levels simultaneously. It assumes human interaction motivated by chance, ambiguity, and uncertainty. It recognizes that whatever stories or people seem to say on the surface in sequential, grammatically and temporally linear fashion, a subsurface meaning emerges from metaphoric and symbolic associations. Altman's movies tell stories that reflect this relationship between manifest and latent significance, and readers of these stories must construct implicit or symptomatic meanings from the tensions between textual signifiers and "hidden," "deeper," "disguised," or "repressed" meaning.

Such narratives constitute a loose series of representations that evoke the omitted detail, the missing logic, the absent fullness of another world grasped only by metaphoric association, intuition, and struggle. Classical Hollywood cinema's plotting through the full storied world taken for granted by the narration reflects an ideological and psychological realm of human separation and desire (inflected conventionally by the different genres) that the narrative seeks to order and regulate, to realize and unify through the fantasy of control. "Subliminal reality" designates a more diffuse, splintered, ambiguous field of knowledge, where the unmet desires and traumas of life exist beyond the easy control of expression or logic in either the story or its narration. It articulates a worldview where life exceeds its speaking or its telling, where human behavior transcends intelligible motivation, where meaning outstrips consciousness.

Subliminal reality, then, motivates modes of storytelling at odds with traditional Hollywood narratives and demands similarly divergent strategies of reading. In particular, Altman's films require attention to loose or broken narrative coherence, to multiple and illusive characterization, and to self-conscious reflections on systems of entertainment. A simple scene in *The Player* dramatically illustrates how we may read such narration. Griffin Mill (Tim Robbins), the studio script executive, has killed a writer whom he suspects has been threatening him for not accepting his story proposal. Subsequently, he begins to date the dead writer's girlfriend, June Gudmundsdottir (Greta Scacchi). Late in the film, when Mill takes June, the film's ice-blond object of desire, to a desert resort that was once a popular hideaway for Al Capone, their dinner table bears a reservation card marked "mr. 'm.'" Narrative referentiality, character identity, and Hollywood entertainment are the cognitive patterns routine in Altman's work, and they provide broad rubrics for constructing the meaning of this scene.

In terms of narrative causality, the card suggests that Mill has previously established this status of incognito authority in concert with the establishment. It hints at his economic power to contract such disguise. It intimates that his retreat to the desert follows a well-worn trail of misdemeanor, masquerade, and deception, first on Capone's part, now on Mill's. It thus suggests, on one hand, Mill's infidelity to his girlfriend Bonnie (Cynthia Stevenson) in the film's story of romance and, on the other hand, his legal guilt as a fugitive from justice in the larger story of crime. Trying to read for plot causality, the audience must associate the card with discreet secret identity and thus with a number of presumed but not clearly specified strands of realistic representation—of action, of character, and of thematic tensions. Reading this plain element of mise-en-scène for its explicit significance encounters numerous gaps and overdetermined motives.

In terms of social identity, the name card also serves to identify the couple as individuals who define themselves and are defined by the larger social world they inhabit. That identity privileges the authority of the male, "mr.," who has arranged and apparently directs this rendezvous. It further locates him as a cipher midway along the arbitrary but socially legislated order of letters in the alphabet. It posits personality as a relationship between economic and linguistic exchange—the power to buy this letter and its repression of verbalized identity. The reservation card "holds a place" for the characters, and the viewer, paid in advance and awaiting their arrival, a seat reserved by power but situated partway between desire (for sex later in the evening and success later in the story) and fear (of the law and of loss). Personal identity is thus implied to be a tension of recognition and misrecognition, of authority and anxiety, situated variously between a simple identifying letter and a complex set of social identifications.

In terms of storytelling itself, the "m" also asks to be read as representative allegorically of something else within the film's reflexive study of the film industry—thus perhaps *male,* or *money,* or *movies.* Generally, it evokes stereotypical Hollywood stories of powerful and predatory studio executives and beautiful young girls waiting expectantly to be discovered for stardom on the silver screen. Specifically, it echoes from the immediately preceding scene the movie poster in Mill's production office for the early German sound film *M* (1931). It thus invites comparison with successful foreign film history. It reminds that the current film, like *M,* is a thriller and may thus harbor psychosis, and it colors this whole scene with the judgmental slogan from that ad: "the worst crime of all." The crime in Fritz Lang's film as well as in Altman's film is violent and illicit desire, but M's crime in both films reflects the crime of the movies themselves, storytelling that sells the manipulation of audience desires and fears for money and power.

Conveyed to the audience in pointed close-up, the reservation card is a formal, realistically photographed object in the mise-en-scène of the film's fictional world. But its meanings derive less from the clarity of its relationship to the cause-effect chain of actions that organize the audience's construction of the story world than from its multiple echoes of significance within both the story and the discourse of the narrative. The audience is situated for a moment in a classical manner that conveys realistic information and in an ambiguous way that suggests self-conscious expressionism. "M" is a signifier of discreet deception, of transgression, and of authority. Holding a place for the lovers, it also lets the audience "in on" the display of duplicity rather than just the duplicity itself. As writing, it momentarily disrupts the visual pleasure of participating vicariously in the fullness of the storied visual moment. It breaks the imaginary realism of the fiction by asserting the alphabetic, the writing, the authority whose arbitrary but ordered chain of signification situates character and audience, cipher and reader. It motivates divergent reading strategies that link this moment to the rest of the film in affective, multidirectional, metaphoric, and contradictory ways. Dinner in the story here precedes disembodied sex between Griffin and June, which precedes mud baths the next morning in tomblike chambers. What does it all mean? "M" is "mud for thought," says Altman *(The Player).* The audience must simultaneously engage models of narrative organization, social psychology, and modernist reflexivity in order to follow the logic of these strands of significance. "Subliminal reality" at once denotes a method of narration in Robert Altman's films and the complex of demands that art-cinema method places upon spectators who view the films for pleasure and understanding.

The signature "Robert Altman" as film director since the appearance of *Countdown* in 1968 evokes numerous schemata for the production of cinematic meaning. Popular audiences and movie critics who read films through the patterned expectations of classical narration look for central characters in explicit situations of social conflict, complication, and conventionally happy resolution. They take for granted a character psychology of individuals with explicitly shared desires and goals that moti-

"M" for movies, money, murder, and Mill *(The Player).*

vate heroic endeavor and eventual success. They expect a transparency of discursive narration that foregrounds the reality of the fictional world, the causal connectedness and efficacy of human behavior, and the certainty of human values that authorize and guarantee such realism and such action. Quality movies for this audience positively correlate with these expectations, and for more than thirty years the popular American audience has dismissed Altman's films as insignificant, dissatisfying, and unreadable.

Since 1968, thirty-three Altman films have consternated producers, audiences, and critics with a challenging narrative practice and worldview. The films' field of knowledge confounds Hollywood's drive toward a fantasy realism with happy endings. The films resist conventional understandings of the real and regularly tell stories with a lyrical strategy of lacuna, fragmentation, and indirection. They develop an understanding of social subjectivity as splintered, diverse, heterogeneous. They reflexively call attention to themselves as movies and critique the role of the entertainment industry in the inculcation of social values. Although the early films were widely recognized for their experimental energy in the renewal of Hollywood cinema in the early seventies, the films Altman has directed since 1990 (when he was sixty-five) provide a continuing impetus to an examination of how the subliminal reality of Altman's art cinema demands active strategies that read narratives implicitly and symptomatically for process, incoherence, and ambiguity. *Kansas City* in particular depicts yet again the symbolic relationship of power, personality, and performance in both the reflection and the construction of gendered subjects. Like the other films, it employs disruptive discourse to convey stories about the contradictions, competitions, and negotiations of cultural identity. It explores the location of artistic imagination and form—in painting, movies, fashion, and music—among the modes of production, distribution, and consumption. Like Cathryn's story of unicorns in *Images* or Willie's pool paintings in *3 Women* or Camille's direction of *Salomé* in *Cookie's Fortune,* it at once resists and represents art as a resistance against the inconclusive and debilitating pressures of society even as its vision also contributes to those pressures. And like the troubled identities of men and art in *Vincent & Theo,* the exuberant irony of Hollywood success in *The Player,* and the exultant fashion of nudity in *Prêt-à-Porter,* it examines problematic gendered subjectivity in relation to the culture industry. *Kansas City* provides a case study of the strategy of "subliminal reality" and demonstrates the terms of reading demanded by art-cinema narration.

## Breaking Narrative Coherence

Cues for constructing the story in every one of Altman's films challenge the dominant narrative schema of Hollywood movies, whether the classical films of the 1960s or the "blockbusters" of the 1970s and 1980s or the "high-concept" films of the 1990s. Their discourse first of all tells multiple stories in what seem like chaotic ways when measured against classical narrative cinema. Modernist narratives regularly operate in a context of former wholes, prior forms of orderly discourse no longer relevant or even possible in a world of modernity described by modernist poets as a wasteland. Classical and postclassical Hollywood films deploy small casts of stars playing interesting, goal-oriented individuals in end-directed and reachable quests with thematic confidence in both the value of the end and the efficacy of heroic endeavor to achieve it. Perhaps the quintessential form of this discourse, popular narrative film genres rehearse these structures with such confidence as to reach the heights of ritual and celebration—solving the mystery, completing the adventure, making the couple. The authority of classical narrative frequently emerges in the transparency of story characters, actions, and locales. In contrast, working in television during the 1960s Altman "learned to say things without saying them" (McGilligan 136), and his films frequently work like limit cases to subvert the terms of traditional clarity and value.

Films like *Nashville, A Wedding,* and *The Player,* with their casts of multiple personae, demonstrate the movement of Altman's films away from central characters and credible or sympathetic characterization. They demonstrate the loose, alogical, meandering plot structures of a writer who approaches a script, as one distraught television producer exclaimed of Altman in the 1960s, by "rewriting it sideways" (quoted in McGilligan 170). *Kansas City* exemplifies Altman's loose story structures. Across city election day in 1934, it tells crisscrossing stories of lower-class desperation, African American jazz, and white politics. It tells the stories of Babe and Johnny, Johnny and Blondie, Blondie and Red, Pussy and Heinie, Seldom Seen and the black ghetto, Boss Tom Pendergast and FDR, Lester Young and Coleman Hawkins—indeed, of Charlie Parker and Robert Altman. All of these stories seem marginal. All of them reverberate out into regions beyond the confines of the film. And they frustrated the reading competence of audiences, who avoided the movie, and critics, who panned its "almost irrelevant plot" and its "strange amalgam of material, none of which seems to belong together" (Fine Line). The requisite reading strategy for *Kansas City,* in which the discourse occasionally puts effects before causes in the story, recognizes the metaphoric rather than the metonymic association of characters and events. According to Altman: "I tried to write this film like jazz and I tried to shoot it that way. In other words, I have lines and there is a plot with definite suspense. There is a beginning, a middle with stopping points, and an ending, but in between, I let the actors go off on these riffs, just like they do in the music." Indeed, he says, the story is just another song in the music of the film (quoted in Fine Line).

The music provides the basis of a narrative constructed by that sense of "subliminal reality." According to Altman, "The whole idea was not to be too specific about [the story]." The film "runs through feelings, moods, unspoken emotions. It didn't call for a literal interpretation but rather for a sort of . . . jazz." Some cultural historians have succinctly summarized the "discontinuous universe" of the modern world as "Freud, Einstein, and jazz," and have cited jazz as both an influence and an apt metaphor for the modernist dispensation. Altman himself suggests that jazz provides a template for constructing meaning out of the discordant range of characters in *Kansas City*: "The simplicity of plot gives the actors freedom to depart from it, to weave their ideas about their characters improvisationally around the basic story. It's film jazz"(quoted in Fine Line). Ironically, the same effect that Krin Gabbard describes as the disarticulation of sound and image in the representation of jazz in film appears in *Kansas City* with strikingly different results. He notes: "Since narrative is indisputably what most audiences crave, then a film about jazz or a film with jazz cannot dwell on the music for too long. The music gets shoved aside to make way for the action, or worse, the music continues, barely audible in the background while the actors talk" (*Jammin'* 6). Consequently, the displacement of jazz performance in classical cinema reinforces the dominance of narrative discourse. Here, however, the displacement of the jazz performances not only irritates the jazz fan, it serves as a metaphor for the nature of jazz itself and as a metaphor for the inventive dissonance of the story.

A popular model of narrative film posits the effect of narrative order as a function simultaneously of the expression and control of masculine anxiety through the display and mastery of the female image. Certainly this paradigm seems to motivate the minimalist plot in such films as *MASH, Images, Nashville,* and *Cookie's Fortune.* Indeed, in his biography of Altman, Patrick McGilligan describes many of the director's notorious disagreements with television and movie producers as his refusal to follow the script. McGilligan argues that this refusal in Altman's career is motivated by insecurity, an anxiety of influence with his father, famous movie stars, and especially writers. More recent feminist criticism has expanded this concern with narrative mastery, however, to see a film as a plurality of social voices brought under the hierarchy of a dominant voice. Reading against the grain of this centripetal energy discovers the narrative as a site of many voices, of numerous discourses, of divergent roles frequently evident and competitive within the representation of different characters. Such reading strategies recognize that strong centrifugal forces work against the unity of narrative constantly to produce texts broken by other voices, other desires, other places, other points of view, other stories.

*Kansas City* clearly illustrates this narrative activation of such a cacophony of voices as constantly to confuse, frustrate, and dismay audiences reading for coherence of plot, consistency of story, and development in characterization. Its juxtaposition of divergent personalities and social levels makes clear that character is not so much a matter of representation within the story as construction by the discourse and asserts that human agency is motivated by both palpable and latent motivations, all of which are never always knowable. The film reminds us that communication is always informed by different ideological and political pressures, by conflicting social and cultural values, by diverse individual and group relationships, by competing exigencies among multiple communities. *Kansas City* works to subvert the force of homogeneity and liberates the play of voices and social strata that constitute personal identity, both in the story and in its telling. The multiplication of characters within the story forces a juxtaposition of many social inflections: the politician, the ward boss, the hoodlum, the musician, the saloon keeper, the housewife, the gangster, the working girl, the servant, the unwed teenage mother. Even as the voices associated by roles crash against each other in the story, the discourse develops character as a kind of morphing from one verbal face to another, the interplay of many voices that rise, fall, shift across the representation of any character. Thus Seldom Seen (Harry Belafonte) is "frequently heard" in many guises—subservient darky, angry militant, contemplative philosopher, influential businessman, hostile social critic, joking companion, cold-blooded gangster. And we hear all of these voices as traces of prototypes only minimally resident in the film, part of the centrifugal force that spins any one moment in the narrative off to the margins of cultural negotiation and social signification. Narrative comprehension of this multiplicity of voices and perspectives must be constantly alert to implied but never clearly articulated relationship and causality. "Nothing runs on nothing," says Blondie in her untutored but intuitive recognition of the second law of thermodynamics and the nature of subliminal reality in the film, "Whatever you do, you're always using something up."

## Unfixing Social Subjectivity

The narrative practice and the philosophical vision of Altman's films cue the audience to construct the story in terms of a plural, conflicted, and unstable social identity. They understand the social subject as a site of contradiction, where identity is constantly in the process of construction and constantly threatened by competing and powerful voices in the social formation. Caught particularly between gendered concepts of success and economic necessity, male characters appear frequently as striving inconsequentially and ineffectually to achieve nebulous or impossible goals: Brewster McCloud constructing the wings of Icarus in the Houston Astrodome, Pudgy McCabe managing a whorehouse in the Northwest woods, William Cody searching for his identity in the fantasy figure of Buffalo Bill, Jack Tanner running for president—these figures describe a masculine subjectivity in bewildered bravado and inappropriate assertiveness, sadly inclined toward death or defeat. Films such as *McCabe & Mrs. Miller, Images, 3 Women,* and *Fool for Love* variously examine the identities of women constructed as submissive in terms accorded them by male aggression, dominance, and authority. From the hysterical Cathryn in *Images,* to the assassinated Barbara Jean in *Nashville,* to the self-imposed silence of Willie in *3 Women,* to the self-delusions of Mona in *Come Back to the 5 & Dime,* indeed to the whole cast of female characters in *Short Cuts*—the women in these films move in defensive anguish against the desire, egotism, treachery, jealousy, indifference, alcoholism, and presence of debilitated and debilitating men. Altman's films routinely construct images of the feminine as dependent, insecure, and abject. Like the men, Altman's women are caught in contradictory social formations of power.

*Kansas City* dramatically illuminates this modernist perception of the individual as a social subject contradictorily constructed by cultural forces. Critics in the past have complained about Altman's films for their representation of a largely white world where issues of race and class seem unrelated to these terms of gender, but this film employs familiar narrative patterns, cinematic style, and forms of social identity to explore an unusual mix of racial tensions, lower-class sensibility, and gendered identity. At the top of the cultural order in 1934 Kansas City stand the representatives of the law: the real FDR is president, the fictional Henry Stilton (Michael Murphy) is his adviser, Guy Park governs from the state capitol, and Tom Pendergast runs Kansas City. Their office is the Northside Democratic Club, where drinking, smoking, gambling men wait in the dark of night like firemen to carry out the orders of the bosses. Their actual presence is marked in marginal, shadowy moments by the film, yet their authority appears everywhere—most notably in the fact that the diegetic length of the film is measured by the activities of election day. Seldom Seen reads to us from the pages of the newspaper in his first scene, telling the viewer that the election will settle the "battle for the control of the city."

The social identities subsumed by, contained within, or simply parallel to this political scene are ones of relative powerlessness constituted in a black jazz club run by Seldom Seen, in the crossroads represented by the Kansas City train station, in the boardinghouse operated by Addie Parker (Jeff Feringa), in a residence for black unwed mothers, and in various locales on the streets of Kansas City. At the bottom of the social hierarchy in this world reside Blondie (Jennifer Jason Leigh) and her husband, Johnny O'Hara (Dermot Mulroney). He's a petty crook who initiates most of the narrative conflict by holding up one of Seldom's customers, and she's a Western Union clerk whose efforts to rescue her husband from Seldom constitute the central narrative line that most mass-media critics dismissed as trivial and insignificant in their reviews at the time of *Kansas City*'s release. Blondie's desperate efforts to free her man, however, occasion the multiple glimpses the film affords of a complex intermingling of marginal individuals in an underworld permitted and overseen by the larger world of local and national white politics. Blondie desperately loves Johnny, but the narrative obscures the nature of their relationship because white Johnny spends the bulk of the story foolishly robbing a black customer of Seldom Seen's jazz club and then awaiting his death in retribution for the robbery. Blondie seeks frantically to rescue him, because "I'd be nothing without Johnny." He never talks about her, and she talks about him in the clichés of 1930s Hollywood romances, from which, as Virginia Wright Wexman describes, she has learned "appropriate courtship behavior" (*Creating* 5). His desperate crime and her desperate effort to free him reflect their tenuous social identities between the black entertainment world and the white political forces of Kansas City during the Depression.

As in so many of Altman's films, the central couple appears in sharp relief against the background of other couples. The major foils to Johnny and Blondie are Carolyn Stilton (Miranda Richardson), known as Red—whom Blondie kidnaps to pressure the city political machine to free Johnny from Seldom—and Henry Stilton, Red's politician husband. Red and Henry's relationship is distant, cold, perfunctory; she retreats from the reality of their life together through laudanum, and he devotes his energy to politics. The narrative clearly underlines the emotional differences between the two couples, Red and Henry, Blondie and Johnny, in a scene where Blondie and Red are going to sleep at Addie Parker's boardinghouse. Blondie plaintively describes her feelings for Johnny, "It's like the two of you was one, ya know?" and accuses Red of failing to understand what she's talking about. Her companion can only stare wordlessly at the ceiling. The narrative organizes the story as Blondie's desperate efforts to rescue her Johnny and restore their perfect union, but at the end it describes that union as possible only in their deaths. The film develops a portrait of the romantic couple as absence, two women, each differently alone, halves of some impossible unity.

Christine Gledhill observes that film, "in constructing a recognizable fictional world, draws discourses circulating in society and in other cultural forms into the fabric of the film" ("Image" 118). In *Kansas City,* the roles of gamblers, jazz musicians, unwed mothers, hairdressers, machine pols, maids, clerks, and society matrons are woven into a rich tapestry of social referentiality. Rather than subsuming the class and racial issues of social antagonism, the film exposes race, class, and gender as a complex competition of power and discourse within a context below—and permitted by—the white male power structure. In the art cinema, the viewer must construct the significance of social identity out of the subliminal representation of conflicting and divergent, contiguous and disconnected performances of personality.

## Critiquing Systems of Entertainment

The oppressive contexts of mass-media entertainment are everywhere in Altman's films: Las Vegas in *California Split,* radio detective dramas in *Thieves Like Us,* rock and classical music at the Hollywood Bowl in *A Perfect Couple,* television talk shows and news in *Health* and *Tanner '88,* the commercialization of painting in *Vincent & Theo,* the fashion industry in *Prêt-à-Porter,* even ironically in Easter church pageants in *Cookie's Fortune.* Films like *Nashville, Buffalo Bill and the Indians, Come Back to the 5 & Dime,* and *The Player* explore the dynamics between what the Producer in *Buffalo Bill* calls "the *Show* Business" and personal identities.

Several Altman films portray the negative and debilitating writing of the female subject as a project of the entertainment industry. In earlier films *Nashville* and *Come Back to the 5 & Dime, Jimmy Dean, Jimmy Dean* and in more recent films *The Player, Prêt-à-Porter, Kansas City,* and *Cookie's Fortune,* Altman's work analyzes the pressures of film, fashion, and acting in the direction of the identities and the behavior of women. Form, performance, ideology, and audience values provide equivocal contexts in these films to depict the energies of entertainment as both protective and debilitating, enabling and disabling, inspiring and deceiving. These films lyrically, metaphorically, disjointedly construct sad, haunting stanzas of women seduced and abandoned by the appeal of dramatic fantasies, by the images of Hollywood.

Many critics of *Kansas City* read the world of Blondie and Johnny as separate from the world of the jazz music in which the film attempts to re-create a famous historical interaction among future jazz greats Bill Basie, Bennie Moten, Jimmy Rushing, Lester Young, and Coleman Hawkins. The fiction is deemed inconsequential and distracting to the replay of this legendary moment in American music history. The remarkable aspect of the film's evocation of these diverse discourses, however, is the extent to which Altman's films explore the relationship between cultural subjectivity and the entertainment business. Krin Gabbard indicates that in his work on jazz and film he seeks to clarify the interaction among "race, gender, sexuality, and the discourses of art" (*Jammin'* 32), and just this amalgam resonates through *Kansas City.* The film not only occasions an examination of the relationship between gender and entertainment but aggressively adds race to this mix.

*Kansas City* focuses centrally on social identity and entertainment and references three separate forms of show business: weekly radio comedy, classical Hollywood cinema, and jazz. These three forms offer discursive possibilities for lives tenuous in both their social substantiality and their narrative delineations. Jazz has played an important historic role in the sexual empowerment of black males: "Especially for male jazz artists, the music provides a unique opportunity for sex and gender display. Part of what has made jazz so intriguing is the number of alternatives it has offered to conventional notions of masculinity and male sexuality . . . elegance, vulnerability, and romance alongside the more conventional desiderata . . . as power, technical mastery, and cool strutting" (Gabbard, *Jammin'* 7). In *Kansas City,* jazz affords its audiences and especially its performers an identity of energy, invention, competition, and a semblance of authority. What means more to the black community, says Seldom, is not what's going to happen on the dawn of election day, but what's going to happen the night before. On election eve in the Hey Hey Club occurs the "Battle of Jazz" in which Hawkins and Young compete to determine "Who is the King of the Righteous Riff?" Jazz and the club also seem to provide a kind of permanence as well, as from dusk to dawn for two days, before the beginning and after the end of the story, coterminous with the discourse, the jazz goes on. Seldom admonishes his captive Johnny: "Listen to that music. That Bill Basie—a part of the reason you ain't dead yet." Jazz, in contrast to the political economy of the white world, provides its own staying power.

The constructive possibilities of jazz for racial identity emerge in the space jazz occupies between, on one hand, the abject feminine world of Addie Parker, mother of future jazz great Charlie Parker Jr., who works as a cleaning lady and runs her home as a retirement boardinghouse for old couples and tries to contain young Charlie Jr., and, on the other hand, the powerful domain of Seldom Seen. The jazz, the club, the homes for old people and for wayward girls are all sites of refuge. Part of Addie's authority derives from these feminine positions of mother and caregiver, but as a cleaning lady, she occupies a position of marginal visibility. Socialite Carolyn Stilton can hardly distinguish Addie from her personal maid, Rosie. And when Blondie urges Addie to keep silent in the face of the kidnapping, Addie abjectly observes, "Nobody's gonna ask me nothing. They never do."

Seldom, on the other hand, is the most authoritative figure in the film, with the power to dispense booze, money, life, and opinions. He is the impresario, the producer, offering a highly successful entertainment venue for jazz and gambling. He affords audiences and performers a racial, gendered, alternative voice for invention and competition, for artistic display and psychic release. A ruthless gangster, he is offended by the violation of his power by white Johnny's robbery of one of his black customers. He also describes an important tension in his position when he characterizes Johnny's victim, Sheepshan Red, as "a loser, and losers have got to be respected. That's the backbone of my business." Whereas Addie moves through the narrative spaces of the film in weary abjection, the discourse gives Seldom a long monologue that runs like the jazz as a repeated refrain throughout the middle of the film. Critics of the film have declared that we have heard his critical litany all before—critiques of black poverty, black exploitation, black power—but the film accords the black male entertainer the voice to express these social analyses.

Seldom also exerts power over Johnny, whose more egregious crime than robbery has been his transgressive theft of blackness.

Johnny is a cheap, insolent hood who reflects the economic instability of his own social position by appropriating the persona of a black man. The poor white who needs the even lower black man to bolster his identity, he echoes the racism that reverberated initially through minstrel shows and in the golden age of radio played weekly in the whiteface drama of *Amos 'n' Andy.* Had he only taken money, Johnny may have lived, but Seldom sees his bigger crime as the racial insult of pretending, in the example of the radio program, to be black. It absorbs Seldom's attention and his anger through most of the film and measures the extent of the radio program's offensiveness to black identity. Seldom reminisces about his mother's suffering and her anger toward white people. "My mother would have cut your balls off," he says, and continues in a dramatic association of music and castration: "Woman went right to the point. She never, ever missed a beat. But of course you've never been treated as badly as she was treated for so long." The power and historic significance of jazz provides a constant backdrop to the doomed media-oriented efforts of both Johnny and Blondie to establish their own sense of social place and dignity. The film critiques the role of show business in its erroneous depiction of reality when Seldom observes to Johnny:

> You come swinging in here like Tarzan, right in the middle of a sea of niggers, like you're in the picture show. You like picture shows? . . . Maybe you're a radio man . . . all that Amos and Andy. In the movies and in radio white people sit around all day long thinking up that shit. And then they believe it!

*Amos 'n' Andy* provides Johnny a modus operandi for continuing racial insult, and the result of the subjectivity afforded him by radio make-believe is death.

Simultaneously, the film develops Blondie through a series of indirect references to her job as a clerk at Western Union, her past as an unwed mother forced at age seventeen to give her child up for adoption, and her clinging relationship with the handsome and shallow Johnny. While he mimics the blackface of *Amos 'n' Andy* and while black men turn to jazz for forms that shape their behavior, Blondie turns toward the movies, and particularly the films of Jean Harlow. Contemporary film criticism has been concerned to define subject positions constructed by the cinematic apparatus as well as those filled by real audiences, and *Kansas City* provides its own analysis of the relationship between need and mediated images of desire. Blondie is a young, lower-class working girl with no family or education who consumes the fantasy of the silver screen as does the Mia Farrow character in Woody Allen's *Purple Rose of Cairo* (1985). She watches the movies out of desire for a personality, a life, and a romance beyond the borders of her limited experience. And she aggressively identifies with the daughter of a dentist from Kansas City who became Hollywood's Blonde Bombshell in the mid-1930s. "Blondie learned how to behave by watching Jean Harlow in *Platinum Blonde* or *Bombshell*," claims Altman (Fine Line), and in the middle of *Kansas City* she retreats to the silver solace of Jean Harlow's romance with Clark Gable in *Hold Your Man* (1933).

The Harlow persona itself was another mix of divergent discourses. In the films from the early 1930s she played a movie star, a gold digger, a social climber, a gangster's moll. She variously portrayed a dangerously aggressive woman from the wrong side of the tracks who uses sex to get her way, a gullible and spoiled rich brat who falls for the wrong guy, and a sensitive and beleaguered movie star who wants to have a family. In that long line of popular culture stars of sensuality stretching from Clara Bow to Cindy Crawford, Harlow's loud, brassy, assertive, tough sexuality contrasted with a warm, sweet, comic bravado. And this contradictory subjectivity finds a needy audience in poor, high-strung, unattractive Blondie O'Hara. She tells her kidnap victim that she has seen *Hold Your*

Seldom Seen—black power in the jazz club *(Kansas City).*

*Man* six times. If Jean Harlow can stand up over and over again for her jail-bound lover, Clark Gable, then Blondie can stand up for Johnny O'Hara. The capture of her man by Seldom Seen motivates her performance of a fantasy female personality in a very dangerous male milieu, the one black with its own tenuous and illegal existence under the benevolent enfranchisement of the other white power that hardly takes notice of the Blondies and Addies of Kansas City.

Altman frequently observes that audiences understand reality in terms of the movies and the character roles ritualized in them. When Blondie kidnaps the wife of Henry Stilton, adviser to FDR, she puts on the persona of Jean Harlow. Blondie O'Hara and Red Stilton constitute a strange pair of women who turn to the opiates of popular narrative romance and laudanum in reaction to lives lived on the margins of male authority. They mock each other's dependency. Red ridicules Blondie as someone low and cheap, one of those people who "frequent movies" all day. She greatly hurts Blondie's feelings when she calls Jean Harlow "cheap and brassy and common, . . . low-class is what I'm trying to say." Blondie contemptuously derides Red's constantly drugged stupor. Nevertheless, the two women develop an inevitable bond in the context of an aroused masculinity.

Altman's art cinema routinely requires a reading strategy that watches simultaneously for a discourse of liberation and another, generally suggested by juxtaposition, that anticipates troubled subjectivity. Critics' repeated assertions that Jennifer Jason Leigh's performance of Blondie is "over the top" are responses to the film's representation of her urgency, desperation, and instability. A particular symptom of Blondie's problematic appropriation of the Harlow look is her hair. From the beginning of the film, Blondie's close-cropped hair contributes significantly to her image as an unattractive woman. When she reveals that its length is the result of too much peroxide, which made it all break off at the roots, the film suggests indirectly, subliminally, the emotional and psychic damage that results from imitating the star persona. Blondie's need is fully marked in the final sequence of the film, when, with Red's help, she completes the transformation from O'Hara to Harlow, from funny-papers comedienne to dramatic heroine. As she steps from the bedroom in her new platinum hairdo and white dress, she poses for Red and asks, "Spittin' image, right?" Blondie drives desperately around the streets of Kansas City in the guise of Jean Harlow. Brazen, tough, and absurd, she embarks upon a journey to rescue her worthless boyfriend and ends in a pool of blood that critiques the image of Hollywood's Blonde Bombshell.

For a while, Blondie's aggressive confrontation of Seldom and her demands to exchange Red for Johnny seem to work. But when Blondie appropriates the aggression of Jean Harlow and kidnaps the presidential adviser's wife, she not only steals a signifier of masculine power, she tellingly transgresses federal law. In one of the major scenes of the film, in the cavernous Kansas City train station, the childless Red and Blondie bond in their mourning for the dead child of Charles Lindbergh—that "beautiful couple, beautiful baby"—and spend the night in a nurturing relationship on a waiting-room bench. The scene is moving and ominous, because it also reminds us that Blondie has violated the "Lindbergh law," the new federal law against kidnapping. The penalty for this transgression is death. Adviser Stilton interrupts his return to Washington ostensibly to pressure the state and city political machines to intercede in Blondie's behalf with Seldom. But such intervention is doomed to failure because "tomorrow's election day. . . . Everybody's going to be distracted." He tells Blondie, "To some people the outcome of this election is more important than your husband." In effect, the bosses only stall her demands "until the polls close." The bosses humor her demands to ransom Red for Johnny just long enough to control the tensions of managing the elections. Then, just as inexorably as Seldom focuses his venom on Johnny, the political strongmen move to liberate Mrs. Stilton. Blondie has innocently watched the magical efficacy of Hollywood romantic comedy and tragically misread the reality of masculine power.

"Forget the plot and the people; just soak up the feel," one critic writes about *Kansas City* (Joan Ellis). But the film's lyrical exploration of the unequal distributions of power along the lines of race, class, and gender has an ominous feel. The two-day slice of life in Depression-era Kansas City is punctuated momentously by the municipal elections and annoyingly by the transgressions of Johnny and Blondie. At the end of the narrative, the bosses maintain their power and magisterial seclusion, the jazz plays on, and Seldom counts his money in the black ghetto. Johnny, playing the Kingfish, and Blondie, playing the Blonde Bombshell, are dead.

The subliminal reality of *Kansas City* ambiguously links Jean Harlow and jazz, and suggests that both constitute forms of resistance. The "music is a reason not to die," Altman claims. But the show business in *Thieves Like Us, Nashville, Buffalo Bill and the Indians, Come Back to the 5 & Dime, The Player,* and *Kansas City* can kill you. *Kansas City* suggests that Blondie's kidnapping of Red motivates the bonding of a female buddy picture. It develops jazz along another track that asks to be read as a musical where Coleman Hawkins and Lester Young (or Craig Handy and Joshua Redman) put on the show. But during the presidential campaigns of Bill Clinton and Bob Dole, the political story of Tom Pendergast, Henry Stilton, Governor Guy Park, and even Harry Truman—all marginal figures in the film—asks to be read like *Nashville, Health, Secret Honor,* and *Tanner '88* as an election-year film that examines the complex circulation of masculine political authority. *Kansas City* explores the construction of female subjectivity as a complex competition of discursive voices in a site contained and licensed by male jurisdiction. Johnny assumes the white fantasy voices of race from *Amos 'n' Andy,* and his extended execution occurs at the hands of black vengeance motivated by black anger at the white entertainment industry's theft of history. Blondie assumes the fantasy voice of feminine authority, and her death occurs at the sympathetic hand of another woman trapped in loveless marriage to a pol in the democratic machine. Both are killed by oppressed others. Elections, jazz, Hollywood—even the glossy hard-edged realism of the sets and cinematography of this film—are polished facades that cover one kind of power and constitute another, the one coercive, the other illusory. *Kansas City* thus illustrates the complex strategies and the critical vision of Robert Altman's art cinema.

The past thirty years of Hollywood cinema demand multiple historical, economic, and aesthetic analyses of the relationships among production, financing, storytelling, stardom, fantasy, and ideology. Altman's films from *That Cold Day in the Park* in 1969 to *Dr. T & the Women* in 2000 constitute a rich source of data for comprehending the movement from a Hollywood renaissance in the 1960s to the high-concept cinema of the 1990s. Examining these films reveals the narrative devices of containment that the fantasy business employs to mask the terms of social insecurity. Altman's films reveal a particular figure of cultural storytelling, social referentiality, and industry consciousness across the complex currents of those thirty years. They appropriate the modernist force of art-cinema narration not to capture in form and thus redeem the radical debilitations of modernity, but to employ open forms that refuse narrative closure. Altman's art films play with the possibilities and fluid chance of life. Their representations of social subjectivity convey both the insecurity and the resistances of the individual: Mona, Sissy, and Joanne playing the McGuire Sisters and singing "Sincerely" from the imaginary space of the five-and-dime; Richard Nixon shouting, "Fuck 'em!" from the fictive space of history in *Secret Honor*; Blondie's assertive transformation of herself into the platinum-blond movie star—"Spittin' image, right?"

Altman's subliminal reality charts a cultural play between lack and desire in its ambiguous discourse. The art-cinema narration works against the idea of an ending, because "the only end I know about is death," says Altman (quoted in Kloman et al. 22). The notion of the social subject recognizes the possibility of efficacious individuality ("my mother," says Nixon in *Secret Honor*; "my star," says Ned Buntline in *Buffalo Bill*; "me pap," says Popeye), but these figures are illusions or cartoons, entertainment fantasies projected by the need to cover the insecure, ineffective personae of social lack. Reflexive cinema wants a humane, inventive, engaged, redemptive entertainment industry but finds instead the crass, exploitative, cruel, and destructive worlds of Nashville and Hollywood, the music and the movies of business. A constantly remarkable feature of Altman's films is their alterity to a Hollywood cinema whose margins, outskirts, and back alleys they clarify and highlight. They are not alone in the continuation of a narrative practice that has roots in Eisenstein and branches in the contemporary films of Atom Egoyan, Peter Greenaway, Jim Jarmusch, Mike Leigh, John Sayles, Gus Van Sant, and others. Subliminal reality plays with the mainstream audience's expectations and literacy in Hollywood narrative. It reflexively interrogates the values promoted by that dominant discourse. It implies its own complicity in the narrative promulgation of reactionary values, and it does so by embracing and celebrating the forms and contents of contemporary popular culture. *Kansas City* reflects the complexities of representation inspired by Altman's conception of subliminal reality and illustrates the reading strategies demanded by its conflicting and disconnected stories.

## 2. New American Cinema and *MASH*

Film histories variously find in the late 1960s a "new Hollywood" (Thompson 711), a "new American cinema" (Cook, *History* 626), and a "Hollywood Renaissance" (Mast and Kawin 431), and they all characterize the period with a list of names. Glenn Man says in his book *Radical Visions: American Film Renaissance, 1967–1976,* "The films of Arthur Penn, Mike Nichols, Sam Peckinpah, Stanley Kubrick, Robert Altman, Peter Bogdanovich, Martin Scorsese, Bob Fosse, and Francis Ford Coppola scrutinized the moral and mythic landscape of the American scene in original, bold presentations that operated as uncompromisingly as possible within the heavy commercial demands of the industry" (1). Thomas Bohn and Richard Stromgren write of this period: "The 'discovery' of the director as star [represented] . . . a reassessment and shift in audience attitudes, industry policy, and perhaps most importantly, critical evaluation. . . . Helped by the decline of the studio system, the director *as an individual* with ideas he wanted to express in film became a significant force in the American film of the Sixties and Seventies" (460). The identification of the director as author reflects an energy that brought increased respectability for film in relation to the other arts, with both the popular audience and the academic audience. The names of these new American "auteurs" are held to be important precisely because their films bear the marks not just of entertainment for a mass audience but of art for an educated audience. Part of the prestige value in this critical move identified the new American directors with the older generation of international filmmakers whose work challenged the formal practice of the classical Hollywood cinema. This cinema of directors situates the auteur as central to the concept and the practice of the art cinema.

One of the most highly esteemed brand names of this new cinema was Robert Altman. With films like *McCabe & Mrs. Miller, Nashville,* and *3 Women,* he enjoyed recognition as "one of the most innovative American film-makers of the past thirty years" (Cook, *History* 642). Critics and reviewers variously compared him to the European art-cinema directors Godard, Antonioni, and Bergman (Man 90). When John Belton and Lyle Tector analyzed the "aesthetics of the zoom lens" in 1980, they praised the "usually next-to-subliminal" use of the zoom in Altman's films in the company of Godard, Rossellini, and Chabrol (13). Altman's reconstruction of the traditional semantics and syntax of genre film, his critique of contemporary mores, his independence within the Hollywood production system, his indebtedness to various European cinemas, his experimentation in technique and style certified his role in the reawakening of American movies in the 1970s. Robin Wood in 1975 explicitly delineated "the centrality of Altman's work to the development of the modern American cinema. . . . Because of its distinction, because of the presence of a clearly defined creative personality, it brings to a sharp focus most of the features that characterize that development" ("Smart-Ass" 2).

The "sleep" usually described as preceding the films of Altman and his fellow renaissance directors is that period of precipitous decline in the Hollywood film industry during the 1950s and early 1960s. Three major events gave impetus to this decline: the U.S. Supreme Court's rulings that broke up the Hollywood studios' vertical integration of the film market from the purchase of a script to the screening of movies in the local theaters, the negative images created by the House Un-American Activities Committee's search for communists in Hollywood, and the advent of television in American homes. Furthermore, the importation of the European New Wave cinema to American art-film houses and college campuses in the late 1950s and early 1960s helped to forge a young film generation. And the new Hollywood cinema reached the large new audience of postwar baby boomers, who had begun to enter college early in the decade and by the late 1960s had begun to shape the "counterculture." The new cinema appealed to their "dissatisfaction with traditional authoritarian discourses—patriotism (Vietnam), paternalism (women's movement), racism (civil rights movement), puritanism (sexual revolution)" (Man 65).

Much of the artistic quality in these films also had roots in the international art cinema that dates both from the various post-World War II innovations in narrative form and style and from the artistic projects in modernism of the 1920s. The large influx of foreign films into the United States in the early 1960s was significant for several reasons.

These films demonstrated a cinematic style indebted more to the practice of Eisenstein than to that of Griffith, and they helped to usher into American movies the "discourses of Art and Culture" (Neale, "Art Cinema" 15). The new Hollywood cinema meant not just a rebirth of values from the classical Hollywood cinema but a continuation, with renewed vigor, of the pursuit of art upon which the movies have been embarked since they started to raid the classics of literature in the first days of sound in order to attract middle-class audiences.

Altman's *Buffalo Bill and the Indians* contains a paradigmatic scene of Hollywood's veneration of and sense of distance from the aesthetics of high art. Buffalo Bill and his troupe of western entertainers listen, transfixed, to the operatic renditions in a foreign language of a coloratura visiting the Wild West show's encampment. The camera pans around the space transformed by her singing to reveal the rapture on the faces of producers, actors, technicians: the gaze of the popular entertainment industry fixed with desire upon the performances of high art. By midcentury, "art" also included modernism. Jack Ellis has written for instance, about Altman, "[His] 'modernism' is quite extraordinary, that is to say precedential, with fragmented structure, shifting narrative viewpoint, play with time and memory, and reflexive commentary on film in relation to life" (409). Indeed, it may be argued that these modernist qualities appealed not only to the so-called youth generation but to a young intellectual audience in the academy as well. They also enabled American cinema to compete with the prestige of those names generally associated with the New Wave cinemas—François Truffaut, Jean-Luc Godard, Michelangelo Antonioni, Federico Fellini, Ingmar Bergman, Yasujiro Ozu, Akira Kurosawa—as they simultaneously set Hollywood against itself. Thus Steve Neale observes:

> If cinema has tended massively to exist hitherto as an institution for the perpetuation of the novelistic, then it has historically been the case that it is within the institutional space of Art Cinema that film has most closely approximated that version of the novelistic that we associate with writers like Eliot, Mann, James, and Tolstoi, shading at times into the hesitations of the modernist novel (Faulkner, Dostoevski, the *nouveau roman*), while Hollywood has tended to produce and reproduce the version of the novelistic we associate with the genres of popular fiction. ("Art Cinema" 13)

Robert Kolker explicitly locates the early Altman films along this cultural divide: "Altman dissociates himself from the closed forms of classical Hollywood story-telling, turning the screen into a wide, shallow space . . . , filled with objects and people, with movement, with talk and sounds and music woven into casual and loose narratives that create the appearance of spontaneity and improvisation" (307).

One transition in Altman's films clearly marks the cleavage between those two modes of film practice. The aesthetic distance between *Countdown* in 1968 and *That Cold Day in the Park* in 1969 and *MASH* in 1970 reflects not only a significant change in the stylistic signatures of the Altman cinema but also the seismic shift occasioned in the new cinema. Altman counts his first film as *That Cold Day in the Park* because it inaugurated his career as a director with authority over the "final cut" of his films. *Countdown* was directed for Warner Bros., and the studio fired Altman from the production and reedited the film before distribution. It is a film that reflects all the rule-governed features of the classical Hollywood cinema. On the other hand, *That Cold Day in the Park* and *MASH* both demonstrate what would be central features of Altman's films over the next three decades: a self-conscious and reflexive representation of marginal and insecure characters narrated with what David Bordwell describes as the salient characteristics of the "art cinema as a mode of film practice" ("Art Cinema" 57).

Films of the new American cinema of the late 1960s consciously undertook a rereading of the classical Hollywood narrative. The traditional Hollywood form makes sense in terms of verisimilitude, generic appropriateness, and compositional unity and closure. It asks to be read in terms of the efficacious action of a psychologically defined, goal-oriented central character, and the logical system of narrative rigorously motivates the spatial and temporal systems of the medium. It contains a dual plot structure in which the resolution of the innermost conflict, usually a romantic one, motivates the resolution of conflict in the dominant story. Its quintessential form, the popular genres, ritualistically celebrates both the shared assumptions of this transparent form of storytelling, what Roland Barthes calls a "zero degree of style" (*S/Z* 5), and the shared cultural values that constitute the semantic opposition of each different genre.

In films of the Hollywood renaissance, attention to continuity of story shifts to the rhetoric of discourse. The coherence of cause-effect narrative gives way to loose, open-ended structures motivated divergently by an "ideology of realism" on one hand and by the "Romantic view that Art is subjective expression" (Neale, "Art Cinema" 14) on the other. Bordwell observes that the "broken teleology" of the art cinema is "justified as the intrusion of an unpredictable and contingent daily reality or as the subjective reality of complex characters." And as the director "becomes a formal component, the overriding intelligence organizing the film for our comprehension," the art film is further justified as "the work of an expressive individual" ("Art Cinema" 58–59). These two tendencies yield a cinema that is both documentary and poetry, with narratives that aggressively ask to be read for ambiguity. Moreover, the spatial and temporal systems, no longer motivated by narrative causality, gain parity with the logical system and work to establish complex patterns of rhythm and graphics. Glenn Man succinctly describes the derivative style of the new American cinema:

> It combines in an eclectic way the codes of expressionism and realism, fusing new wave and neorealistic techniques: on the one hand, disjunctive editing, ellipses, fragmented structure, rapid collage montage, closed subjective framing, soft focus, distorted angles, hand-held camera, flashbacks, flashforwards, and mixed genres; on the other hand, long takes, deep focus, wide-screen compositions, tracking/panning camera, grainy cinematography, actual locales, episodic structure, open framing, overhead mike and actual sounds, and a montage of songs and music from the time and setting of the film. (105)

## Classical Narrative Past

*Countdown* recounts a story of space-race politics and technology. Attempting to capitalize on all the drama of the Soviet and American efforts to land a man on the moon, the film was trumped in reality by Neil Armstrong's "giant leap for mankind" prior to the film's release. The plot unambiguously carries the viewer through the tensions surrounding an emergency plan at NASA to use makeshift technology from the Mercury space program for a manned moon launch in the event the Soviet Union launches one before the planned American Apollo attempt. The original military astronaut of the emergency plan is replaced, through a White House decision, by his friend, a civilian astronaut, for a launch whose success depends upon the astronaut's locating and living for a year in a previously dispatched moon shelter until rescued by Apollo astronauts.

Robert Duvall and James Caan develop psychological portraits that work largely and simplistically as a function of national pride, pilot machismo, and personal envy. The cause-effect chain of luck and pluck effortlessly evokes and resolves personal as well as national conflicts and, in the best classical tradition, works unequivocally on behalf of the heroic force of the good, the right, the law. The film generates suspense through what now seem like the major clichés of space-race stories, whether in *Countdown* or *The Right Stuff* (1983) or *Apollo 13* (1995): conflict among the pilots and the chain of command about who should go, tension around the completion of training, suspense over the competition with the Russians, anxiety about the trip in the astronauts' families, the blastoff and flight, the successful landing, and, of course, survival. All this suspense in the main plot action draws the requisite support from the secondary romance plot between the James Caan character and his wife. The narrative resolves the tension between the two of them so that her love sustains him on his important and risky mission. Altman shoots all this "right stuff" in a soundstage milieu with atmospheric shots of NASA facilities at Cape Kennedy and a special effects mise-en-scène of the moon that looks like NASA training sites. From establishing shots to medium shots to close-ups, the film honors all the rules of classical continuity editing and progresses largely through the verbal drama of talking heads. The jingoism of the narrative blatantly rationalizes the entire project. Its pro-American, space-race mentality is exactly that exploded in the prologue of Arthur C. Clarke's science fiction novel *Childhood's End* (popular among members of the "counterculture" movement of the 1960s) when the Overlords appear from outer space to usher humankind past its colonialist thinking about the conquest of space into the transcendental Age of Aquarius.

The Warner Bros. release of *Countdown* and the film Altman had in mind were apparently two different things. The studio objected to Altman's confusing use of overlapping dialogue and, apparently, to his greater interest in the personal lives of the pilots and their wives behind the public and political scene. The first of these "problems" previews one of the noted stylistic signatures of Altman's films, but the other replays soap-opera dramatics. Virginia Wright Wexman notes that "the film's overall formulaic simplicity suggests television, an impression that undoubtedly arises as much from Altman's prior career as a television director as it does from producer Jack Warner's tampering with the editing and final shooting of the film" ("Critical" 26). Altman has claimed that his planned ending for the film would have left the astronaut trudging on the moon, not toward the shelter—as the released version has it—but in the opposite direction, toward death. In any case, none of this is palpable in the existing film, and Altman has renounced authorship of its conventional narrative work.

## Starting Again

Altman marks the beginning of his career as a self-proclaimed auteur with *That Cold Day in the Park,* independently produced by Altman and shot in Canada without Hollywood backing. Lacking the clarity of politics or social realism, the film is largely motivated by the psychological complexity of the central character, Frances, a sexually repressed, middle-aged spinster played by Sandy Dennis. Altman reduces Richard Miles's novel about the interior, first-person perspectives of the spinster and the relationship between two male prostitutes and homosexual lovers (none of this classical Hollywood fare) to an external observation of a woman who inexplicably brings a kinky young man from the Vancouver hippie culture into her apartment, where she imprisons him apparently for sexual purposes. Here is the first of Altman's several films—including *Images, 3 Women, Come Back to the 5 & Dime, Jimmy Dean, Jimmy Dean* (again with Sandy Dennis), *Fool for Love, Kansas City,* and *Cookie's Fortune*—that establish women as the central figures and in which he explores the marginality, psychoses, and silences of women under the dominance of a phallocentric culture. The psychological trajectory of the film suggests a woman raised by a domineering mother and a father present only as wealth. Frances's friends are geriatric. In her single sexual foray, she encounters male virginity, male silence, and male condescension, and her final act is the murder, with a large butcher knife, of a prostitute she procured for the boy. As the film ends, she makes ironic, futile gestures of motherhood.

The verb *suggest* accurately describes the viewer's construction of psychological motivation and causality in the film, because in characteristically art-cinema ways few of the narrative connections are clear. Numerous episodes are only tangentially related to the story's central action, and the pattern of the thriller genre meanders away from suspense into a moody confusion of motive, conflict, and resolution. Apparently gratuitous moments like the boy's romp in the bathtub with his sister metaphorically depict a sexual freedom and casualness sharply distinct from Frances's dry sexual frigidity. When Frances visits a gynecology clinic, the purpose of her visit and her meeting with the doctor are both repressed as the sound track and camera literally eavesdrop, from outside the building, on the conversation of three unseen women about differential sizes of the penis. Such elements require that the audience construct significance from implicit and metaphoric associations. The film structure derives not from any narrative causality but from a five-part look at the inefficacious gaze of a woman, a gaze progressively of separation and longing, of confusion, of betrayal, of desire, and finally of madness in face of the male as an impossible and absurd object of desire. The audience must identify with a subjectivity in which the economic, linguistic, and sexual exchange values of the woman are significantly troubled, if not clearly interrogated.

In addition to the complexities of narrative interpretation that derive from a concern to recuperate meaning with psychological realism, a contrasting level of stylistic expressiveness appears in the sound and cinematography; another structure undergirds the editorial strategies. Classical narrative cinema generally subordinates spatial and temporal features to the demands of narrative time and space. Here for the first time Altman displays the expressionistic style of the art cinema that subverts this subordination. The sound track alternates between stark silences and cacophonous piano and flute music—a sharp and atonal contrast that will continue to mark Altman's films through *The Gingerbread Man* in 1998. Zoom-shot close-ups of lights mark the ends of scenes. Simultaneous pan, track, and zoom shots inexplicably relate characters to the environment and to each other. Glass-brick windows and walls in the art deco mise-en-scène repeatedly provide refracting screens through which to see or beyond which to lose sight of the characters. Numerous mirror shots reflect multiple images of space or character. Such devices study, enlarge, and distort the settings, not for the purposes of story but for the more poetic and painterly effects of mood. Robert Kolker writes:

> Altman begins to develop in this film the opening of the aural-visual space of his narrative, diffusing its center by taking notice of the peripheries. The camera continually drifts away from the main action, zooming past a face into a window to pick up the out-of-focus light reflected on the glass defining the central character and her state of mind by bringing to our attention the otherwise unnoticeable objects and minutiae that surround her. (274)

Describing his work in *Nashville,* Altman has cited one of his directorial role models in the art cinema as Ingmar Bergman, who compared film to music in his famous remarks on the relationship between film and literature. Altman has further sounded a central preoccupation of the art-cinema auteurs: "I don't think we've found a format for movies yet. I think we're still imitating literature and theater. . . . [Film] can be more abstract, impressionistic, less linear. Music changes form all the time. I think if you just establish a *mood* with a film, it might have more impact than anything we've done, just a *mood*" (quoted in Giannetti 428). Looking back at *That Cold Day in the Park* in 1994, Altman identified the music as central to the film's effect, and as late as 1999 in *Cookie's Fortune,* music continues to provide central affective and structural dimensions to the subliminal reality of Altman's art-cinema narration. Psychological certainty, causal connections, and stylistic clarity yield to unspoken and unspeakable complexities of human relationships. Reality is everywhere marked by innuendo, metaphor, and ambiguity.

## A New American Cinema

Authorial expressivity, narrative open-endedness, contradictory points of view, psychological insecurity, and cinematic reflexivity constitute the characteristics of the new American cinema. These features are both famous and notorious in Altman's films, as well as the international art cinema, and they come to their first full expression in *MASH.* A cacophony of moods crisscrosses the film, which rode the antiwar energy of the late 1960s to carry Altman to his only significant financial success at the American box office. *MASH* is one of those "blockbusters," along with *Bonnie and Clyde, 2001: A Space Odyssey* (1968), *The Graduate* (1967), and *The Wild Bunch* (1969) generally named as illustrative of a Hollywood renaissance. Ironically, because of its stylistic and philosophical distance from the television show, it spawned one of the longest-lived series in American television history and generated an income sufficient to maintain Altman's studio, Lions Gate Films, as one of the viable independent Hollywood production companies in the 1970s. In experimental style, in antiestablishment theme, in desultory story, the film displays many of the values of the American counterculture movement of the late 1960s. Indeed, its very popularity reflects a sympathetic vibration with the ethos of the time, as Hayden White argues about experimental fiction: "Such experimentation will find an audience 'programmed' to receive innovative messages and contacts only if the sociocultural context is such as to sustain an audience whose experience of that context corresponds to the modes of message formulation and conveyance adapted by a given writer" (63). The antiestablishment mood of the country provided fertile ground for the seeds of an American art cinema.

*MASH* requires active audience participation in its subversive construction of meaning. The central antagonist is an absent war—the military, medical, and religious establishment that attends it and the constant stream of bodies and blood that flows from it. No single character is the protagonist; rather, the whole MASH unit plays that role—a community that in the four major divisions of the film variously and divergently exposes the religious hypocrisy of Major Burns, restores the sexual potency of the company dentist, attacks the medical incompetence and insensitivity of an army hospital in Tokyo, and subverts the military superiority of the general's football team. The episodic story moves with fluidity and without apparent teleology. Its central structural strategy must be recognized as a doubling motion in which each of the major sequences stands in metaphoric rather than metonymic relation to the rest of the story: the long football sequence reflects on the military enterprise, for instance, and the comic handling of the camp dentist's sexual resurrection stands in marked contrast to a more realistic homophobia. Little segments like the emergency surgery on an Asian-American baby in Japan display an internal narrative coherence without any causal connection to a central story. The unconventional, rebellious personalities of the film motivate attention more than the resolution of any war genre conflict, and the film works to invest these heroes with a moral, sexual, and professional potency superior not to an international but to a national enemy.

Visually, the film represents the vibrant and unusual mix of art-cinema style: medium long shots and extreme close-ups shot with a telephoto lens, distances held together by a zoom lens. It displays an energetic blend of continuity editing that maintains some dramatic unity and editing that accentuates graphic and rhythmic rather than story dimensions. Thus expressive editing, cinematography, and mise-en-scène never simply denote the space and time of the action but develop images that require metaphoric and symbolic reading. The film's blend of somber khaki, greens, and gray in the set design, blurred around the edges of the frames by telephoto lens; the restless, moving camera; the exuberant mix of metaphor and criticism, of laughter, games, and death—all establish a mood that is contradictorily humorous and angry, infuriating and self-aware, tragic and meditative.

Close analysis of the film's use of sound in particular illustrates the complex way in which its narrative form reflects new American cinema's reconstruction of classical Hollywood practice as well as characteristic signatures of the international art cinema. It demonstrates the splintered construction of social identity in those films. It illuminates the reflexivity whereby these films frequently signal their own existence and distance the viewer from the transparent evocation of fictional reality practiced by the classical narrative cinema. As these characteristics distinguish key aspects of the new American cinema, they also signal the beginning of concerns that remain constant throughout Altman's films.

Sound, especially speech, in the classical narrative cinema has been employed since its inception to promote the popular and critical mythology that the essence of film as a form of discourse relates to its ability to capture "literal reality." The film industry has historically devoted a great deal of energy to coordinating the acoustic with the visual apparatus in order to enhance the illusion of realism. John Belton points out in this regard that the evolution of sound technology represents "the quest for a sound track that captures an idealized reality, a world carefully filtered to eliminate sounds that fall outside of understanding or significance" (66). As sound technology has vastly improved technicians' ability to reduce mechanical noise from film sound tracks, leaving a "clean" sound of dialogue, effects, and music, filmmakers' efforts to portray "true-to-life" fiction have also greatly improved. Merely to scrutinize the lengthy credits that have been placed at the ends of Hollywood films since the 1960s is to become aware of the large number of technical personnel—sound recorder, sound editor, sound rerecorder, sound effects editor, music recorder, music editor, and so on—required to construct this quality of realism.

A popular critical generalization about Robert Altman's films credits them with advancing the state of this "art." Speaking of Altman's *McCabe & Mrs. Miller,* for instance, one author states: "Sound is often stacked on sound, voice on voice, but stacked in new ways so that we get an incredible sense of *being there*—in a different place and a different time. The texture is so real that we feel the rain and the cold wind and even smell the smoke" (Boggs 181–82). According to Rick Altman, the "complex, thick, multi-layered" sound in *Nashville* reinforces "the notion that we are witnessing not a fiction film but a media report of a real event" ("24-Track" 6). The loudspeaker enhances the same reality effect in *MASH.* And the constant overlapping of ambient sound and dialogue is another striking characteristic of sound in the film that may be heard as contributing to this effect. When Hawkeye (Donald Sutherland) and Duke (Tom Skerritt) arrive at the mess tent at the beginning of the film, for instance, the sound track is filled with the hum of many voices in dinner conversation and the sounds of clattering silverware and plates. During the twelve scenes in operating rooms—which punctuate and structure the film in much the same manner as the loudspeaker announcements—we hear the constantly overlapping dialogue of doctors and nurses and the sounds of surgical tools from the several operations usually occurring at the same time.

Despite the fact that Altman's films, like those of such other American directors of the 1970s as Coppola, Cassavetes, Kubrick, Scorsese, and Penn, work to disrupt and criticize the traditional style of the classical Hollywood cinema, the various categories of sound in *MASH* may thus be recognized within the functional boundaries of conventional narrative characterization. As the sound engineer for *Health* observes, "Altman demands a full, rich, multilayered track which will color, highlight and augment his story . . . , one which will give nuance to each character" (L. Levin 368–69). The film employs onscreen and synchronous sound that emanates from some source within the space enclosed by the frame and is synchronized to that source. It uses offscreen and simultaneous sound regularly to support classical shot/reverse-shot editing wherein we watch the face of a listener while we hear a voice, sound, or music whose source is offscreen—that is, not visible within the frame but occurring simultaneously with the dramatic time of the listener. Viewers thus share the act of audition with a character in the fiction; the offscreen voice elicits interest in the character psychology that motivates classical causality, and the fictional space is extended beyond the borders of the frame.

But whereas onscreen sound works realistically in dialectic with offscreen sound, synchronous and simultaneous sounds posit another, more complex aspect of temporal order that is nonsynchronous or nonsimultaneous. Sounds not associated with the apparent time of the action visibly occurring at any given moment in a film require us to distinguish between those sounds deriving from some other story time than that visually present and those sounds deriving not from the story time at all. The discontinuity inherent in this technique corresponds to other disruptive tendencies in art-cinema narration. Two striking examples of displaced diegetic sound occur in *MASH.* Story sound that is earlier than the time of the image is audible in the scene where the colonel, Duke, and Hawkeye discuss Burns and the new chest surgeon. The flow of sound categories here is remarkable: the onscreen, synchronous dialogue among these three actors becomes offscreen and simultaneous as the camera cuts to a shot of the colonel's ante-office to show Radar entering the colonel's office. The camera holds on this space as we overhear Radar's message to the colonel, then cuts to a scene later in the pre-op ward, where Hawkeye and Duke check patients while their voices and the colonel's continue on the sound track.

| Shot | Dialogue |
|---|---|
| 1. Medium, three shot: Duke, colonel, Hawkeye around the colonel's desk. Cut to | DUKE: We got to get an A-1 chest cutter in here quick or we're gonna |
| 2. Medium shot of colonel's outer office; operator at switchboard to left; Radar enters right, crosses, exits left. Cut to | be in a helluva lot of trouble.<br>COLONEL: Forget it. No MASH unit has a chest surgeon, and we're not about to get one.<br>RADAR: Excuse me, Sir; They're behind in OR and the |
| 3. Medium shot of pre-op ward with Duke and Hawkeye bending and checking wounded as they weave their way among the nurses and large number of wounded all over the floor. Camera pans left to follow their progress. | pre-op ward is all jammed up. The helicopters and ambulances are coming in full.<br>COLONEL: You guys are going to have to go to work early today.<br>DUKE: What! Add overtime to a twelve-hour day! What the hell is that? The union will raise all kinds of Cain with you, Henry.<br>HAWK: Boy, Henry, you work those kind of hours you sure need your rest. You can't get it with a sky pilot jabbering away to heaven all night.<br>COLONEL: Major Burns will be out of your tent in twenty-four hours. Tell 'em that Captain Pierce and Captain Forest are on their way.<br>HAWK: Henry, you're forgetting something—a chest cutter!<br>COLONEL: I'll try, dammit! |

Here is the increasingly complex style of the new American cinema. The sound in shot 1 is simple diegetic, onscreen, and synchronous. In shot 2 it is still simple diegetic but has become offscreen and simultaneous, and in shot 3 it is offscreen, nonsimultaneous, and displaced diegetic. The effect of this sound shift is to show that while in continuous dialogue the surgeons argue about ways to improve their and the unit's operating efficiency, in action the narration jump cuts in time and space to show them already moved to meet pressing medical needs. The narration thus works complexly to add a deeper, more positive resonance to their characterization as we simultaneously hear them badger the colonel for improved medical conditions and watch them work sympathetically and professionally with the wounded soldiers.

Robert Altman, as a major innovator of such realistic sound technology during the 1970s, might have been a candidate for praise in the industry, but the opposite was the case. Jack Warner fired Altman from the production of *Countdown* because of this "new way" of constructing sound. Although it may increase some sense of "being there," it vastly complicates the viewer's ability to follow the story, and classical cinema gives precedence to dramatic realism and credibility over the capturing of literal experience. Overlapping sound and dialogue was not new in 1970. Such filmmakers as Howard Hawks and Orson Welles employed it with dramatic effect in the 1930s and 1940s. But Altman's impressionistic practice violates a boundary with regard to the traditional foregrounding of story. James G. Stewart, one of the principal sound engineers during the "golden age" of Hollywood, writes in respect to this boundary:

> I do not go along with the present trend to see how difficult you can make it for an audience to understand the dialogue. There is a definite limit past which you must not go, or you lose the attention of your audience. Once you have lost that you have ceased to communicate. There is a basic principle: before you can communicate you must have the attention of the listener or the viewer. In poor intelligibility there is an element of irritation which causes the audience to reject what you are telling them. (62)

Altman's films demonstrate an interest in a dense texture of sound that from one perspective may be more realistic—that is, more like the act of listening in actual experience—as it requires the viewer to select from among the conflicting number of sounds that are heard. Rick Altman observes, "Usually mixed at levels permitting comprehension of individual tracks in spite of the continued presence of multiple sound sources, Altman's sound mix thus replaces Hollywood's familiar intermittent sound editing patterns by alternation of attention on the part of the auditor" ("24-Track" 6). But Altman' s attitude toward sound in the service of subliminal storytelling diverges significantly from the classical linkage of sound to drama. He has said:

> Sound is supposed to be heard, but words are not necessarily to be heard. I am trying to divorce the audience somewhat from literature and from theater, which is based on literature. In those areas it's the words that the character uses that is important. I think in film it's what the character does not say, what you don't hear. (quoted in Leyda 6)

One of the most notable and well-known sound devices used in *MASH,* the camp loudspeaker, reflects the complex use of sound for both realistic and expressive purposes, which has been a trademark of nearly all Altman's films and one of his contributions to art-cinema stylistics. The voice can be synchronized with its apparent source, the loudspeaker, only by the editorial juxtaposition of the mechanically reproduced voice and a close-up shot of a loudspeaker, but it has a variety of diegetic functions: to convey the larger presence of the camp compound beyond the visually truncated spaces delineated by the camera, to establish an effect of militarylike realism, to provide a dramatic continuity across contiguous shots of discontiguous spaces. The twenty-one different pronouncements from the loudspeaker also serve structural, comic, and thematic functions and work overall to give the film the kind of unity frequently achieved by the nondiegetic musical score that accompanies the story in classical narrative film. They simultaneously employ realistic sound as an expressive device in the characteristic manner of art-cinema discourse.

A simple illustration of the loudspeaker's function as diegetic continuity is the three-shot sequence that shows (1) the sexually-aroused Major Burns (Robert Duvall) after an embrace with Hot Lips Houlihan (Sally Kellerman), (2) Burns and Hot Lips mailing their joint letter to headquarters, and (3) Burns saying good night to Hot Lips outside her tent. Across these shots is heard the unbroken announcement from the loudspeaker that three cases of amphetamines have been stolen from the base pharmacy for the third time in a month: three shots, three separate times and spaces whose integrity derives from the coherence of the announcement. This juxtaposition motivates a number of metaphoric readings: the pious Major Burns contemplating adultery linked to the medical component of the military that runs on drugs—an ironic mix of positive and negative values associated with both "heroes" and "villains" that gives preference to neither.

Directors of the Hollywood renaissance influenced by international art-cinema directors such as Fellini, Bergman, and Godard value narrative realism less than authorial expressivity. This cinema puzzles the viewer not by enigmas developed in the story but by questions raised in the act of storytelling, in the process of narration, in the dissonance perceived within the cinematic apparatus itself. One of the most striking examples of this destablization of diegetic reality occurs at the very beginning of the film, with the *MASH* theme playing over the opening scenes of helicopters bearing wounded soldiers on stretchers: What is the relationship between these initials shots of the diegesis that denote war and the nondiegetic lyrics of the lilting theme song, which delights in the changes occasioned by suicide? The questions generated by the nature of the commentary on the story offered by this music are multiplied in the first dialogue of the film:

> Medium long shot, zoom in to medium close on Colonel Blake and Radar, staring offscreen right, apparently at the arriving wounded seen in opening shots, rotating helicopter blades out of focus in extreme left foreground. Both characters speak at once.

| | |
|---|---|
| COLONEL: Radar, get a hold of Major Burns and tell him that we're going to have to hold a couple of surgeons over from the day shift to the night shift. Get General Hammond down there in Seoul; tell him we gotta have two new surgeons right away! | RADAR: I guess I'd better call Major Burns and tell him to put another day shift in our night shift. I'll put in a call to General Hammond in Seoul. I hope he sends us those two new surgeons; we're sure going to need 'em! |

This dialogue summarizes the effects that large numbers of newly arriving wounded have on the MASH unit. In turn, it becomes the cause that motivates the arrival of Duke and Hawkeye in the next scene—except that these words so crucial to the viewer's understanding of the initial situation in the story, which sets in motion the whole cause-effect chain of the narrative logic, are spoken by both characters simultaneously and are incomprehensible. It is possible only after several listenings to decipher fully the content of their speech. Laughter at what becomes part of the comic business in the film, the overlapping of the colonel's commands with Radar's simultaneous statement of them, occurs at the expense of clarity in the development of the story. At the crucial stage of its beginning, this shot disrupts causality, what David Bordwell calls "the armature of the classical story" (*Making Meaning* 13). In describing such disruptions in films of the international art cinema, the authors of *The Classical Hollywood Cinema* argue: "The author comes forward chiefly as patterned violations of the classical norm. Deviations from the classical canon . . . any failure to motivate cinematic space and time by cause-effect logic—can be read as 'authorial commentary'" (Bordwell et al. 374). One engineer describes this sense of commentary in Altman's use of multiple dialogue tracks in terms not of story, but of painting: "His wish was to create a condition figuratively similar to that of a painter who might coat his canvas with layer upon layer of color, allowing each brush stroke to give character and texture to the final rendering" (L. Levin 336).

In classical Hollywood cinema, sound traditionally functions to establish dramatic time and scenographic space as a context subordinate to the causally connected action of fictional characters. The viewer anticipates that sound will especially cue a sense of story character as part of the classical "*mise-en-scène* of bodies" (Doane, "Voice" 37). Sound has been used aggressively to naturalize characters, to animate them, to give them a greater degree of life and at the same time to guarantee not only their presence but the validity of the story, the reality of the fiction. In the context of classical practice, the new American cinema's disturbance of the sound-image relationship upsets both performance and narrative coherence. Altman's films continually focus on the instability of social identification, and many of the discontinuities that ground the comedy of *MASH* also reflect the splintering of individuals, both as subjects and as bodies. Altman's use of sound in *MASH* reveals not a concern with presence, a concern to authenticate and valorize presence, but a realization of fragmentation. Coherence of story is broken into the four major sequences, none of which is linked to any of the others by any narrative causality, and coherence of personality is fractured into disconnected action. This depiction of fragmentation and brokenness in the social subject reflects the film's antiwar theme. It marks the renegade director whose work disrupts classical canons of style, and it reveals not only a hostility toward military authority but a profoundly contradictory attitude toward the authority of discourse as well. Sound particularly marks this expressive fragmentation and its consequent refusal of presence.

One of Altman's approaches to sound recording technically is the use of radio microphones hidden in the actors' costuming rather than the more traditional boom mike. They "pick up speech (and body tone) *before* it is projected—that is, before it can acquire spatial properties." They lend "a surfacy quality to the image . . . which plays havoc with more traditional, illusionistic notions of space" (Rick Altman, "Moving Lips" 69). New American cinema works routinely to distract the viewer from an easy reading of the horizontal axis of story, to disrupt the viewer's engagement with the fiction's fantasy. Thus, like the flattening effect of the telephoto lens, the initial process of literally recording the sound in *MASH* works less to authenticate the existential, dramatic presence of the speaker than to distance the viewer from the three-dimensional wholeness of the narrative space and its personae. Robert Kolker describes the contradictory effect of employing both telephoto lens and the wide screen of Panavision "as rendering an experience of claustrophobia, a sense, on the viewer's part, of being locked into an observation of a *mise-en-scène* which refuses to open up or to give way, to yield immediately to the viewer's investigation of it . . . supported and exacerbated by the sound track. . . . The effect is an aural space that parallels the decentralization of the visual space" (342). The effect also contradicts the traditional Hollywood representation of the actor-character relationship, like that of the character-audience relationship, as one of clarity, integrity, and identity.

These fragmentations of story, style, personality, bodies, and identification share another concern of the new American cinema that also emerges from analysis of the sound track. Contemporary film theory asserts that audiences invest much psychic and ideological energy in the pleasurable stabilities certified by traditional narrative coherence. As Doane writes, "The aural illusion of position constructed by the approximation of sound perspective and by techniques which spatialize the voice and endow it with 'presence' guarantees the singularity and stability of a point of audition, thus holding at bay the potential trauma of dispersal, dismemberment, difference" ("Voice" 45). Art-cinema discourse constantly has recourse to the psychoanalytic understanding of human identity as splintered and divided along lines of sexual influence and insecurity. The dislocations of presence and the psychic motivations of *MASH* demonstrate a modernist sense of hostility, uncertainty, and ambiguity about the nature of authority, and that authority is repeatedly configured in terms of unstable sexuality.

Modern psychoanalytic film criticism posits a variety of signs as signifiers of authority in patriarchal culture. Specifically in film, the male voice and the male gaze have received extensive analysis as loci of dominance in sexual politics. The overarching symbol for this power is the phallus. Kaja Silverman writes that "the phallus is a signifier for the cultural privileges and positive values which define male subjectivity within patriarchal society," values indicative of "paternal power and potency" (*Subject* 183–84). The fear of homosexuality is one marker of a sense of male inadequacy in *MASH.* The entire second sequence of the film involves elaborate efforts to redeem the camp dentist, Painless (John Schuck), from his momentary impotence. A great deal of the sound track also reflects concern over the physiological representation of this potency, the penis, and its powerlessness, its lack.

Aural references to the penis abound. Early in the film, the loudspeaker announces: "Attention, attention. All noncommissioned officers will report for short arm inspection at 0400. That is all." Here is an association between military command and penis size and a paranoid sense of deficiency in the face of authority. In the scene that introduces Painless as the "best-equipped dentist in the army," Hawkeye's voice goes offscreen and then fades off-track while he is talking about "a great samossa" he saw once in medical school during an autopsy of a drowned man. The reported size of Painless's masculinity evokes a story, almost repressed from the film narrative, about a dead penis. One of the most figurative moments of dialogue in this regard is almost buried in the buzz of onscreen and offscreen conversation among medical personnel in the operating room scene framed by Hawkeye's and Hot Lips's evaluations of the nurses on his shift. Without seeing Hawkeye, we overhear his voice in conversation with the priest who asks if a patient on the table will be all right. Hawkeye replies that he's going to live but that someone needs "to be around tomorrow morning when he wakes up to tell him he hasn't got anything between his legs anymore." The aural register here specifically reiterates the modernist theme of physical debilitation that results from war, but the image of castration reflects a larger concern in the film with sexual prowess and inadequacy in the role of male authority. The MASH unit asks not to be understood classically as the source of comic stories about war, but as an imaginary site where fantasies of rebellion and anxieties about sexual potency can be metaphorically played out.

The omnipresence of war, the shattering of the body, the aural decentering of human presence, the hostility to established and arrogant authority, the fear of impotence—these interrelated issues in *MASH* reflect the new American cinema's development of inventive style to convey issues of ambiguity, anxiety, and broken communication that course throughout films of the late 1960s. Part of the authorial—or directorial—expressivity in *MASH* lies in the innovative reflexivity of the film, in those moments when the film as discourse addressed to an audience, rather than simply a series of story events unrolling innocently before our eyes, becomes apparent. When the black singer performs "Suicide Is Painless" during the last supper scene, the sound of the song is heard from within the story, rather than in voice-over as it is during the opening credit sequence. However, the singer looks directly into the lens of the camera as he sings and performs not for the other characters in the scene but for us in the audience. This direct address of us with his eyes deflects our attention from the "reality" of story events onto the artifice of the filmic discourse. The film again self-consciously places the audience in the position of the camera and thus the addressee of the scene where Hawkeye, ostensibly speaking into a newsreel camera, looks directly at us and says, "Hi, Dad!" At another point the film actually foregrounds the whole process of narrational sound—the unseen, offscreen placement of a microphone to eavesdrop on characters speaking to each other in ignorance of the audience listening and watching on the other side of that invisible wall that separates us and them—in the scene when Radar places a microphone under Hot Lips's bed.

Across the film the announcements on the loudspeaker shift from the function of establishing diegetic space to a diegetic commentary on the action. A realistic effect is achieved when announcements about camp movies are heard, but the nondiegetic function is simultaneously served by the fact that all of the movies screened in this MASH unit are war films, recalling reflexively that *MASH,* too, participates in this genre. The humorous anachronism of the announcements is apparent only to the viewer who knows that although *When Willie Comes Marching Home* (1950) is a film about World War II, the film *The Glory Brigade,* like *MASH,* is about the Korean War and was released in 1953, a year later than the time of the story in *MASH.* The concluding announcement of the film marks the end of the story as the diegetic sound becomes the nondiegetic summary (and anachronistic anticipation) of the film we have just seen: "Tonight's movie has been *MASH.* Follow the zany antics of our combat surgeons as they cut and stitch their way along the front lines operating as bombs—[laughter] as bombs and bullets burst around them, snatching laughs and love between amputations and penicillin. Follow Hawkeye, Trapper John, Duke. . . . Starring Donald Sutherland, Elliott Gould, Tom Skerritt. . . . That is all."

Self-reflexive narration has long been a staple of both classical film comedy and art-cinema narration, as evidenced by films such as Buster Keaton's *Sherlock Jr.* (1924), which "is, above all, a movie about a movie—a film within a film within a film" (Mast 133), and Woody Allen's *Purple Rose of Cairo,* in which much of the humor emerges as the diegetic and nondiegetic voices of the film actually converse with one another. The gradual shift toward reflexivity of loudspeaker announcements moves its locus as a voice within the story to a voice in the narration of the story. Rick Altman points out that the effect of synchronized sound in classical Hollywood cinema transfers "the origin of the words, as perceived by the spectator/auditor, from sound track and loudspeaker to a character within the film's diegesis" ("Moving Lips" 69). *MASH* achieves exactly the opposite effect by pointing the camera at the loudspeaker. Unlike classical cinema, which works progressively to reduce the signs of its omniscience, the voice of *MASH* asserts its presence more and more self-consciously; the resulting voice is transparently narrative and discursive. The audience no longer takes the military of the story as the author of the loudspeaker's voice but recognizes its source to be in the nondiegetic work of discourse.

The counterculture, the antiwar movement, and the new American cinema, like the doctor heroes of the story, resist established authority. *MASH* particularly refuses the established authority that shapes Hollywood stories in traditional ways. Silverman notes about the Oedipal development of the male that "if everything goes according to cultural plan, he identifies with his father by internalizing the latter's authority or 'voice.' . . . The male child will henceforth measure and define himself in relation to this repressive paternal representation, and thus to his society's dominant values" (*Subject* 141). The characteristic gesture of Altman's films seems partially to accept but finally to refuse the very authority for which it creates place. At the end of the credits to *The Magnificent Ambersons* (1942), Orson Welles puts the image of a microphone on the screen and identifies himself as the narrator and author: "I wrote the script and directed it. My name is Orson Welles." But the narration in *MASH* points the camera at the loudspeaker and concludes the film with a reflexive joke ("Tonight's movie has been *MASH*") that conceals authority and returns us to the imaginary world of the MASH unit even as we leave it.

Stephen Heath observes that "the sound cinema is the development of a powerful standard of the body and of the voice as hold of the body in image, the voice literally ordered and delimited as speech for an intelligibility of the body, of people—agents and characters—fixed in the order of the narrative and its meanings, its unities and resolutions" (*Questions* 191). At one level the storied world of *MASH* contests and unfixes human desire with violence and death. But just as its characters struggle against the constraints of military authority, so the film struggles against the rigor of classical narrative order. Nowhere is this combat more apparent than in the acoustic refusals of fidelity, clarity, and synchronization with the visual scene. Sound calls attention to itself as a separate register disconnected from the coherence of narrative voice. Asking to be heard in distinction from rather than in collusion with the image, the sounds of *MASH* convey a complex and cacophonous range of aural discourse. They work traditionally to create a story of human characters. They work nontraditionally and expressively to distance the presence of those characters. They echo the fragmentations of war, and they fragment the authority of narrative heroes. They subvert the pomposities of power and laugh at the subversion.

Film historian David Cook writes about all the innovative energy of 1968 and 1969, "It had seemed for a time that America was headed for a major cinematic (and social) renaissance. But neither came to pass" (*History* 634). J. Hoberman chronicles the transition that occurred during the seventies:

> As Hollywood passed mid-decade, nostalgia was in the air; minority tastes were swept aside by a new cinema of consensus. . . .
>
> Altman, Peckinpah, Kubrick, and company were succeeded by the generation of television-bred (and, in some cases, trained), film school–educated directors known as the "movie brats." . . .
>
> As the seventies wore on, it became apparent that the overarching impulse was less an attempt to revise genres than to revive them. . . .
>
> . . . A massive youth market had emerged, for whom *The Graduate* and *Easy Rider* were ancient history. The time was right for a bubble gum blockbuster and *Saturday Night Fever* was followed in the summer of 1978 by two other epochal youth pix: *Grease* and *Animal House*. . . .
>
> By 1975 it was apparent that the extraordinary period that saw the formation of an indigenous avant-garde, the so-called New American Cinema, was finally over. ("Ten Years" 36, 38, 45, 52)

By the middle of the 1970s the counterculture was dead, and Hollywood under the sign of the "movie brats" Coppola, Spielberg, Lucas, and Scorsese had begun to find the formulas that would "revivify classical cinema by directing films that were wildly successful" (Thompson 8). The new cinema of directorial names became another part of Hollywood marketing. Product differentiation now included the Steven Spielberg film, the Robert Zemeckis film, the James Cameron film, industrial auteurs who "shied away from the experimentation encouraged by the art-cinema vogue of the late 1960s and early 1970s" (Thompson and Bordwell 710). Yet Altman's *Prêt-à-Porter* in 1994 or *Kansas City* in 1996 or *Cookie's Fortune* in 1999 no less demonstrates the formal, stylistic, and philosophical commitments of this renaissance than the early Altman films that helped to establish that historical moment. More than just an American wave of cinematic innovation, however, the new cinema shared many of the formal, stylistic, and philosophical elements of the international art cinema. Steve Neale asserts, "It now appears that there is a relatively permanent genre towards which Art Cinema internationally has begun to gravitate" ("Art Cinema" 29). Specifically, according to David Bordwell, the genre "represents the domestication of modernist filmmaking. The Art Cinema softened modernism's attack on narrative causality by creating mediating structures—'reality,' character subjectivity, authorial vision—that allowed a fresh coherence of meaning" ("Art Cinema" 62).

In the three films analyzed in this chapter, Altman steps from journeyman television director in the classical storytelling tradition to director as auteur in the art cinema. This older director, who was forty-four at the time of *MASH,* helps usher in the emergent form and style of the "Americanized art cinema" (Thompson and Bordwell 710): graphic and rhythmic dimensions of editing and cinematography have come unstuck from narrative logic; story moves psychologically from apparent external to obscure internal motivation; plot becomes a project that is open-ended, ironic, ambiguous; generic formulas interrogate genre and traditional social values; unfamiliar and unusual actors play against the star system. The innovative expressivity of the auteur director produces a discourse occasionally reflexive, often moody and contradictory, and generally oblique in its narrative voice rather than the effaced zero degree of style in the classical narrative cinema. These early Altman films mark the distance between the cinema of the golden age of Hollywood and its modernist, if still marginal, successor, the new American cinema, and figure centrally in a period rightly designated a renaissance.

# 3. Art-Cinema Narration: *3 Women*

In the 1950s, the critics of *Cahiers du Cinéma* began a significant rereading of Hollywood movies. The French New Wave directors employed their readings of Hollywood to give vital energy to the European film practice that produced the international art cinema. While drawing upon the avant-garde and modernist tendencies of the other twentieth-century arts, the art cinema as a model of film production predominantly defines itself within the context of the classical Hollywood cinema. Its work amounts to an homage, a reading, a critique of that cinema; moreover, its films proved to be highly influential on American filmmakers of the 1970s. In particular, the structures, styles, and ideological characteristics of Altman's films ask to be seen as extensions of the Hollywood tradition reread through the practice of the international art cinema.

Defined formally, the "canonic story" of classical Hollywood cinema foregrounds the logical system of narrative causality that subordinates and rigorously motivates the other filmic systems of time and space. It focuses attention on the actions of a few dramatic personae whose goal-oriented behavior motivates conflicts, deadlines, suspense, crises, and resolutions. It deploys a story that moves linearly from stasis through disturbance to restoration and achieves closure through the efficacy of a central character, the hero, a star. Story action precedes along an axis of cause-effect logic, initial causes "in the beginning" producing effects that in turn cause subsequent effects until the chain achieves "the end" as a final effect. Narration and style work transparently and conventionally to cue the construction of a homogeneous and unambiguous story world. Intelligibility in the classical cinema involves viewers' acceptance of temporal and spatial continuity and causal verisimilitude projected for the viewer as an authentic, realistic, and ideologically stable social universe. Classical narrative situates the viewer, voyeuristically safe and distanced, as a passive, unself-conscious consumer of a story that seems to tell itself.

The international art cinema, on the other hand, seeks to liberate the spatial and temporal systems from subservience to narrative cause and effect. It portrays a graphic, rhythmic, and reflexive heterogeneity that challenges the homogeneity of character sociology, of causal order, and of thematic certainty conveyed by the classical model. It calls attention not to some *story*, that implicit chronology of realistic events, but to *narration*, to the explicit manner of the film's presentation. Its narrative and stylistic opacity construe the naturalized world of the filmic reality as an effect of the play of signifiers ordered, structured, distressed by the forces of language, ideology, and psychology. The art narrative is poetic. It foregrounds graphic and rhythmic systems. It emphasizes visual and temporal discontinuity. It employs symbolic, nonobjective imagery. It asks to be read vertically rather than horizontally, metaphorically rather than sequentially.

Just as in the novel, the separation between classical and modernist film marks the aesthetic distance between the "great tradition" of the nineteenth century and twentieth-century literary modernism: the word gradually loses its preeminent role as the sign for reality and increasingly appears as a symbol of reality. Like the nineteenth-century novel, committed to a middle-class ideology, classical narrative cinema explores but then effaces materialist and psychological contradiction. It assumes the possibility of communication and persuasion and asserts a unified social identity grounded in the secular humanism that optimistically posits "man" as the position of intelligibility, meaningful action, and ethicality. Offering the viewer a stable subject position from which to view, read, and understand, the classical cinema is a story cinema whose aim is to entertain. Modernist cinema, on the other hand, presupposes the world as splintered and centerless, meaning as imprecise and indeterminate, morality as divisive and illusory. It asserts that the human being is neither an autonomous individual nor a meaningful unity, but a process of divergent and contradictory forces, both internal and external. It suspects the power of communication in the face of human greed, alienation, estrangement, and self-destruction. Rather than encouraging viewer identification with a coherent character psychology, it delineates a variety of contradictory subject positions that critique privileged intelligibility. The modernist cinema is a materialist cinema whose aim is distanciation.

Between these poles, between the "zero-degree" style of classical directors like D. W. Griffith, John Ford, and Frank Capra and the polyphonic montage of modernists like Sergei Eisenstein and Jean-Luc Godard, lies the realm of the international art cinema. Salient features of this cinema do not derive from a priori assumptions of film theorists but evolve variously from the critical practice and film production of early Soviet cinema, Italian neorealism, and the French New Wave, and from such directors as Bergman, Ozu, Ray, Kurosawa, Dreyer, and Fellini. Throughout the last half of the twentieth century, numerous scholars in literature and film gave analytic, historical, and theoretical voice to these broad tendencies, which have avatars in all the twentieth-century arts. In film particularly, David Bordwell has extensively examined the terms of cinematic narration and provides one of the most specific analytic descriptions of art-cinema narration written to date. Bordwell points out in *Making Meaning*: "The practical critic possesses an underlying schema that proposes which textural features can carry abstract meaning. Most members of the critical institution share that schema, and those features become common property, like semantic fields" (180). His research articulates a number of widely shared "knowledge structures" that illuminate the practices of modern film narrative—in particular the designation of the procedural schemata "objective realism," "expressive" or subjective realism, and narrational commentary to "explain the various narrational strategies, and their instanciation in syuzhet and style, characteristic of this mode of filmmaking" (*Narration* 205). Specifically, he identifies the "new aesthetic conventions" that "motivate a loosening of cause and effect, an episodic construction of syuzhet, and an enhancement of the film's symbolic dimension through an emphasis on the fluctuations of character psychology" (*Narration* 216). These categories in the context of the cultural energies that sparked the Hollywood renaissance illuminate clearly the practice of Altman's films from *That Cold Day in the Park* in 1969 to *Dr. T & the Women* in 2000, more than thirty years later.

As "objective" realism, these films demonstrate a verisimilitude of space, time, and behavior. Although films like *McCabe & Mrs. Miller, Buffalo Bill and the Indians,* and *Kansas City* work through set design and costume to convey historical realities, as *Quintet* conveys an imagined future, a great number of Altman's films employ the real world of the contemporary United States and other nations as their settings: Reno gambling parlors in *California Split,* Opryland in *Nashville,* the Don Caesar Hotel in St. Petersburg for the health food convention in *Health,* the Houston Astrodome in *Brewster McCloud,* those famous French poppy fields in Arles for *Vincent & Theo,* the suburbs and streets of Los Angeles in *Short Cuts,* the former studio office of Francis Ford Coppola in the Hollywood film *The Player,* the contemporary ephemera of Paris fashion in *Prêt-à-Porter,* "present-day" Savannah in *The Gingerbread Man.* The films occasionally adopt a documentary mode in the representation of people and locales. In both *Nashville* and *The Player,* real country-western performers and real actors cross the stages of real Tennessee and Hollywood environs, the actual locales of these entertainment capitals. *Tanner '88,* which was produced for cable television, mounted a fictional presidential campaign for Jack Tanner during the 1988 political season that carried the characters through each of the actual primaries in New England, the South, the Midwest, and California, with occasional stops in Washington, D.C., and conversations with numerous individuals, from Bob Dole to members of the Fiske University choir playing themselves. The eleven-hour series put Tanner in debate with the major Democratic Party candidates, Michael Dukakis and Jesse Jackson, and the last sequence in the series brought Tanner to the actual floor of the Democratic National Convention in Atlanta, where he apparently lost for real to Dukakis. Kitty Dukakis, playing herself, made an appeal at the end for Tanner's support of the Democratic ticket in the fall elections of 1988.

This commitment to shooting in actual locales as opposed to using studio sets complements the tendency of the art cinema to work with unfamiliar actors. Altman's films also employ the star system in uncharacteristic ways: working against typecasting, using hero/heroine images in unglamorous roles, casting "box-office" unknowns, employing actors with unusual physical appearances in star roles. In his analysis of the fragmentary quality of filmic systems, Noël Burch stresses the effort that filmmakers must exert to achieve the illusionary reality of the classical narrative cinema ("Institutional Mode" 92). This fragmentation is especially clear in the clashes among actors, their bodies, their careers, and the individual characters they develop in separate films. The human actor as a sign specifically situates the major dichotomy between a "realism" signified in the story, the "character" of a "personality," and the opacity of convention that constantly signifies the individual actor. That is always Humphrey Bogart playing Duke Santee, Sam Spade, and Charlie Allnut. That is always Marlene Dietrich playing in *The Blue Angel* (1930) and *Touch of Evil* (1958). That is always Paul Newman performing in *Cool Hand Luke* (1967), *Exodus* (1960), and *Hud* (1963). The dynamics of the star system work to incorporate the actor's persona and the fiction's character, so that the weight of a career or a viewer's experience with that career becomes invested in the energies of the current role. The art cinema refuses these classical dynamics, however, by casting unknown actors, actors without star appeal, or actors whose appearances remind the viewer of the constructed theatricality of character.

The tendency to employ Hollywood stars in unusual ways and especially to use individuals with body types that audiences are unaccustomed to seeing in starring roles is a predominant aspect of Altman's efforts to remodel classical storytelling techniques. Stephen Heath has noted that the figure (in its rhetorical but especially its physical sense) "is a shifting circulation between agent, character, person, and image, none of which terms is able to contain or to settle that articulation" ("Film and System" 105). The logic of classical narrative works essentially to maintain that flux: if the presence of glamorous actress or handsome actor subverts attention to narrative movement, the seamless narrative nonetheless makes important use of the beautiful body in the illusory world of the story. Altman's films, however, make unusual use of stars in strange, nonempathic roles, such as Burt Lancaster and Paul Newman in *Buffalo Bill*; Warren Beatty in *McCabe*; Mia Farrow in *A Wedding*; the international stars of *Quintet,* Paul Newman, Fernando Rey, and Bibi Andersson; Susannah York in *Images*; Jack Lemmon in *Short Cuts*; Julia Roberts in *Prêt-à-Porter*; Richard Gere in *Dr. T & the Women.*

One scene in *McCabe & Mrs. Miller* illustrates this practice and its effects in particular. Reacting to his frustrating relationship with Mrs. Miller (Julie Christie), McCabe (Warren Beatty) is drunk and sits facing the camera as he mumbles his unhappiness and tries without success to close his pocket watch. As we watch the Hollywood star and western hero in this inebriated state, he unambiguously burps and farts the heroic prototype into a modernist oblivion and reinforces that film's deconstruction of the western genre. The gross distortion of Beatty's glamorous image signifies a different western realism, represented as often by the film's close-ups of the back of Beatty's head as by the diminishment of the hero's traditional peacemaker to a concealed derringer.

Similarly, *Quintet*'s enshrouding of the lithe and well-known body of Paul Newman in heavy winter, medieval-like garments opposes the new filmic image to the familiar signification of Newman's person. Embedded in the hypnotic pace and obscure structure of *Quintet,* the traditionally heroic impulse that looks to the future against impossible odds still breathes. And somewhere within the somnambulistic role of Essex (Newman) lies the ideal embodiment of that impulse. However, the optimistic theme, the traditionally forward-looking face of the dominant model in science fiction, and the heroic body usually signified by this genre are all subverted.

Moreover, like the films of other art-cinema directors, Altman's films from *That Cold Day* in 1969 to the Altman-produced ABC television series *Gun* in 1997 employ an Altman repertory company: Michael Murphy, Geraldine Chaplin, Bert Remsen, Allan Nicholls, Henry Gibson, Lily Tomlin, Paul Dooley, Rene Auberjonois. The use of unique physiognomies such as those of Sissy Spacek, Bud Cort, Keith Carradine, Shelley Duvall, Sam Shepard, Linda Hunt, Stephen Rea, Jennifer Jason Leigh, and Embeth Davidtz continually disrupts the anticipated uses and gratifications afforded by the prototypes of beautiful bodies in popular culture. The films undercut the images of heroes or heroines with male and female physiognomies so unconventional for such roles that attention to the dramatic action is constantly threatened. Keith Carradine in *Nashville* and *Thieves Like Us* or Paul Dooley in *A Perfect Couple* hardly fits the Hollywood paradigm of a leading man. Dooley is middle-aged, paunchy, and round-shouldered, with a craggy face, double chin, and thinning hair. Marta Heflin is twentyish, skinny as a rail, with a big nose, a wide mouth, and bulging eyes. Their bodies signify the painfully plain; their roles signify ideal couple. This characteristic dissonance subverts narrative coherence by throwing fictive character as well as theme into a new register. As in much of the international art cinema in which Altman's films have their roots, the diminished glamour of actors renders story more lifelike: "real couples" are more like Dooley and Heflin than they are like Clark Gable and Claudette Colbert or Doris Day and Rock Hudson. While subverting the illusionary realism of ideal couples, Altman's actors portray a couple uncomfortable to watch, difficult to identify with, and thus more credible in the loneliness that constitutes their initial meeting by computer-date service. The film represents one of Altman's most traditional uses of classical structures, but the unlovely physiognomies of Dooley and Heflin create a dual spectator position—the viewer desires the generic success of love triumphant in the romance while remaining distanced from the lovers themselves.

Nowhere is the resistance between the actor and the fiction more apparent than between the depiction of the nude body and the significance of that depiction. The naked body, on one hand, indicates the absolute refusal of the body to portray any character other than itself. And nudity is always defined within and by a context of shifting cultural values, a system of conventions assimilated by the viewer. The short scenes that display in particular the nude female body and the unusual or atypical physiognomy of actors in Altman's films are practices that deflect and revise conventional systems of narrative characterization. They at once narrativize the body and subvert narrative coherence and diegetic meaning. Thus they further reflect the expressive realism of the art-cinema practice. The nudes in these films move within the diegetic discourse of dramatic action and within a social discourse of physicality and sexuality. They dramatize the bifurcation of the human subject that frequently provides the thematic center of these films—a dissonance between the character as a role or disguise and the body as an object or resistance to desire.

The nude female body constitutes part of the attraction of the international art cinema for American audiences raised on the visual chastity of classical Hollywood cinema. But the depiction of the body in Altman's work complements the unique physiques of the Altman repertory company to establish a form of communication that Roland Barthes describes as "discontinuous, indifferent to the story and to the obvious meaning" ("Third Meaning" 61). It is "the epitome of a counter-narrative" (63) and urges self-consciously the recognition of cultural and narrative conventions. It represents one of those moments of difference, of heterogeneity, of excess in the use of the body in the work of the film to maintain a homogeneous narrative illusion.

More than any other figure, Shelley Duvall signifies the bizarre, socially unpopular physiognomy. She illustrates Barthes's observation that there is "an eroticism which includes the contrary of the beautiful" ("Third Meaning" 58). Perhaps the most audacious use of the body as a signifier to disturb easy spectator position in these films is Duvall's nude bathing scene in *Thieves Like Us.* Her tall, skinny body in a conventionalized pose of nude bather signifies nakedness, an abject revealing of her self in a moment doubly dissonant: as she modestly shares both the glances of the spectator and her lover, the viewer recognizes that Bowie (Keith Carradine) sees her as nude: "To be nude is to be seen naked by others and not recognized for oneself. A naked body has to have been seen as an object in order to become nude" (J. Berger 54). At a larger level, Duvall and Carradine contrast sharply with the alienated but lovely Cathy O'Donnell and Farley Granger of Nicholas Ray's original film version of *Thieves Like Us,* titled *They Live by Night* (1949). Throughout the film, Duvall represents the awkward, lonely, inexperienced personality whose body guarantees—as perhaps its cause—the social alienation of the personality. Unable to see her as an erotic object, the spectator experiences the social dichotomies between the pathetic body as subject and the beautiful body as object; the viewer focuses reflexively on the distance between the pleasurable looking afforded by romance even in a film noir and the painful (almost embarrassed) looking afforded by Altman's movies.

Altman's films employ this signifying quality in very different ways in two other of Duvall's six major roles. In *Nashville,* Duvall is the freaky and freaked out L.A. Joan, who constantly changes from one outlandish costume to another. Her bizarre appearance is epitomized in the scenes where she displays her body in a skimpy bikini while trying on wigs over a stereo headset. Her appearance is constantly changing, constantly startling in the film, but the narrative finally cues a perception of coherence between Duvall's physiognomy and the bizarre, unsympathetic character she portrays. Her role as Millie, the central character in *3 Women,* establishes the lack of erotic appeal signified by her body as a thematic key to the heterogeneous narrative in the film. The film casts Duvall as the focus of the troubled sexual and economic exchanges in this very modernist film. As the ego persona of the Pinky-Willie-Millie symbiosis in the film, the Duvall character may be the author of the film as a dream text whose center is the fear of sex, of sexuality, and of childbirth. She makes a fetish of following the recommendations in women's magazines for transforming woman—her body, her actions, her dwelling—into the erotic object of male desire. The profusion of mirrors in the film constantly demonstrates the dual self-concept of woman as both an object for male observation and an observer of herself as such an object. She is exploited by the mass-media images of the "thoroughly modern Millie," but she lives in a body that conventionally signifies not the beautiful but the ordinary. She is constantly ignored by the men whose glances she covets. Betrayed by the images of advertising, the feminine identity depicted in *3 Women* is captured by the artist Willie as reptilian, repulsive, and defensive before the image of the phallus. The dissonance between Shelley Duvall's physique and the characteristics that normally signify "leading lady" in a Hollywood story significantly informs the narrative dissonance between Millie's traumatic self-concept and the attractive sex object she longs to be. Duvall received an academy award nomination for this role (appropriately in the company of such star bodies as Vanessa Redgrave, Jill Clayburgh, and Jane Fonda), even as it epitomizes the Altman subversion of traditional narrative codes. The body as a signifier in Altman, to use Roland Barthes's language, "radically recasts the theoretical status of the anecdote: the story (the diegesis) is no longer just a strong system . . . but also and contradictorily a simple space, a field of permanences . . . whose false limits multiply the signifier's permutational play" ("Third Meaning" 64). Altman's films hardly redefine the social concept of the beautiful body, but their unusual interest in atypical physiognomy and the curious display of the body at once deflects and renews the essence of cinematic narrative.

This commitment to a "multifaceted reality" also motivates a different kind of storytelling, characterized by a loosening of cause-effect logic, a blurring of story problems, a shortage of deadlines, a tenuous linking of actions and scenes, and an open-ended and episodic chronology of events. Modernist fiction generally recognizes that "the human imagination forces coherence on the existential void by telling stories, ultimately meaningless, which compose delusively neat teleological wholes with beginnings, middles, and ends. Life, after all, does not tell stories" (Stam 8). A tendency to tell unfocused stories, because, as Altman has routinely remarked, "that's the way life is," addresses one of the most characteristically unpopular features of Altman's films. Narration structures the films without the discursive order, the continuity of story that is the cornerstone of the Hollywood model and that still conditions audience reactions to film and television drama. The open-endedness of films like *MASH, California Split, Nashville, A Wedding,* and *Short Cuts* is perhaps Altman's most famous—or notorious—trademark with the popular audience. During an interview in 1975 on the television news show *60 Minutes,* Mike Wallace harshly interrogated Altman at length regarding his failure to tell stories and literally asked him to justify his "hostility" to storytelling films. His justification for experimenting with meandering, unfocused, ambiguous narrative forms is the ubiquitous resolution of the clash between realism and form in the art cinema: that's the way it happens in real life. "We are looking for a reason," he said in response to the widespread criticism of the narrative structure in *Nashville.* "We demand logic, but it doesn't necessarily have to be there" (quoted in Bryne and Lopez 25).

The audience encounters delayed exposition everywhere in these movies, so that understanding what moves the story from initial stasis to disturbance remains frustratingly remote. Why does Blondie kidnap Red in the opening scene of *Kansas City*? What does the bird lecture have to do with anything in *Brewster McCloud*? Orson Welles's famous long shot in *Touch of Evil* concluded with Janet Leigh and Charlton Heston's interrupted honeymoon kiss, which the narrative seeks to conclude at film's end, but what action does the eight-minute shot at the beginning of *The Player* activate? What causes the tension and hostility

A parody of happy endings *(The Player).*

between Eddie and May in *Fool for Love*? The viewer remains as puzzled by this question as May's date, who enters the story in its last act. Marcello Mastroianni buys identical Christian Dior ties in Moscow in the opening of *Prêt-à-Porter* and uses them as means to set up a clandestine meeting with a famous designer in Paris, but neither these nor any other actions of the Mastroianni character ever seem to make story sense in the entirety of this film. *The Long Goodbye* languidly intercuts Marlowe's quest for cat food with Terry Lennox's driving through the night and then rapidly puts the two of them in a car at the Mexican border, only the first of many times the viewer wonders what's going on in this detective story. And so it goes in almost all of Altman's movies, which, as Helene Keyssar expresses it, "rarely leave us with a conceptual conclusion or with the satisfaction that the world projected is complete and distinct from the world in which we live" (16). According to Bordwell, "The viewer must therefore tolerate more permanent causal gaps than would be normal in a classical film" (*Narration* 296).

The large casts of multiple characters in films like *Nashville, A Wedding, Health, Tanner '88, The Player, Short Cuts,* and *Prêt-à-Porter* further generate this sense of the realistic. Confusion derives from Altman's practice of developing dozens of stories in relatively limited social spaces with large numbers of individuals whose paths and lives cross in only willy-nilly ways. Much as daily life occasions numerous chance encounters between people whose lives only momentarily touch, the numerous plots in these films seem linked at best by chance as the audience's dependence on a single line of story disappears. Moreover, the large number of stories mean that few characters can ever be developed in depth, that specific problems and deadlines and resolutions become blurred in multiplicity. Thus the films replicate the fluid, unexpected, accidental, and sometimes portentous dimensions of the flow of daily existence. At the same time, the recursive evocations of the multiple stories detail the rich density and interactive possibility of that existence. Different politics and talents and fortunes and motives coalesce into ironic, tragic, or just complex tapestries of American entertainment. Diverse economic classes, religious perspectives, sexual orientations, and ethnic associations somehow merge in the humorous or pathetic rituals of social functions surrounding weddings. Multiple sexualities in silly social intrigues evolve around the big-business pomp and glamour of the fashion industry. Like William Faulkner's modernist model, these films demonstrate the remarkable fertility of social motivation and understanding that somehow combine at surface levels of life to create a recognizable if not coherent fabric of shared social existence. And in every case, Bordwell observes, "the narration asks us to unify the story by appeal to the plausible improbabilities of 'real life'" (*Narration* 207). Altman argues that "we ask for reasons in life, but that there are no answers, only chance" (in Kaplan and Dorr).

Although "objective" realism motivates much of the open-endedness of such narratives, art-cinema narration also results from the filmmaker's interest in portraying a certain kind of character. Rather than the heroic individual "certain of certain certainties" and possessed of the physical and mental attributes necessary to fight for the right or the girl or the country, this cinema portrays characters who lack clear-cut traits, motives, and goals, who slide passively from one situation to another, who display "psychological effects in search of their causes" (Bordwell, *Narration* 208)—like Pinky in *3 Women* or van Gogh in *Vincent & Theo* or Eddie in *Fool for Love* or Mona in *Come Back to the 5 & Dime, Jimmy Dean, Jimmy Dean* or Cora in *Cookie's Fortune.* These narratives are motivated by a concern with psychological as opposed to sociological realism. They subjectively portray psychologically confused, conflicted, alienated characters, enmeshed in frequently aimless plots constructed not on action but on inaction and reflection. Altman's movies present a large gallery of such complex and often aberrant personalities: the hero of *Brewster McCloud,* who lives in a bomb shelter at the Houston Astrodome, where he is building a set of wings so that he can fly away from society; the homicidal, schizophrenic heroines in *Images* and *That*

*Cold Day in the Park*; the decidedly unheroic John "Pudgy" McCabe and his dope-smoking business partner, prostitute Constance Miller; the splintered personalities in *3 Women* of Willie, Millie, and Pinky, who together perhaps represent a whole personality in symbiosis.

Narrative causality and ease of comprehension frequently collapse because of such psychologically diffuse individuals. Nondirected plot is a function of questioning, uncertain, alienated, sometimes crazy central characters. The meandering quality of plot in *McCabe & Mrs. Miller* aptly follows from the indecisive personality of McCabe. The general plotlessness of *Buffalo Bill and the Indians* detours narrative resolution into the labyrinth of the hero's inability to maintain the tension between his identity as William F. Cody and his show business role of Buffalo Bill. Unlike the hero of western mythology, this Buffalo Bill can hardly separate imagination from fact and so is lost in the confusion. Barbara Jean's nervous feats strung together between her private and public lives motivate much of the kaleidoscopic energy in *Nashville*. *California Split* evokes and resolves no conflict but rather lyrically muses over the manic Charlie and the depressive Bill, two sadly humorous and obsessive gamblers, who are, as Leonard Cohen's song asserts about McCabe, looking for that one last great winning hand. Redundancy in the classical narrative derives largely from the very fact of narrative structures and traditional genres. In art-cinema narration, however, redundancy diminishes as cause-effect logic is subverted. Information increases, but the comprehensibility of dramatic action itself declines as a marked signifier of the hero's confusion.

As these new probabilities come into play and narrative contiguity and extension diminish, the viewer is further compelled to construe character less in terms of coherent behavior and motivation and more in terms of comparison with other characters similarly displayed in minimal ways. The four parts of *MASH*—the humiliation of Burns and Hot Lips, the resurrection of Painless, the visit to Japan, and the football game—ask to be read metaphorically as replicating similar masculine fears mastered through the mastery of others. The dizzying gyre of family relationships among fourteen individuals in *A Wedding* permits the conception of the Corellis as a family whose basic dysfunctions remain hidden in wealth and drugs and the Brenners as a family burdened by religious and sexual hypocrisies. The jazz singing of Tess and the classical cello playing of Zoe in *Short Cuts* establish two separate styles that allow viewers to construct paradigms of character: the motorcycle cop and his family, the chauffeur and the waitress, the pool cleaner and the phone-sex mom replay lives of jazz. The clown and her husband, the doctor and the painter, the weatherman, his wife, and dying son echo the cello's dirges. Parallelism rather than causality becomes the dominant structural device in the films of multiple major characters, "impelling us to compare agents, attitudes, and situations" (Bordwell, *Narration* 207).

A characteristic structural device of modern fiction since the short stories of James Joyce in *Dubliners* has been the epiphany. A religious concept related to the revelation of divinity, it denotes that sudden intuitive flash of the subjective apprehension of reality, as when Joyce's young hero in "Araby," in a sudden moment of understanding, sees both his trip to the bazaar and his love for Mangan's sister as childish, foolish, and humiliating. Epiphany further denotes a narrative structure organized to flow toward or around such moments of illumination. Modern theologians and philosophers such as Paul Tillich identify such moments when individuals simultaneously recognize their nonbeing and the ground of their being as boundary situations. The international art cinema abounds in such moments—perhaps most dramatically memorable in Ingmar Bergman's *The Seventh Seal* (1957) when the Knight, who is playing a film-long chess game with Death, sits in a sunny meadow and shares strawberries and milk in an epiphanic moment of communion with Jof, Mia, and their child. "Crises of existential significance" course through all of Altman's work: when Marlowe learns that his friend Terry has lied to him in *The Long Goodbye;* when Barbara Jean sings her first song, "In the Garden," in the hospital chapel in *Nashville;* when William Cody measures the gap between himself and his public relations image as Buffalo Bill; when Griffin Mill contracts to make a movie called *The Player.* Such moments produce the light of understanding that illuminates character behavior beyond the order of cause-effect logic. Like the sunlight reflected off the milk as the Knight lifts nature's holy communion bowl in *The Seventh Seal,* these instants suffuse and inform in multiple, nonlinear directions the representations of character in these films.

Bordwell argues that such concerns for expressive or subjective realism mean that "inquiry into character becomes not only the prime thematic material but a central source of expectation, curiosity, suspense, and surprise" in the art cinema (*Narration* 209). Moreover, it further motivates the use of cinematic style to shape temporal and spatial representations as reflections of subjective states. Nearly all of Altman's films share the art cinema's elevation of temporal and spatial systems to parity with the narrative system. Relationships of time and space still work generally, as in the classical Hollywood cinema, to support the demands of the logical system, but as narrative continuity and closure go awry, spatial and temporal articulations ask to be read not dramatically but metaphorically. In *Images,* the camera's play over mirrors, prisms, and wind chimes makes sense less as the dramatic context of Cathryn's actions than as the metaphoric representation of Cathryn's schizophrenia. A transparent wall of glass provides the looking glass in *Come Back to the 5 & Dime* through which character, camera, and audience move to see the past as an explanation of the present and to explore the nature of the past in the present. The doubled fluidity of this scenographic space emerges as a remarkable metaphor for the subjectivity of memory, of passion, of betrayal, of deception. Production design in *Vincent & Theo* alternates the dark and somber interiors of the brothers' various abodes and Theo's galleries with the brilliant, sunny colors of the natural world and Vincent van Gogh's paintings. In *Dr. T,* the mise-en-scène alternates between the bright colors of upper-class women's fashion and the monochromatic play of gray, green, and yellow skies forecasting the tornado that will blow Dr. T away from the Oz of contemporary Dallas. Modern jazz replicates the rhythms of *Kansas City* in the 1930s; it comments on the perceptive worlds of Seldom Seen and Blondie; it shapes the narrative of the film, motivates script development, and captures the subjective emotions of all its characters.

To the critical schemata of "objective" and "subject" realism Bordwell adds a third category he calls "narrational commentary":

> In applying this schema the viewer looks for those moments in which the narrational act interrupts the transmission of fabula information and highlights its own role. . . . The marked self-consciousness of art-cinema narration creates both a coherent fabula world and an intermittently present but highly noticeable external authority through which we gain access to it. (*Narration* 219)

Such narration becomes opaque to the story, blocks easy access to the story through intrusive, reflexive devices that call attention to its telling. It makes the viewer aware of a process of shaping and manipulation. It employs connotative and symbolic means of expression and linkage. It distorts temporal reality and calls attention to the profilmic event as a construct, "as the narration's restaging of history" (*Narration* 211). Indeed, it constitutes the "puzzle movie," in which "the very construction of the narration becomes the object of spectator hypotheses: how is the story being told? why tell the story in this way?" (*Narration* 210).

Altman's films confront audiences with these questions everywhere. Vilmos Zsigmond's sensuous cinematography in *McCabe & Mrs. Miller* may write a poem to autumn that lyrically chronicles McCabe's last days. At the same time, however, it illustrates a tendency in Altman's films for temporal and spatial constructions to motivate aspects of narrative. The descent of winter in the mountains of Calgary, Canada, where the film was shot, visually motivates McCabe's death as much as does the cause-effect logic of his encounters with Mrs. Miller and the mining company. Altman has asserted that he chose Leonard Cohen's music for the sound track of the film because it had been played constantly during production and had in the minds of the production staff determined the editorial and dramatic rhythms of the film (Kass 111–12). Although the chaotic, multifaceted energy of real life in Nashville motivated the open-endedness of Joan Tewkesbury's script for *Nashville,* the narrative randomness of the film also results from the editorial matching on ubiquitous media equipment: telephones, cameras, television sets, and tape recorders. In *Quintet,* Altman's futuristic script develops through the color, mood, and tone achieved through the use of an old still-photography diffusion filter discovered accidentally during preproduction camera tests. Each of these events asks to be understood in metaphoric relationship to the story nevertheless unfolding on the other side of narration.

In *The Long Goodbye,* the camera is never still. Kolker argues that "Altman so radically and subtly manipulates the perception of cinematic space that the viewer becomes aware of this manipulation through a sense of discomfort and uneasiness" (319). The camera pans, zooms, tilts, and reframes in very noticeable ways. "It's never in the right place," according to Altman *(The Player).* When Marlowe and Roger Wade converse on the Malibu beach, the camera tracks in oblique arcs. It zooms in off-centered ways to capture the two speakers, and the cutting between shots conveys a rhythm of movement that constantly disrupts, even overwhelms the conversation itself. When Marlowe interrogates Eileen Wade, the camera captures the two of them first in a medium shot, then begins a slow zoom to their heads in close-up only to continue slowly zooming past the two of them through the window behind them to the tiny white figure of Roger wading into the ocean. Why is the camera working like this? Kolker asserts that "throughout the film the movement insists that there is more to be known, catches us up in an instability and an incompleteness" (319).

*Vincent & Theo* opens with an enhanced video shot of the auction at

Christie's in London of a famous close-up painting of sunflowers by van Gogh. The narration holds this shot as the bidding proceeds from five million pounds to fifteen million pounds. Then it shifts to a scene of two arguing men, whose clothing indicates some nineteenth-century past. As the shot conveys their dispute over the painter's work and his brother's financial support of that work, the sound track continues to play the sound of the twentieth century until the painting is finally sold for the remarkable sum of twenty-two and a half million pounds. What are the relationships between these two temporal orders? Why does the narrative aggressively foreground itself to begin the film in this way?

*Kansas City* juxtaposes the performance of jazz from the Hey Hey Club with the antics of Blondie as she tries to free her man from Seldom Seen. Critics of the film routinely dismiss the latter story and praise the jazz or enjoy the story but fault the jazz. How do the two strands relate to each other? What does Count Basie's "Solitude" have to do with the scenes from Blondie's story to which it is linked? Moreover, why do the contemporary jazz musicians who play the music of the 1930s interpret that music in the modern rhythm rather than attempting to replicate the sound of the thirties, especially in light of the set design, which works meticulously to duplicate the look of history?

Such considerations of stylistic matters may determine impressions about psychologically diffuse characters and aimless plots in the narrative. They may convey the mix of both objective and subjective reality. But sometimes graphic and rhythmic dimensions in Altman's films come unstuck from story logic, place, and time altogether. Wexman writes, "In Altman's plots, the principle of causality frequently gives way to a fascination with randomness, a method that can produce images of rapturous intensity because they have the aura of having been discovered at the moment of their creation" ("Critical" 20). At one level, *3 Women* aggressively asks to be read as a study in yellow and purple, colors that run throughout the set design in a range from pure abstraction to polychromatic puns. The film also writes an extended essay on the aesthetics of the zoom lens in its array of long shots, close-ups, oblique angles, pan shots, even the classical shot/reverse-shot continuity, all subsumed to the energy, if not the logic, of the zoom. *McCabe & Mrs. Miller,* too, is a motion painting in blue/green and red/gold, from the initial designs of deep greens partially illuminated by gold to the pointillistic blend of white and gold in the penultimate scene and the imagistic suffusion of gold and red in the final scenes. Ingenious criticism can always recuperate such details to the service of narrative coherence. More broadly, however, Altman's films reflect the exuberance of musician, painter, poet, and storyteller—in short, the expressivity of the artist, the art-cinema director.

It is especially the unity imposed by an expressive auteur in the art cinema that partially replaces the unity in story and character generated by psychological realism. The consistency of the classical production system, of story continuity, even of genre conventions yields to the consistency of the director's style and vision. This mixture of psychological realism in story and authorial expressivity in narration in Altman's films has earned them a limited audience, as it has for most directors in the art cinema. Popular with critics and film educators, Altman's films almost never succeed at the box office, a fact central to the mistrust of Altman by Hollywood production companies. One aspect of his work that has angered audiences and even many critics, and that actually draws verbal reactions of hostility from theater audiences, further characterizes the art cinema as a mode of discourse. The juxtaposition of psychological realism in the narrative with the frequently self-conscious expressionism of the director results in a contradictory clash of cinematic modes. David Bordwell asserts: "The surest signs of narrational omniscience . . . are the least capable of realistic justification. Contrariwise, to push the realism of psychological indefiniteness to its limit is to create a haphazard narrative in which an author's shaping hand would not be visible. In short, a realistic aesthetic and an expressionist aesthetic are hard to merge" ("Art Cinema" 70). Wexman further designates a particular aspect of this conflict in Altman's films: "This tension is often expressed in terms of the contradictions inherent in art itself between the static order of aesthetic forms and the constantly evolving life processes that the forms represent" ("Critical" 21). Such contradictions are resolved in the art cinema through narrative open-endedness, formal irony, and ambiguity. The art cinema demands a reading strategy that looks not for resolution but for multiplicity, not for linear causality but for indeterminacy. The art cinema asks to be read in its ambiguity.

The clash of modes is striking in Altman's films. On one hand, there is the approach to a heightened realism that results from shooting on location (in *Images, McCabe, Brewster McCloud, California Split, Nashville, Tanner '88, Vincent & Theo, The Player, Prêt-à-Porter, Cookie's Fortune*), enhanced frequently by vividly "real" cinematography, "an aura of documentary-like tangibility" (Wexman, "Critical" 19). The apparent concern with naturalness in acting in these films has led to the erroneous belief that Altman works in production by improvisation, but the

Blending the real and the fictional *(Prêt-à-Porter).*

impression of improvisation is part of the code of realism in the art cinema. Altman's long experimentation with overlapping sound cumulating in an eight-track recording system also seems largely motivated by a desire for a more natural, more "real," if less comprehensible, reproduction of dialogue and ambient noise.

On the other hand, however, Altman's films strikingly illustrate that the art cinema is a mood cinema, a poetic as well as narrative art. The cold palette of gold and green in *Images,* the lyrical zoom and pan shots in *Nashville* and *3 Women,* the pointillism of the final sequence in the blizzard in *McCabe,* the exuberant colors and sounds of fashion in *Prêt-à-Porter,* the ominous and nightmarish repetition of red and black throughout *The Gingerbread Man*—these reveal the eye of a painter rather than the voice of a narrator. Indeed, Altman has repeatedly insisted that what he wants to achieve in his films is an emotional rather than an intellectual effect: "I look at film as closer to a painting or a piece of music; it's an impression . . . an impression of character and total atmosphere. . . . The attempt is to enlist an audience emotionally, not intellectually" (quoted in Kass 21). On other occasions he has described all of his films as musicals *(The Player).* Altman's films never simply depict unresolved stories as much as they represent life's ambiguities.

## The Art-Cinema Text

Henry James's short novel *The Turn of the Screw,* written in 1898, provides an illuminating model of ambiguity in modern narrative cinema. This famous ghost story develops sufficiently unclear character psychology that it has generated a long critical debate over the reality of his fictional ghost. The narration shifts the reader's attention from the realism of the story to the more subjective realism of its plot, its telling, and, at a further remove, the very production by James of the novel itself as a ghost story. Individual interpretations as to whether the ghosts are real or not, whether the narrator is mentally unbalanced or not, whether the frame tale is central or not cannot subsume the complexities of the narrative. Moreover, James's assertion that he wrote the novel as a self-consciously calculated exercise in narrative construction, making it in some ways a parody of his other novels, drastically drives the reader's attention away from a reading of the story as signified to the novel as a play of conventional fictional signifiers structured in tension with each other.

James's novel creates a narrative reality that asks to be read in its ambiguity. A central feature of modernist literature that proceeds from the Jamesian strategy is "a tendency to foreground and create a conflict between the two basic courses of action in a text, the narrative or dramatic movement and the presence of an authorial voice seeking to take up some stance towards the dramatic material" (Altieri 88). The art cinema similarly relies on modern literary practices to produce ambiguity depending on the interaction of character subjectivity at the level of story and authorial vision at the level of narration. Where the classical narrative cinema endeavors to foreclose an unstable reality by subordinating spatial and temporal systems to the necessities of narrative logic, the art cinema attempts to liberate spatial, temporal, graphic, and rhythmic dimensions from narrative altogether and accentuates the process of signification itself. Art-cinema narration achieves a balance between classical closure of cause-effect logic and modernist diversity; it serves as the meeting ground of the realistic and the expressive. Altman's film *3 Women* dramatically illustrates the central reading strategies demanded by the art cinema: a comprehension of the play among divergent signifying systems as the dialectic between fictive characterization and artistic expressivity that ultimately renders more ironic, more complex, and more ambiguous the realism portrayed in the narrative.

Classical narrative film functions through the authority of a central point-of-view character, but the art film obscures the locus of narrative voice, like a detective story with no detective, no surrogate to solve the mystery presented to the viewer's curiosity. For instance, the narration's pervasive use of mirrors in point-of-view shots in *3 Women* effectively undermines the direction of glance and space and thus destabilizes the continuity of narrative perspective achieved by point-of-view structures in the classical film. The audience for *3 Women* that seeks narrative perspective as given, fixed, and credible is consigned a position of confusion from the outset of the film. The hazy quality of the opening shot;

the bizarre, serpentine images of the murals; the haunting sounds of a woodwind quartet—all suggest a reading of meditation or hallucination. And the sharp clarity of the second shot, a close-up of legs in a pool, recuperated at last as Pinky's (Sissy Spacek) as she stares in trance-like fixation at Millie (Shelley Duvall) at work with patients in a geriatric center, establishes a range of at least four points of view: external and perhaps dreaming narrator, Pinky as the subject of mediation, Millie as the dominant object of attention, and Willie (Janice Rule) as a silent, elusive figure whose murals nevertheless obtrude enigmatically everywhere in the diegetic spaces of the film.

The subsequently equivocal nature of characterization and filmic voice exemplifies how the art film moves the viewer's focus from what happens in the story to the representation of those happenings. As the hermeneutic code involves the psychological enigmas of the narrative voice, its fears, its origins, the viewer encounters the broken teleology of the art cinema. Temporal continuity no longer oversees the straightforward drive of the cause-effect chain, but is subordinated to the perplexing aberrations of character psychology. In *3 Women* the confusion of points of view geometrically expands the sense of diegetic conflict. Is the central opposition in the film between Willie and Edgar (Robert Fortier), between Millie and her social world, between Pinky and her parents? Among the three women? Between the three women and Edgar? As it suggests all of these, the story dramatizes a central reading strategy of the art cinema. The viewer's inability to identify the protagonist thwarts any attempt to follow the meaning of events, which consequently must be interpreted from all the ambiguity of mutually interdependent individuals.

*3 Women* graphically illustrates the tendency of the art cinema to achieve ambiguity through the tension of systems within the work. Its advertising sold ambiguity in the first place when it proclaimed: "1 woman became 2; 2 women became 3; 3 women became 1." The trailers promised, "It will make you examine everyone you ever wanted to be." In addition to the numerous enigmas in its story—about Pinky's motivations, about the relationship between Pinky and her parents, about Pinky's attempted suicide and subsequent appropriation of Millie's identity, about the death of Edgar—the film mobilizes a systematic disruption of coherence and meaning. The narration regularly punctuates the story with images from three different murals painted by the Willie character. The structure and content of these visual representations within the film constantly highlight artistic expression as a commentary, as a gloss on events.

These images open and close the film and appear paradigmatically to describe the interaction of the three women and Edgar. The murals all portray two women protecting a third, pregnant woman from a male figure, which is variously depicted as insignificant or phallically dominating. Careful examination of the murals, however, reveals a variety of different interrelationships among the characters, some of which occur in the diegesis and others of which do not. Furthermore, the narration's juxtaposition of mural image to individual character in the editing now parallels, now contrasts story character with mural character. And the overriding situation in the murals, conceived before the story's end, depicts with marked temporal distortion the dramatic situation achieved only at the story's end. What appears initially to be a graphic symbol that clarifies the narrative logic works ultimately to heighten the tension between events and their artistic depiction and to confound even further a confident reading of these events.

The film disrupts causality by editing together sequences of ambiguously related images—as in a scene that cuts from a shot of Pinky's aged parents making love to a close-up of Millie's observing face, then to a shot of Willie shooting holes in her snake paintings, then to a shot of Willie shooting holes in the head of a male target, and then to shots of

"Mother," "daughter," and art *(3 Women).* The Museum of Modern Art/Film Stills Archive.

Pinky's awakening from her coma in the hospital. The narration disrupts temporality in the dream sequence by conveying situations that will not occur until later: the shot of Millie and Pinky in bed together after the dream, the image of Millie with outstretched bloody hands after the stillbirth of Willie's baby. It further depicts events that occur only in the dream: Edgar and Willie dancing, Millie dancing with the cops, Pinky lying stabbed on the floor. The persistent wave motion that appears throughout the dream occurs at key moments across the diegetic action from the beginning of the film to the end of the childbirth scene and suggests that everything prior to the long telephoto shot of the yellow Coke truck rolling across the desert floor be read as a dream. Similarly, the spatial truncations of the narrative ambiguously locate the various locales of the story: geriatric center, hospital, Dodge City bar, Purple Sage Motel—all isolated and discontiguous points in the desert. The preponderance of the colors yellow and purple—in the cars, the sets, the costuming, the paintings and murals, the foliage of the desert itself—suggests that the film story takes place not in real spaces but in the space of expressive ambiguity. The constant languid zoom motion of the cinematography replicates the camera movement in the dream and reflects what Edward Branigan calls the "ambiguous and unclaimed voice in the film" (*Point of View* 53). In similar ways the ominous, somber tones of the woodwind quartet call puzzling attention to themselves as they rise and fade at inexplicable moments in the narrative.

The dream modes of *3 Women* resort to the popular device of ambiguity in the art cinema, whereby the levels of diegetic discourse are confused and temporal/spatial configurations distort the narrative chain of cause and effect. Dreams serve this purpose dramatically in such art films as *8½, Persona* (1966), *The Discreet Charm of the Bourgeoisie* (1972), and *The Conversation* (1974). Indeed, Marsha Kinder argues that "dreams and myths provide the crucial battle ground" for a modernist defense of the self, and that "in cinema some of the most powerful auteurs," such as Bergman, Fellini, Altman, and Resnais, "are waging this battle" ("Art of Dreaming" 12). In *3 Women* the dream that appears two-thirds of the way through the film is attributed to the subjectivity of both Millie, by the point-of-view structure that precedes the dream, and Pinky, by her dialogue that follows the dream. The point-of-view structure and camera movement within the dream seem to designate Pinky as the dreamer. The preponderance of yellow in the set design, props, and costumes seem to indicate that the dreamer is Millie, with her strange and humorous fixation on that color. Thus the narration problematizes which of the two characters is dreaming. Moreover, the crescendo of dominant camera movement and musical signatures from the entire film up to Willie's final statement, "I just had the most wonderful dream," suggests that the film be read as a dream within Willie's larger dream and further clouds the identity and behavior of story characters. The inner dream, as it presents times and spaces that will occur only after its conclusion, as it reveals times, spaces, and events never depicted elsewhere in the film, also reveals the hand of a directorial persona. Indeed, the wave motion superimposed over events at particular intervals throughout the film indicates the authorial expressivity that finally suggests the entire film be read as a dream text. The hallucinatory inner dream, then, of doubling, death, and aggression is a dream within a film that is itself presented as a dream. Thus the dream content, the surface of the film, hides the dream work, the depth of the film.

Nick Browne, in explicitly describing a central aspect of this category in point of view, also captures an effect of *3 Women*:

> A spectator is several places at once—with the fictional viewer, with the viewed, and at the same time in a position to evaluate and respond to the claims of each. This fact suggests that, like the dreamer, the filmic spectator is a plural subject: in his reading, he is and is not himself. ("Spectator" 36)

*3 Women* requires the viewer to psychoanalyze a dream motivated by the subjectivity of all three major characters as well as the personal dream that Altman claims originally inspired the film. Dreams in the art cinema echo the modernist concern with subconscious verisimilitude and complicate the problem of textual voice by urging the question, Who is dreaming this and why? By failing to differentiate dream reality from nondream reality in the rest of the film, or by failing to bracket the dream reality with clues to the identity of the dreamer, dream devices in the art cinema generate ambiguity.

This interplay of narrative, spatial, and temporal elements in the art film further displaces interpretation from the tale to its telling. The ambiguous meanings of such films stand over against the clarity of diegetic realism in the classical cinema, which establishes the viewer in the position of spectator. The shift in focus from story to discourse confounds the closure of critical meaning. Like the post-Jamesian novel, the art-film narrative is consciously indeterminate, refusing to give its materials secure meaning or to establish the viewer in the position of comprehension. The films of the art cinema exist quite explicitly as puzzles to be solved by the viewer, but puzzles also constructed to prevent easy solution (Susan's unfinished puzzles in *Citizen Kane* establish the paradigmatic metaphor). At best the film presents the terms of a game to be entered into by the audience. The art film, however, is not an easy game for an audience conditioned to the rules of the classical narrative cinema, with its goal-oriented hero who moves in a world of clearly defined oppositions and who acts to resolve the conflict.

For a tutored audience the development of the art cinema means the advent of film as a twentieth-century art form. Founded on the ambiguity that results from the convergence of psychological realism and artistic expressionism, art films join company with such modernist writers as Joyce and Faulkner, Eliot and Wallace Stevens, for whom meaning is a play of language, a play of shifting perspectives. As realism came to be perceived as a mode of representation in the century of Sigmund Freud and Werner Heisenberg, ambiguity emerged as a focus on the process of perception itself. For the traditional audience of the classical narrative, positioned before the "natural" flow of "an imaginary reality," the art cinema makes significance tenuous. Constructed, like most modern art, in Walt Whitman's "diffused faint clews and indirection," the art cinema positions the spectator as game player for whom meaning is not given but half perceived and half created.

The art cinema invites participation in its recalcitrant, equivocal play of signifiers, but it is a play with risk, for it reveals the unstable grounds of human enterprise, the irresolute demands of human interaction. Roland Barthes's analysis of Balzac's "Sarrasine" (in *S/Z*) and Stephen Heath's analysis of Welles's *Touch of Evil* (in "Film and System") uncover social and personal fears that classical narrative realism seeks to control and repress. Barthes and Heath analyze these works as "limit texts" precisely because they indicate the extent to which they purchase homogeneity at the cost of disruptive heterogeneity. The art cinema generates its ambiguity as a result of appropriating as subject and form the very problems that constitute the limits of classical narrative and its efforts to comprehend objective realism through the pressures of subjective desire. The limit text breaks apart in its effort to recapture in a final unity the disorder that initiates narrative movement. It only partially succeeds in positing a harmonious world of reality characterized by equivalence of sign and referent, the wholeness of individual identity, the efficacy of human agency, the confidence and security of economic exchanges. The distressed aspects of these qualities constitute the art cinema, its ambiguity a function thematically of troubled sexuality, troubled economy, troubled discourse. What emerges as the excess, the logic of dispersion that exceeds control by the economic narrative in the classical cinema, is given textual primacy by the art film.

Problems of sexuality abound in this cinema. Sexual innocence, guilt, experience, desire—regularly repressed by the classical film—repeatedly ground the ambiguous relationships of men and women. *3 Women* defines Millie through her desperate need to create herself with cooking, clothing, and decorating skills in the image of *Ladies' Home Journal* and *Redbook* and her desire to be noticed sexually and domestically. Willie's murals are partly motivated by her fear of her husband's phallic aggression, his six-gun a parody of his sexual power. For Millie and Pinky, physical satisfaction is possible only through transgression of the bounds of Willie's marriage. Themes of latent homosexuality underlie Pinky's attraction to Millie, but this attraction equally reflects the desire for a parent-child relationship free of the frightening demands of heterosexuality. Willie's murals reveal a fear of pregnancy, and the trauma of stillbirth seems the only fruition of sexual relationships in the film. Thematically, the art cinema frequently evokes and leaves unresolved such tensions and uncertainties of sexual identity.

Problems of economic exchange are another particular feature of the art cinema's content. Ambiguities of sexual identity parallel concerns of the self as exchange value, not only in terms of desirability, but in terms of self-worth, the value and purchasing power of the individual as a commodity in the marketplace of ideas, of society, of religion, of art. A significant aspect of *3 Women* revolves around Millie and Pinky as unskilled workers in the California geriatric service industry, whose product is prolonged old age. Millie's total ineptness as a social animal is ironically and harshly contrasted with her principal role as consumer of all the plasticity guaranteed by Madison Avenue to produce a "thoroughly modern Millie." Pinky's innocence is demonstrated by her lack of a social security card. And the only galleries for Willie's art are the bottoms of swimming pools in the middle of the desert that defines the parameters of the women's social milieu. All three women in this film are denied sexual and economic productivity and socially admired exchange value.

The ambiguity created by the considerable dissonance between plot and story also appears thematically in the art cinema in the troubled communication that results from the problematic relationship between language and its referent. The fissures that separate thoughts, objects, and language constantly shape modernist art. The failure of both words and images to communicate exactly is a repeated theme in the films of such art directors as Bergman, Fellini, and Antonioni. And here the art cinema makes clear its sympathy with the modern crisis in the romantic conception of the artist. Hailed in the nineteenth century as the unacknowledged legislator of the world, the Poet with his divine imagination was the arbiter, the seer, the prophet. Through the unique power of his art, the artist achieved a reconciliation of opposites. But the economic, political, and cultural discord that informs the history of the late nineteenth and early twentieth centuries results in the famous literary vision of a modern wasteland. The subjective genius of the artist and his vision of alienation, despair, and psychosis coalesce in the powerful, paradoxical works of art that communicate the impossibility of communication. Addressed now to a limited audience, this art, like James's ghosts, is ambiguous, motivated as much by the progressive concern to revitalize artistic expression as by the problems of delineating the modern situation. *8½, Persona,* and *Blowup* (1966), no less than works by Joyce, Eliot, Proust, and Faulkner, self-consciously experiment with efforts to impose the author's artifice on the discontinuities and anxieties of contemporary life. If they are constituted in irony and ambiguity, they are also graphic in charting the disjunctions between objective reality and its subjective perception, between perception and its aesthetic articulation.

In this context, *3 Women* delineates the ambiguous product that results from the artist's escape into the privacy of art as a defense against the failures of communication. The film repeats essentially the same theme and structure of the earlier Altman film *Images*; both obscure and expressionistic films make personal statements about the necessary but perhaps insufficient role of the imagination in the estrangements of social reality and personal identity. At the level of character subjectivity, schizophrenia in the earlier film and dreams in the later represent the psychological defense against fears of personal inadequacy and the demands of sexuality. Within the narrative of both films, art obliquely reflects the confusions of distressed relationships. Cathryn's sexually symbolic fairy tale, *In Search of Unicorns,* in *Images* and the Freudian violence of Willie's murals in *3 Women* portray artifice as a hermetic refuge from the difficulties of inter- and intrapersonal communication. At the level of authorial expression, the obscurity of the art within the films mirrors the obscurity of the films themselves. The difficulties of both films may be read as authorial retreats, like Cathryn's and Willie's, to art's ambiguous and defensive exploration of the interaction of sexual fears, social worth, and efficacious communication. Both films reveal the tendency of the art cinema to offer the ambiguity of its own face as a testimony to the troubling disjunction between sign and referent in modernist art and in modern life.

Yet just as the classical narrative cinema produces films that display the limits of story "realism" through the gaps and ruptures of narrative continuity, so the art cinema at its limits produces a symbolic order, provides clues toward narrative clarity either in the expressive vision of an author or in a sense of psychological verisimilitude, presents moments when the sliding of meaning asks to be read in its identity with the frictions of the signified story reality. In such moments the narrative cues the audience in its ambiguous clash of filmic systems and its disorder of events to read the film as a narrative rhetoric of explanation. *3 Women* moves in a dreamlike drift through the first two-thirds of the story and dramatizes several heterogeneous relationships among the major characters. It confuses their connections, and it refuses the clarity of narrative conflict. Point of view and narrative voice remain ambiguous. But the movement from Millie's angry explosion over Pinky's spoiling her dinner party to Pinky's attempted suicide, her coma, and finally her usurpation of Millie's personality suggests a narrative schema of cause-effect logic that may replace the ambiguous tension of the dream work with the authority of a coherent, homogeneous position of intelligibility. It grounds the ambiguity. It demonstrates the terms of the film's puzzle. It provides the viewer as interpreter with keys for an effective psychoanalysis of the film, wherein, as Krin Gabbard discovers, "the three women have regressed from the normal exigencies of life, but . . . their new existence is a dream come true" ("*3 Women*" 263).

Rather than attacking the ideological basis of narrative realism, the art cinema establishes through its ambiguous play of signification more complex relationships among author, film, viewer, and realism than does the classical cinema. Norman Holland argues that "form manages content." It acts out for its audience something in the nature of a "defense" by imposing a logic and coherence on the "conflicts that inhere in the deeper content"—as in the classical narrative, for example, by formally arousing and satisfying audience expectation through the systematic opening and closing of enigmas. But if the anxieties of content, of authorial vision, if the conflicting and the debilitating demands of the diegesis are significantly disturbing, their displacement to the form of traditional narrative homogeneity, with its subsequent "feeling of mastery or control of ordering," will only undermanage that content. Thus in the art cinema the frustration of narrative clarity, the internally contradictory structuring of meaning "reinforces the displacement of our involvement from content onto form. We say the particularly 'arty' techniques 'call attention to themselves.' More accurately they displace our attention from content to the logic of the techniques themselves, which thus become doubly strong ways of managing content" (*Dynamics* 150–51).

Yet, as Holland argues, such forms hardly lack significance, any more than dreams do. *3 Women* develops "an enactment rather than a disquisition on fears relating to loneliness, fragmentation, fruitlessness, and rootlessness. These stories are about the self divided from itself, but also about the self divided from others" (134). And as such they reveal defensive madness, dreams, and art in the film's characters, but in their puzzling, lyrical, nonrational mode of presentation they represent the displacement to form of "a fearful fantasy from an artist's point of view about barrenness, from a human point of view about pointlessness, from a male point of view about procreative uselessness" (Holland, "Unity" 131). Marsha Kinder argues that *3 Women* affirms the regeneration of self, the affirmation of "self over structure" ("Art of Dreaming" 18), and that affirmation emerges in the complex and puzzling form of the movie. Art offers an alternative to madness and dreams as a safety valve for the pressure of psychological trauma. The film never unites all the splintered aspects of character psychology, but the formal management of story by aesthetic discourse affirms the willed control of life's anxieties and necessities that is the production of art.

Ultimately, these techniques and the reading strategies they demand in *3 Women* reveal the art cinema's commitment to "realism." It establishes a play among its various levels of discourse not, finally, to destroy a meaningful diegesis but to present a verisimilitude more complex than that of the classical cinema. The limits of its evocations of sexuality, economic exchange, and language in distress are those of contemporary psychological therapy, whether Freudian or behavioral: there are meaningful, comprehensible traumas, uncertainties, ambiguities that derive from the pressures of living in the modern world, which at the bottom is the Real World of the California desert. *3 Women* produces an ambiguity that at last must be recuperated within the narrative, not in opposition to it. Steven Neale describes this tendency in the Hollywood renaissance as it reached its zenith in the mid-seventies: "Ambiguity and open-endedness are sustained and articulated within the limits of the dominant discourse, within the text" ("New Hollywood" 120–21). Compared to the more radical heterogeneity of modernists like Straub and

Godard, Altman's films offer a reformist critique of the classical cinema. Like James's *Turn of the Screw,* they ask the viewer to enter into an aesthetic play, to engage with strategies of discontinuity, to struggle with their limited range of heterogeneous structures.

Classical Hollywood cinema subscribes to a liberal humanism that sees human essence as the origin and source of meaning, knowledge, and action. Its ideological practice is "to present the position of the subject as fixed and unchangeable, an element in a given system of differences which is human nature and the world of human experience, and to show possible action as an endless repetition of 'normal,' familiar action" (Belsey 90). In this view, formal and thematic changes, even if only cyclical, are inevitable and, in the mass media, necessary to satisfy the audience's taste for the new within the context of the familiar. Historically, at the end of the 1960s the art cinema provided a source of new stories, new techniques, new stars for the Hollywood system and the old ideology. By virtue of the large financial success of *MASH* in 1970, Robert Altman and his studio, Lions Gate Films, emerged on the fringe of the Hollywood system during the 1970s as an experimental voice challenging its techniques, revising its genres, interrogating its values in the post-Vietnam, Watergate, Bicentennial decade. The box-office failure met by all of Altman's movies during the last half of the decade—*Buffalo Bill, Quintet,* and *A Perfect Couple*—the refusal of Twentieth Century Fox to release *Health,* and the advent of the blockbuster phenomenon with films such as *Rocky* (1976), *Star Wars,* and *Superman* seemed to mark the end of Altman's role as an innovator and gadfly within the Hollywood system. But the energetic continuation of Altman's movies through the decade of the 1990s and into the twenty-first century reflects the continuing possibility of an American art cinema. Thomas Schatz has observed, "What is so fascinating—and finally so unique—about the American cinema is that it has generated both the 'formulaic' and the 'artistic,' the conventional and the modernist, within the same commercial industry" (*Old Hollywood* 28). By submitting to social criticism the faults of contemporary cultural experience and challenging its underlying ideology, by employing the spatial and temporal aspects of film coequally and metaphorically with the cause-effect logic of narrative, by assuming a self-consciously expressionistic stance toward narrative voice in an effort to enrich, renew, and elevate the humanistic perspective of the classical narrative cinema, Altman's films describe an American art cinema.

# 4. Generic Art: Romance and Adventure

Film scholars have routinely observed that many of the characteristics attributed to art-cinema narration participate similarly in the definition of modernism in the arts, especially in literature. American literary history narrates a continuum that runs through the nineteenth and twentieth centuries from romanticism to realism to naturalism to modernism to postmodernism. Each of these categories is vast and vague at the outer limits of abstraction, but each posits a particular perspective on "actual" life, a certain content, a specific narrative structure and style, a definite philosophical worldview. Modernism, for instance, is formalist in structure, reflexive in subject, experimental in expression, ironic in worldview, and conservative and pessimistic in philosophical stance as it surveys an early-twentieth-century "wasteland" of modernity in Western culture, economy, politics, and morality. It calls attention to its artifice as an interrogation of realism. It asserts the value of aesthetic as opposed to moral absolutes. It seeks a dispassionate and detached voice to speak about passionate and traumatic matters. It experiments with the limits of artistic form to discover new and fragmentary forms of expression. It takes an existential stance toward the disruption, alienation, and despair that it takes to characterize contemporary life.

Insofar as film has since its invention constituted part of the array of modern mass media, however, its easy identification with modernism is problematic. Andreas Huyssen argues, "Modernism constituted itself through a conscious strategy of exclusion, an anxiety of contamination by its other: an increasingly consuming and engulfing mass culture" (vii). Modernism is characterized by "its insistence on the autonomy of the art work, its obsessive hostility to mass culture, its radical separation from the culture of everyday life, and its programmatic distance from political, economic, and social concerns" (vii). Genre film in particular, however, participates in the mass cultural recirculation of popular story forms, popular icons, popular values. Arising in their modern form during the late eighteenth century, the genre forms of mystery, adventure, and romance demonstrate both structural and thematic consistency as well as continuing evolution. Cultural scholars track the growth of these forms in terms of a growing population, a growing literacy, and a growing necessity for society at large to communicate its values to the increasingly dispersed members of that culture. Genre films rehearse abiding issues central to the community's sense of identification—freedom versus authority, country versus city, wilderness versus civilization, tradition versus imagination, salvation versus redemption, guilt versus grace, present versus future, industry versus sloth, beauty versus ugliness. Genre films ritually celebrate a hierarchy of presumably shared values in the resolution of their conflicts.

Evolution in the genres revitalizes or revises or satirizes both popular narrative traditions and cultural values to which the genres respond and that they simultaneously extend. They continuously reflect the shifting interactions among artistic vision, popular values, audience anticipation, and social change. Individual genre films constantly ask to be read in the context of their genres' histories and forms. Unlike the modernist valorization of autonomous art, genre filmmaking in the realm of commercial mass culture "is a matter of successfully reinventing established conventions in a way that satisfies the filmmakers' aesthetic sensibilities without violating their expectations. . . . [A]ctually commercial film production, while heavily bound to story formulas and narrative conventions, demands continual innovation, variation, and stylization in the retelling of its mythic tales" (Schatz, *Old Hollywood* 14).

The new American cinema's adaptation and development of such popular narrative forms as the western, the melodrama, the mystery, the gothic, and the romance thus seem uncongenial to the antipopular moods of modernism. Yet as they appropriate many of the attitudes of modernism and at the same time many of the forms and thematic concerns of postmodernism and continue to employ classical Hollywood's most successful brand names, the popular genre narratives, the films of the Hollywood renaissance make a particularly American contribution to the art cinema. Just as directors in the international art cinema such as Chabrol, Godard, and Truffaut employed popular genre formats to make personal films, the American directors of the late 1960s and 1970s especially employed a modernist sensibility of aesthetic innovation "to subvert, question, accentuate, deconstruct, or critique the codes and conventions of established genres" (Schatz, *Old Hollywood* 240). Directors of the new American cinema bring a modernist sensibility to the business of generic storytelling. Where the classical narrative genres once provided audiences with a conventional, familiar syntax and semantics that allowed an easy reading of the story, the genres provided auteurs in the American art cinema structural frames within which to arouse and then challenge rather than satisfy audience expectations. As Schatz notes, "The effect is to distance the viewer from the immediate narrative and consequently from the genre's traditional interpretation of American history, thus encouraging the viewer to renegotiate the values and belief systems underpinning that standard interpretation" (*Old Hollywood* 240).

This chapter examines the way three of Altman's films interrogate the possibilities of love in one of the broadest and most persistent of the Hollywood genres, the romance, and looks at Altman's specific deformations in two of the classical adventure genres, the western and science fiction. *A Perfect Couple* ironically celebrates the idealistic couple of romance by exaggerating the nature of family opposition in the lives of "star-crossed lovers" and the cliché that "opposites attract." *Popeye* renders romance as a cartoon for children. And *A Wedding* magnifies the ritual moment of transformation from the single to the married state in order to expose and parody the complexities of the narrative moment that precedes "happily ever after." *McCabe & Mrs. Miller* turns the vocabulary, the syntax, and the semantics of the western inside out as it simultaneously debunks the idea of western heroism and progress and poetically evokes the beauty of a painterly West. *Quintet* warps us into a postapocalyptic future to a scene pessimistically penultimate to the heat death of the universe and the human race. All these films reveal an iconoclastic stance toward narrative coherence that complements a critical analysis of contemporary social identity as insecure, splintered, unstable. They reflect an aesthetic sense that is lyrical as well as narrative. Moreover, as they diverge from the canonical forms, as they lay bare the terms of generic readability, these generic films call attention reflexively to themselves as products made by the entertainment industry.

An emphasis on resolution is central to definitions of popular genre generally; indeed, insofar as this feature corresponds to Claude Lévi-Strauss's famous observation that myth reveals its structure "through the repetition process" and has as its purpose "to provide a logical model capable of overcoming a contradiction," generic patterns of conflict resolution establish the formal basis for a richly incisive approach to genre in terms of myth and ritual. As Lévi-Strauss observes, in ritual "there is an asymmetry which is postulated in advance between profane and sacred, faithful and officiating, dead and living, initiated and uninitiated, etc., and the 'game' consists in making all the participants pass to the winning side by means of events, the nature and ordering of which is genuinely structural" ("Science" 443). Yet when popular forms fail to satisfy such conditions in plot, they are said to constitute either more sophisticated or antigeneric forms of communication and consequently confront us with that distinction between entertainment and art that has generally relegated westerns, thrillers, and science fiction to the category of pulp fiction.

Transformations of conventional role conflicts to the point of formal self-consciousness and nonresolution relate these popular works to those canonized in the academy as modernist art, committed to a vision of ambiguity, contradiction, and paradox rather than resolution, unity, and harmony. These works constitute ritual for a smaller, more intellectual audience of communicants for whom significance resides in tension and question rather than answer and resolution. Although the popular audience may not identify with this community, the elite audience is not always distinct from the popular, along with whom, as a part of which, it too has acquired, perhaps unconsciously, a familiarity with the historical method and form of popular genre. As Leo Braudy has written: "Genre forms and conventional forms are generally deceptive because they are so accessible. If you haven't seen them before, you still have a good chance of having culturally absorbed their aesthetic canon" (116). Even while the genre discourse of Robert Altman's art cinema, then, seems to eschew plot itself in favor of poetry, or to employ plot to short-circuit discernment, the popular conventions of romance, western, and science fiction provide many of the images, forms, and values with which the art cinema conjures. The works described here aspire to the level of artistic invention as opposed to formulaic convention, but they are all nonetheless recognizably popular genre films, and as such create a bridge between formulaic and artistic fiction.

The impulse in art cinema that elevates the director to the role of expressive artist, one who imposes an "authorial signature" on the ambiguous clash of "objective" realism and subjective "truth" across a body of works, establishes the director himself as a kind of genre. The director's "trademark signature" cues the spectator to see any single film as belonging to a larger body of work. Thus "Robert Altman" names a genre with a paradigmatic social stance that opposes dark humor to the deathward inevitability of life. The syntax of this genre fails to cohere causally, but it persistently juxtaposes laughter with a sickening violence—in *MASH,*

*Brewster McCloud, Nashville, A Wedding, The Player, Short Cuts,* and *Kansas City.* Its semantics routinely include unusual, offbeat central characters, as in *California Split, The Long Goodbye, Thieves Like Us, 3 Women, Fool for Love, Prêt-à-Porter,* and *Cookie's Fortune.* The psychoses that make *Images* and *3 Women* oblique variations on the traditional psychological thriller represent the displacement of sexual and artistic fears, a defense that belongs both to the fractured personae of the stories and to the expressivity and psychological concerns of the Altman film. And where *McCabe* and *Buffalo Bill* violate the traditional codes of the classical genre narrative, their visual lyricism, their generally truncated narrative logic, their strange mixture of gentleness and cynicism reflect the Altman trademark.

Schatz asserts that although the generation of new Hollywood filmmakers in the 1960s and early 1970s chose "to work quite near the limits of narrative logic and viewer accessibility, only Robert Altman has gone over the edge," that in his manipulation of traditional genre films Altman "has come close to that synthesis of classical mythmaking and modernist demystification, creating films which can be read as popular storytelling even as they create a narrative subtext which, at least for those viewers responsive to their modernist impulses, call into question the nature of classical narration and the ideology that it enforces" (*Old Hollywood* 243–44). Altman's films have interrogated a wide range of American values and traditions even as they have employed the storytelling conventions of the classical narrative cinema.

Leo Braudy analyzes this process and its effects in the international art cinema:

> If what the New Wave brought into film can be described in one word, that word might be "self-consciousness" at all levels: a self-consciousness about film history and tradition, a self-consciousness about the act of making a film, a self-consciousness in the audience that approaches the film more as a cultural artifact than as an entertainment for which the mind was turned off, and, perhaps the most important aspect, a self-consciousness about the role of the director, matched with the audience's increased awareness that the director is a "star" too. Inspired by the sense of tradition and formal self-awareness that marks genre films, the New Wave at its best treated convention seriously, as it treated technical devices seriously. (166–67)

This engagement with form means at the same time serious concern with the social issues always at stake in generic discourse. During the

1970s in particular, Altman's genre films reflect what one scholar has described as central to generic form: "a heightening of the conflict between the cultural and countercultural aspects of entertainment" (Cawelti, *Adventure* 41–42). The structural possibilities and thematic concerns of the western, the musical, and the detective film, of war movies, gangster movies, science fiction, and romance provide aesthetic paradigms that Altman's cinematic practice borrows and transforms. Military and medical belligerence and violence generate bloody humor in *MASH.* Putting on the show in the musical *Nashville* becomes a social, political, and personal metaphor for cultural schizophrenia. The romance of crime and the ingenuity of its detection in gangster and detective genres are energetically undermined, even ridiculed, in *The Long Goodbye* and *Thieves Like Us.* The tension and suspense of psychological thrillers are reduced to poetic ambiguity in *Images* and *3 Women.* The nostalgic glow of the vanished western frontier is seen as the public-relations haze of mass-media promoters in *Buffalo Bill,* and the visual lyricism of *McCabe & Mrs. Miller* transforms the heroic action of the western into ironic insignificance. The traditional tensions of the thriller in *The Gingerbread Man* dissolve into a limit text repressing the image of abusive fathers. Indeed, despite their use of conventional iconography, Altman's films interrogate the viability of the generic contract.

## Imperfect Romance

Robert Altman's films contain a variety of dialectical structures that formulate and characterize a persistent double vision. Their art-cinema narration of traditional genre formulas to shape and reverse viewer expectations, their penchant for mirror images to reflect troubled dualities of personality, their marked juxtaposition of narrative and poetic modes, and their self-conscious sense of cinematic play are ubiquitous features of thematic ironies and ambiguities. But the modernism of these features is generally grounded in a traditional social reality that focuses the possibility, but seldom the actuality, of the romantic couple. Classical narrative cinema overwhelmingly employs romance as a primary story or as the requisite secondary story whose conflicts and resolutions variously parallel, analyze, and motivate the tensions and conclusions of the primary tale. The regnant value system supporting the possibilities of couples in this cinema is romantic. Virginia Wright Wexman argues that "in most Hollywood films, romantic love is a major concern" (*Creating* 3) and cites Raymond Bellour's claim that creating the couple "organizes, indeed constitutes, the classical American cinema as a whole" (4).

John Cawelti posits romance along with mystery and adventure as one of the major "archetypal story patterns" of popular narrative discourse that "reflects the construction of an ideal world without the disorder, the ambiguity, the uncertainty, and the limitations of the world of our experience" (*Adventure* 13). He asserts that the "crucial defining characteristic of romance . . . is the development of a love relationship, usually between a man and a woman." He argues, "Since romance is a fantasy of the all sufficiency of love, most romance formulas center on the overcoming of some combination of social or psychological barriers." Thus he defines the "moral fantasy of the romance" as "love triumphant and permanent, overcoming all obstacles and difficulties" (41–42).

In this context Altman's films pose a number of narrative difficulties for romance. They tend routinely to confront the viewer with the "ambiguous, uncertain, and limited world" of mimetic representation in the art cinema rather than the formulaic representations of classical Hollywood cinema. They tell stories of insecure, marginal, and unattractive characters. They favor fragmented, open-ended story lines that seldom propose reachable ends, such as the happily wedded couple. As Wexman writes, the Altman film "lacks faith in any rationally constructed standards that could support integrated social or personal identities" (*Critical* 11). Nevertheless, the preoccupations in these films with the act of creation, with biological reproduction, with insecurity and loneliness and death regularly surface around the socially constructed drive toward pair-bonding.

Wexman charts the transition in the "meaning of the romantic couple" across the twentieth century "from an acceptance of the Victorian notion of separate spheres to the companionate ideal to the validation of romance as a key to individual identity" (*Creating* 13). Certainly as sexual mores became more liberal during the latter half of the twentieth century, as the divorce rate steadily increased and the "traditional" American family with a loving couple at its head declined dramatically, Altman's films over the past thirty years have further identified sexual politics as one of the most pressing difficulties of this social period. The majority of these films represent negative variations on the generic formula of love triumphant.

The "display of the united romantic couple" at the end of the popularly acclaimed 1946 film *The Best Years of Our Lives* perfectly illustrates the social importance of the predominant resolution in traditional romance (Wexman, *Creating* 159). The final sequence of the film begins with a close-up of the prosthetic hands of the paraplegic war veteran and the hands of his sweetheart, the girl next door; then the camera dollies back to reveal the ceremony under way to unite this couple in a wedding that also reflects the nation's as well as the bride's acceptance of the disfiguring wounds of war. Waiting in the wings is another marriage, this one sealed in the promise of the story-ending kiss, between the daughter of the bank officer and the once-married, older man from the other side of the tracks. Moral tensions, class differences, and individual antagonisms, indeed the very wounds of world war itself, all dissolve away before this powerful evocation of romance. Edmund Leach describes the function of ritual at work in such popular narrative genres: "Most ritual occasions are concerned with movement across social boundaries from one social status to another. . . . The ceremonies concerned have the double function of proclaiming the change of status and of magically bringing it about" (77).

Weddings mark this transformation in romance, even though they usually appear as the concluding rather than the transitional moment. Altman's *A Wedding,* like his treatment of the ritual western transition from wilderness to civilization in *Buffalo Bill and the Indians,* takes the ritual and symbolic moment of change as its central focus. Rather than a celebration of the resolutions achieved in the formulaic narratives of romance, the film instead offers a critique of what Helene Keyssar describes as a "catalogue of contemporary human foibles and resistances to dominant practices" (291) that explores marriage as a kaleidoscope of unresolved emotional, religious, moral, racial, sexual, ethnic, and economic tensions. Rather than concluding them, the narrative explodes these tensions. *A Wedding* opens with parallel editing that shows the death of the family matriarch and the beginning of the wedding ceremony. It closes with the fiery deaths of the surrogate young couple who sneak away in the bride and groom's wedding car. In between, the formal event becomes the occasion not to resolve but to reveal the wide range of social attractions and conflicts, desires and infidelities, contracts and subversions that course through the lives of the attendant families.

The titles of *A Wedding* and *A Perfect Couple* suggest the goals toward which many of the major characters in Altman's stories aspire, but in reality the stories seldom achieve these goals. As they accept the potential of the romantic couple, the films valorize a whole cluster of values central to the dominant ideology from which Hollywood films emerge and that they in turn support: true love, marriage, the home, the family, and so forth. These values, however, constitute a background to be parodied, satirized, mourned, and only occasionally approved and revitalized.

Patricia Waugh argues that when genre fictions—which normally "provide collective pleasure and release of tension through the comforting total affirmation of accepted stereotypes"—are parodied, "the release effect of such forms is to do with *disturbance* rather than *affirmation*" (81–82). Altman's art-cinema romance routinely recognizes social debilitation and locates its audience in unstable and uneasy positions of intelligibility and affirmation.

*A Wedding*'s glimpse of the contemporary ritual that celebrates the establishment, socially, religiously, and legally, of a new couple satirically probes the difficulties in pair-bonding that involve meshing together three different families. It thus examines the social differences that stand in the way of a smooth course for true love: the groom's family is midwestern upper-class; the bride's family is southern middle-class. The groom's father was an Italian waiter and a phony aristocrat; the bride's father was a truck driver. One family is Catholic, the other Baptist; one is supercilious and secretive, the other crass and loudmouthed. As the celebration continues, the narrative reveals many unhappy facts that contradict the happiness of the event. The groom was born out of wedlock. The mother of the groom is a dope addict. The sister of the bride is pregnant, perhaps by the groom. The matriarch of the groom's family is solicitous about the secret affair between her daughter and the black valet. The mother of the bride has a passionate encounter with the uncle of the groom. Although the narrative treats this conflict of motives and values with satiric good humor, it nonetheless recalls the tragic dimension of reality never far from the surface in any of Altman's movies. The beautiful couple—loose, carefree, engaging college friends of the bride and groom—die in a flaming auto crash on a Chicago expressway. *A Wedding* celebrates the marriage vows in their isolation and describes the making of a modern American couple as a patchwork of duplicity, hypocrisy, and manipulation of conflicting values in which the stability of romantic love appears like an old-fashioned fantasy. As William Butler Yeats defines this modern landscape, "Love has pitched his mansion in / The place of excrement."

In *Dr. T & the Women,* a wedding again becomes the social event that uncovers a fractured world of gendered identities in contemporary Dallas. The wedding at the end devolves into social and emotional chaos as a storm destroys the outdoor ceremony simultaneously with the lesbian bride's affirmation of her love, not for the groom, but for her bridesmaid. The film works reflexively by employing and revising the familiar terms of the generic contract for romantic comedy—in particular the star-crossed lovers who resist social convention and expectation to establish the happy couple at the end. The film revises both this narrative structure and the cultural iconicity of its central actors. Richard Gere as Dr. T reprises the role of the rich and powerful central male from *Pretty Woman* (1990), whose plot ends happily in the dashing Prince Charming's last-minute realization of his love for the prostitute with a heart of gold. In that film, according to the best romantic tradition, Edward (Gere) climbs to Vivian's (Julia Roberts) balcony to offer the love that will redeem and authenticate her existence.

The two central women in Dr. T's life react very differently to the power of this male largesse. On one hand, the narrative depicts his wife, Kate (Farrah Fawcett), as the victim of too much love. The emotional bonds of the happily married couple cause a disease called the "Hestia complex," in which too much male adoration leads to Kate's mental breakdown. On the other hand, Helen Hunt as the golf professional Bree brings to the film the cool, sharp-edged, self-sufficient persona of Jamie Buchman in the popular television series *Mad About You* and her tough, independent roles opposite Jack Nicholson in *As Good as It Gets* (1997) and opposite tornadoes in *Twister* (1996). Bree is an assertive and successful professional—frank, self-confident, free. As his world splinters around the debilitation of his wife and the dissolution of his daughter's wedding, Dr. T suddenly seems liberated to accept his love for Bree, and he races madly through wind and rain to give her his hand and his beneficence. In part the film is motivated to portray just this conflict in romantic representation, the clash of the Hunt and Gere personas and their conflicting generic configurations. It seems in particular designed to resist the expectation of a passionate happy ending. When Dr. T at last offers Bree married happiness, dependency, and financial security, she arches her eyebrows to ask incredulously, "Why would I *want* that?"

## Star-Crossed Love and Cartoon Passion

At the center of *Short Cuts,* the Jack Lemmon character delivers a long monologue of confession and justification about the thirty-year past infidelity that broke up his marriage, removed him from his home, and rendered him the absent father in the life of his son, to whom he now tells the story as his grandson lies dying in the hospital. The story reflects the forces that come between people to prevent, confuse, disrupt, and shatter romantic relationships. It further reflects the paradigmatic tension that figures in each of the nine stories woven together to generate the diegetic world of the film. Every story relates a marriage relationship, and every relationship is troubled. Stormy Weathers and Betty are going through an angry divorce. Gene and Sherri fight around his lies and infidelities. Ann puzzles over Stuart's ability to ignore the body of a murdered young girl discovered on a fishing trip. Ralph obsesses over Marian's one-time affair with another man long ago. Jerry listens as his wife disinterestedly sells telephone sex. Honey and Bill drift away from each other in desire for other lives. Doreen and Earl quarrel over his cycles of getting drunk and staying sober. Howard and Ann hold a deathwatch over the bed of their son. Lost birthday cakes, lost dogs, lost fishing time, and lost furniture variously signify the lost youth, lost sex, lost confidence, lost stability, and lost love that characterize pair-bonding in the film. In the opening sequence, helicopters spray Los Angeles with pesticide, and in the last scene a minor earthquake jars the city. Infested by fruit flies and shaken by nature's violence, the modern city holds death and suicide in the heart of romantic relationships.

Given such negative perceptions, the fantasy of old-fashioned romantic love in *A Perfect Couple* and *Popeye* seems like the most definite, and most uncharacteristic, among Altman's movies. Only these two films of all Altman's work assert the absolute possibility that love will be triumphant. Even then, permanence is another story, and the art-cinema penchant for unglamorous personalities and body types motivates central characters who hardly engage audience identification. *A Perfect Couple* obviously reveals the stable trajectory of the traditional genre narrative. Its conflict is basic—the Montagues versus the Capulets. Alex's family is ethnocentric Greek, nuclear, and hierarchical; family members are proprietors of a fashionable antique business, committed to the art of classical music, and wealthy. Sheila's family comprises the musicians, roadies, and groupies of a rock and roll band called Keepin' 'em Off the Streets. Although their leader reveals the same parental tyranny as Alex's father, the band lives in a warehouse and, on the road, in a double-decker bus; its members are culturally heterogeneous and its existence is tenuous. The same symmetry of conflicts appears here as in *A Wedding,* in classes, ethnic backgrounds, and cultural tastes. Both of the lovers, as lovers, are unconventional in appearance: Alex (Paul Dooley) is middle-aged, overweight, and jowly. Sheila (Marta Heflin) is tall and skinny, with straight hair, large nose, and protruding eyes. They find each other through a computer dating service that matches his upper-class, patriarchal Greek family with the heterogeneous group of rock musicians that is her family. Alex's real family is rigid and classical; Sheila's surrogate one is loose and modern. Both Alex and Sheila, however, chafe against the authoritarian discipline of father and band leader, and both share simple romantic needs. Sheila says on her dating service tape that she just wants to "share some experiences with somebody." Alex is looking for an admittedly trite relationship that is "meaningful." Loneliness and a computer dating service bring hero and heroine together; patriarchal authoritarianism, cultural diversity, class prejudice, and limited sexual mores are the villains that drive them apart.

The narrative establishes the tension between possible and impossible couples again in the contrast between the clearly bleak, orthodox marriages of Alex's brother and sister and the liberated couples in Sheila's band, one composed of two loving lesbians who are planning to have a baby, the other of the band leader (Ted Neeley) and his wife (Heather MacRae), who, with their baby, share work space and living space alike. Alex's baby sister Eleousa (Belita Moreno) is a cellist for the Los Angeles Philharmonic who breaks from the dominating control of her family to move in with her lover, Mona (Mona Golabek), a pianist for the orchestra. Both her courage and her premature death provide catalysts to Alex's final break with his family in an assertion of his love for Sheila. She energizes him to seize the day, kick off the traces of family convention and musical snobbery, and return to the arms of love. In this ancient boy meets girl, boy loses girl, boy gets girl ritual, Altman employs another traditional conceit: the sister's vision of freedom and particularly her death motivate the new life of Alex and Sheila. Moreover, her death becomes the event that harmonizes the divergent music of the hero and heroine as well. In the last scene of the film, the L.A. Philharmonic and Keepin' 'em Off the Streets play a musical memorial called "Goodbye My Friend" for piano, orchestra, and rock band.

The final scene of the film further underlines the narrative's uncharacteristically romantic affirmation of a love that transcends the differences in the two lovers. In the final analysis, the film reflects the contradictory impulse of the art cinema. The concluding image of lovers in *A Perfect Couple* clearly celebrates what John Cawelti calls "the moral fantasy of the romance . . . love triumphant and permanent, overcoming all obstacles and difficulties" (*Adventure* 41–42). At the same time, the unusual physiognomies of Paul Dooley's jowly, middle-aged countenance and Marta Heflin's beanpole body and disproportional facial features are far away from the idealized romantic couples of classical Hollywood. *A Perfect Couple* is a musical comedy whose conclusion celebrates love triumphant in unlikely personal and social terms. It nevertheless employs the classical paradigm described by Schatz, in which the generic conflict and its resolution function to transfer some specifically cultural conflict into expressive terms and to resolve the struggle in a way that ritually celebrates both the individuality and the social relationships of the central characters (*Old Hollywood* 133–35).

*Popeye,* in its hybrid mix of musical, comedy, romance, and adventure, similarly acclaims the values of social order, social initiation, and integration, but in a fantasy world of cartoon characters. The film at once celebrates true love, romantic pair-bonding, and old-fashioned heroism. In light of such earlier Altman films as *Nashville, McCabe & Mrs. Miller, 3 Women,* and *Buffalo Bill* in the 1970s, Robert Evans (prolific producer of such popular blockbusters as *Chinatown, Marathon Man,* 1976; *Black Sunday,* 1977; and *Urban Cowboy,* 1980) correctly observed: "*Popeye* doesn't sound like a film Evans and Altman would make . . . , but it does sound like a film Disney would make" (quoted in Perry 89). It develops a story with a straightforward chronology, and it celebrates the kind of heroic action central to children's stories and popular genres alike. Plot conflicts are resolved in a delightful chase and successful combat with a monster and a bully. The conclusion is specific and positive. The heroic action is unambiguous. Popeye (Robin Williams) is an orphan abandoned at an early age, and in search of his father he enters Sweethaven, a community isolated from civilization and living under the oppression of a mysterious and dictatorial Commodore, his brutal enforcer, and his omnipresent tax collector. When villainy in the form of Bluto (Paul L. Smith) fails to gain Olive Oyl's (Shelley Duvall) hand in matrimony, the tax collector descends upon the family. The hero's search for his father involves the discovery of himself. Swee'pea's mysterious abandonment results in the creation of new lovers and the establishment of a new family unit. A hidden treasure chest contains proof of the hero's parentage. The hero's victorious confrontation with evil in this film is synonymous with the triumph of love. He drives villainy into the ocean; as a new father, he discovers and reunites with his own father (Ray Walston), and at the end he is integrated into the community that he has liberated by his heroism. Thus the film focuses and exorcises many adult as well as childhood fears about authority, belonging, identity, self-worth, security, and love.

The film represents a crescendo of narrative unity and action that clearly distinguishes it from other Altman films. Altman and his producer, Robert Evans, have explicitly described the film as a "morality tale." In adapting E. C. Segar's cartoon strip to the movies, Altman says, "the only thing we're doing . . . is showing a microcosm of an oppressed society. The whole key to Popeye is Segar's 'I yam what I yam'" (quoted in Linderman 84). And in the middle of this traditional, sentimental family romance beats the heart of a loving couple. As Popeye and Olive argue over who would be the best parent for Swee'pea, they discover their love for each other, a love marked by their reversal of gender roles ("If I'm his mudder, den youse have to be his fadder," exclaims Popeye) and by their harmonizing of difference: "Sail with me," he sings as she sings, "Stay with me" (Perry 144). True to the form of classical narrative, the resolution of this romance in the innermost narrative predicts and motivates the successful resolution of the quest narrative.

Nevertheless, in its evocation of atmosphere, the style of *Popeye* locates the story in the impressionistic and contradictory space between reality and cartoon and creates "the mood that is a cartoonist's imagination, that strange, childlike state of mind that causes grownups to invent make believe worlds with their own laws of gravity and foolishness" (Siskel, "First Rate" 17). One of the film's magical moments evokes the lover's dreamy affirmation of love in classical musicals, but Olive Oyl's awkward dancing and off-key singing of "He Loves Me" simultaneously parodies and celebrates movie romance. The film subtly questions heroic viability in a cartoon world, and Williams's Popeye and Duvall's Olive convey the credible delineations of multidimensional individuals whose romance emerges within the two-dimensional possibilities of Sweethaven. At one level, the film suggests that heroism emerges simultaneously with a reduction of social complexity. As the hero enters the cartoon world of his fame, Popeye's success emerges first because he discovers himself and ultimately because he and Olive discover love and gain family. The film ritualistically celebrates those events, but in a world of cartoon fantasy. In effect, it details the prehistory of the famous cartoon hero and seems to trace the devolution of a hero in its depiction of a real man becoming a two-dimensional cartoon character. At the end, Bluto is beaten, but Popeye's song of self-affirmation in the middle of the film, "I Yam What I Yam," becomes the famous cartoon melody "I'm Popeye the Sailor Man," in which he even affirms a taste for spinach, despite his hatred of it throughout the film. Although the narrative evidences the affection between Popeye and Olive, their union as a romantic couple is never explicitly demonstrated. Thus this Walt Disney production may be read as subtly questioning some of the very values of heroism and romance that on the other hand it so obviously promotes.

A central facet of the critical work performed by these uncharacteristic romances rests in their constant depiction of the plight of star-crossed lovers. The optimism of *A Perfect Couple* and *Popeye* at the end of the 1970s is overshadowed by more pessimistic depiction of the possibilities of the romantic couple in Altman's other films. The openness of their stories and of their cinematic style frequently discourages attention to couples as central in these films, despite the fact that the typical failure of viable couples constitutes much of their plot tensions. *Kansas City* in 1996, like *That Cold Day in the Park* in 1969, ends with death in romance. And *Fool for Love* in 1985 like *The Gingerbread Man* in 1998, documents the destructive infidelity of the father to the mother. When narration and story become fragmented in the art cinema, when causal connectedness goes awry, when the logic that grounds understanding in the narrative rhetoric of explanation becomes alogical, then the fiction of romance can no longer plot the coherent trajectory of "creating the couple." Lacking further the linguistic rules and regulations of traditional generic semantics and syntax, these narratives pick up the shards of romance scattered on the cultural landscape. "A perfect couple" is only a humorous possibility in *A Wedding*; a tragic impossibility in *McCabe & Mrs. Miller, Fool for Love,* and *Kansas City*; a symbiotic necessity in *3 Women*; a cultural fantasy in *Come Back to the 5 & Dime, Jimmy Dean, Jimmy Dean*; a dream of the past in *Quintet*; and an illusion of freedom in *Thieves Like Us.* It is homosexual in *California Split* and *Dr. T,* aggressively heterosexual in *Nashville,* and unisexual in *The Long Goodbye.* It is pathological in *That Cold Day in the Park* and *Images.* The "perfect couple" is dressed, addressed, redressed, cross-dressed and undressed in *Prêt-à-Porter.* It is fraternal in *Vincent & Theo.* It is a cartoon possibility in *Popeye.* It is the goal of Hollywood happy endings in *The Player. Dr. T* conveys the dissolution of one couple, the aftermath of another, and the impossibility of yet a third. *Short Cuts* maps unhappy couple on top of couple and links them together in frustration, insincerity, selfishness, anger, desire, infidelity, alcoholism, and self-doubt. Sexual attraction beheads the object of desire and romantic longing motivates suicide in *Cookie's Fortune.* Robert Kolker describes Altman's films as "nothing less than an inquiry into the images of contemporary America, as those images have been set by our films and our politics. . . . His films . . . reflect from us and back to us the images we hold of ourselves and our culture" (273). The tension between the image of wholeness possible in human pairing and its negative image of loneliness and incompleteness is central in three decades of Robert Altman's films and shares with the generic communicants of romance a disquieting depiction of contemporary American life.

### Painting the Western

Altman's films employ the ritual function of popular genre discourse as a base, from *That Cold Day in the Park* in 1969 to *Dr. T & the Women* in

2000, for examining and articulating much of the discontent and social disruptions of the intervening decades. Two of Altman's genre films—*McCabe & Mrs. Miller* and *Quintet*—particularly illustrate the innovative surgery performed on the classical narrative genres by the art-cinema appropriation of mass-media forms and consciousness. As they appropriate the syntax and semantics of the western and science fiction, they simultaneously reflect the art cinema's displacement of the hero from a subjectivity of efficacy and authority. They display the self-conscious reworking of narrative structure and social identification that characterize the whole range of art-cinema qualities in Altman's films.

Popular narrative genre films communicate a culture's hierarchy of values to individual members of that culture. They ritualistically celebrate the shared beliefs of a culture. Indeed, they work to establish the identity of community. Heroic resolutions of the relative core conflicts of the different genres rehearse contemporary ideological proscriptions for socially accepted and defining behavior. Individual genre films are always tacitly reflexive as they reference the presupposed set of semantic and syntactic codes of the particular genre. The bare bones of action, of conflict/climax/resolution, constitute the essence of such genre films. Arthur Danto analyzes this narrative structure as the rhetoric of explanation, in which the middle is logically antecedent to and explains the movement from the beginning of a story to the end (231–41). Schatz has further argued that the function of popular genres "is the ritualization of collective ideals, the celebration of temporarily resolved social conflicts, and the concealment of disturbing cultural conflicts behind the guise of entertainment" ("Structural Influence" 309). The resolution of the plot conveys the classical "message" in the genre narrative in general. In the western, for instance, this resolution settles the "conflict between the individual and the group, between self-realization and communal conformity, between the anxiety and loneliness engendered by the feeling of the self and the security of passive identification with the crowd . . . in favor of the community" (T. Sobchack 201).

The western has provided an especially rich pattern of heroic action because of its potential for resolving the civilization-wilderness conflict, not only toward the values of civilization but against them as well. John Cawelti argues that "it is in the changing treatment of this [civilization-wilderness] conflict, so basic to American thought and feeling, that the western most clearly reflects the attitudes of its creators and audiences at different periods" (*Adventure* 194). *Buffalo Bill and the Indians* employs the pattern of dual resolution itself as a subject. It tends not toward a settlement for eastern or western values but captures the confusion attendant on the historical moment of transition between the two frequently celebrated in the western ritual and reflexively calls into question the nature of any resolution. The film develops a wilderness-society conflict in terms of a hero caught between a sense of his personal identity and the demands of his increasingly successful and rigid media personality. As Buffalo Bill struggles in vain to maintain a superior position against Sitting Bull, the writers, producer, and public relations agent struggle to possess the hero's image. The real enemy is not the Indian but the eastern tastemakers. The forces of civilization win the West once more. Buffalo Bill becomes "America's National Entertainer," but the demands of popular entertainment consume the history of white and red man together, leaving the Wild West show where heroes and the wilderness once stood. Altman's concern is not simply the debunking of a mythical Buffalo Bill to fit a contemporary sense of historical truth; rather, confusion and ambiguity are the informing moods in his representation of the classical western's East-West conflict.

Insofar as the story reminds the audience of the tenuous nature of any resolution at all, it represents a more "artistic," as opposed to "popular," celebration of western ritual. The most popular stories achieve an unambiguous conclusion to the tension between wilderness and civilization. Less popular yet aesthetically successful westerns equivocate not only the resolution but the terms of the conflict as well. The concept of resolution is perceived by many contemporary authorities as absolutely crucial to the structural definition of the popular western, as demonstrated by John Cawelti: "The most basic definition of the hero in the Western is as the figure who resolves the conflict between pioneers and savages" (*Six-Gun* 95). Cawelti isolates other factors aside from heroic action in this resolution: "The almost wholly commercial circumstances of its creation, the fact that it is defined as entertainment, and the broad popular audience to which it appeals place a premium on the resolution of conflict and the affirmation of existing cultural values" (74). When popular forms fail to satisfy such conditions in plot, they constitute reflexive forms of communication and consequently confront the viewer with that distinction between entertainment and art that has generally relegated the western, detective narratives, and science fiction to subliterary status. Here Leo Braudy says the "implicit self-consciousness of plot" in popular genre becomes "explicit self-consciousness of form" (114).

None of the early Altman genre films so radically interrogates popular genre form and content as the western *McCabe & Mrs. Miller.* None so clearly develops the art-cinema play of temporal and spatial style.

Edmund Naughton's novel *McCabe,* which the film adapts, had already begun to critique the classic western plot: the "hero" McCabe is a gambler and the operator of the town whorehouse whose reputation with a gun makes him the protector of a weak community. The owners of the mining company kill him because, for no stronger reason than pride, he stands in the way of their expansion. In the film, the gambler McCabe (Warren Beatty) rides into the far northwestern mining town of Presbyterian Church, sees a business opportunity for gambling and drinking, and enters into a partnership with the more savvy Mrs. Miller (Julie Christie) to operate a brothel as well. When mining officials come to town to buy out the property, the drunken McCabe vainly exaggerates its value and miscalculates his strength. McCabe confronts the gunmen ultimately sent to town by the company to remove him by force and ends up dying in the blizzard that concludes the film.

What the film finds readable in the novel amounts to the lack of motivation in the hero's behavior. It proceeds further to challenge other dominant motives of the classical western: it devalues the hero-villain conflict. It portrays McCabe as a shallow, vain, barely competent gambler who dies for his bravado. It represents the woman as the stronger of the two title characters. It depicts gambling, not the church, the prostitute, not the school marm, as the good, if weak, forces of civilization standing against the bad and powerful energy of greedy corporations. All these changes rung on the western widely earn the film's critical reputation as an "anti-western." Schatz, for instance, argues that "the quintessential New Hollywood Western, and one which manages both to honor and to utterly subvert the genre's conventions, is Altman's *McCabe and Mrs. Miller*" (*Old Hollywood* 248). In particular, the film subverts the celebration of community everywhere. As McCabe's body is slowly covered by snow, the townspeople, who have hitherto ignored the building, celebrate their successful containment of a fire at the church that was started during the extended gunfight, and Mrs. Miller retreats into an opium haze in a Chinese drug den.

When viewed historically, dramatic changes in the portrayal of the western hero and the wilderness-civilization conflict such as those in *McCabe & Mrs. Miller* delineate significant moments of social change and cultural reevaluation. Diminution of heroic endeavor, denunciation of the corporate enterprise, cynicism about religious values, candidness about the role of women as prostitutes—these perspectives in the film contrast sharply with the creed of traditional westerns. They reflect as well the national political malaise of the Vietnam War era. An elegiac quality has always characterized accounts of progress in the western, and the relationship between John McCabe and Constance Miller participates in this mood of finality. The cryptic and mournful lyrics of Leonard Cohen's music configure metaphorically the itinerant life of the weary gambler as a journeying Joseph seeking room at the inn and a driven card player seeking the final wild card to win the game of life. When Constance Miller wanders away into the blue light at the end of the film the night before John McCabe's death, the music laments the romantic relationship that never develops in the film.

It may also be read narratively as a lament for the prostitute, tragically dependent on the indifference or inadequacy of men as impotent as the women are. When Cohen sings about the nurturing sisters of grace and mercy as McCabe brings the prostitutes to Presbyterian Church and the cross is attached to the church steeple against a brilliant golden sunset, the narrative evokes an eerie kind of religious nostalgia for the prostitutes from Bear Claw even as they arrive. The film's reconstruction of the western genre reflects contemporary historical research that shapes new understandings of the West by listening to the divergent, hitherto ignored, voices of western history, in particular the voice of the prostitute. The plight of women caught in prostitution emerges with dramatic clarity in Clint Eastwood's western *Unforgiven* (1992), in contemporary historical investigations, and hauntingly in *McCabe & Mrs. Miller.* Historian Patricia Nelson Limerick seems to be describing this film when she writes, "Acknowledge the human reality of Western prostitutes, and you have taken a major step toward removing Western history from the domain of myth and symbol and restoring it to actuality" (133). Altman's work in the demythologizing of the western depicts powerless, marginal individuals far removed from the image of noble cowboys and pioneers who "won the West" in classical Hollywood westerns. "When prostitutes tried to find stability in marriage, they found their partners in an unpromising pool of saloon owners, pimps, and criminals, men who were often violent and who were neither inclined nor able to rescue their spouses from their rough lives" (Limerick 131).

But these interpretations essentially focus on narrative content. They reflect certainly the ways in which *McCabe & Mrs. Miller* debunks and revises the optimistic ideology of manifest destiny so central to the western traditionally. Such interpretations reflect the influence of classical narrative paradigms and reading strategies that subordinate film's spatial and temporal systems to the service of the story logic. The ambiguities and gaps in the story, its representation of weak and insecure characters, its metaphoric use of song and atmosphere are all seen as the practice of the new Hollywood cinema to tell stories in innovative ways. Art-cinema narration, however, subverts the classical relationship between story and style, not to destroy story, but to activate visual and rhythmic systems as counterpoints to the story as well as supplements to it.

Altman asserts his understanding of the art cinema against the classical story forms:

> Film, to me, is all based on literature and reading. But film isn't that; it's more like painting. They should be more like murals. They're all too articulate, and everything is told to you too many times. You're not allowed to glean anything from it or get impressions. . . . But with paintings, you stand and look at them as long as you want and walk away, and every time you look at them, your own experience is bringing something additional to the information that you're looking at. Music is the same way. (quoted in Phipps).

The film's mournful melodies and ambiguous lyrics remain oblique, diffuse in their significance for the story. The music punctuates and rhymes across the film. In particular the sensuous image from Cohen's song "Sisters of Mercy" of hair woven of fire, gold, and dreams seems to motivate dominant visual motifs in the film. In this regard the film asks to be read not so much on its syntagmatic, horizontal, narrative axis, but on its paradigmatic, vertical, metaphoric axis.

*McCabe & Mrs. Miller* is in part a poem to autumn. It records the temporal progressions of the end of fall in the American Northwest, where the "fruited plain" gives way to mountains and the giant redwood becomes the major crop ripe to harvest. The lush green height of the tree towers over the human space in the film, and its warm red heart colors the human habitat. Against this green and red the deciduous trees turn yellow and then drop their leaves before the advancing winter winds. The season runs from mid-autumn rains that turn to mud and freeze to the first snow flurries that flutter finally down as flakes that culminate in blizzard. The mid-season sunlight, by turns soft and harsh, plays richly across the work that turns trees into buildings and disappears at last behind the leaden-gray winter sky. The camera rack focuses, zooms, and pans across the end of a season.

The visual and spatial representations of the film frequently appear to pursue a course independent of the central story. While the town of Presbyterian Church grows along with the story of McCabe, the viewer may watch this development as the construction of the profilmic set as well, finished only as the film ends. The fact that the narrative tends to obscure rather than establish diegetic space at the beginning of scenes promotes a sense of confusion that the labyrinthine set encourages. The viewer can hardly map the geographic relationships of buildings and communities in the space of the story and may recuperate this disorientation as a reflection of the uncertain direction of the story events. But the narrative's fluid, contradictory, ambiguous construction of space also suggests another more graphic and painterly scheme for its comprehension in the film.

Critics of *McCabe & Mrs. Miller* have regularly noticed its rich palette of complementary blues and greens, reds and golds. Robert Kolker, for instance, notes that "conventional association offers this as the light of warmth and security, contrasted with the cold blue of the exteriors." Inevitably such readings are reinvested into the economy of the story: "This is a film in which warmth and security are shown to be delusions and snares and community a fraud" (327). The red-gold colors reach a crescendo of warmth in the birthday celebration in the brothel before falling way to the darker moods of withdrawal, avoidance, and isolation in Mrs. Miller's drugged reverie at the film's end.

But these colors call attention to themselves as well in ways disinterested in the story. The play of lamps from shot to shot seems to motivate camera placement and editing—matches on action replaced by graphic matches, shot/reverse-shot sequences edited around the placement of lamps. The whole sequence when the mining negotiators come to town may be read as an abstract play of this stylistic pattern. Marked at either end by the strong red/gold glow of the brothel, where prostitutes and customers dance to Christmas music, the scene occurs in the nearly dark, muddy streets of town. The viewer can hardly follow the action, which pits a miner against men who have insulted his mail-order bride and concludes with an eventually mortal blow to his head. But the viewer can easily follow the momentary spots of golden red light that derive from lamps, reflections of lamps on faces, sudden shafts of the late sunset in the background, and the supper fires in front of miners' tents. The significance of the miner's injury to the story is suppressed both in this scene and during the middle section of the film as he lies dying, but the construction of colors urges another kind of attention.

The film also asks to be read in its painterly replication of the nineteenth-century visual arts. The opening scene of the gambling table in Sheehan's saloon replicates the peasants and miners playing cards in Vincent van Gogh's *The Potato Eaters*. The scene of bathing prostitutes singing "Beautiful Dreamer" in the red-tinged glow "of smoke and gold and dreaming" in the bathhouse recalls Adolphe-William Bouguereau's lush treatments of nymphs and madonnas, paintings that blended the gaze of the "lecher and the mystic" (Canaday 153). The sharp-edged landscapes set against the confusion of buildings in the cold autumn light repeat the romantic blend of nature and social decay in the paintings of Caspar David Friedrich.

Moreover, artistic motivation cues the viewer to understand the play of green and blue and red in particular as the effects of a set design with ideas of its own beyond the diegetic needs in the story of John McCabe and Constance Miller. When McCabe first spreads the red felt cloth over the saloon table in the opening scene of the film, the narrative announces its concern, like the French academician painters of the late nineteenth century, to employ red in the demarcation, structuring, and organization of space. From beginning to end, the film explores the changing values of red, much as will *The Gingerbread Man* more than twenty-five years later. In the small glow of McCabe's cigar at the distant end of the swinging bridge when he first arrives in Presbyterian Church, in the red hole that marks the entry of the derringer bullet into the killer's head at the end of the film, in the glowing raw red wood of the newly constructed buildings, in the rich warm interiors of the "red-light house," in the electronically added red flecks in the pointillistic snow falling during the final shootout, in the visceral red surface of the small jar scrutinized by Mrs. Miller's drugged eyeball—the changing values of red absorb the viewer's interest as much as the outcome of the shootout or the church fire. As Noël Burch writes: "What this principally involves is the creation of a truly consistent relationship between a film's spatial and temporal articulations and its narrative content, formal structure determining narrative structure as much as vice versa" (*Theory* 15). The film sings and paints and rhymes as well as tells its western tale, and in so doing energizes the elegiac voice of the western genre at a whole new level of artistry. *McCabe & Mrs. Miller* reconstructs this most typical Hollywood film genre as an art film.

## The Future as Absolute Zero

The science fiction film *Quintet* similarly situates the viewer at the complex intersection of poetic art and popular entertainment. Its genre work parallels the energies of the new wave in science fiction, which, just as the art cinema must be seen against the classical Hollywood cinema, asks to be read against the form and history of the "golden age" in science fiction. Thematically, its negative vision of future civilization on earth resonates with many of the experimental concerns in the science fiction new wave while it also cues the viewer's comprehension of *Quintet* and illuminates the place of genre in Altman's work.

Definitions of the science fiction that developed under the influence of editors such as John Campbell during the 1930s, 1940s, and 1950s read very much like the descriptions of the classical Hollywood cinema. Both in novels and in short fiction published in magazines like *Astounding Stories of Super Science* and *Amazing Stories,* these narratives tell stories of psychologically motivated individuals whose conflicts resolve generally through the efficacious action of strong central characters. They mix this element of popular adventure with representational realism in well-plotted, linear, and end-directed stories. Their generic semantics deploy an interaction of the physical science and technology of biology, physics, geology, and chemistry with the life sciences of psychology, sociology, and political science to convey a future infused with both scientific and humanistic optimism. This fiction matured in the same years often described as Hollywood's golden age and, like the stories of classical Hollywood, it reveals a formal and philosophical anachronism: science fiction conveyed a futuristic content in a narrative form derived from nineteenth-century literary realism, and Hollywood movies employed a modern technological medium to replicate that same form. Moreover, both golden-age science fiction and Hollywood fiction aggressively celebrate heroic individuality in a century when modernist art depicted the individual as alienated, isolated, insecure, and ineffectual.

Both art forms similarly experienced major formal transitions in the late 1960s, and the science fiction new wave parallels very much the movement described by the international art cinema. This new fiction reveals a literary self-consciousness with greater attention to technique. Its frequently opaque discourse disturbs a coherent sense of story. It employs symbolic and metaphoric modes of expression in order to emphasize private or subjective perspective. It elevates style to a status coequal with the logic of story. It brings a more pessimistic perspective to bear on contemporary social issues. It seeks to balance the representation of an empirically measurable, scientifically explainable universe with subjective experience and the personally observable. Like the art cinema, it achieves this contradictory amalgam through the discourse of ambiguity.

Science fiction proves to be a more difficult genre to define than the western or detective story because it lacks the formulaic syntax of other forms. It nevertheless owns telling paradigms. Mark Rose argues that one of two major patterns in science fiction is "that in which we are launched into an unfamiliar world" (27) yet one that nevertheless remains cognitively ordinary. This element of the unfamiliar constitutes part of what Thomas Schatz calls the "static nucleus," the central and defining semantic opposition that lies at the heart of every popular generic form (*Hollywood Genres* 31). In the detective story, guilt resists detection, crime opposes punishment; in the gothic tale, the normal confronts the horrific abnormal; in the western, civilization duels wilderness. In science fiction, the semantic core contains the distinction between the human and the nonhuman, an opposition that "defines the semantic space, the field of interest within which science fiction as a genre characteristically operates" (Rose 32). Rose further delineates four major categories of this semantic opposition—space, time, monster, and machine—of which the first two provide the most significant schemata for an understanding of *Quintet*'s divergent art-cinema form and its negative representation of social subjectivity.

One of the film's most striking elements is its bleak, oppressive, and depressing setting: the ruins of a vast, futuristic city, once housing five million people, surrounded by ice and slowly succumbing to a deadly ice age. As Grigor (Fernando Rey), the Quintet game master, says: "There's nothing but water, and soon that's all there will be left. The planet will be enveloped in ice, and that will, mercifully, be the end of this history." Throughout the entire film the sound track echoes with dull explosions that convey the sense of this world cracking and breaking under the strain of ice. Ice is the nonhuman other, the void space that has thrust itself cataclysmically upon human order. Nature in *Quintet* denotes a magnificently bleak and frozen wasteland. It recalls too what Vivian Sobchack describes as the basic iconography of the science fiction film during the 1950s and the 1960s: "What creates the terrifying wonder and pessimism of [such films as *It Came from Outer Space, Them!* and *The Monolith Monsters*] is not primarily the giant ant or spider, not the creature, not the alien invader . . . [but] the terrain of Earth itself . . . , the terrifying blankness in the eyes of what he thought was mother Nature" (112). Everything, even the lights, shimmers under a coating of ice in *Quintet,* and the film opens and closes on shots of an immense, blank, frozen landscape appropriate to a modernist vision of the contemporary. The film thus develops not only the category of space but of time as well. Every action of the characters is frigid, slow, belabored. And time is running down; "the entropic will to chaos" seems to rule even the movement of the plot. The energy of *Quintet* moves toward absolute zero. One of the characters remarks, "In a few months, a few years, all dying will be done." The city, civilization, humanity draws to a conclusion here, and the film participates in one of the genre's classic structures—apocalypse.

The second law of thermodynamics and the pessimism of apocalyptic entropy have coexisted with a religious element in science fiction since its modernist incarnation as a genre. Similarly, the biblical image of the Fall has filled the pages of science fiction since Mary Shelley's characterization of the scientist in *Frankenstein.* Altman's film pessimistically includes the clergy on the list of the fallen. In *Quintet,* St. Christopher (Vittorio Gassman) is the priest who, alternatively dressed in black or in white, runs a sort of rescue mission for the all-but-dead of this fallen city. Located in the lowest level of ruins in the five-tiered city, St. Christopher becomes the hero's most apparent antagonist. Paul Newman's character, Essex, must descend to this lowest level to confront and ultimately to kill St. Christopher as he wends his way, Dante-like, toward the first level, the casino, home of the game master Grigor. The film gives St. Christopher the longest speech in the film, perhaps one of the bleakest speeches, actually delivered as a sermon, in Altman's work. He describes an obscure five-sided universe with a sixth space in the center:

> What is the sixth space? It's empty. It's blackness. Void. In other ages, equally ignorant, it was said that an eternal fire would follow death. But I tell you there is no fire. . . . No, my sons, the emptiness . . . is the total horror of madness, the awareness of nothing. So your wretched lives are supremely happy. It is your reward. You must cherish your tortured lives because it is a pause, an interruption of the void preceding and following it.

The narration's apparent hostility to the values of St. Christopher's religion and Grigor's game also evokes a generic structure beyond that of apocalyptic science fiction, according to which the thematic values of *Quintet* become meaningful. A variety of theorists posit an evolutionary model of generic structure that sees the form move from a social, ritualistic stage to a more formal, self-conscious stage. Rose calls the self-conscious phase of science fiction one that leads "to interiorization and to emphatic metaphorization in which spiritual or psychological correlations replace simple external action" (81). Wexman links the self-conscious structures of Altman's work to aesthetic game playing: "His technique is directed toward exposing the artificiality of his audience's conditioned attempts to see the neat conventional patterns of art as refections of reality. For this reason, many of his films are based on generic models, which he treats as games" ("Critical" 15).

The external game in *Quintet* is science fiction, the rules of fiction, cinematic storytelling itself. The internal game, Quintet, directs character relationships and behavior. It emphasizes protecting one's own life at the expense of others; it establishes a metaphor of life as entertainment while waiting for death. Everyone in the city plays the game in the hopes of being, paradoxically, a survivor. Quintet shapes and consumes everything; its game master, Grigor, "adjudicator, judge, referee," reigns as a local deity who explains that his function is "to keep the game alive. The game is all that is important. The only intelligent expression of life is Quintet. All the elements of life are contained in it—our art, our philosophy. All things of value fit the game. The game is the only thing of value." Like the games of football and poker and "the game of life we all must play" in *MASH,* like gambling in *California Split,* like the game of mythmaking itself in *Buffalo Bill,* the game of entertainment in *Nashville,* the game of marriage in *A Wedding,* like the game of moviemaking in *The Player,* the fashion game in *Prêt-à-Porter,* and the games of chance and wit in Seldom Seen's basement in *Kansas City,* the game in *Quintet* consumes human energy in deadly competition. Even the structures of the city and the shapes of Altman's set design derive from the playing board, the levels, the metaphysics of Quintet.

Darko Suvin's definition of science fiction as "cognitive estrangement" substitutes the concept of cognition for science: "Cognition must be understood as embracing the polarities of human intelligence; that is it is at once logical and imaginative, rational and empirical, systematic and skeptical" (Parrinder 21). The game Quintet stands in metaphoric relation to cognition in this equation, at once rational, rule governed, determinative, and baffling. The narration only partially shares Essex's point of view with the spectator; for him the game seems rational, but it is also a cipher, its players, its rules, its structures oblique and confusing to the spectator. Like the art cinema, its rhythms, mise-en-scène, and structure create a maddening puzzle. As in *Nashville, A Wedding, California Split, 3 Women, Fool for Love,* and *The Player,* as in so much of the modernist aspect of the art cinema, the narrative of *Quintet* seems linear but works figuratively.

"Do you still have hope?" Ambrosia (Bibi Andersson) asks of Essex during the film that raises the same question. An indirect answer resides in the film's color codes. Just as in *McCabe & Mrs. Miller,* the cold colors of blue and green dominate the locales of *Quintet.* Very early in these films, both under the art direction of Leon Erickson, the narration begins to punctuate and illuminate this grim, cold setting with the golden red of firelight and sunset. *Quintet* is dominated visually by a variety of bleak grays, greens, and browns that graphically display the desolateness of situation and action. Here again the warm glow of golden, red lights mark the narrative space throughout in ways that doubly signal the false warmth of the casino and the true warmth of human relationship. During the night they spend together in the middle of the film, Essex and Ambrosia share warmth, memory, and meaning. The scene begins with a close-up shot of a round golden lamp filling the entire screen; then two cameras gradually zoom in to give us at last extreme close-ups of the characters' faces in a striking shot/reverse-shot sequence. In the morning, Ambrosia verbally marks the significance of the previous evening by describing a dream of her mother that caused her to awake with a rare smile of her face. The scene dissolves from a close-up of her face to another golden light in a bar; a tilt down reveals a grayish-green painting of a goose in flight. At the end, the narrative associates the warmth of fire, like the fire extinguished at the end of *McCabe,* with the false values of Grigor and his game. The game master stands framed in hellish flames as Essex renounces the city for the same instinctual drive that compels the goose to fly north, the image of spring with which the film begins, the sign of hope. He trudges off in the end into the frozen north, following the example of a lone goose whose northward flight symbolizes the springward turning hope of life.

This paradigm locates the central configuration of *Quintet* as both generic innovation and modernist vision that was extremely unpopular with audiences, who applauded instead the positive vision and heroics of *Superman* and *Close Encounters of the Third Kind* (1977). Paul Newman's acts of revenge in *Quintet* hardly approximate the space-opera heroics of *Star Wars* or the certainty of meaning in *Close Encounters.* Altman's take on heroism in this frozen confrontation with death and emptiness at the heart of life directs the hero to denounce the evil and nihilism of the game, to reject its killing and pessimistic view of civilization, and to return to the wilderness. As the film ends, he disappears into the icy wasteland. Christian conceptions of the apocalypse promise the possibility of redemption. In the archetypal story of winter or satire, there also follows the potential of the city's renewal. *Quintet,* however, gives no reason to expect that Essex will find anything but death beyond the horizon of the city. The final gesture of this hero seems a faint echo of the romantic refusal to go gentle into the dark night, a still, small voice of human affirmation. The heroic stance of *Quintet,* like the body of its star, is disguised beneath the heavy modernist robes of alienation and despair and the obscurity of the narrative itself.

In 1970, the black comedy of *MASH* fit perfectly a public mood shaped by the Vietnam War. The negative, cynical views of *The Long Goodbye* matched similar public moods during the Nixon years. By the end of the decade, however, the bleak, cynical pessimism of *Quintet* seemed misanthropic and intolerable. Critics of all persuasions agreed that the film was one of the worst ever made. The same period witnessed a significant number of science fiction films of another mode, the blockbuster—*Star Wars, Close Encounters, Superman, Moonraker* (1979), *The Black Hole* (1979), the first *Star Trek* movie (1979)—all goal-oriented, heroic, upbeat, and optimistic. *Quintet*'s somnambulistic pace and Tom Pierson's gothic score complement the modernist view of entropy. The vague metaphysics of the film's central metaphor, the apocalyptic endgame constructs a puzzle worthy of the most ambiguous art film. Essex's denunciation of the nihilism and murderous pessimism in the heart of the dying civilization could hardly compete with the enthusiastic heroics of Luke Skywalker, James Bond, and the crew of the Starship *Enterprise. Quintet* conveyed an all-too-disturbing view of the end on the eve of the Reagan years in American politics. Jack Kroll of *Newsweek,* almost alone in his appreciation of the film, praised its "great beauty and hypnotic rhythm" and its "shimmering tapestry of image and sound" and called Altman's "a true vision, both poetic and startlingly real: he makes you feel fire and ice coming together in the scorching chill that's overtaking the human heart" (88). Paul Newman's heroic disappearance into the icy wastes at the end displays the modernist mode of alienation that Robert Kolker calls "singleminded desolation . . . an experiment in despair" (334).

Alan Wilde conceives of "suspensive irony" as an aesthetic effort "to create, tentatively and provisionally anironic enclaves of value in the face of—but not in place of—a meaningless universe" (148). Such creative negentropy characterizes Altman's genre films. *Brewster McCloud* explodes the detective film by telling the story from the sympathetic point of view of a modern Icarus protected by a bird woman who murders with bird shit. *Quintet* explores new wave science fiction to discover a depressing distant future. *McCabe & Mrs. Miller* paints a lovely canvas of the ineffectuality of individual endeavor and mythic narrative. *The Gingerbread Man* hides the unspeakable under the gloss of narrative closure. *Dr. T & the Women* banishes the romantic hero from his professional and familial harem of women in the Dallas land of Oz and sends him via tornado not back to the black-and-white reality of Kansas but to the brown-and-white desert of Mexico. The long helicopter shot that concludes the film leaves the Richard Gere character delivering a male child in the middle of a desolate nowhere.

John Cawelti asserts that a key function of popular genre formulas is to "assist in the process of assimilating changes in values to traditional imaginative constructs" (*Adventure* 36). Transformations in Altman's films of conventional genre patterns in the 1970s reflected the turmoil in values attendant upon the Vietnam War, Watergate, and the Bicentennial decade. But by the end of the decade, the cultural climate had changed. The social liberalism of the late 1960s was in retreat. On the eve of the Reagan presidency retrenchments became the norm in politics, in economics, in lifestyles, in Hollywood narratives. Audience taste for innovative or complicated films declined dramatically, and the studios were disinclined to produce such films. *Quintet* and *A Perfect Couple* were failures at the box office, and Twentieth Century Fox refused to release *Health.* The film environment into which *MASH* was released included *Easy Rider* (1969), *Five Easy Pieces* (1970), *Medium Cool* (1969), *The Last Picture Show* (1971), and *Little Big Man* (1970). The film environment for *Popeye* included *The Empire Strikes Back* (1980), *Kramer vs. Kramer* (1979), *The Jerk* (1979), *Airplane!* (1980), *Coal Miner's Daughter* (1980), and *The Blues Brothers* (1980). Ronald Reagan told America, "People who say there are no heroes anymore just don't know where to look." The deconstructive, experimental, resistant moment in Hollywood filmmaking proved short-lived. The advent of the blockbuster film inaugurated both a narrative and an economic energy that continues to dominate the Hollywood industry at the beginning of a new century. The *Superman, Rambo, Rocky, Star Wars, Indiana Jones,* and *Lethal Weapon* films, and even the *Home Alone* movies, reflect an upbeat return to action-oriented, hero-dominated, goal-driven narratives. The modernist pessimism of films like *Nashville, Quintet, Short Cuts,* and *Kansas City* remains unfashionable and unpopular.

Altman sold Lions Gate Films in 1981 and retreated to New York and Paris and the production of stage dramas for most of the 1980s. Adapting plays by Marsha Norman, David Rabe, Ed Graczyk, Sam Shepard, and Harold Pinter, Altman during this decade exchanged the interrogation of traditional genre forms for the enclosed spaces and prescribed dialogue of the stage. Altman's movies returned to popular critical attention in 1990, but more aggressively with art-cinema rather than generic forms: *Vincent & Theo* is an art film about art that depicts the famous relationship between the van Gogh brothers in aggressively art-cinema narrative and style. Altman's films of the 1990s eschew traditional genre altogether until the noir thriller *The Gingerbread Man* in 1998 and the comic romance of *Dr. T & the Women* in 2000. *Vincent & Theo, The Player, Short Cuts, Prêt-à-Porter,* and *Kansas City* represent the least generic, most open narratives in Altman's work. They reflect more personal and more reflexive observation, more exaggerated stories and characters, more satiric and playful, although nonetheless pessimistic, cinematic discourse. Robert Altman's genre films constitute the art-cinema strategy that variously interrogates generic form in film, audience anticipation and contemporary values, and the conventions of the film industry. They depict life as confusing and contradictory. They gently confront Hollywood's urge to tell stories and wander off into poetic thickets of meaning in the manner of the films of such international art directors as Truffaut, Fellini, and Bergman. They eschew the narration of straightforward complications and resolutions of the human romance. Altman's films of the 1980s and 1990s generally cease to remodel the popular narrative genres, but they continue to reflect a commitment to the modernist impulses of irony, experimentation, reflexivity, and social critique; they consistently represent the merger of realism and expressivity that asks to be read in ambiguity; they characteristically examine the disruptions of the ego and the fractured forms of the self. They reflect the ongoing vitality of art-cinema narration in American cinema.

# Part II. Identities in Patriarchy

# 5. Masculine Subjects: Nixon, Tanner, and the Gingerbread Man

Jacques Maritain locates the apotheosis in "the Advent of the Self" in European romanticism during the first half of the nineteenth century, a self with roots in Christian revelation, "a creative Self endowed with immortal intelligence, pursuing deliberately willed ends, and capable of sensing beauty" (30). This creative self, in conceptual conjunction with Descartes's "I think, therefore I am" in the eighteenth century, conveys with theological and philosophical certainty the power of human individuality. As modern industrial capitalism developed under the impetus of science and colonialism, the confidence that supported the conception of individual, rational, imaginative, capable, progressively evolving social identity slowly eroded from this height. By the beginning of the twentieth-century, modern psychology announced the distance between the conscious and the subconscious. Physics described the theory of relativity of time and space and the indeterminacy of observing subatomic particles of the molecule. Social science charted the coercive influence of economic class and environment. The death of Queen Victoria in 1901, Mahler's First Symphony in Berlin in 1909, the New York Armory Show of experimental art from Europe in 1913, and the "guns of August" in 1914 announced the end of something. The concept of the self triumphant at the dawn of the French Revolution began to break up on the shoals of a modern sensibility marked by splintered politics, uncertain science, atonal scales, and fractured vision. Yeats described it well: "Things fall apart; the center cannot hold; / Mere anarchy is loosed upon the world." When an entire generation of young French, English, and German soldiers died on battlefields like Flanders, any romantic "song of myself" had become the modernist dirge "Human voices wake us, and we drown."

Robert Altman's films reflect the modern sense of the individual as a social construct, a signifier of relations composed of the roles determined by social conditions. They afford case studies of the "declining vitality of the self" that has, in the words of Robert Langbaum, "accompanied a loss of confidence in the individual and individual effort due to mass production, mass markets, mass media, to increasing urbanization, industrialization, specialization, and to the increasing alienation of the self, according to Marx's analysis, from all specialized functions" (53). By the time Popeye, for instance, achieves his specialized function as hero at the end of that film, he has overcome his earlier alienation from the community of Sweethaven. But entering into his role as the comic strip "Popeye"—son, lover, father—he becomes alienated from the multiple, humanized Popeye who initially enters the film in a quest for his father. By the time Opal begins to comprehend the meanings of events in *Nashville,* or Kitty Potter manages to explain the fashion scene in *Prêt-à-Porter,* the viewer has long since become lost in the replication of subjectivities that denies the possibility of constructing coherent understandings of the films. Internal and external personal relationships meander along unmarked routes and suddenly make unexpected links into other lives that merge and diverge by chance in the myriad directions of *Short Cuts.* As Silvio Gaggi observes, "It is the inconsistencies and ambiguities, the slidings of voice from character to character, the unexpected intrusions of alien voices, that challenge the integrity of the *cogito* and threaten the reader's own confidence in his or her ability to fully master the text" (*From Text* 45).

This chapter illustrates the broken subject of art-cinema narration. In particular, three of Altman's films reflect his innovative use of form to characterize central male figures as unheroic, insecure, diversely constructed figures whose individuality and authority are problematic or illusory. The starkly interior *Secret Honor* develops a psychological portrait of a suicidal Richard Nixon, whose justification for Watergate proves to be the disabling cacophony of voices that shape his persona. *Tanner '88* extends through eleven televised parts of a docudrama whose central character is a discursively and diegetically made-up politician running for president alongside the other, "real" politicians of the 1988 presidential campaign. *The Gingerbread Man* recycles film noir to portray the insecurity of apparently successful masculinity undone by the unspeakable details of childhood sexual abuse. The subliminal reality in these movies consists of the links that integrate their internal voices, the cues that distinguish reality from fiction, the causality that links desire, violence, and control. All three films feature fractured images of male lawyers displaced from positions of power and ironically separated from the figure of the law that their gender, their profession, and narrative order would traditionally authorize.

If the self is posited traditionally as a center of meaning and action with a public demeanor undergirded by a rich inner life, then Altman as filmmaker may be arraigned for contributing to that crime of radical depthlessness frequently charged to the modernist worldview. Nathan Scott calls its "desolate frontier" and narrow focus on the self constructs of "estrangement and alienation," a "literature of metaphysical isolation" (8). The loss of self, that inner authenticity that guarantees integrity to the public persona, is magnified by an art form that can access the unconscious states through dream imagery more easily than it can portray the self-conscious ego. Even in his most formally accessible films, however, such as *A Perfect Couple* and *The Gingerbread Man,* Altman reveals a marked fascination with physiognomy and behavior as clues to a complex, contradictory, unspeakable inner identification.

One of the most characteristic signatures of the subliminal reality in Altman's art cinema is the use of the zoom lens in shots that begin at a medium distance and then zoom in slowly to gaze close-up in desire and separation at a character's face. Such probing shots seem to promise a growth in audience knowledge about individuals but finally end only in appropriating the mask and the distance between the gaze and the galvanizing spirit in the object of the gaze. In another mode, many films perceived widely as "Altmanesque" generate large rambling stories with many characters. In films like *MASH, Nashville, A Wedding,* and *Short Cuts,* the multiplicity of characters resists any narrative possibility of story development sufficient to reveal, explore, or explain individual motivations and desires. Even as these films have developed narrative and stylistic strategies that imply the buried self, the inner life of another persona beyond the surface images and behaviors and their social determinations, their multiple stories resist any representation of coherent, stable, "round" characters. Such strategies display yet another set of surfaces, of course, but the different images suggest different levels of authenticity and construct selves of multifaceted identities. Gone are the narrative perspectives of classical realist fiction, with its knowing and confident authorial voice. Gone are those narrative voices of stability, of ordering, of making meanings that share cultural knowledge and value with equally stable and understanding readers. Gaggi again is instructive in his analysis of the concomitant dissolution of the self:

> When replication and multiplication decenter the world by depriving it of reference that grounds, that "authorizes" those replications and multiplications, the subject itself reflects that decenteredness, as it does when viewing a painting that contains multiple, inconsistent vanishing points or when reading a novel that consistently shifts voice. (*From Text* 61)

A familiar subjectivity in Altman's art cinema configures the ideological voices of gender relationships in modern American society. The films specifically constitute a continuing critique of patriarchical authority and reflect marked desires and anxieties about the kind of dominant masculine sexuality regnant in the macho roles of Clint Eastwood, Charles Bronson, Sean Connery, Sylvester Stallone, Bruce Willis, Tom Cruise, Harrison Ford, and Mel Gibson. Altman's films explore a troubled masculinity, perceived as a refusal, a fear, a lack, a breakdown of authority. In *McCabe & Mrs. Miller,* the inner nature of John McCabe counters the braggadocio of his public demeanor. He is insecure, doubt-filled, inept, and fragile, and he breaks apart on the shoals of big business and its macho enforcers. In the classic western showdown, when he kills the oversized hunter who chases him with an oversized buffalo gun, his weapon is no bold pistol but a tiny derringer. Its small force spent, McCabe dies meaninglessly in the snow. The portrayal of "Pudgy" McCabe as weak, unimaginative, and sadly laughable challenges the dominant masculine myths of popular genre heroes—as do Marlowe in *The Long Goodbye,* Essex in *Quintet,* and William F. Cody in *Buffalo Bill.* Altman's male characters frequently give the lie to any sense of macho pride; indeed, they show a fear of, a shrinking away from that sense of self—Bowie in *Thieves Like Us,* Bill and Charlie in *California Split,* Brewster in *Brewster McCloud,* Griffin Mill in *The Player,* Rick in *The Gingerbread Man.* In *Short Cuts,* the doctor, the weatherman, the baker, the fx intern, the pool cleaner, the helicopter pilot, the motorcycle cop—all reflect debilities that interfere with their professional, personal, and social well-being.

*Buffalo Bill and the Indians, or Sitting Bull's History Lesson,* perhaps the most interrogative of Altman's films, asserts the difficulty of any unified, coherent identity for the self or any unified meaning in a text. William F. Cody's struggle to express himself confronts the competing authors of that self, the babel of voices that authorize Cody as literally a textual other. The film dramatizes a tension between William F. Cody as an apparently whole individual capable of meaning, knowledge, and action and the image of Buffalo Bill as an ensemble literally of conflicting historical, psychological, and ideological forces, a creation of divers authorial hands, and the product of divergent media of communication and art. Ned Buntline, for instance, the first author of the long-lived series of Buffalo Bill dime novels, recounts his first encounter with the young Cody as a predetermined textual idea:

> I'm eager to write about somebody 'cause I got a batch of excitin' plots I might take to Hickok but I'm mad at him, so I tell the kid from now on his name is Buffalo Bill and in six months the whole country's gonna know about you. . . . Sure enough, these stories come out and are a big success and the kid comes lookin' for me, scared to death about the legends I created but real excited with his new fame. (Rudolph and Altman 22)

The film constantly focuses the issue of personality by contrasting shots of William F. Cody and images of Buffalo Bill. As William Simon and Louise Spence observe:

> Bill is represented through numerous, often contrary modes: what people say about him, what people write about him, what he thinks and says about himself, artists' images, publicists' blurbs, Wild West performances, mirror images, dreams, and hallucinations. By the film's end, Bill has been presented in so many ways that he himself no longer has a firm grasp on his identity. (71)

From the outset, the film works to deconstruct the ideological and psychological projections of a stable subjectivity in mass-media entertainment. William Frederick Cody is constrained by a variety of subject positions variously articulated by the demands of history, popular mythology, psychology, and economics, as well as the media.

The critical viewer, when looking for meaning in such art-cinema narratives, for an interpretation, discovers a multiplicity of subject positions within the film that echo a similar contest of critical voices that situate his or her viewing. As John Caughie writes, "The crack in the singular text's self-containment is opened wider by questions of subjects other than the purely textual subject—social subjects, sexual subjects, historical subjects who are constituted in a plurality of discourses (in an intertextuality of other texts) of which the single text is only one moment" (206). Contemporary textual analysis is aware that the death of the author has meant the birth of many authors, the death of the self supplanted by many selves. *Buffalo Bill and the Indians* designates "Buffalo

Bill" as the site of conflicting codes of meaning, as the site of numerous codes through which, as Jonathan Culler states, "the subject is deprived of his role as source of meaning . . . , the self is dissolved as its various functions are ascribed to impersonal systems which operate through it" (*Pursuit* 33).

The film represents a range of responses to this situation. At one end of the spectrum, William Cody succumbs to the public image of himself demanded by the arena, offered by the symbolic systems of entertainment. But at the other end, the film reflects a series of narrative conflicts that have little confluence and are impossible to resolve. One approach to such conflict in identity is the classical drive for containment and narrative closure—a recapitulation of the heterogeneous discourse under a larger homogeneity. On the other hand, the art cinema asks the critical viewer to comprehend the contradictions in a story, the mix of codes, structures, and languages in a film, as a function of broken subjectivity, fragmented individuality, centerless egos. An inevitable effect of the symbolic is to naturalize the process of signification and thus to assert the legality of its discourse, its efforts to control the differences, the desires, the absences of the imaginary. At the other end of this spectrum is the modernist response, which accepts the plural narrative in all its ambiguity and indeterminacy. Altman's art cinema constantly reflects the pressures that unfix the subject in a context that demands stability.

## Failure in the White House

Biography has the effect of re-creating the past as a new present. Its retelling establishes a new reality, a different portrait, a story different from the original. Barbara Johnson tells us that rereading questions the "very idea of identity, infinitely deferring the possibility of adding up the sum of a text's parts or meanings and reaching a totalized, integrated whole" (3–4). Biography thus, even as it works popularly to deliver the "real" person, effects a defamiliarization of its original. Biographers and filmmakers reflect their own values, concerns, and knowledge as they reappropriate the past in an effort to catch the portraits of individuals borne further away by time and representation. They make the old new again; they create anew; they extract a new readability from the unreadable or unread dimensions of historic narratives and lives.

One of the most fascinating political lives and social stories of the recent past is that marked by the historical name "Richard Milhous Nixon." Nixon's career as a politician and president during the tumultuous 1960s and 1970s has constantly provided material for biographers seeking to describe and capture the real man: Jules Witcover's *The Resurrection of Richard Nixon,* Gary Wills's *Nixon Agonistes: The Crisis of the Self-Made Man,* William Costello's *The Facts about Nixon,* and Fawn Brodie's *Richard Nixon: The Shaping of His Character* all seek to convey what Bela Kornitzer sought in one of the earliest biographies, *The Real Nixon.* As the titles of their volumes indicate, these authors also seek to effect a new image, a new explanation, a new Nixon, or, in the most recent effort by Anthony Summers, to expose "the arrogance of power" and the "secret world of Richard Nixon." Perhaps nowhere are these simultaneous energies more clearly demonstrated than in the antiestablishment portrait of Nixon in Emile de Antonio's film *Millhouse: A White Comedy* (1971). Herbert Klein, Nixon's longtime press secretary, describes the inevitability of Richard Nixon as an example of the concern and effect of biography: "When one looks at the history of Nixon and his relations with the press, 'new Nixon' comes out almost like code words. I lived through 'new Nixon' after 'new Nixon'" (quoted in Wicker, *One* 497).

Tom Wicker reveals this dual effort to capture the real man Nixon and to read differently the story of Nixon's career. His biography *One of Us: Richard Nixon and the American Dream* raises the question, why would the journalist who in his own words "was more often his critic . . . than his admirer write this new book on Nixon?" The book reveals the surprising efforts of a longtime political reporter and liberal editor of the *New York Times* to achieve a more journalistically balanced and just portrait of the man, to give the puzzling political story of Nixon an explanatory plot. Wicker's rereading of the events of Nixon's career from 1954 to 1974 are motivated by a vision of the "authentic man": "As his entire career had demonstrated, he was an uncommonly driven man in his desire for greatness, achievement, recognition; but these are more nearly the drives of someone uncertain of his own worth, eager to prove that worth to himself, than of a man comfortable in his identity" (427). The power of the presidency could perhaps "erase the past, make him whole against the wounds and slights of a savage world, perhaps even bring about through his efforts the peace on earth which at last would earn his mother's love" (206). Wicker seeks to explain: "I can safely assure my readers that he is not the product of oddly perverted thinking. . . . I saw his form pass by—appealing—significant—under a cloud—perfectly silent. . . . It was for me, with all the sympathy of which I was capable, to seek fit words for his meaning" (x).

Similarly, Altman's portrait of Nixon in *Secret Honor* seeks a recovery and an explanation, but one whose rereading contains all the contradictions. The film's sympathetic representations derive from the stylistic and structural strategies of art-cinema narration in other Altman films, which show a repeated empathy for splintered integrity and uncertain independence in narrative authority. On an evening following the collapse of his presidency, as a heavily drinking Nixon (Philip Baker Hall) contemplates suicide, he exposes, rehearses, and evaluates the multiple strands and contradictory voices of his life's story. He describes a feeling of shame over his political beginnings at a meeting of the Republican elite in 1946: "I sold my soul in Bohemian Grove for shit!" He also expresses the tension frequently revealed in Altman's films and in Altman's career between personal integrity and public endorsement. At stake here is the freedom to author one's own narrative, one's own blueprint, one's fiction—to be captain of the story and master of the discourse. Selling out means "power and money—lots of it." And the work, the job description is simple: tell *their* story, write *their* fiction. Adjust your life to the dominant system of meaning. On the mythical morning in 1972 after the greatest electoral mandate in American history, the clandestine force behind his campaign, the Committee of One Hundred, declared to the reelected president, "Here is the plan, Richard!" One context for the comprehension of this story is the film career of Robert Altman. The perception of Altman's films' eccentric and perverse stories and style, their marked divergence from the Hollywood narrative, their failure at the box office—all contributed to Altman's estrangement from Hollywood during the 1980s and his continued reliance on so-called independent companies for production and distribution of films during and since the 1990s. The cost of not telling *their* story, as it is in this Nixon's loss of power, is lack of respect, banishment, the loss of power and money.

Like *Buffalo Bill and the Indians, Secret Honor* investigates and interrogates social identity as the relationship between competing narrative authorities. Indeed, it portrays narrative as a major site of political conflict. It examines the relationship between multiple conceptions of identity and the competition of narrative voice so central to art-cinema narration. It reveals the depths of masculine insecurity in the "highest office of the land." It particularly reveals a struggle between surface stories and stories of hidden motivation—as in *Brewster McCloud,* which represents the U.S. national anthem as patriotic discourse supported by show business. In that film, a black band rehearsing the anthem with a white lady wearing red, white, and blue refuses to play it again and instead breaks into a spirited rendition of the "black national anthem," thus calling attention to an alternative patriotic narrative, a competing political story. It reveals surface texts as motivated by subtexts, as facades developed for larger purposes. Thus, too, the story of "Richard Milhous Nixon" is a construct of the "China Plan." Just as Nixon claims that he "would have had to invent John Dean," so the Committee of One Hundred produced RMH: "Wanted, young man to run for Congress."

Within such contexts, *Secret Honor* symbolizes a struggle central to the art cinema generally and to many of Altman's films in particular. Here is pessimism and paranoia about the forces that silently coerce our lives. Here is the rhetorical strategy of a surface story designed to subvert the hidden master narrative. A central focus of the film is Nixon's story of Watergate as a counter to the story about a politician named Nixon being told by the economic interests of hidden, plutocratic power, represented as the authority behind his career, the Committee of One Hundred. Both stories are fictions with a purpose. The Committee's story, "Stick with Dick in seventy six," is motivated by and conceals another story, which is the plan to carve up the markets of the Pacific Rim and divide them with the Chinese. Nixon's story of Watergate is a "load of chicken-shit charges" invented to "lead the public to the tip of the wrong iceberg." Altman's story (the film's story) of Nixon works to diffuse cinematic perceptions of identity as coherent narrative. Nixon's invention of Deep Throat was a way "to orchestrate the [Watergate] tapes like a great drama," a secret strategy to subvert the master narrative written by the authors of the China Plan. The film's representation of Nixon similarly works to subvert both narratives, that of the Committee of One Hundred and that of Deep Throat, with yet another narrative, of presidential admission, confession, and rebellion. And Altman's dissembling story of the film's story of Nixon is designed to diffuse cinematic perceptions of identity as coherent narrative.

We can follow the presumed chronology of events in the Committee's biography of Richard Nixon, the political "blueprint" for his life from 1945 to 1976, and we can follow its rewriting by Nixon from 1972 to 1974. But the rambling, digressive, broken discourse of the film does not coherently or chronologically present these stories. Rather, this eighty-six-minute chronology of Nixon's revelation of the "face under the mask" is motivated by a perception of cause-effect, of personal identity that is overdetermined and contradictory. The China Plan is an elite secret strategy to control the world's markets for power and money, "millions for Bohemian Grove, and billions for the Mob." That plot requires four more years for the Nixon presidency, to be bought at the polls with "blood bribery" from the prolonged Vietnam War, during which time Nixon is to effect a treaty with the Chinese against the Soviet Union to establish worldwide economic hegemony. But this story involves truly impeachable acts—treason, bribery, and other high crimes and misdemeanors: "You understand what it means if they catch me. It would mean the firing squad." So the third-rate break-in at the Watergate Hotel provides him the opportunity to get out of the dangerous scenario. Deep Throat spins out another tale generating Nixon's "public shame" for the good of the nation.

But a sympathetic understanding of the pressure to sell out to a dominant narrative authority does not extend in Altman's art cinema to the production (like Wicker's or Nixon's) of a competing order—a better, more compelling plot. Rather, Nixon's "secret honor" is revealed by the film as a constantly interrupted and interrupting discourse, full of unspoken and unspeakable intentions, fears, and hostilities—multiple strategies of desire, conflicting, unrealizable, unresolvable, unspeakable. The difficulty in piecing together the Nixon biography, of following its plot, results from the broken surface of the text, which reflects the broken surface of the man. Nixon is depicted as the site of many discordant and competing voices that converge and disperse across the short length of the film.

What Nixon stutteringly calls "the prayer, uh, the pre . . . , uh, the prologue" of his revelation is instructive. Its subjects are first of all a gift for the gardener's sick wife: "Tell her it's from . . . uh, uh, tell her it's from . . . uh, the, uh, from friends of a free Cuba!" Nixon then rambles through a dozen subjects, ironically instructing his office assistant twice to erase the tape "of all that crap." Here is the list of his concerns: the pardon, the Warren Report on the assassination of John F. Kennedy, the Kennedy brothers, Nixon's brothers and his parents, the health of the family and the California climate, recollections of his childhood, quotations from his memoirs, the supportive influences in his life, his presidential acceptance speech, the presidential election of 1960, his six crises, the Checkers speech, *Hamlet,* his high school days, his dislike of women, the Orthogonian Society, his strategy about Watergate, the impeachment proceedings, the theories of his involvement in Watergate, and the elitism of the founding fathers. There are yet other subjects, but this list sufficiently demonstrates the digressive character of the Nixon monologue.

Not only do these subjects vie for attention in the film, the displacement of one by another is accompanied by a number of roles that appear and disappear, contend and change, merge and dissolve. These are the voices in which Nixon speaks, and by which he is spoken. The central voice of defense attorney establishes Nixon in a dual relationship with himself, first and third person. The distinction between "Your Honor, my client" and "Your Honor, I" is not a stable one. This voice, however, most explicitly designates the narrative as a defense—of a client "from a poor family, a boy who never had a break or a chance." It also promises an admission: "Your Honor, . . . today my client is going to reveal to you the reasons behind the reasons for the Watergate affair." At other times the voice we hear is that of the writer, as Nixon reads to us from his memoirs about the face of an American child or as the writer replaces a more strident, intemperate voice; for example, aggressive assertions like "I used to lie awake at night trying to figure out how the hell I . . ." yield to empathic longing—"When I was a child the sweetest sound I ever heard was the sound of the Sante Fe Railroad."

Occasionally the voice echoes the oratorical style of the politician: "I ask you to help me make that dream come true for millions to whom it is an *impossible* dream!" At times he is the high school organizer: "You know what I did? I founded the Orthogonian Society—all boys, no girls, just square shooters." At other times his role is that of the entertainer, dancing around the room, singing, playing the piano. At other times he is the raconteur: "That [Congressman] Patman was so funny! He said, he said, he said, 'Where . . . is all this [reelection] money coming from?!'" There are touching moments, too, as when during his recollection of the Alger Hiss case he becomes a consoler, almost motherly as he leads a distressed Whittaker Chambers through his "Now I lay me down to sleep." Nixon further plays confessor and moralist: "My life ended that night. God help me. . . . This was the crossroads. I knew I was making a pact with the Devil." He voices impotence in handling the Committee of One Hundred, "so that is the reason we had to invent Deep Throat and use Watergate to get out with a pardon. . . . Oh God!" Nixon also is the voice of the little boy who pleads, "I wish you would come home right now, Mother." And he is also a dog, literally kneeling on the floor and barking for his master's approval.

Nixon assumes a most telling voice when he asserts, "It was *me* who was Hamlet!" "My drama teacher in school used to say I was the most melancholy Dane he had ever directed." With a loaded pistol on his desk, he pointedly intones lines from the "to be or not to be" soliloquy. Hamlet is also an apt role for Nixon to assume in other ways than this contemplation of suicide, for despite his inaction, Hamlet resorts to acting, to disguised behavior in order to discover the guilty authority of the king. Both dramas develop the conflict among surface stories, secret stories, and stories of subversion. Both chronicle debilitated men examining the terms of their own confusing subjectivity.

Conflicting stories, conflicting roles—*Secret Honor* further presents a kaleidoscopic array of tones and moods. These Nixon personas whine, plead, rail, and whisper. He is self-righteous when he maintains, "I did it for Maggie and Jiggs, the little people, my kind of people . . . , the forgotten American, for the silent majority." He is defensive when he admits, "I may have done and said some things [up at Bohemian Grove] that came back to haunt me twenty-five years later when the real China card was played." His tone is also plaintive: "I was always running, trying so hard to make the team that I was always offsides." Yet he can arrogantly, aggressively assert, "I *am* the American Dream! Period. . . . I *am* the system! Period!" He bitterly and hostilely attacks the eastern rich, the liberal press, and the founding fathers. His anger frequently reduces him to inarticulate splutterings of rage. And his venomous cursing of Henry Kissinger nearly brings him to hysteria. The viewer struggles to comprehend an exhausting range of energies and personalities woven into the fabric of this film, and in doing so activates those familiar reading strategies demanded by art-cinema narration to follow a bewildering number of narrative threads and competing personas.

*Secret Honor* brims over with stories. Its miniature vignettes, full-blown plots, teasing allusions, static tableaus, partially glimpsed conflicts, and imaginary scenarios feed, on one hand, into the master strategy of the China Plan and its deflection by Deep Throat. On the other hand, they constitute the unresolvable mix of moods, voices, and experiences specified as the identities of Richard Nixon by the film. The stories reveal, admit, and confess; they deny, conceal, and affirm, justify and accuse. They vacillate between stances of security and insecurity, confidence and uncertainty, prowess and impotence. Stories about Nixon's Black Irish family, for instance, involve his sense of being poor and unlucky, not "to the manor born" like the Kennedys, and sick: "They came to California for the climate and all died anyway." Whereas the Kennedy family represents a political clan, Nixon declares, "My goddamn family alone could have ruined me." Yet that family is also the source of pride, Quaker morality, and the encouragement "to dream the impossible dream."

Stories about studying and practicing law similarly direct our attention in two conflicting directions—Nixon's recollections of himself as "Iron Butt" and third in his class at Duke, and his recollections of being out of his league when applying for a job in a high-class eastern law firm. Stories about football, however, clearly evoke a sense of power. One of the memorable moments in the film occurs as old number twenty-three sits at his mother's piano between the portraits of Washington and Lincoln, playing the Notre Dame fight song. His delight in power, too, is quite evident in his recollection of calling in plays to the coach of the Washington Redskins on the Oval Office white phone and bombing missions in North Vietnam on the red phone: "That was fun!"

We hear that his coach had wished he could run the ball as well as he could run his mouth as a debater. And we learn that he won that first debate in high school: "Resolved: girls are no good." Numerous stories about women circulate through the film—about girls in school, about his wife, about Jackie Kennedy, about the prostitutes at Bohemian Grove—and reveal his sexual insecurity. His narratives linked to women always break down, he begins to stammer, sentences go awry, never finish. "You know how they are when you're uh, uh . . . ." "Naturally, I couldn't get any. . . ." "During all those years, I was . . . , I didn't . . . ." Of Helen Gahagan Douglas, his first Senate opponent, he manages a fuller articulation: "She was beautiful. . . . She was the kind of . . . uh, woman . . . . I liked her." The various stories of his "gentle Quaker mother" are the most complete, perhaps because, as he tells us, "You I owe, Mother, only you."

The predominant number of stories, of course, involve politics. Nixon's narration moves rapidly and repeatedly over all the years and events between 1945 and the present: the Committee's ad in 1945, the senate campaign in 1950, the dirty jobs for Ike, the Checkers speech, the debates and the Chicago vote fraud in the 1960 presidential election, the landslide election in 1972. The film interlaces this welter of historical narratives with moral tones. Nixon divides the presidential portraits according to good and bad presidents and constantly passes judgment on the actions of others. We may read his Deep Throat narrative as motivated by ethical concerns to save the presidency, or more cynically as motivated by the paralyzing fear that "they will put me in a cage." Throughout the film, stories collide and compete with each other, stories about dreams of success ("I really did want to grow up to be Abraham Lincoln") and dreams of failure ("To make it in this rat race you have to dream of failure every day").

In the film's effort "to understand," the art-cinema dimensions of

*Secret Honor* generate not a straightforward story—with a central conflict, a clear-cut beginning, middle, and end, and a single efficacious protagonist—but a "meditation" on the multiple, shifting, contradictory personas that constitute the subjectivity of Richard Nixon as a mixture appropriately of fact and fiction. Nixon's invention of Deep Throat develops out of fear and aggression. It grows from a desire for an authoritative narrative, one of sufficient power to feed the public's desire for plausible fictions, a story of sufficient power indeed to organize the conflicting drives of Nixon himself against the treasonous plot of the Committee of One Hundred. Speaking of himself in the third person, Nixon states, "He took the hardest possible way. . . . He chose . . . secret honor and public shame." This impulse to organize, to narrate an escape from the Committee's control reflects Nixon's expression of desire conveyed to the image of his mother at the end of the film: "I just wanted to have power . . . to be a man, not your dog."

During the 1980s, while variously directing off-Broadway and cable plays in New York and drama and opera at the University of Michigan, Robert Altman directed ten films that are adaptations of works written for the stage. These adaptations reflect at once a dramatic focus divergent from the discordant productions of the 1970s and a continuation of structural and thematic deconstructions of authority that have marked Altman's films. The ten films—*Come Back to the 5 & Dime, Jimmy Dean, Jimmy Dean*; *Streamers*; *Two by South* (1982); *Secret Honor*; *The Laundromat* (1985); *Fool for Love*; *Beyond Therapy* (1987); *The Dumb Waiter* (1987); *The Room* (1987); and *The Caine Mutiny Court Martial* (1988)—are "small" dramas. Subsisting on small budgets, featuring small casts, enjoying small distribution, achieving small success with critics and audiences, they represent major departures from the big-budgets, ensemble casts, and studio productions like *MASH* and *Nashville* of the decade before or *Short Cuts* and *Prêt-à-Porter* of the decade after. The narrative energies of these films focus on restricted spaces—a dime store, a motel, a barracks, a study, a laundromat, a basement—and they seem to drive coherently and linearly toward climax and resolution.

A familiar subjectivity in Altman's films is nevertheless apparent in *Secret Honor* and these other adaptations of contemporary plays. They depict the familiar themes of the art cinema—the alienated, angst-ridden, socially constricted characters of a debilitating contemporary existence only momentarily held at bay by the confines of mise-en-scène. Fractured identity appears in the central lines, the central diegetic conflict, the central strategy of *Secret Honor*—"public humiliation, secret honor." Under the paranoid pressures to act out a political drama authored and produced by a "Committee of One Hundred," Richard Nixon contrives the Watergate conspiracy as a false, misleading, and coherent narrative designed to derail the ideological objectives of hidden power and to feed the public's desire for plausible if disturbing fictions. The issue in these films is power. The apparent aimlessness and chaotic good humor of the earlier Altman films is burned away here, but the gesture of hostility and defiance shouted by Nixon at the conclusion of *Secret Honor* derives from the same refusal of authority that motivated the black comedy of *MASH.*

*Secret Honor* is equally motivated to deflect the master stories that seek to organize our social knowledge, but unlike Wicker's concern with carefully illuminating the conflicted Nixon, its strategy is a refusal of the authority that resides in narrative. It turns away from an ordered and ordering rhetoric of explanation. It seeks instead a form that interrogates order. It develops a portrait of personality as heterogeneous and fluid, contradictory and in flux. Tom Wicker's adaptation of Nixon seeks to explain the "flaws of character [for which] he came to grief personally, and [which] left incomplete the soaring structure of peace he envisioned" (*One* 661). But Altman's narrative is a disordered reflection of the subterfuges of control concocted by politicians (like the soldiers, cowboys, detectives, countergirls, musicians, and schoolteachers in Altman's other films) who are impotent, paranoid, confused, and isolated. Wicker has empathy for a man whose "strengths and weaknesses, his virtues and deceits, his lack of grace in his self-willed ascent to the summit suggest how many Americans sensed, if they did not fully understand, that he was 'one of us' and the more to be embraced for that" (687). *Secret Honor* empathizes with a figure so insecure that his very efforts to confess and explain collapse into a contradictory and hypnotic portrayal of subjectivity as a babble of competing voices. The multiple images of Richard Nixon emblemize heroism in the art cinema.

## Doonesbury for President

Four years after Altman's fractured fictional portrait of the real Nixon was released, *Tanner '88* presented a documentary portrait of a fictional politician. During the 1988 presidential campaign, Robert Altman and comic strip artist Garry Trudeau linked their satirical skills as commentators on contemporary American values to produce a miniseries for HBO on cable television called *Tanner '88.* The eleven-part series ran intermittently in conjunction with the various presidential primaries, beginning in New Hampshire during the winter and ending during the summer on the eve of the Democratic National Convention in Atlanta. The series documents the presidential campaign of Jack Tanner; it stages a docudrama on the backstage life of that campaign, fictionalizing the race for president in 1988. The Altman/Trudeau production is a narrative that meanders along with the chronology of Tanner's life during the winter, spring, and summer of 1988 and shows that meandering to be fiction. But this fictional campaign crosses paths constantly with the actual movement of the primaries through New England, Iowa, "Super Tuesday," and California, and ends in Atlanta. The effect is a production that constantly calls attention not to itself as a fiction, but to the reality it mimics as fiction.

Moreover, the eleven-hour production depicts in "Jack Tanner" a subject who desires to be the major representative of the law in the United States, a political subject in process of construction by the divergent voices of the diegesis and a fictional subject who is literally the construct of media representations—an imaginary fabulation of the cross-currents of special interests that determine corporate subjectivity in the United States at the end of the 1980s. The series depicts the persona in politics as a composite of insistent public and private voices. It depicts the political self as a collage of representations resident in television genres. It depicts the political ego enthralled by the law as a function of desire, and it describes the social subject, like television, as the site of competing, contradictory discourse. Gone is the cogito of classical realism. Interpreting the series engages the art cinema's parodic representation of social identity as multimediated fictions.

At the most obvious level of textual intention, *Tanner '88* works as a political satire and thus participates in the art cinema's interrogative stance toward social interaction. Trudeau's popular cartoon strip *Doonesbury* is so widely perceived as political satire that many newspapers carry it on their editorial pages rather than on their comics pages. Representations of the Kennedy-like lawyer in *McCabe & Mrs. Miller,* of public police and elected officials in *Brewster McCloud,* of Bicentennial politics in *Nashville,* of the schizophrenic paranoia of Nixon in *Secret Honor* mark Altman's movies as kindred to the counterculture politics of *Doonesbury.* The collaborative creation of Jack Tanner is an extended satire of presidential politics. Candidacy for election means developing a social persona split under the demands and expectations of diverse public audiences. The production lampoons all these groups. It parodies the media reporters who follow campaigns as cynical, vain, vicious, and voyeuristic. It satirizes the production of campaign advertising as the bizarre mix of ideological zealots, earnest poly sci majors, uncontrollable filmmakers, and fuddy-duddy college professors. The electorate emerges as a collection of local-color rubes for whom politics is either media hype or media entertainment: the New Hampshire housewife who only collects polaroids of the candidates (it's Margaret Crooks down the road who collects campaign buttons); the ladies' sewing circle, for whom the candidate is another patch on their common quilt; the audience at the Nashville picking parlor, who really came to hear the band New Grass Revival; the suntanned revelers at a glitzy California pool party, for whom *political* means simplistically to vote. The candidate is followed by his disapproving father, managed by a professional Washington handler who is constantly being called by Joe Kennedy for advice, engaged secretly to a senior staffer for the Dukakis campaign, and accompanied by his college-student daughter, who is running on her own anti-apartheid platform. His campaign speeches for the most part comprise a half dozen empty sentences, and his major claim to "generational leadership," by his assertion, rests on his understanding that John Lennon was the most important member of the Beatles.

But *Tanner '88* cannot simply be read as parody and satire of the presidential selection process because, as it engages the objects of its criticisms, it reprises that process by becoming a campaign in its own right. *Tanner '88* is a real campaign for a fictional candidate. This point was strongly marked by the fact that the series appeared in a somewhat random schedule on HBO much in the same way evening news programs were intermittently filled with "Campaign '88" reports from the primary elections as they occurred throughout the first half of the year. Then, on the eve of the California primary, HBO reran the six episodes that had been shown randomly up to that point in one marathon screening hosted by Linda Ellerbe, playing herself as television news commentator. While marking the fictionality of Tanner, this production had the effect of summing up the current success, apparently, of the Tanner campaign. Each episode was introduced by a clip from the speeches of the other candidates still in the running: Bush for the Republicans; Dukakis, Jackson, and Tanner for the Democrats. The presentation of their words and images was undifferentiated stylistically, and indeed HBO ran an actual poll throughout the three-and-a-half-hour show ("call 1-800-323-VOTE") for viewers to register their support for their favorite candidates, to "choose from a group of presidential candidates, one or more of whom is not a real person." Tanner appears with "real" candidates. The program is hosted by the "real" Linda Ellerbe. HBO conducts "real" viewer polls. Thus the *production* isn't fiction (my own response to the telephone poll appears as part of the announced totals for the different candidates). Tanner won the poll that day, with 38 percent of the forty-one thousand votes cast, followed predictably by Bush with 22 percent, Jackson with 21 percent, and Dukakis with 19 percent. The fact remains that to parody the process, Altman, Trudeau, and HBO threw their own hat into the ring and launched a "real" campaign for Tanner '88.

What results, then, is a viewer subjectivity, familiar in art-cinema narration, of vertigo, disorientation, instability occasioned by the simultaneous representation of multiple televisual realities. Kitty Dukakis asks for Tanner's support after the Democratic National Convention. Ralph Nader explains his support for Tanner's policies. Jack Tanner shakes hands with fellow campaigners Robert Dole and Pat Robertson in New Hampshire. Tanner debates Jackson and Dukakis in California. Real toads in imaginary gardens? Or imaginary toads in a real garden? The effect of the production is regularly the eerie disorientation that recognizes then Arizona governor and "presidential hopeful" Bruce Babbitt as a fiction and Jack Tanner as real. Tanner's campaign aggressively foregrounds this phenomenon as an object and goal of its persuasion. Its initial slogan, "The Future Is Now," gives way after the first episode/primary to a revised representation: "Jack Tanner: For *Real.*"

*Tanner '88* thus demonstrates what John Fiske calls the "producerly text":

> It draws attention to its own textuality, it does not produce a singular reading subject but one that is involved in the process of representation rather than a victim of it, it plays with the difference between the representation and the real as a producerly equivalent of the writerly mixing of documentary and fictional modes, and it replaces the pleasures of identification and familiarity with more cognitive pleasures of participation and production. (95)

This process of audience disorientation works as productively here as anywhere in Altman's art cinema, which always demands active viewer response to an open and interrogative discourse. The humor of the television production begins in its engaging mix of the real and the fictional. *Tanner '88* explores the ways "Jack Tanner" is a fiction because, within the diegetic world, he is a composite of other voices. His fluid subjectivity emerges as a textual weave of the advice, opinions, demands, pleas, and laments of others. This fact appears divergently valued in the series: members of the test audience for an early campaign film criticize Tanner because, "instead of just coming out and plagiarizing like Biden, he puts old faces around him. It's the same thing, not saying anything, just letting other people speak for him." The question "Where's *his* ideas?" marks an idealistic desire for a candidate who speaks for himself, as an individual, speaks his own ideas, speaks authentically. The movie star Rebecca De Mornay, playing herself, asks Tanner at a California rally, "How do I know you're not just another like we get on TV?" And in Tennessee, Waylon Jennings, playing Waylon Jennings, tells a reporter: "I'm a country boy, and I like people who are real. Well, he seems real to me."

At the same time, however, Tanner constantly appears in scenes where his gaze is simply the mediation point among different speakers giving him words to say. This representation of the political candidate as a sponge absorbing discourse from the environment is particularly marked in the episode centered on a Washington fund-raiser. The dramatic space is filled with real people—actual Washington insiders, presumably offering real advice to a candidate being briefed and primed by his brain trust: "Define yourself in relation to the other candidates." "You've got to be the outsider." Hodding Carter, cousin to the former president and a Washington insider, observes: "The biggest idiocy is the guy who says we don't need another actor like Reagan. You should be so lucky as we will put you forward as another actor—so long as you're an actor like Roosevelt." Before the presidential debates, the Tanner team hires a new consultant who promises, "In just a few days, I can show you how to go on the tube and project strength and decisiveness and uncommon commanding presence the people have been asking for." At the end of a session intended to help Tanner remodel his television image, Tanner looks directly into the camera and reflects his marked distance from the concern for racial authenticity in the politics of Jesse Jackson, whose community litany he restates as a question: "I *am* somebody?"

The multifaceted diegesis of *Tanner '88* thus explores the making of the presidential subject as a process, both positive and negative, of blending the divergent voices of campaign expediency, political integrity, professional idealism, and public need. The real candidate Jack Tanner is both a fictional representation played by actor Michael Murphy and a representation like the quilt being sewed by the ladies in New Hampshire, a patchwork of many pieces, produced by many hands, competing but patterned social voices. Moreover, from the perspective of television as medium, *Tanner '88* further develops the perspective of subjectivity as the effect of generic discourse—the styles, the scenes, the orientations of different modes of television.

At the broadest level of distinction, *Tanner '88* mixes documentary and fiction, news and drama, and thus of course marks the discourse of the whole series as a self-conscious play, a tension, even a contradiction between reality and representation. Here is a distinction between a series of looks that construct and attend to social situations and the community—the construction of social identity within the constraints of conflicting pressures—as opposed to the series of looks characteristic of classical narrative cinema, which establishes a logic of causality among characters and events and displays them according to an ideological hierarchy of values. On one hand, the Tanner series offers itself to be read as documentary survey of the multiple energies, issues, people, and places of one political subject in the midst of one American presidential campaign. On the other hand, Jack Tanner is the focal point for the character psychology of goal-oriented actions—a race to be the "leader of the free world"—organized on a causal chain marked by a continuing series of conflicts and resolutions, whose ultimate end will come on election day in November.

At times, then, the viewing subject watches the news, conveyed by reporters in the field holding microphones and addressing the camera. The viewer watches videotape footage of public events, being taped simultaneously by other network reporter-camera teams, and listens to news voice-over commentary explicating the handheld camera images presented on the screen. The viewer also watches the documentary coverage (offscreen and thus again more "real") of the news teams themselves, as colleagues, competitors, hardworking reporters in unglamorous lives on buses following in the wake of the news story that will produce a sound bite for the evening news. The viewer watches the efforts of campaign managers to construct newsworthy material, media events that will bring headlines for their candidate, and occasionally the viewer gets the actual sound bite, newspaper headline, or larger story itself.

The documentary realism of *Tanner '88* is further established by other television news genres. We first meet the character Jack Tanner as the subject of an interview on *New Hampshire Closeup,* a weekly talk show that deals with news and politics: "My guest this week is Jack Tanner, . . . a serious candidate for president." The narrative presents his political positions during a televised debate among Tanner, Jackson, and Dukakis, although, given that the debate could not have happened, it presents the event both in documentary fashion from backstage, from the point of view of an observer in the reporters' pool, and through images of the questioning reporters and the individual candidates on the backstage television screens. The effect of the real in all these generic styles and forms participates in the "You are there," "See it now" quality of television. Thus the representational terms of the medium itself work to establish the realism of the fictional Congressman Tanner. We watch the way television constructs the real person out of the imaginary parts.

Other generic contexts establish Tanner's multiple subjectivity in ways less real but no less effective and credible or productive of credibility. The narrative focus on Tanner depicts a more or less efficacious character worthy of interest because, like most presidential contenders, he is successful, popular, and good-looking. His presidential subjectivity resides in his image: he *looks* and *sounds* presidential and, because much of what we consider to be good looks is mass-media determined, he also looks like a soap opera character. Indeed, the dominant narrative style working in opposition to the placement of the viewer before documentary realism is that of the soaps: the ongoing tale of Jack Tanner's tensions with his twenty-year-old daughter, offspring of a broken marriage, whose fragile health as a child caused Jack to drop out of politics to nurse her back to health; the surreptitious romance between Jack and the beautiful campaign aide to Dukakis and its dramatic discovery by the news media; the candidate's querulous, senile father, once a famous general, who relates to his son only as an observer during congressional hearings; the sudden wedding decision during the midst of the presidential campaign by a major candidate and the just as sudden cancellation of these plans on the eve of the wedding. One man's family, the private life of the very public man—all this is the familiar fare of the television soap opera, and this play with genre and the levels of realism and expressionism is the stuff of art-cinema narratives.

On one hand, soap opera as a genre of fiction may be perceived to work further against the representation of political subjectivity as real. Where documentary and the news work to stage the fictional Tanner as a real candidate, the soap opera form and substance of the series stage the presidential subject as the object of melodrama. Once again, however, the generic form sustains a view of the subject in contradiction. Fiske notes particularly that soap opera represents "aspects of our social experience in such a way as to make that experience meaningful and pleasurable to us. These meanings, these pleasures are instrumental in constructing social relations and thus our sense of social identity" (78).

*Tanner '88* illustrates the simultaneous play of multiple realities that constitute much of Altman's subliminal realism. It confronts the fictional world of real politics in its generic discourse of realism and confronts the realistic world of fictional drama in its discourse of imagination. The series offers the viewer an expressive narrative, a parodic narrative, and a plural narrative that calls attention beyond its diegetic rendering of "Campaign '88" to the construction of subjects under the law as a mix of other voices and divergent modes of representation. Jack Tanner is thus not unlike another fictional presidential candidate named Chauncey Gardner, whose mediated "being there" represents sufficient reality to authorize a powerful and thus presidentially possible subjectivity. The prevalent recognition of the news and the soaps, the two dominant modes in the series, as masculine and feminine gendered discourse further marks Tanner as a site of dissonant textual representation. The masculine, task-oriented world of politics and the pragmatic world of the news clash with the feminine world of romance and relationships, the intimate world of the soaps.

Tanner is a site of contradiction, a site of both conflicting television genres and conflicting desires. Although the representation of the presidential candidate is fictional, the motivation of the image is real. Tanner is the representation of politics as the shaping force of desire. One reporter remarks: "This guys wants to be the most powerful person on the planet. We're not dealing with 'well adjusted.' . . . We're dealing with an obsession." In the face of a hostile father, the military hero who publicly criticizes the ability of the son who always disappointed him, Tanner represents a narrative nostalgia for the efficacious and liberal male hero. The advice from Bruce Babbitt is telling: Don't take the safe course of listening to your advisers. Challenge the "silver screen of unreality" in presidential politics and speak honestly. "Take a risk!" Tanner opposes the law and is arrested in a Washington demonstration against apartheid in response to his own moral view of the law. And the only speech of substance that Tanner delivers in the narrative appeals for spiritual and physical cleansing, renewal, salvation of the environment. The narrative runs Tanner not because of his silly claim to know who the most important Beatle was but because he believes he can lead. The ad campaign that sparks his candidacy "for real" develops from his impassioned chronicle of the political fathers who brought bold and vital leadership to America in the past. "It's time for that leadership now," he insists, "I'm not sure if it's me, but I'd like the chance to find out!"

His proposed cabinet in one way satirizes the lost hegemony of the liberal democratic coalition of the underempowered and in another expresses a desire for the very political sites thus parodied. In a striking documentary fantasy of liberal victory, Tanner announces his cabinet choices at a news conference, which is conveyed to the viewer on the evening news: Lee Hamilton for secretary of state, Robert Redford for secretary of the interior, Studs Terkel for secretary of labor, Gloria Steinem for secretary of health and human services, and Ralph Nader for attorney general. The audience watches these people, "as themselves," express a real desire for an illusory Tanner, one "who brings an outsider like me inside," says Steinem; who appreciates that there will be remarkable opportunities to change international relations because of Gorbachev, says Hamilton; who appreciates the legacy of Walter Reuther, says Terkel; and who appreciates that the Reagan administration has been criminally weak in its enforcement of civil rights laws, says Nader. The fiction of the Tanner campaign affords these individuals, who have come to speak prototypically in social affairs, the expression of a political subjectivity diversely authored by their desires and their political agendas.

The idealism of the series of course constitutes its fiction, the subliminal absence from the realm of the politically real. The idealistic desire for a subjectivity that renews a Democratic coalition and empowers the powerless is nowhere more apparent than in the poignant central episode of the series, which takes Tanner into the black ghetto of America's motor city, Detroit. And perhaps at no other point is the viewer so confronted with the demands of an urban actuality that highlights Jack Tanner as a powerless actor named Michael Murphy. The narrative gives place to a number of black voices that speak in plaintive appeals beyond the formalized fictions of television, that for a moment speak in the gap opened by the silence of the fictional Tanner. The episode begins with images of a robotics exhibition mixed with the voice-over recitation of a rap poem that repeats the angry, insistent phrase, "We need some changes, some changes . . . ." The neighborhood rally where Tanner is scheduled to speak begins for the television viewer before Tanner's arrival to hear a black father named Earl Henderson, "as himself," read this poem:

> So sad
> When they die so young,
> In a city where nobody cares.
> Why should it take hundreds of lives

To make people see
That only in death is there equality. . . .
I've never held ill feelings for anyone,
Till I found my daughter dead,
Till I found my daughter dead. . . .

The HBO production team either captures or organizes an actual rally of the organization SOSAD (Save Our Sons and Daughters), where the fictional candidate can listen to the real problems of the ghetto. Here the representation of real poverty, devastation, drugs, high suicide rates, and the gunshot death in the past few years of seventy-seven Detroit children under the age of sixteen—all this reality threatens the fictional facade of political subjectivity. The cameras keep cutting from the face of actor Michael Murphy surrounded by neighborhood blacks describing the "blood . . . in the streets" to the silent and tragic face of Clementine Barfield, the founder of SOSAD, who mourns the death of her sixteen-year-old son. As the episode ends, Tanner discovers on the way back to his limousine the body of another young African American lying in the weeds and debris of a ghetto vacant lot. Is the body "real"? Is SOSAD an actual organization? Is the ghetto there? The pain and anguish of this community interrogates the make-believe of this HBO production, just as elsewhere the fictional representations of *Tanner '88* interrogate the circus of presidential politics.

The conflicting surfaces of reality and genre characterize the discourse of the art cinema. While the documentary power of television challenges any desire for authenticity and presence that motivates the representations of Jack Tanner, the sexual politics of the soap opera further undermine his representation as the subject of female others. Tanner is centered as the focal point of multiple female interests: Alexandra, his loving daughter; Andrea, the political groupie; T.J., the dedicated manager; Joanna, the loving enemy. These women constitute a harem where adoration in one way authorizes Tanner's centrality. The male subject has his eyes on the political prize, while the female subjects find their identity in the male. Fiske points out "that the cultural formations of patriarchy constantly reproduce and revalidate these differences, and soap operas work more explicitly than most art forms to connect with women's decentered subjectivity, their social relations in patriarchy, and the structure of texts that are popular with them" (194).

Reading for the contradictions of subliminal reality, however, is illuminating. At the same time that Jack Tanner represents an image of desire, the discourse also situates him as a kinder and gentler candidate than Jackson or Dukakis, with a "wonderful quality about him," says T.J., "steady, concentrated, you trust him." Fiske notes that although such mediated images "are clearer, more impressive than the reality they claim to represent . . . they are also fragmented, contradictory, and exhibit a vast variety that questions the unity of the world of experience" (116). The nostalgia for the efficacious male hero of classical narrative cinema or male-gendered genres like the cop show is finally resisted by the soap opera persona of Tanner as the sensitive male, by the professional and public status of the women on the Tanner team, and by the refusal of narrative closure in the last episode. Even as Tanner has lost the nomination to Michael Dukakis, his team, under the direction of T.J., has begun to test the waters for a fictional independent campaign against the real Democratic candidate and the real Republican, George Bush.

Reading between the lines, connecting the gaps of this series reveals the textual subject as a site of contradiction. Just as the art-cinema representation of absence, subordination, and multiplicity emerges in the conflict of television genres, in the tension of masculine-feminine, in the opposition of real and fictional, the series further reveals its double articulations in two metadiscursive characters—Hays Taggerty, the newspaper reporter, and Deke Connors, the filmmaker. These men are only slightly disguised doubles for the two major authors of *Tanner '88,* Garry Trudeau and Robert Altman. Hays is the gentle, protective, responsible reporter concerned with seeing the whole candidate and hostile toward sleazy reporting motivated by a kind of *National Enquirer* mentality. One cynical reporter denounces Hays's work as "fuzzy, warm, he's-only-human, humanistic profiles." Moreover, his thoughtful questions to the candidate, the daughter, the father, the girlfriend reflect an awareness of subjectivity as complexly and contradictorily determined: "It's the only way to understand the man. . . . It's easy to evaluate the manager, but the leader, that's something else. You have to determine not just what the candidate is, but why. You have to ask what drives him. . . . I haven't joined the character cops yet."

On the other hand, Deke is the "East Village pitch artist," the experimental filmmaker (with a Vandyke beard, literally an Altman look-alike) concerned, as he says reflexively, with making "neorealist political film documentary." Like his real-life other, Deke is less concerned with the conventions of political advertising or the concerns of his employer or the norms of television news videography than he is with experimenting with the boundaries of his medium. He produces two political biographies, the first of which alienates its intended audience, the second of which angers his boss and gets him fired, and both of which again mirror the documentary/soap opera dichotomy of style in the larger series. He also makes the successful campaign ad that at once promotes Jack Tanner as the candidate "for real" and ironically employs an art-cinema style that is expressive, fragmentary, and disruptive: "It's rough. It's real. It's unexpected."

Trudeau and Altman have framed a parody of contemporary politics that simultaneously explores the pluralities that constitute political subjectivity in a mass-mediated society. *Tanner '88* further demonstrates the "producerly" qualities characteristic of the cultural economy of television:

> decentered, diverse, located in the multiplicity of its modes and moments of reception. Television is the plurality of its reading practices, the democracy of its pleasures, and it can only be understood in its fragments. It promotes and provokes a network of resistances to its own power whose attempt to homogenize and hegemonize breaks down on the instability and multiplicity of its meanings and pleasures. (Fiske 24)

At the same time, however, the Tanner series neither emphasizes the differences between its satire and the routine fare of television nor addresses itself to a radical political minority. Its motivation, as elsewhere in Altman's work, is a liberal, not radically committed, interrogation of the politics of cultural identity. It engages the discursive competencies of viewing subjects to take pleasure in the recognition of fractured televisual and political subjectivity.

## Insecurity and the Abusive Father

Art-cinema narration constantly vacillates between realistic and expressive modes of discourse. It frequently appropriates a seemingly random, superficial, discontinuous reality as itself revelatory of the difficulty of coherent expression. Modernism's fixation with the relationship between nightmare realities and the subsequent dislocation of the personal recurs throughout Altman's films. Their representation of nonheroic, powerless males conveys an anxiety and a vulnerability that is comic in *MASH,* tragic in *McCabe & Mrs. Miller,* and especially ironic in films where the male figure is a figure of the law. In *Secret Honor* and *Tanner '88,* the dislocations of the president and the presidential candidate from the authority they ostensibly command clearly capture the mix of multiple and fractured narratives, expressive style, and pessimistic themes that characterize the art cinema. Character debility in the art cinema frequently results from psychological fears and fixations that are generally unstated but that, as these films reveal, seep into the fabric of the text everywhere. *The Gingerbread Man* employs the traditional codes of the film noir, the most narratively disruptive, thematically bleak, and psychologically irrational of the Hollywood genres. Its dark and moody narrative of mystery and resolution set in the middle of a hurricane in contemporary Savannah appropriate the darker moods of the American 1950s. Although duality and deception in the film document a desire to tell an effective thriller, they also reflect a confusion of culprit and prey in the narrative discourse. Its superficially traditional drive toward the thriller's revelation of the facts, exposure of the truth, development of a public knowledge conceals a personal knowledge that cannot be expressed. Its interrogation of masculine guilt suppresses a dark night of the soul that destablizes surface reality, events, and personality.

Popular criticism following the release of the film identified its style and complexity with the proliferation of neo-noir films released during the same decade (Ansen, "Neo-noir" 68). This distinction evokes titles such as *Basic Instinct* (Paul Verhoeven, 1992), *Pulp Fiction* (Quentin Tarantino, 1994), *Red Rock West* (John Dahl, 1994), *The Underneath* (Steven Soderbergh, 1994), *Bound* (Larry and Andy Wachowski, 1996), *Lost Highway* (David Lynch, 1997), *L.A. Confidential* (Curtis Hanson, 1997), and *Fargo* (Joel and Ethan Coen, 1996), but it also evokes a sense of the disruptive syntax and semantics that criticism has come to associate with film noir as a genre. It reveals much of what Janey Place identifies as the modernist worldview of the noir film: "paranoid, claustrophobic, hopeless, doomed, predetermined by the past, without clear moral or personal identity," and the expressive visual style of darkness, "silhouettes, shadows, mirrors and reflections" ("Women" 51). Film scholars variously characterize the contradictory impulses, the "thematic oppositions or recurring cultural conflicts" in noir films: between the marginal white male and the dominant law, between the nuclear family and the dark forces that threaten it, between the repressive stories and the resisting images of women, between "modernism and blood melodrama" (Naremore, *More* 40). In particular, reading *The Gingerbread Man* in the context of 1990s neo-noir requires the same symptomatic reading against the grain, reading for the subliminal realities of classical noir, to ask how the figure of the femme fatale continues to reflect masculine anxieties about women.

J. P. Telotte pointedly describes "a deeper identifying characteristic" of film noir as "a compelling urge to understand, formulate, and articulate the human situation at a time when our old formulations, as well as the means of expression underlying them, no longer seemed adequate" (14). These words seem to characterize the art-cinema narration and style of earlier Altman films more than *The Gingerbread Man,* and none more so than the other noir film in Altman's work, *The Long Goodbye.* Its experiments in style, its reflexive send-up of Hollywood, its inept detective as the sad fate of hippie nonchalance in a sadly repeating world of bleak stories—all reflect the dissonance between vision and expression that Altman characterizes as "those cultural comments about the early seventies" *(Gingerbread Man).* Then, at the end of a decade in which the art-cinema narration of Altman films like *Short Cuts, Prêt-à-Porter,* and *Kansas City* aggressively challenge "high-concept," blockbuster films like *Jurassic Park* and *Titanic, The Gingerbread Man* seems narratively and stylistically classical. It hardly seems to assert the inadequacy of contemporary discursive formations. Its continuity editing, mise-en-scène, and cinematography work clearly and dramatically in the service, Altman asserts, of a "straight-ahead" story with a definite beginning, middle, and end. Kenneth Branagh plays a slick, successful, powerful lawyer, vulnerable in his sexual weakness to the seductive scheming of a working-class girl, manipulated into killing her father, and ultimately reprimanded for his guilt in her mercenary plot, as the narrative finally sends the girl off to appropriate incarceration.

In many ways the film seems to deliver the uncluttered truth of a traditionally transparent and closed story, its narrative suspense easily read and its moral sentiment neatly pointed (male sexual philandery gently condemned and the woman's crime punished) in what Altman calls "a traditional wrap-up" *(Gingerbread Man).* It employs conventional elements of narration to raise and tantalize audience curiosity, obscure character motivations, withhold pertinent information, and delay the distribution of full knowledge. This process of selectively revealing and withholding certain information opens numerous questions, generates classical narrative suspense, and carries the viewer easily along the causal chain of events. That chain ostensibly constructs Mallory Doss (Embeth Davidtz) as the antagonist who uses Rick Magruder (Branagh) in a scheme to acquire authority over her father's property, with its thirteen million dollars worth of walnut trees.

Noir film criticism, however, urges reading for the "conflicting discourses" that expose how "the work of the film has revealed to viewers the way men distort women and also offered a warning against too ready acceptance of male ways of seeing" (Kaplan, "Introduction" 19). Closer scrutiny of the story reveals that ambiguities of discourse outrun the story logic and raise more questions than the revelation of Mallory's guilt resolves. Where the story sets Mallory up as the typical femme fatale who lures Rick into her plot against her father for monetary gain, the discourse establishes Mallory as a woman under psychological distress, whose actions deliberately emphasize the contradictions among discursive levels. It suggests that Mallory's desire to be rid of her father goes deeper than greed and that we understand Mallory not as the victimizer, the greed-driven seductress, the femme fatale of "cold calculation and sensuality" (Naremore, *More* 20) who must eventually pay for her crimes, but rather as the victim, who seeks requital for injuries she has suffered. She reflects what Christine Gledhill identifies as the contradictory noir discourse in which the hero is "not sure whether the woman is honest or a deceiver, but the heroine's characterisation is itself fractured so that it is not evident to the audience whether she fills the stereotype [of the treacherous woman] or not" (*"Klute"* 31).

When *The Gingerbread Man* muddies the question of who set up Rick Magruder and why, it opens a complex trail of motivation that leads back not only to Mallory, but to her father Dixon Doss (Robert Duvall), and ultimately and paradoxically to Rick himself: the trail that leads to Rick first as a tool of Mallory's greed, then as a target of Mallory's revenge, finally approaches Rick himself as the cause of the scheme against him. The film suggests that Rick is the object of a seduction aimed at the elimination of the father, and that Rick is a target of both Mallory and the narration, not only as another, but also as the ultimate figure of the bad father in the film. Richard Dyer has argued that noir film is "characterised by a certain anxiety over the existence and definition of masculinity and normality . . . [and] may be taken to constitute the films' problematic" ("Resistance" 115). At the core of *The Gingerbread Man* lies a tension between the two figures of the father, one of whom, as a lawyer, is also a figure of the law in direct contestation with other figures of the law in the police. Frank Krutnik traces the degree to which classic noir films "often cast male subjectivity adrift from its mooring with the Law of the Father and this results in a functional dislocation between desire and (culturally-specified) identity" (242). *The Gingerbread Man* moves through a series of transformations that threaten to expose the broad array of narrative motivations in the film as a nexus of guilt, arrogance, and anxiety, all resident in the figure of the father. That figure is at base Rick, but his guilt as a victimizer rather than the victim of Mallory's plot amounts to the major social disruption that the narrative needs to contain.

Telotte's incisive analysis of film noir points out the extent to which noir films represent both a "resistance to the dominations of power in society" and a "symptom . . . caused by the same desires and powers that propel our culture and our lives" (12). *The Gingerbread Man* works a resistance to the power of the law characterized by the slick, arrogant, ethically suspect "snake-oil salesman" in the very masculine figure of Rick. One of the most dramatic scenes in the movie follows his arrest. The scene opens with a close-up of the flashing red lights of a police squad car and the sound of a typewriter, which is recording Rick's story of events leading to the death of Dixon Doss. The sheriff interrogates Rick and indicates the depth of his legal culpability. In many ways the scene asks to be read as a culminating moment in the emotional economy of the film. It represents an interrogation of Rick at a number of levels and marks him as the major target of the discursive strategies of the narrative. As a lawyer who has successfully defended clients by undermining police evidence and procedures, Rick faces the sheriff's hostile challenge to his understanding of the legal grounds for self-defense; indeed, the sheriff ironically evokes the "founding fathers" on property rights before telling him, "You got yourself in a whole bucket of shit here, Magruder. If I were you, I'd damn sure find myself a good lawyer." As their professional colleague and boss, Rick suffers the shocked dismay at his behavior of his legal assistant and private investigator. As a father, he must listen to the report of his children's terror during the kidnapping ordeal his actions occasioned. And as a father, he must face the anger and hostility of his ex-wife, who tells him she will seek to bar his contact with the children. She explicitly asserts, "The last thing you've been to them is a father, and if I can't trust you to keep them safe, so help me if I fight tooth and nail for full custody without visitation." Arrogant, self-confident, egotistical, Rick here is finally reduced to tears of humiliation, regret, and loss. The scene arraigns him as both the killer of the father and a bad father, a failed figure of the law and of the family.

This hostility to the figure of Rick carries the narrative far away from Mallory's initial concern with ridding herself of an abusive father and possessing his property, and before its closure the narrative must recuperate this disruptive image through a return to Mallory's behavior as the venal desire to capture the wealthy lands of her father and to her punishment by the diegetic law of Savannah and the discursive law of the narrative. But the excessive overdetermination of Rick's guilt in this scene derives from a disruptive, destabilizing force that momentarily displaces the central cause-effect logic of Mallory's greed; it furthermore lays bare the unspoken dimensions of the film's subliminal reality in a series of textual displacements that emerge alongside the enigmas of her plot.

The most striking transformation in the movie is that of the lawyer becoming the outlaw. Two scenes strikingly chronicle this change. The first, when Rick successfully argues for the incarceration of Mallory's father in a mental institute, marks the only time in the film when Rick appears in the role of courtroom authority that warrants his success as an attorney. The second occurs when a judge appoints Mallory, accompanied by Rick's associate Lois (Daryl Hannah), as the custodian of her father's property. Rick watches this scene in a visual disbarment from outside the courtroom, his face mirrored in the reflection of the glass door that separates him both literally and metaphorically from the site of his authority. As Krutnik writes of the criminal-adventure thriller, "The hero of such films is a male over-achiever who seeks through his defiance of the law to set himself above it" (138). Rick knows the law, yet in his smug arrogance he assumes his superiority to it. He takes his children out of school when he does not have the right to do so, he punches a grade school security guard, and he kills Doss.

The issue of arrogance that seems to permeate the movie resides even in the title. "The Gingerbread Man," the title of a nursery tale, hardly reflects the titles of classic noir films, which often allude to sexual violence *(Kiss Me Deadly)* or existential fatalism *(They Won't Believe Me),* but the main point of the nursery tale is that the end for someone consumed with pride is eventual destruction. The Gingerbread Man scene of Mallory's nightmare and Doss's escape is the most revealing and significant scene in the movie. It illustrates what Krutnik describes as an "italicised" noir moment that conveys, "in a displaced manner, the effects of extreme violence, perverse or corrupt sexuality or moments of psychic breakdown" (20). Here is the stylistic complexity of the art cinema that reflects the ambiguous dualities of the story and reveals the number of overdetermined motivations at play in the narrative.

The formal construction of the scene is quite complex. The initial dialogue passes over quickly and obscures a complicated range of legalities regarding the situation involving the Georgia courts, Rick, Mallory, and Doss, who has just that day been committed to the Georgia Regional Hospital for "acute schizophrenia." A series of images depicting, first, Rick initiating a sexual embrace of Mallory, then shadowy men running through an eerily lit graveyard full of blooming red camellias, then Rick caressing the naked back of the sleeping Mallory and putting on his red robe, then a zoom-in close-up of her troubled face, convey a disjunction of time and place held together by the continuity of cacophonous sounds and gothic music. Throughout the remainder of the scene, the camera cuts constantly back and forth between the space of Mallory and Rick's darkened bedroom and the hospital into which Doss's cronies cut their way and from which they release Doss and other mentally disturbed inmates. The sounds of the fence cutting echo and carry over into the shots of Mallory, whose moans and whimpers carry over to the scenes of Doss's escape, and the sounds of the approaching storm carry over to the scenes of Mallory's restless sleep. She awakens in panic from her nightmare entangled in the window screen, resists Rick as he tries to comfort her in bed, and finally lies in his arms as she recounts both her recurring dream and the recollections of her father from her childhood.

This scene is saturated with dualities that result from the play of mirrors, the continuous play of editing between scenes, and the play of aural and visual links. It reflects the expressive power of art-cinema discourse to suggest a quality of doubleness and to assist the narrative in creating a character of the father that is split between Rick and Doss. The narrative employs the legal issues of inheritance as part of the motivation of character action in the story, but its constantly murky delineation, particularly marked here, establishes a scenario of repression that this scene dramatically illustrates. When Rick's arms encircle Mallory in sexual embrace, the ominous gothic music rises on the sound track and throughout the scene progressively mingles with the sounds of the approaching hurricane. This shift in music both reflects a subjective negativity toward

Outside the court and the law *(The Gingerbread Man).*

Rick's sexual desires and establishes the mood for the remainder of the scene. The discursive sequence of three shots—Rick's caresses, Doss's henchmen darting through the cemetery, Rick's leaving the bed and the sleeping Mallory—represses the scene of sex between the two (as also happens in the initial seduction scene earlier in the film) and replaces it with ghostly images of men emerging from a graveyard. In the place of sex come images of ghastly return. The narrative repression of sex here parallels Mallory's repression of the past in the story. The black cemetery with red camellias glowing eerily in the night is replicated in the bedroom, where the darkness is slashed by Rick's scarlet robe. And Mallory awakens in fear of a dream about her father's escape.

The reason for that fear is unspeakable, and its repression leaves its impression everywhere in the violence of this scene, in the disruptions of family relationships throughout the film, and, as the hurricane builds in fury, even in the conditions of nature itself. "It's always him" in the dreams, Mallory tells Rick. "When I was a kid, he used to tell me stories, and they became stranger and scarier, and he'd come into my room, and he'd sit on my bed, and he'd. . . ." Altman's commentary on this moment in the film asserts that the viewer must "read between the lines" because Mallory "is telling you that she was abused by her father as a child" *(Gingerbread Man).*

Whatever happened between her and her father in the past is unspeakable in the present. The echoes and distorted space that exist between these two scenes assist in the creation of a dreamlike atmosphere that links the actions of Doss and his gang to Mallory's nightmare. As the members of the gang cut through the fence and enter the grounds of the institution, Mallory screams at the invasion. When the men creep around the grounds, Mallory runs to the window and fights with the screen, seemingly attempting to escape. After the red-robed Rick brings her back to bed, she resists him. Here the narrative cuts to one of the most striking of a number of imagistic shots in the film that generally work to heighten emotional tension and narrative suspense. In a three-second shot, the camera zooms back out of a tunnel created by coiled barbed wire and tacitly, metaphorically signals the sexual violence of male penetration and female resistance. As a result of the connection of the scene of invasion, the entrance, the image of withdrawal, and the escape of Doss and his men with Mallory's nightmare, the scene suggests that the unspeakable for Mallory resides in fear of the father. Moreover, because of the textual dualities linking Doss and Rick, Rick also becomes linked with the father as a sexual victimizer of Mallory.

Like other scholars of noir, Telotte points out that a central structural feature of the film noir is its use of the subjective, first-person voice-over flashback that runs in counterpoint to the more objective realism of the cinematography. In many ways this works with the expressive ambiguity of dreams in other art-cinema narratives. Telotte's analysis of the device is illuminating for an understanding of this key scene from *The Gingerbread Man*:

> Embedded within a larger narrative structure, such sequences invariably seek to violate diegetic normalcy, to suggest an eruption of the subjective in a world that we initially see in a conventional, objective manner. However, as a kind of partially glimpsed truth, that eruption qualifies and even raises questions about the larger narrative context, in the process suggesting other possibilities for truth and a sense of this world's complexity. (15)

This observation in part can be applied to the way noir films use this voice in an effort to speak the tensions and debilitations of living in the bleak world of the modernist vision. Frequently, in traditional noir films this voice encompasses the entire narrative length of the film and seems to provide answers to the difficult issues raised in the discourse. Here the voice is tellingly shrunk to a small story told in the middle of the film; equally telling is that the first-person narrative is a child's nursery rhyme. Its recounting fills the ellipsis in Mallory's narrative of the father's aggression against the child, the space left by her repression of that past.

Fairy tales convey moral codes, but Bruno Bettelheim, as well as other child psychologists, has documented how fairy tales speak to children's basic fears: "The fairy tale . . . takes these existential anxieties and dilemmas very seriously and addresses itself directly to them: the need to be loved and the fear that one is thought worthless; the love of life, and the fear of death" (10). "The Gingerbread Man" is a well-known story whose mix of instruction and resistance is richly ambiguous here. It warns, of course, against pride that blinds a person to danger and destruction, but the Gingerbread Man's pride—I've evaded everyone who would eat me up—displaces a vulnerability: the water of the river would break him up, the surrounding natural world would devour him. The character's famous mantra—"You can't catch me, I'm the Gingerbread Man"—is a defense against the anxieties of vulnerability. In Mallory's story, however, it also works as a threat: "My daddy used to warn me that it was just as easy for little children to disappear as it was for gingerbread men." The reason for the threat is unspoken, but it locates vulnerability in the force of the father. The gingerbread man scene effectively details the repression of the father's abuse of the daughter and displaces that figure of violence onto Rick as the father's double. The effect of abuse is represented as the character of the father split between Rick and Doss. The unspeakable in the film reverses the story's representation of Rick as the victim and identifies him with the victimizer.

Part of the craft in *The Gingerbread Man* appears in its expressive range of art-cinema dualities and displacements. Yet the ambiguity of all this duality emerges from a multiple motivation, from a concern on one hand to tell an effective thriller and from the disruptive pressure, on the other hand, of a silence. Its ambiguity confuses the viewer as a condition of entertainment, but its dualities deceive the viewer as the effect of a repression. Here continues the modernist perception of social and psychic disruption that emerges as the complex discourse of art-cinema narration. While we watch Mallory's playacting as the target of her violent father in order to steal his wealth, we discover her to be the actual victim of his past behavior, and although her initial intent is the desire for power of attorney, her repressed desire is to kill him. Rick is tellingly situated to kill the father, but the power of the narrative reflects the traditional noir trajectory of blaming and containing the disruptive force of the woman. As Mary Ann Doane points out, "The power accorded to the femme fatale is a function of fears linked to the notions of uncontrollable drives. . . . But the femme fatale is situated as evil and is frequently punished or killed. Her textual eradication involves a desperate reassertion of control on the part of the threatened male subject" (*Femmes* 2). Here that sexuality is from the outset tangled up in anxiety about the father. When Rick first enters Mallory's life, after the apparent theft of her car and the invasion of her house, he asks, "What'd I walk into here—an old boyfriend, a jealous husband, or what?" Mallory answers, "My daddy," and signals the emotional center of the story. In *The Gingerbread Man* the law and the family are sites of struggle over the desire and the power of the father. The narrative closure of the film on one hand ignores Rick's killing of the father and restores his only slightly tarnished power. But the slow displacement of Mallory's sexuality into a fragile childishness reestablishes the threatening figure of the father even as the end reasserts Rick's authority. At the end of thirty years of narratives whose weak and ineffectual male characters motivate the meandering and inconclusive plots of the art cinema, this film exposes the apparently coherent narrative as complicit in the repression of a masculine anxiety that stimulates sexual violence and guilt.

Peter Lehman has remarked often on the humorous asides about small penis size that abound in Altman's films; he notes that "penis jokes are usually throwaways with unattractive male characters as their object" (*Running* 122). The female hygienist in *Short Cuts* who takes urine samples from pilots after they spray poison on Los Angeles to kill fruit flies taunts one character about his need for tweezers to hold his penis. A central sequence in *MASH* depicts a mock last supper in anticipation not of the impotent dentist's resurrection but in hope of his renewed erection. In *The Gingerbread Man,* Rick's brain size is compared to his penis when his assistant alludes to his womanizing tendency to "think with the other end." Sullivan Travis at the end of *Dr. T & the Women* delivers a baby boy, and the last shot of the delivery is a close-up of the infant's penis, a contradictory metaphor that at once signifies new birth and the shrinkage and displacement of Dr. T's authority.

The diminution of male power and its attendant anxieties further demonstrates one of the most significant aspects of masculine authority depicted in Altman's art cinema. The silence and loss of what has embodied masculine authority appear in the weakening of narrative order and structure, in the multiple randomness of point of view, in the mix of divergent voices within the narratives, in the negative depiction of male heroes. Even the apparent coherence of *The Gingerbread Man* interrogates the arrogance of masculine power in its diminishment and works to position the male victim as the guilty figure of masculine threat and ineffectualness. Together with the exploration of the displacement of women from roles of social power and control, these films develop a subjectivity of the guilty male, insecure and defensive, in retreat from the very phallic authority to which by his gender and the tradition of modernism he is the social heir. Even as *The Gingerbread Man* rescues Rick's authority in the story's conclusion, he remains under suspension from the law and arraigned by the narrative, just as Olive Oyl charges Popeye's father: "He's a crook, a thief, a kidnapper, and a bad father and more!"

Catherine Belsey points out that "classical realism tends to offer as the 'obvious' basis of its intelligibility the assumptions that character, unified and coherent, is the source of action. Subjectivity is a major—perhaps the major—theme of classic realism" (73). What she calls the "interrogative text" discourages audience identification with any unified subject of the diegesis. Indeed, although Altman's art cinema posits a recognizable world of human action, the representations of character critically establish a subjectivity that, like the films themselves, reveals "the multiplicity and diversity of its possible meanings, its incompleteness, the omissions which it displays but cannot describe, and above all its contradictions" (Belsey 109). Such interrogation presupposes divergent conceptualizations of identity and individuality, the self and the subject, the cogito in twentieth-century modernist and art-cinema discourse. Silvio Gaggi summarizes these perspectives:

> If the classical subject was quietly confident in its fixity, the modern subject . . . is not so sure of itself. . . . Moreover, in the postmodern world the ubiquity of mass media representation—where the subject is reduced to a surface, a mask, and a commodity—shifts the challenge of philosophy and linguistics from the level of theory to that of the lived experience of everyday life. The modern subject bemoans the diminution of the self, in the face of mass society, industrialization, and closer Cartesian scrutiny. (*From Text* xiv–xv)

Not just Nixon and Tanner and Magruder represent the sense of loss, rebellion, refusal, and insecurity that characterize the masculine subject in Altman's art films. The significant social subject is diminished in the films that multiply the ensemble of major characters from two or three to twenty-four and forty-eight. The figure of masculine and professional success and wealth in *Dr. T,* while not the bad father, is rather a caring husband whose love promotes disease and whose success the narrative works to destroy. Efficacious male action becomes precarious, threatened, doubtful, suspect in Brewster McCloud, in Philip Marlowe, in Essex, in Vincent van Gogh, in Griffin Mill, in Rick Magruder, in Sully Travis. Singularity of purpose is splintered, challenged, circumvented, impossible in *Buffalo Bill,* in *McCabe & Mrs. Miller,* in *Short Cuts,* in *The Gingerbread Man.* Self-knowledge, self-confidence, self-certainty, and self-assessment are all casualties in Altman's art-cinema narratives. The loss of self marks the modernist dispensation everywhere.

## 6. Resisting Women: Madness, Dreams, and Art

*MASH* at the beginning of Altman's Hollywood career and *Dr. T & the Women* toward the end of that career have generated significant charges of misogyny against the representation of women in his films. *Dr. T* in particular focuses the critical balance between an interrogative and a complicit representation of women in cultural discourse: How can narrative depict troublesome social constructions in a way that calls them into question rather than replicates, reaffirms, and reinforces the problematic conditions? Altman's commitment to the open-ended, diffuse, and ironic representations of subliminal reality compounds the nature of this question. Incoherent narratives, contradictory subjectivity, and coercive systems of entertainment shape and characterize his decidedly antagonistic stance toward much of the contemporary status quo. Thus *Dr. T*—like *Charlie's Angels* (2000), *A Thousand Acres* (1997), and *A League of Their Own* (1992)—may represent "a suspiciously similar gender configuration: A man plopped down in a nest of women, who flutter and preen" (Keller and Wilmington 5.1) or "an essentially misogynist plot—a studly man forced to fend off the fluttering attention of beautiful women who, without him in the center of their lives, are sad, empty wrecks" (Keller 5.1). It may also be a satiric representation of a male figure "desperately wanting to do the right thing, not sure he knows what that is, baffled by a woman who does not seem to need him" (Ebert, "Dr. T") in an artificial social space characterized by wealthy, affected women struggling for self-worth.

Satire and irony always offer the terms of such contradictory readings. Nevertheless, the diegesis of the film conveys a trajectory of masculine security and feminine dependency that significantly unravel and deteriorate. The film suggests a play on the story of Job, as it inflicts a series of losses on Sullivan "Dr. T" Travis (Richard Gere)—his wife to mental breakdown, his children to uncertain independence, his patients to riotous desertion, his nurse to professional baking, and his lover to self-sufficiency. The film may be read as multiple images of pathetic, vacuous, and humiliated women—most notably represented by the scene in which Dr. T's nurse (Shelley Long) hides under his desk in her slip after throwing herself, unnoticed, at the doctor. But the film develops many divergent portraits of contemporary women: wives with absent husbands, single mothers, lesbian lovers, unhappy professionals, community activists. Their various modes of innocence and seductiveness, dependency and aggression, humiliation and pride convey the contradictions of masculinist fantasies about women in the culture.

The male world is essentially the limited hunting ground of golf clubs, shotgun practice, duck blinds, and turkey shoots. The film seems to give Gere a role of warmth and sincerity perceived by many critics as parallel to the star persona of Cary Grant late in his career. Sympathy for the male and animosity toward the female, however, is never an obvious stance of Altman's films. Indeed, he asserts that "if you want to look at whom we're making fun of in this movie, look at the guys in these silly duck-hunting outfits trying to shoot at ducks, turkeys, golf balls." In particular he says of Dr. T, "Someone decided to test him. And he's not properly prepared. . . . He's been looking at women from the wrong end all his life" (quoted in Sragow). For all his tenderness, Dr. T has been the center of a personal, professional, and social world that inexorably falls apart across the story. Accustomed to having women wait for him and depend on him, he is frustrated, puzzled, and hurt by the dissolution of his authority. Dr. T is ultimately blown away by a tornado from the security and success that derives from gynecological control over the female body and is abandoned in a Mexican desert, where he can deliver a male baby to a Latina mother in utter foreign solitude.

At the same time, the film explicitly references *The Wizard of Oz* (1939), where the woman asserts her own strength after she discovers the male to be the manipulative and impotent power behind the screen of illusion. Each of the major women in the story has a moment in which the audience is asked to understand her sympathetically. One daughter struggles to maintain her independence, the other to accept her homosexuality. Dr. T's sister-in-law, Peggy (Laura Dern)—who works to parent her three children while going through a divorce and drinks too much—reveals her quiet distress at one moment when she longingly remarks to herself the importance of turning within for strength. Perhaps clearest among these portraits is that of Kate, Dr. T's wife. Played by former sex star and pinup queen Farrah Fawcett, she performs a slow strip in a mall water fountain in front of the Godiva chocolate shop and simultaneously reinscribes the voluptuous body of past cultural desire and the inappropriateness of its display. Her behavior precedes her confused refusal to have sex with her husband of many years, and she subsequently is institutionalized in a mental hospital.

The logic here simultaneously narrates the role of women as inscribed in the mode of dress and as the legally proscribed object of the male gaze. The reference to Godiva recalls the story of female nudity as a resistance to male authority. It restates the violation of female sanctity by the character Peeping Tom, immortalized in our culture as the figure of voyeurism. The popular pinup body of Farrah Fawcett and the naked body of Kate Travis incarcerated by the law and institutionalized by medicine suggest the paradigmatic condition of women in the film and in the movies. Her doctor tells Sully that Kate is suffering from a Hestia complex, which he self-centeredly reinterprets to his family as the result of his loving her too much. But Hestia was the Greek goddess of the hearth, who gave up the home in resistance to divine masculine authority and became the guardian of virgins. Screenwriter Anne Rapp asserts: "When you look at that Farrah character, what you see on the outside is this fragile sadness that she is a lost soul and longs to return to childhood. But you also see Farrah become happier and happier—in some odd, twisted way she's empowered herself. She has made this choice, like the goddess Hestia" (quoted in Sragow). The golf professional Bree (Helen Hunt) especially focuses this energy of independence and resistance. When Sully asks Bree if he makes her happy, she asserts that she is "just a happy person." When he asks her to make his life complete by running away with him, she rejects the need for dependency he describes, asking, "Why would I *want* that?" And when he assumes that she refuses him because she is with another man, she asserts, "I'm not *with* anybody!"

After the release of *The Player*, an interviewer suggested to Altman that "there seems to be a pattern in your films of women being humiliated," and that "feminists have given you a hard time about this before." Altman replied, "I'm not showing you the way I think things should be, but the way things are. That is the way women are treated. . . . it isn't the way that I treat women, that's the way I see them treated" *(The Player)*. The most systematically ambiguous and psychologically subjective of Altman's films explore conditions of women enervated by subordinate positions accorded them within American culture. They generally represent the image of women in terms of dependency, desperation, and defensiveness induced by the values of patriarchal authority. Whereas the men represent various retreats from that authority or defeats from its power, the women reveal its debilitating ubiquity. Keyssar writes that in "Altman's 'women's films,' a sexual paradox is expressed; all of these films focus on women who are peripheral to the societies they inhabit, and men in these films are peripheral to the films' attention" (200). These films vividly articulate the fragmentation and violence that result from the alienation in feminine self-consciousness.

Robert Altman's films have constantly developed a pattern of social analysis and understanding that posits women as marginalized, codependent, and disabled by the coercive power of patriarchal influence. Many of these women reflect Kaja Silverman's analysis of the female family structure in *3 Women.* The central characters develop a relationship of grandmother-mother-daughter, in which the weakest, childlike persona has rebellious impulses but not the strength to live alone. In the resultant family the child finds a mother, and these two support the older woman, an artist whose work constitutes a defense as well as a representation, an actualization of the social coercion of identity by dominant society (*Mirror* 126–29). *That Cold Day in the Park, Images, 3 Women, Jimmy Dean, Kansas City,* and *Cookie's Fortune* present stories in which the anxieties of the major characters are measured by the puzzling, defensive nature of the aesthetic forms onto which they are projected. In all but the last of these films, the disturbing quality of the story situations is reflected by violation of formal, narrative, rational expectations in Altman's art-cinema construction of irrational, emotional, lyrical forms, and the tragicomedy traumas in *Cookie's Fortune* motivate incongruous church theatrics. These films shape intense personal narratives into poetic reflections that mirror and complement each other. They present the fear, isolation, and fragmentation of personality that generate madness, dreams, and art within the demands and debilitations of the patriarchy. The films express the need to overcome the isolate and multifaceted personality in terms of the urge and fear of sex and the necessity, both psychic and aesthetic, of creating an identity that protects against the inevitable disjunctions between self and others, between inner and outer, spoken and unspeakable reality. Schizophrenia in the earlier films, dreams and fantasies in the later, and Easter service theatricals in the last constitute defense against the anxieties of personal insufficiency and the demands of reproductive sexuality.

The confusing coalescence of fantasy, dream, literal reality, and artistic reality in the six women's films can only express, without resolving, problems of female identity in contemporary society. Characterizations like those of Barbara Jean in *Nashville* or Blondie in *Kansas City* provide paradigmatic ways of conceptualizing a central issue in Altman's art cinema. These characters are represented within a dominant culture that is aggressive, competitive, and materialistic. It is manipulative of words, objects, and people. It is sexually and economically exploitative. It is the environment of phallocentrism. This chapter looks closely at *Images, 3 Women, Jimmy Dean,* and *Cookie's Fortune* as illustrations of the nexus child-adult-artist that grounds their complex and unconventional patterns of discourse. Art-cinema narration consciously and aggressively disrupts and interrogates the style, the narrative structures, and the social themes of containment and disability in classical narrative cinema. It employs unusual and often puzzling structures as iconic signs of life's confusing and subliminal connections. It obliquely and symbolically plumbs depths of psychological realities that reflect and deflect social realities. These four "women's films" portray dichotomies of security and vulnerability as they depict conditions and effects of social pressures. They illustrate an art-cinema preoccupation with the terms of feminine subjectivity in a society of engendered self-recognition, of male dominance and female submissiveness, and they dramatize the traumas generated in women who are displaced and dislocated by the power of that dominance.

Feminist film criticism has been particularly interested in the fact that the classical narrative cinema offers a relatively stable subject position for the male spectator situated before a transparent and naturalizing discourse that relegates women to positions of absence, silence, and marginality. Classical male heroes frequently provide male viewers idealized portraits of authority and command that provide easy sites of identification. The traditional female spectator, on the other hand, receives only images of powerlessness and victimage that reinforce cultural mandates of subordination and inferiority. David N. Rodowick describes the numerous "binary machines" of much institutional discourse, such as classical narrative realism, which construe maleness as an "imaginary coherence" and femaleness as a "negativity," and asserts that to the contrary modern psychology works "to understand the range of scenarios that describe the different experiences of division and loss where sexual positions are constructed" (68). Similarly, Altman's films examine these same sites. Like the art cinema generally, they critique regnant social values. Like feminist criticism in particular, these films examine the effects of a system that identifies women as the objects of male desire, dependent upon male awareness, and the position within the symbolic order that such a system affords the female subject.

If there is fragmentation and doubleness, doubt and failure in Altman's images of the male self, his images of women are more distressed. They graphically convey the crisis in verbal, sexual, and economic production and exchange that constitutes the social subject in all of Altman's films. Particularly, the films about women reveal the construction of the self as an action of retreat from the self-determining pressure of the phallocentric culture. For these women their sexual anatomy as the predominant terms of their exchange value has become a trap. Their potential as mothers, as producers, has become problematic or even abhorrent. As Catherine Belsey observes:

> Women as a group in our society are both produced and inhibited by contradictory discourses. Very broadly, they participate both in the liberal humanist discourse of freedom, self-determination and rationality and at the same time in the specifically feminine discourse offered by society of submission, relative inadequacy and irrational intuition. The attempt to locate a single and coherent subject-position within these contradictory discourses, and in consequence to find a non-contradictory pattern of behavior, can create intolerable pressures. (65–66)

Altman's women's films make quite explicit the conflict between a weak inner self and an outer persona dominated by machismo, the phallus, the white father, the law.

In *That Cold Day in the Park,* the viewer watches the woman of class, respectability, and money as she approaches and accommodates middle age and spinsterhood. While pressured to marry by her older friends, social arbiters by appearance and manner, she retreats from the stuffy and boring pursuit of a fatherly lover into the crazed imprisonment of a sexy young man who stands bemused and silent before her ineffectual efforts to possess him. At the end of the film she procures a prostitute for the young man; the final scene, in which she kills the prostitute in the midst of sex with the man, is a gruesome depiction of sexual self-hatred and surrogate suicide.

In *Kansas City,* Blondie performs another Jean Harlow role as she turns the trauma of loss into a tragic gesture of defiance. Uneducated, plain, nervous, haunted by memories of the child she was forced to give up for adoption in favor of romance, she tries to "stand by her man." She tries to play Harlow to Clark Gable. As her Johnny faces death for defying the authority of the black crime world, Blondie kidnaps the wife of an important machine politician in an effort to coerce the white political world into helping free her husband. The center of the film conveys the image of two women, one desperate to restore the man who gives meaning to her life, the other drugged to forget the meaninglessness of her life. The world of white male power cares more about its own regeneration of authority on election day than about any squabble between powerless women and blacks and almost casually restores order to their marginalized worlds at the end of the film. In perhaps the final irony of the film, Blondie's death at the hand of the drug addict wife of a Missouri politico results from her disruption of the positions of self-defense established by other women.

A common rhetorical strategy for the presentation of character in art-cinema discourse gives characters individual stories to tell. The effect of turning diegetic figures into narrators is multiple: it tends to naturalize or efface the external discourse of the text by deflecting attention from authorial control to the discourse within the diegesis. It works to give greater depth to the character by extending his or her "existence" into another scene, by authenticating the character's presence with a past. It presents significant causal data from the "past" that explains or motivates actions in the "present." It locates character within the intertextual codes of social roles. Susan Alexander in *Citizen Kane* illustrates this nexus of contradictory pressures. She is established early as a knowledgeable voice, a credible storyteller, a woman with a present/presence because of the story of her past. But her story is requisite to establish an even larger presence, that of Kane, whose desire and lack summarized in the word "Rosebud" are also personified in Susan herself. And her presence in the diegesis falls under the larger regime of the external storyteller (Thompson), which relocates her place in the discourse to become not the first but the penultimate voice in an explanation of the rise and fall of Charles Foster Kane, who desires and fears her: "I love you, Susan" becomes "You can't do this to me."

There are two dimensions to this narrative process in art-cinema narration: the external discourse, the voice of the text, narrates the fictional characters; the internal discourse, the voice of the character, further authorizes itself and neutralizes, disguises, represses the voice of the author. From the structural perspective of subjectivity in linguistic discourse, the *I* both speaks and is spoken by the subject position afforded to it by language. Similarly in fiction, the character who narrates is both engendered by the role it speaks and simultaneously engenders that role. The analysis, then, of internal narratives is particularly useful in understanding gender roles naturalized by the stories characters tell. Whose voice is enfranchised to tell stories? Who is authorized as a storyteller and why? What are the stories told? To whom are they told? The answers to such questions, especially as they relate to the portrayal of women, isolate the relative weight ascribed to women characters in the development of the diegesis. They focus attention on the roles presupposed for the women characters. They describe a permissible range of action, behavior, and presence for women. Social significance appears from this perspective as a function of narrative voice.

What isolates the films analyzed here are, on one hand, the large roles set for women characters by the external narratives of the films themselves and, on the other hand, the nature of the narrative voices given to these female characters within each diegesis. The narratives voiced by the women in *Images, 3 Women, Jimmy Dean,* and *Cookie's Fortune* describe a subjectivity that reflects a troubling of language, sexuality, and economics, "the three major forms of exchange by which society reproduces itself . . . , each of which requires a fixed positionality (addressor-addressee; masculine-feminine; buyer-seller)" (Coward and Ellis 58). The instabilities of identity undermine the terms of these dichotomies in the external stories of these films. Existing within an economic marginality or dependency, the internal narrators displace the debilitating terms of male-female relationships ultimately onto the signifying system of narrative discourse. What is at stake in the critical project of these films is not simply the dramatization of alienated, neurotic women characters but the tension between competing narrators and between the different levels of narration, a tension both reflecting these neuroses and predicting them for spectatorial identification. These women faithfully narrate their disorientation, their disablement, their dis-ease. Within the diegesis of each film the women become intradiegetic narrators who produce a variety of hypodiegetic worlds—Cathryn's tale of unicorns, Willie's murals, Joanne's demythology of immaculate conception, and Camille's dictatorial interpretation and production of *Salomé.* The films further reveal the strategies of an art-cinema narration concerned formally and experimentally to reflect both the crisis in modern identity construction and the concomitant necessity of narrative deformations to convey the problematic and frequently unspoken energies of that formation.

## Portraits of Splintered Identity

Narratologists, whose concern it is to designate these various differences, note that internal narratives serve a number of functions in relation to the narrative within which they are embedded (Kozloff 53). In these films they work metaphorically as thematic functions. *Images* develops a story about schizophrenia in which by contrast the external narrative represents a desirable (indeed, almost in classical narrative terms) alternative to the negative demands of sexual subjectivity posited within the diegesis. *3 Women* develops a story about female silence and marginality whose internal diegesis is a *mise en abyme* in which the inchoate images of the murals and inner dream mirror and reduplicate the almost unreadable dream of the diegesis. *Come Back to the 5 & Dime, Jimmy Dean, Jimmy Dean* unfolds a story in which the illusory and debilitating structures of Sissy's and Mona's internal narratives are contrasted with another *mise en abyme,* the hypodiegetic narrative of Joanne's voice, a voice of disruption that must radically assume lack in order to speak and that reduplicates the overall thrust of the diegesis, which reconstitutes the narrative space as an illusion initially founded upon but finally bereft of the authoritative presences of Joe and James Dean—father and son. In the diegetic world of *Cookie's Fortune,* Camille desperately attempts to control appearance, decorum, and power in the face of a community represented significantly as the local police force. The internal fantasy of her rewriting and production of Oscar Wilde's *Salomé* situates the heroine to procure the silence of male prophecy as the cost of the king's illicit desire.

The analytic paradigm of the mirror stage in psychological development helps to illuminate these narratives. In the undifferentiated phase of infancy, the imaginary phase of growth, individuals come to a sense of self perceived in the mirror stage as unique and separate from the being of the perceiver. Identity, thus, is a form of self-alienation, the spectral image representing a fullness lacking in the individual. Subsequent entrance into the symbolic phase of social discourse and authority means the acquisition of a linguistic subjectivity that systematically organizes the differences between perceiver and image under a legal system of sexual difference, around the notion of the phallus, "a signifier for the cultural privileges and positive values which define male subjectivity within patriarchal society, but from which the female subject remains isolated" (Silverman, *Subject* 183). The reading affect generated by the overarching narratives in these films implicates the viewer in imaginary relations—the simultaneous discovery of identity and estrangement—within the frames of metaphoric and real mirrors. The spectator experiences the female characters of these stories dialectically as they re-create, on one hand, these spectral relationships under the pressures and the authority of the symbolic and as they seek, on the other hand, to negotiate and escape from the dichotomies of the imaginary—the self and the other, the contingencies of identity, its attendant lacks and differences—through a stabilizing discourse of narration and a subjectivity as storyteller.

In *Images,* Cathryn (Susannah York) not only sees herself frequently throughout the film as her double, her mirror image, but the shape that that double predominantly takes is male. One image accuses her of fearing her sexual fertility. Another accuses her of both fearing and greatly desiring sex. She recognizes herself, then, in mirrored image as male observations of her inadequacy. Identification with herself takes the form of self-hatred, and her hallucinated murder of the male images represents an attempt to eradicate these voices of accusation as she discovers an inability to escape the terror of multiple images of her self. At the fantasy level of this story, Cathryn's personal insecurities, the frustration of her sexual needs, and the impossibility of conception and new birth result in violence and death. Her inability to have children drives Cathryn into extramarital affairs with two men and fills her with guilt over her biological failure and her infidelities. She tells one of her lovers, Rene (Marcel Bozzuffi):

> Why do you think I let you touch me in the first place? . . . All I ever wanted from you was a baby. I couldn't bear you. I wanted a baby for us, Hugh and me. I used you. I use to close my eyes and say there's nothing wrong with this. I'm not really feeling anything. This is for my marriage. That's all it was. I didn't cheat.

These emotions are managed organically by the madness of schizophrenia, which projects Cathryn's fears and guilt onto the images of her husband, Hugh (Rene Auberjonois), and her two lovers. The killing of the two lovers in her imagination leads in her confusion of objective and subjective reality to the attempted murder of her split personality, her fiction-writing double, and results in the apparently real murder of her husband. The metonymic displacement of Cathryn from an object of desire to an object of incompleteness occurs at the end of the film as the castrating image of terror and death motivated by her sense of lack.

The power of her neurosis appears as the fracturing of her personality into three personae: the homicidal wife Cathryn, her adult double and writer of children's fairy tales about monsters and escape, and her childhood double, the young girl Susannah (Cathryn Harrison), who is the reincarnation of her own golden, innocent youth. Cathryn's insecurity results in her regressive tendency to identify with the child Susannah, a tendency that configures the imaginary "desire of the mother" and the appropriation-alienation aspect of the mirror stage of development. The child represents the unformed, incomplete, embryonic subjectivity finding an image of herself as a desirable wholeness in the central female character, who at the same time experiences extreme difficulty with the negative patterns of female sexuality acquired upon entrance into the symbolic, into language, into subjectivity.

This insecurity also motivates the other dominant form of representation in all these films, the symbolic discourse of art, the subjectivity of the artist, the positionality of storyteller. Within the violent disorder of her fears, Cathryn's artist persona retreats from the confusion of realities into the children's tale *In Search of Unicorns.* As a writer she sublimates her relationship with Hugh into the story of a heroine named Una and her quest for a unicorn, that medieval figure of innocence, purity, and virginity, a quest that requires the assistance of "Lord Hero Fairbeard" in avoiding watery pits and the "snorkeling trumpetings of Hammoth, the mammoth." At the same time, her childish ego Susannah sublimates her loneliness, her fear of sex, the infidelity of her mother, and the insecurity of unstable and sexually promiscuous parents into her movie-long attempt to put together Cathryn's childhood jigsaw puzzle of a house, a tiger, and a unicorn. While Cathryn's schizophrenia leads her into murder, Susannah's search for the last missing piece of the puzzle and the writer's attempt to complete the fairy tale come to simultaneous fruition at the very end of the film and imply that these projections onto external form represent a more successful, or at least a less violent, management of Cathryn's fears than that provided by the homicidal schizophrenia.

Throughout *Images,* the storytelling voice of the central character weaves in and out of the film narrative, indeed vies with it for authority, and is arguably the dominant or external of the two stories. Susannah York published the book *In Search of Unicorns* prior to the production of the movie, so that the two authorial voices, York and Altman, female and male, actually vie across the lines of this text. The traumatic images of Cathryn's schizophrenia are doubled by the trials of her fairy-tale heroine Una in her contradictory quest for the generic male Hero and for an aesthetic purity represented by the unicorn. This dialectic tension between the two diegeses punctuates key moments in Cathryn's relationship to the images of herself and others in the external story. A central moment of pain in the inner tale graphically captures its metaphoric relation to the external tale as well as the frightening dualities of Cathryn's confrontation with herself:

> Out of Una's breast shot a tiny blue bird, straight to the sacred bonfire where it hovered and spun over the flames. It was Una, Una who felt the pain—like flames scorching her heart. She knew that the little blue bird had always been part of her, lodged inside her since she began, and the pain of being without was more than she could bear. Oh my soul! My soul! Give me back my soul! (53)

The literal image of herself terrifies Cathryn throughout the film, and the sense of identity split across conflicting images and desires remains unresolved at the end of the film. Beginning and ending with the tale of unicorns, this narrative threatens entirely to subsume that of Cathryn, Hugh, and Susannah. Only the fact that the latter story involves a world of human characters rather than images of fantasy justifies calling it the external narrative. The story of Cathryn and Hugh, indeed, never concludes but merely stops on the images of schizophrenia and murder. On the other hand, the child's story concludes happily on images of innocence, happiness, and unity. Bruce Kawin, writing about "feminism and the dis-covery of self," describes this phenomenon: "Because the writer confronts herself and the world both as creator and as subject, writing is a special and charged means of defining and healing the self. This is one reason 'Every woman who writes is a survivor'" (*Mind* 303). As the film opens with Cathryn writing her story and concludes as the story concludes, the diegetic world becomes successfully enclosed between the "once upon a time" and the "happily every after" uttered by the interior storyteller. Significantly, the final shot of the film captures the completion of the jigsaw puzzle simultaneously with Susannah's voice and an intrusive male voice on the sound track reading "the end" to Cathryn's story of unicorns as the film's "the end" is superimposed over the image. Survival and containment are simultaneous.

## Three Women Become One

*Images* is a more interior, more claustrophobic film than *3 Women,* but the desire for and fear of sexual communion, the impotence of individual and incomplete personalities, the frustration of new life, and the place of self-expression constitute similar preoccupations in both. Millie's social ineptness at the Purple Sage Motel occurs against the ironic backdrop of water imagery in the Desert Spring Rehabilitation and Geriatric Center, the hot sterility of the desert, and her desperate retreat to the Dodge City bar where the men ride dirt bikes and practice marksmanship at a pistol range. Millie's sexual desires, are, like Cathryn's, tied up in the insecurity of her self-concept and express themselves in her attempt to create a persona from the plastic clichés of modern advertising. The sexual fears that in *Images* result in a search for unicorns are here depicted by Willie in three surrealistic murals that link three female images, one of whom is pregnant, in mutual defense of the pregnant figure against the violence of a male figure. And Susannah's quest for companionship and security is repeated by the childish instability of Pinky in *3 Women.* In the earlier movie, schizophrenia produces the ego-splintering disintegration of Cathryn's personality apparently isolated in three separate and incomplete individuals. In *3 Women,* psychic integration and personal wholeness seem at once to rest on and be frustrated by sexual engagement with Edgar, the gun-toting character identified as the former stunt double for a television western hero: Willie needs protection from the male sexual image, Millie reaches in guilt and desperation for the same figure, and Pinky seeks the adult identity of Millie—a circular quest for identity and sexual security that courses through the images of dreams and the nightmare of attempted suicide and stillbirth. The final, perhaps dreamed, symbiosis of Millie, Pinky, and Willie seems the result either of Edgar's accidental death, sublimated as in a dream to the film's off-screen space, or of their combined murder of Edgar.

Here is the art cinema's recognition of reality as a shadow of subliminal relations. What actually constitutes reality in both films is distanced, distorted, fractured, and displaced—by madness and art in *Images,* by dreams and art in *3 Women*—so that for the characters of both films the fears of reality take on the quality of the surreal or the unreal. A central complexity in *3 Women,* as in *Images,* is found in the confusing relationships among these three different female personae. Despite the fact that three actresses actually portray the central characters of the later film, compared to a woman and a child earlier, the adult-child-artist configuration is even stronger in *3 Women.* Again the internal narrative works as a displacement of problematic accommodations of female sexuality within the public and symbolic domains. The external framing of the film as a dream is not clearly grounded in a dreamer from within the diegesis of the dream, so that all three women are potentially dreamed doubles of the dreaming subject. The implications of emerging, splitting relationships in the context of the mirror stage are everywhere suggested by the constantly repeated motif of mirrors and the recurring image, visual and verbal, of twins. While Willie appears in only two of the twenty-three different mirror signatures in the film, the majority of the remaining mirrors reflect images of Millie and Pinky by themselves, as double reflections of themselves and each other.

The narrations' constant reiteration of mirror imagery in these films establishes an appropriate metaphor for the art cinema's interest in the multiple nature of personality. The viewer frequently perceives the doubling and tripling of individuals that parallels the compounding of identity deriving from schizophrenia and dreams. The twenty-three mirror images in *3 Women* strikingly parallel the number of shots devoted to the murals and the number of times the haunting musical theme rises on the sound track and variously depict one, two, and sometimes all three of the central characters. The multiple mirror images of the women dramatically convey the splintering of personality; the economic, sexual, and artistic traumas of identity; the insufficiency of Millie, Pinky, and Willie as single, separate individuals. Narrative space, authorial voice, spectator position are all aggressively undermined. Here is that "mirroring within the mirror by which identity (of characters and/or of spectators) is variously doubled, split, and recomposed" (Nowell-Smith, "Note" 238). The self is conceived not as a unity but as a system of relations constructed linguistically, sexually, and economically. This sense of the subject situated externally to the film by the cinematic apparatus

"Never trust a woman with a loaded gun" *(3 Women).*

parallels the sense of the subject within the diegesis. Indeed, *3 Women* depicts the birth of an ego relationship among the three characters as a mutually defining and supportive symbiosis in response to the breakdown of an insupportable if dominant sense of a unified self.

A major trajectory of the dream work in this filmed dream, a metonymy of desire and murder, is the appropriation by the child persona, Pinky, of Millie as her ideal image: "You're the most perfect person I've ever met," she tells Millie. When Millie rejects her, Pinky's attempted suicide results in her literal assumption of Millie's identity. And where Millie fails to achieve the ideal subjectivity constructed for her in the pages of mass-media magazines for women as the desirable object of male desire, Pinky meets with demonstrable success in that same guise. That effort, however, involves both the denial of her past, her parents, and her identity as well as the denunciation of Millie's adequacy. For a moment she becomes Mildred, but the self-negating, self-alienating demands of this female sexuality are impossible to sustain. They collapse in the film's dream within a dream, a nightmare of mirrored identities, doubling imagery, sexual competition, violence, and self-hatred—a dream montage of the same tensions and psychological disruptions that characterize *Images.* This moment in the film marks Pinky's regression to a childlike personality and precedes the stillbirth of Willie's baby, doubled images once more of the inadequacy of female sexuality—infertile and prepubescent.

If once again the demands of the socially symbolic differentiations between male and female sexuality offer no stable or positive subjectivity for the woman, the symbolic order is inescapable. And here, contrary to the complexity of the art-cinema mode that conveys it, artistic discourse provides one of the less demanding and more liberating modes of positive reproduction. Willie as the artist persona has lapsed into almost total silence; she says only two sentences in the whole film. But she continually works on the nonverbal narratives of the three murals, whose content, like that of *In Search of Unicorns,* is coequal with the length of the whole film—from opening to concluding credits—and is expressive of the troubled positionality accorded the female subject under the authority of a phallocentric culture. All of the three murals contain the same basic cast of characters, with the same grotesque, serpentlike human figures arranged in slightly different configurations of relationship. Common to each visual story stands an upright male figure with a prominent and pendulous penis and with his arms upraised in a position of hostility and rage. The three other figures in these murals are women—one pregnant, another small and childlike, the third like the male figure, aggressive and combative. One depicts the male rearing over the pregnant woman, who kneels before him as he confronts the tall woman with the child figure kneeling before her. Another depicts the pregnant figure in a reclining position, with the child kneeling at her side and the combative female figure interposed between them and the angry male. And the third locates the angry woman between the pregnant woman and the child, with her arms around them in a protective grouping as she confronts the male figure. The story told in all the paintings is one of overbearing male aggression confronted by one of three women who is also protective of the other two women. Two central differences among the murals are the movement of the pregnant woman from under the dominance of the male and into the protective cluster of the other women and the diminution in size of the male figure, from that of threat to that of insignificance.

The film conceptualizes the actual and symbolic fragmentations of personality that motivate the experimental energies of art-cinema narration. In her discerning review of *3 Women,* Marsha Kinder asserts that the film works to "reaffirm the existence of the self" and that it "powerfully affirms Self over Structure" ("Art of Dreaming" 18), but that affirmation lies less in characterization than in the form of the film. To characterize the variety of subject positions inscribed in *3 Women* is to recognize that the film never unites all the splintered aspects of personality. It depicts the traumatized self, the discourses that it authors, and the fragmentation of identity revealed by that discourse. Narrative coherence is a linchpin in the concept of the unified ego. The incoherence of *3 Women's* art-cinema discourse, however, sufficiently disrupts the homogeneous subject position to reveal the self as neither unified nor fixed but as a relation, in process, threatened and threatening, a possibility only in symbiosis, only when authorized by an other. The film explicitly and directly may be read as an expression of hostility to the coercion of the ego by the dominance of the phallus and of efforts to establish a variety of more authentic if unstable roles beneath the pressure of images determined by the phallocentrism of culture. Similarly, both narrative structure and cinematic technique in *Come Back to the 5 & Dime, Jimmy Dean, Jimmy Dean* illustrate the way socially derived illusions constitute the public, again, of three women. The critical strategy of the film probes beneath the illusions surrounding the lives of these women and explores the extent to which an honest inner self, a communication with the private self, the acceptance of a self divergently composed is achieved at the cost of phallic renunciation.

## Sexual Facades and Social Alienation

Five women return to the Woolworth's in a tiny Texas dust-bowl town called McCarthy on the twentieth anniversary of the death of James Dean. As members of an old James Dean fan club called the Disciples, their lives are seen in direct relation to the impact of the movie star and teenage idol who came to this back corner of the world during the filming of *Giant.* Two of the women have exchanged their single status for wealth and sexual productivity and escaped to Dallas. Money and children are mutually exclusive for these women, however. Brassy and vulgar Stella Mae (Kathy Bates) has a financially rich but emotionally barren marriage. Edna Louise (Marta Heflin) is mousy and poor but happily pregnant with her seventh child. The major characters of the film are single, and two still remain in McCarthy. Sissy (Cher) is the bouncy, witty, sexy truck-stop waitress whose husband, Lester T., has left her. Mona (Sandy Dennis) is asthmatic, slightly daft in her dedication to the memory of James Dean, and still a clerk in the Woolworth's. She is also mother of the never-seen, slightly retarded teenager Jimmy Dean. The fifth member of the Disciples was Joe (Mark Patton), who has left Texas and had a sex change. Into this setting he returns as Joanne (Karen Black)—sensuous, mysterious, driving in from California in a Porsche, dressed in white, and primed to reveal the deceptions that fill the lives of the small-town Texas women.

The stories of three major women characters indicate efforts to accommodate and control their personal insecurities under the pressure of a phallocentric authority, specifically identified with James Dean. Of the three major stories told about the past, only Joe's enjoys a vantage point of power. As the castrato Joanne, he/she says, "Unlike apparently all of you, I have undergone a change." The film reveals the self-negating power, the positioning of a negative female sexuality in the personal stories of Mona and Sissy. Mona has apparently long since rejected Joe as the real father of Jimmy Dean and constructed her life around the false story of "Mona Magdalene," about how "*I* was chosen the one to bring the son of James Dean into this world." Her narrative reveals an idealized and false relationship motivated by worship of the star: "Did you ever dream what it'd be like . . . to make love to somebody real famous like him? . . . I feel something so deep inside me about James Dean that

I'm not able to get words to come out about it. . . . It's something more than love . . . , something beyond the end."

Sissy's story of the past is equally false, but motivated by a different self-image. Sissy is the sex object, famous for her sexual exploits in the town graveyard, whom the culture compels to see herself in light of the idealized female image of Marilyn Monroe and whose claim to subjectivity derives from the size of her breasts. Her liberation in the drama derives from her admission to a double mastectomy that caused her husband to leave her because of her changed physique. "He worshipped me. He told me I had the biggest pair of melons in the whole goddamned state of Texas." She must admit, however, that after the removal of her breasts, "I was scared to death to tell anybody, especially Lester T. He loved them so much. Every night he would come home and fall asleep with his head on them." Their loss, of course, motivates his desertion of Sissy.

Contemporary reviewers almost unanimously wondered why Altman was wasting his talent on boiled-over Inge-Williams-Albee material, although some made passing allusions to certain general similarities between this film and *3 Women.* The actual likeness rests not simply in the selves constructed around illusions but in the means by which the narrative finally lays these illusions to rest. The teleology of the story and the set design of the film indeed seem intended to explore the depths of subliminal reality in even more detail than the previous film. Tellingly, many of the contemporary reviews speak obliquely about Joanne's role, some under the guise of not ruining any surprises of the plot (although they also complain that the script is so poor as to be completely transparent from the beginning), whereas others simply fail to address the fact that the Joanne of the twenty-year reunion is Joe of the original Disciples. The critics wrote eagerly about Dustin Hoffman in *Tootsie* that same year, but evinced a decided uneasiness about discussing Karen Black as Joe in *Jimmy Dean.* Viewers apparently find the cross-dressing concept of charade more acceptable symbolically than, in the words of Roland Barthes, "the horror consubstantial with castration" (*S/Z* 210). The fear of castration is the fear of a loss of power, possession, and control. The subliminal reality of this art film finds connections that play around this anxiety. We confront uneasily a willing acquiescence of masculine authority.

In the film, Stella Mae expresses fascination with the mechanics of the sex-change operation, and Juanita (Sudie Bond), the longtime manager of the dime store, explicitly conveys her disgust with Joanne, but Sissy sees another side of herself in Joanne's change. Joe has given up voluntarily what Sissy lost against her desire. Sissy's empathy with Joanne provokes the story of her mastectomies. She reveals that what she has proudly announced as "the biggest bosoms in Texas" are in fact prostheses. The false front of her body and the sexual assertiveness of her speech conceal the loss, the pain, and the loneliness self-imposed by her acceptance of the social view that only the shapely female body has exchange value.

Anthony Wilden conveys this perception of loss in phallocentrism:

> The castration fears of men in a culture which equates virility with force, violence, aggression, killing, and the objectification of the "other" sex, are quite serious enough. But the fears of the master cannot be equated with the effect of those fears on his psychosocial and socioeconomic slaves [women]. It is probably true that the phallus is indeed the general equivalent in most of the psychosocial exchanges in the pathology of our culture. The devastating effect this Imaginary identity has on women is that the phallus becomes the imaginary equivalent of the woman herself. (*System* 288)

By voluntarily giving up the phallus, the signifier of desire, Joe has not merely established himself as a lack, but has constituted Joanne beyond the system of sexual exchange. Sissy, on the other hand, sees herself quite literally in terms of her physical attributes. But Mona denies the actual terms of physicality and sexual relationship altogether. Her story of one night with James Dean is a fantasy. Her assertion of Dean as the father of her retarded son is a fiction of divine intervention, an illusion of immaculate conception that idolizes the remote cinematic object of desire and rejects the true father. Sissy internalizes the cultural values of sexual identity. Mona idealizes them. Joe is destroyed by them. Joanne is a new identity composed in part by the memory of the sexual other.

Probing behind the destructive personas imposed by society, *Jimmy Dean* displays the metaphors of mirroring employed by the art cinema to represent psychological effects of interactions that dramatize the positive and negative differentiations of male and female sexuality. With the characteristically metaphoric constructions of the art cinema, it provides an internal voice to a central female character that at once reflects and undermines that set of differences. Castration, sex change, discarded male images most explicitly represent the need to achieve personalities apart from the oppression of the dominant culture. The set design exemplifies the technical construction of this complex self. The production uses two identical sets, back to back, one the mirror, reversed image of the other. A see-through mirror separates the two halves of the set, and when lights are used behind it, the second set becomes clear through the now-transparent glass. *Images* and *3 Women* employ mirrors extensively in the mise-en-scène to suggest multiple personalities. *Jimmy Dean* extends the metaphoric doubling suggested by mirrors into a literal image: the mirror becomes a window. Early in the production of the play on Broadway, which Altman directed also, he decided not to use younger actresses to play the teenage selves of the major characters. The actors in the back set were the same people who performed in the front set. Nor in making the film did he resort to postproduction editing techniques to dissolve from the front to the back halves of this set. Dramatic time between these two spaces is largely continuous and present.

These facts help us to understand how the scenes representing the Disciples in the five-and-dime twenty years ago are to be read: the change of lighting with the resultant shifting of the viewer's attention signals not a move from the present reunion on the front set to actual events of a twenty-year-old past on the back set, but a move from outer reality to inner memory. Here is the graphic display of the psychological expressivity of the art cinema focused on a reality whose presence is motivated and determined by an unspoken and subliminal other reality. The mirror becomes an entire wall of the dramatic space and occasionally the frame of the screen itself, where all of the major characters identify themselves with spectral images that represent an idealized and alienated image from the past. The mirror is the site of both self-recognition and misrecognition, of wholeness and difference, of the spoken and the unspoken. The mirrored images of the characters in the present time reflect not the past so much as the way that past has been internalized, particularly by Sissy, Mona, and Joanne. And again those identifying images of completeness and separation are retroactively perceived through the economic and sexual significations accorded them in symbolic differentiation. Part of the force in this film rests on this technique. When the camera zooms slowly through the dusty pastels of this set to a close-up of a character's face, it can continue past the surface of that character into an inner present of memory and desire.

The film thus complicates classically tutored reading strategies. As the facades of deception break down under Joanne's probing, the subsequent vulnerabilities are modified by our knowledge of both public and private selves as they have stored up images of the past. The former camaraderie of the Disciples in general represents a collectively held movement of ego development in adolescence—unchanging, enthusiastic and fearful, sentimental and painful. It establishes at once a metaphor of youthful energy and a deceptive model for living in the adult world. The inner image of Sissy hardly differs from her exterior demeanor. Her wisecracking sensuality is an old disguise against the physical disfigurement she reveals at the reunion. Mona's half-crazed worship of James Dean icons—which fight Juanita's neon-lit portrait of Jesus on the walls of this dimestore shrine—is undergirded by a memory of excitement and devotion to the dead movie idol. All of the characters are literally visual doubles of themselves—except Joanne. What she remembers is Joe. Sissy's physical facade and Mona's idealistic one originate in the same context as Joe's painful confrontation of his sexual inadequacy. All three reveal the falsehoods of personality played out against the pressure of socially determined sex roles.

Joanne's sex change is both a dramatic retreat from the phallus as an equivalence of exchange and an assumption of knowledge. Becoming female, she is not simply the castrato but the Tiresias, the truthsayer, the seer who has lived both lives. What knowledge she brings to McCarthy, Texas, is difficult to bear. The same feeling of exhaustion pervades the end of this film that colors the conclusion of *Who's Afraid of Virginia Woolf?* (1966). After so much delusion and catharsis, so many pieces of ego to hold together, where can these characters go? Altman's films about women assert the necessity for the female ego to struggle against the dominance of phallocentrism. But it is a struggle waged at great cost and seldom won. Death and schizophrenia result from this conflict of inner and outer selves in *Images* and *Nashville.* In *3 Women,* the traumatized self carves out small spaces of new existence: Millie, Pinky, and Willie create a parent-child symbiosis in the California desert. In *Come Back to the 5 & Dime,* the struggle ends without the formation of any public image but with another symbiosis, this time mental: the three old friends Mona, Sissy, and Joanne one at a time step around into the back set, not into the past but into a shared inner present, where they form a chorus line to sing together, as the McGuire Sisters, "Sincerely," a song of desire, longing, and escape.

Where *Images* and *3 Women* represent displacements of troubled individuality onto a story for children and a collection of murals fading under a chlorinated pool and the sun of Southern California, here the energies of storytelling are not limited to one character and are reinvested into the social matrix. Rather than the singular, discordant, and defensive discourse of one woman, the internal stories of all three major characters in *Jimmy Dean* indicate efforts to accommodate, to narrativize the imaginary images in the mirror. Just as clearly, however, these narratives are all governed by the pressure of a phallocentric authority. That authority is specifically identified with James Dean, and nowhere is the gap between the individual and the mirror image more striking than under the gaze of Joanne, for when she sees herself in the mirror, she sees Joe. And as Joe, the real father of Mona's baby, he is forced to recognize his inadequacy before Mona's imagined conception of the baby with James Dean. Joe/Joanne as the literal configuration of sexual difference can see how the power of the phallus, the law of the culture, the figure of the father significantly shapes the misapprehensions of the self in the individual's imaginary image.

The art cinema assumes both formal and thematic postures of social resistance, frequently in modes that reflexively implicate narrative in its bill of particulars. Ironically, the proclamation of Joe's difference leads first to a denunciation of the power of the father by Mona. When Juanita exclaims, in the mirror, "We have searched our Bible from cover to cover to find an excuse for his behavior, and there is none. In the eyes of God, he does not belong!" Mona responds, "Then God is wrong! God made him, didn't he? If God doesn't accept him, then . . . I don't accept God. He's not my God! I don't want him! I hate him!" But the power of the father configured in movie star James Dean reinforces Juanita's proclamation of Joe's difference; Mona rejects Joe's fatherhood of Jimmy Dean and constructs the story of "Mona Magdalene." Her narrative reveals an idealized and false relationship motivated by worship of the star. Joe's return as Joanne brings the pressure of truth—of a counternarrative ("I was there!") that speaks the hitherto subliminal reality—to bear on the request for Mona once more to "tell us the story of being chosen the Virgin Mona." Joanne confronts her at the end of her false narrative: "That is not the way it happened at all, is it?" Sissy's story of the past is equally false, and Joanne provides the pressure that forces Sissy to face the truth about why Lester T. has left her. Joanne asserts that Sissy's "very believable explanation" is "unfortunately . . . not accurate," and Sissy confirms that Lester T. left her because of her changed physique.

The distance between their idealized self-images and their recognition of inadequacy lead Mona and Sissy to the strategies harshly described by Mona: "I managed to rise above the attitudes of this town while you lay spread over a grave stone and took them inside you." The narrative explicitly links the town values to male sexuality. The phallocentric culture has defined two prototypical places of individuality for Sissy and Mona, the virgin (above sex) and the whore (full of sex), idealized and physical objects of male desire. In the mirror the initial perception of the self as this other is accepted by the women first as fact ("It *is* real, just deceiving to the eye, that's all") and must be recognized finally as a fiction. *Jimmy Dean* plays out a drama of exorcism—of the ghost of James Dean, of the engendered stereotypes of negative female sexuality, of the power of the patriarchy. The male presence—"law," "money," "knowledge"—is the problem, and rejection of the male brings uneasy, uncertain power. The male is not murdered but sacrificed, transformed to a "thing," a "pervert," a "freak"—a woman. Joe/Joanne comes to reveal that the alienating and full images constructed in the mirror are "just a front . . . , a false front." The exchange value of Joe's penis is Joanne's knowledge and narrative power.

## Directorial Authority and Masculine Silence

In *Cookie's Fortune,* the exchange value for Camille Dixon's sense of family honor is her role as theatrical director. Before Easter weekend is over in Holly Springs, Mississippi, Jewel Mae "Cookie" Orcutt (Patricia Neal) will have committed suicide, left her fortune—house and guns—to her black servant Willis Richland (Charles Dutton), and almost disrupted the placid surface of the southern town to reveal secrets of family enmity, incest, and interracial kinship. Almost, because the most disruptive aspect of this Easter weekend would seem to be the fact that Cookie's niece Camille (Glenn Close) is rehearsing Oscar Wilde's *Salomé,* a play that resonates with the scandalous fin de siècle movements in England of symbolism and decadence. Wilde describes Salomé as the "tragic daughter of passion . . . dancing for the head of the English public" (Joost and Court 107). His concern to attack social hypocrisy and puritan earnestness and his representation of the lurid sensuality of Salomé's desire for John the Baptist's sexy body hardly seems appropriate for the Easter Monday pageant at the local Presbyterian church. But the tension between an unruffled acceptance of the play by the town folk who play its roles and the turmoil in Camille that motivates her direction of the play constitutes the ambiguous center of Altman's film. Its overlay of blues and jazz on Protestant hymnology signals the extent to which this apparently gentle and sunny comedy represents again the divergent layers of art-cinema narration. The incongruity of the play and the place—Oscar Wilde in Holly Springs—characterizes once again a film in which the audience struggles to construct meaning out of the disparate fragments of three women's engagement with the patriarchy.

*Cookie's Fortune* presents an apparently transparent cause-and-effect interaction of three women in the aftermath of Cookie's suicide, but Altman insists it's not really a story, "not so much plot but a character study of these people" *(Cookie's Fortune).* Moreover, the intertwining representation of *Salomé* suggests the subliminal reality at work in the relationships of these women with each other and their society. Camille's anxiety about social appearances, her sister Cora's (Julianne Moore) dim-witted and childlike subservience to Camille's dictations, and the daughter Emma's (Liv Tyler) obdurate resistance to social decorum are configured in Wilde's adaptation of the biblical story of female subversion of male law and prophecy. The play's portrayal of the mother-daughter relationship between Herodias and Salomé and their resistance to King Herod and John the Baptist provides a gloss, a commentary, a mirror on the enervating relationship between these southern women and their culture. At the same time, Camille's claim of coauthorship of the play with Wilde and her production of the Easter performance put her actively and reflexively in the director's chair. The play and her direction of it suggest simultaneously a hostility to masculine authority and a guilty participation in its nonchalant, complacent, and inept dispensations. In the penultimate scene in the film, Camille the director has been jailed for the suicide death of her aunt and symbolically enacts her own suicide.

Adaptation studies have taught that films adapt not only a single antecedent literary text but a range of other social texts contemporary to the adaptation, that the reading of the antecedent text is itself shaped by concerns of interest not only to the director but to a number of other artisans in the production process and indeed to the audience's taste as

Performing *Salomé* in Mississippi *(Cookie's Fortune).*

well. Oscar Wilde one hundred years ago read the story of Salomé through the lens of his interest in the aesthete fashion of decadence and sensuality and his desire to shock puritan sensibilities at the end of the Victorian nineteenth century. His play emphasizes Salomé's inflamed desire for the sensuous John, his intoxicating voice, starkly white body, black hair, and red lips, and locates interest less in any divine prophecy than in his sexual power. Altman's adaptation of Salomé also reads the play through the repeated understanding of feminine subjectivity as a three-part persona of extroverted ego, innocent child, and revelatory artist. Wilde's Salomé reflects this same nexus of personality: She is the popular princess, the social figure around whom all the action of the play revolves. She is also innocent and childlike in her initial desire for John the Baptist—"a white rose . . . cold and chaste . . . a virgin. . . . She has never abandoned herself to men," says the play (Wilde 555). She is also the artist whose performance of the dance of the seven veils denotes seduction, deceit, and vengeance. As one Wilde scholar writes:

> When she desires most to be vindicated as a woman by the conventions of the patriarchy, she is rebuked. To restore her sense of her sexuality and as a rebuke to the patriarchy, she defies the social conventions which confine her. Like her mother Herodias, Salomé uses the only power she has in male society, her body, to bargain with Herod for John's head. In arousing Herod through her dance, Salomé succeeds in reconciling him to her ends, manipulating the patriarchal authority into achieving what she as a female could not. (Zatlin 94)

Here are the metaphoric redundancy and multiple motivations of the art cinema. Part of the complexity in *Cookie's Fortune* rests in the fact of a double adaptation. Altman adapts Wilde, but so does Camille. As both directors' version of the play, the film, like Altman's movies since *MASH,* again asserts a reflexive stance that examines the authority and system of mediated social communication. Indeed, one of the most humorous moments in the film is a shot of the signboard in front of the church that announces *Salomé* as written by Oscar Wilde and Camille Dixon. The question of why Altman adapts Wilde mirrors the question of why Camille very incongruously adapts this play for a southern Protestant Easter pageant. One of the most reflexive lines in the film is Cora's demand of Camille, "Tell me about motivation again." The answer involves a complex and purposefully oblique emotional and behavioral array of concealment and revelation, of confession and liberation in the lives of the three women. Camille and Cora are sisters but seem ostensibly like mother and daughter, and Emma, who believes herself to be Cora's daughter, turns out to be the daughter of Camille as the result of an incestuous relationship between her father, Cora's husband, and her actual mother. The narrative purposively confuses these familial relationships so that the mother-sister-aunt-daughter distinctions blur the women into a single amalgamated persona.

The film ultimately discloses that Cora's husband cheated on her with her sister/mother Camille. It further reveals that the faithful black family retainer Willis is Emma's cousin, because they share the same grandfather. Thus a subliminal reality of complex kinship and lineage links the women and the African American members of the community in a relationship marginal to the white male authority of Holly Springs, which the film consistently foregrounds through the town's one lawyer and its three-man police department. The film shows little inclination to make these relationships clear, however, revealing them so rapidly toward the end as to repress them even as it exposes them. Wilde's play, too, suggests a complex set of relationships that recapitulate in overdetermined ways the affiliation of Camille, Cora, and Emma.

Emma and Salomé function alike as the recalcitrant daughter to the domineering mother, thus Camille doubles Herodias. Cora and Emma both operate like Salomé in their mother-daughter relationship to Camille, Emma as Camille's actual daughter and Cora in the stage role of Salomé as well as in her subordination to her imperious sister. Emma as the apparent daughter of Cora and the actual daughter of Camille thus reiterates the mother-daughter relationship with both women. Emma's similarity with Salomé is further figured in her seduction of Jason (Chris O'Donnell), who is a comic signifier of both law and desire. Camille is at once a representation of the mother Herodias in her relationship both to Cora in the part of Salomé and to Cora in her relationship with men. She is also Salomé herself as the vicarious result of her directing Cora in the role for the play and of her dancing in her jail cell at the end of the film. As Cookie commits suicide at the beginning of the film and Camille contemplates it at the end, both characters resonate with the young soldier who commits suicide in Wilde's play because of his unrequited desire for Salomé. "His suicide foreshadows further violence emerging from the same cause" (Joost and Court 100) and suggests the recurrent issue of suicide in the film, both Cookie's real suicide over the absence of male relationship and Camille's rehearsed suicide over the all-too-present fact of masculine authority. Herod's incestuous desire, both earlier for Herodias (his brother's wife) and now for

Salomé (his wife's daughter), as well as Herodias's incestuous relationship with the king, configures Camille's incestuous relationship with her brother-in-law, Donny, Cora's husband and Emma's father. Cora's seduction of the incestuous father is an act of revenge against the incestuous seduction of her husband by Camille.

This confusing complexity reflects the art cinema's preoccupation with unspoken and multiple determinations of relationships and behavior. All these connections barely emerge during an initial experience with the film. Indeed, the narrative wants to repress them in the same way that Camille seeks to repress Cookie's suicide. Camille's direction of Cora in the role of Salomé seems at once a confession of her guilt and an act of revenge against Cora's husband for seducing her. John exclaims in the play, "Bid her rise up from the bed of her abominations, from the bed of her incestuousness" (Wilde 557). This condemnation of Herodias suggests Camille's personal sense of guilt just as Salomé's request for John's head reveals her hostility to the world of masculine accusation and judgment: "My daughter has done well to ask the head of Jokanaan. He has covered me with insults. . . . Do not yield, my daughter" (Wilde 570). This remarkable tangle of parallel characters and situations centers on Salomé's frustration and anger with John as the quintessential Freudian nightmare of desire and castration. It further reveals that Camille's directing the play amounts to a resistance and Altman's directing the film amounts to another delineation of women whose resistance is symbiotic and limited.

This complexity and its resistance appears clearly in an analysis of Camille's and Cora's dance. Salomé's attempted seduction of John indicates the play of her desire and her sense of betrayal at the refusal of that desire. Consequently, her seduction of the king is an act of revenge, both for herself and for her mother. Salomé's dance also marks her authority over the king, whose desire she thwarts and whose authority she manipulates in her request for the head of John. Her own death is imminent, but as the play ends, Salomé, like Cora, who plays her in the Presbyterian church production, is triumphant: "Thou didst reject me. . . . Thou didst treat me like a harlot. . . . Well, Jokanaan, I still live, but thou, thou art dead" (Wilde 574). In all three versions of Salomé—in the Bible, in Wilde, and in Holly Springs, Mississippi—the central actions signal the consternation of male authority and the silence of masculine prophecy. One of John's most prophetic and ironic lines in the play, repeated three times in the film, conveys the masculine anxiety: "Rejoice not thou, land of Palestine, because the rod of him who smote thee is broken!" (Wilde 556). One scholar has described Oscar Wilde's motivations here: "Wilde's female protagonists are naturally restricted and frustrated by the patriarchal society in which they live. Even Salomé, perhaps the most independent and cunning of Wilde's female characters, must get permission from the reigning patriarch to obtain the head of John the Baptist" (Horan 105).

Wilde's *Salomé* represents women as competitors with each other under the desiring and condemnatory gaze of masculine authority. Their motive ultimately, however, reflects the desire of both Salomé and Herodias, who exclaims in the play, "I should like to see that day" when "the kings of the earth are afraid." Critics have suggested that Wilde's play variously adapts the mythical stories of the "man-devouring Kali," of "Circe the *femme fatale,*" of Cybele's murder of Attis, her resistance to sterile sexual impulses through the subjugation and castration of the male (Joost and Court 100). Cora and Camille in rehearsal literally echo the Wilde impulse to "make afraid the enemy." Salomé's dance thus is self-revelation and performance as murderous resistance. In *Images,* Cathryn writes escapist stories about unicorns. Willie paints murals on the bottoms of pools in *3 Women.* Joanne narrates the story of the past playing on the mirrored walls of the five-and-dime in *Jimmy Dean.* The performance of resistance is a fantasy, a pretense, a covering up of the reality of regicide and patricide that social subjectivity disallows.

Ultimately, the play seems like the dream work of the movie. Its rich play of symbols, displacements, and condensations signal the complexity of anxiety and desire, guilt and hostility of its central women characters. Its central image, Salomé's dance, recurs in several iterations throughout the film—the dance during the church performance, the dance that Camille performs to subvert the police investigations of Cookie's death, and the dance she performs in her cell at the end of the film. Here she appropriates the voices of the play to rehearse the desire for "sweet air" outside the assembly of barbarians, the joy of innocence, and the resistance to suicide: "Yes, it is ridiculous . . . to kill oneself."

Camille's incarceration finally seems neither permanent nor fatal. We observe here, however, another performance of the controlling voices of masculinity where performance becomes a substitute for death. The death of John the Baptist in *Salomé,* the murder of the husband in *Images,* the death of Edgar in *3 Women,* the death of Joe in *Jimmy Dean*—all reflect this same resistance to dominant power and authority. All prove simultaneously limited and liberating. Cathryn confronts her naked self at the end of *Images.* Willie, Millie, and Pinky constitute a familial symbiosis in the desert of *3 Women.* Joanne, Sissy, and Mona momentarily harmonize at the end of *Jimmy Dean.* At the end of *Cookie's Fortune,* Camille contemplates death from a jail cell, where she nevertheless performs another resisting dance of the seven veils. Cora's triumph as Salomé on the stage has occasioned in her a new, strong, and confident identity. Cookie's "fortune" comprises a new family symbiosis in which black male and white female cousins discover each other in self-recognition, and the daughter emerges from the shadow of social confinement to engage Jason, the rookie policeman, in playful sex. In the very last scene, Emma—the sensuous daughter whose face bears the bruise of masculine aggression throughout the film and whose unpaid parking tickets reflect her refusal to accept the force of authority—leaves fishing with the boys, as one of the boys, and strides confidently off to screw the law.

The voices of these films and their narratives constitute point of view as the battleground over which competing female selves contend. Altman's women's films evoke questions about the relationship of the internal to the external narrative voices, of the efficacy of female discourse within a realm governed by the masculine. Feminist film critics have noted that "a discourse which is marked as the possession of the woman is simultaneously marked as seriously deficient in its relation to knowledge and truth" (Doane et al. 12). The symbolic energies of these four films represent discursive strategies of mediation and negotiation aimed at escaping oscillations of the self between deficiency and strength. Under the terms of control offered by dominant social forms, however, the nature of a negative female sexuality risks being reaffirmed rather than reconstituted. The internal narratives of the female in *Images* and in *3 Women* are marginal, existing in silence or for children, despite their continuity from beginning to end with the external narratives that construct female subjects in crisis without resolution. The internal narrative of *Cookie's Fortune* is Wilde's representation of masculine anxiety and retribution in the face of aggressive female desirability. In all these films the fears of sexual identity prevent successful male-female relationships and prevent healthy procreation. Cathryn cannot conceive in *Images.* Willie's child is stillborn in *3 Women.* Mona's child is mentally retarded in *Jimmy Dean.* The central narrative work of *Cookie's Fortune* represses the incestuous fact of Camille as the mother of Emma. Even as these films tie regression to this sexual instability, they constantly align the fears of self-identity and procreation with the act of artistic creation.

Psychic disruptions motivate a divergent and cacophonous discourse that renders story incoherent and produces the art cinema's interrogative text, which, according to Belsey, "disrupts the unity of the reader by discouraging identification with a unified subject of the enunciation. The position of the 'author' inscribed in the text, if it can be located at all, is seen as questioning or as literally contradictory" (91). The central women characters in all four films are the focalizers of each internal diegesis but are not the extradiegetic narrators. The outermost teller of these tales—whether we designate it as "Robert Altman," as the overall textual system of each film, or as the institutions that shaped and determined their production, dissemination, and consumption—speaks with two voices that authoritatively contain and permit the internal voices of the women. It raises two sets of competitive considerations. Do these films, under a surface interrogation of phallocentrism, merely continue the repressive representations of women? Or do they constitute a progressive depiction of female subjectivity?

Inasmuch as these open narratives actualize the female voice within a male discourse, it is possible to read them as further examples of the effort of Hollywood cinema to effect an authority over women. It is also possible to read these Altman films as inversions of the hostility toward woman, demonstrated particularly in the slasher films contemporaneous with much of his work, as reflective of the guilty male, insecure and defensive, in retreat from the very phallic authority to which by his gender he would hold claim. Here the classical repression of the female takes on a new dimension: the extradiegetic voice of these films is itself fractured and positions the male spectator in unstable relationships to feminine need and energy. Male insecurity in a context of masculine authority even further requires the subordination of women. As Naomi Segal asserts, "the norm of male discourse is founded in uncertainty and anxiety . . . a fear not of what women lack but, on the contrary, of what women are" (251).

Art-cinema narration describes the subversive disorientations of teller, tale, and told in these Altman films. It perceives the social subject as a site of contestation and contradiction that is constantly in the process of construction and crisis under pressure from forces in the cultural formation. The subject is a process not yet fixed but open to difference and transformation. In *Images* there is unresolved psychosis, but in *3 Women* and *Jimmy Dean* three women find a unique voice and establish a small if precarious space of their own. Feminist criticism points to the "dilemma of difference" for the woman concerned to deconstruct the feminine self-image as a function of her "being for another": "For the mirror which is delegated to her as the special locus of female subjectivity reflects back to her as she is in the process of theorizing her own, untenable situation under patriarchy" (Doane et al. 14). Altman's female voices are authorized by the male. But their work lies, as Kinder says of *3 Women,* in "reaffirming the self and human creativity on three levels of experience—dreams, conscious artistry, and social interaction" ("Art of Dreaming" 10). Indeed, the most authoritative narrations within these films are Joanne's, whose position of authority derives from the sacrifice of the real penis for the symbolic phallus. If on one hand these films seek once again to control the sense of male fear and desire by projecting terror and fullness onto the female, they also work "neither to destroy difference nor to valorize it, but to multiply and disperse differences, to move toward a world where difference would not be synonymous with exclusion" (Doane et al. 14). They seek at the same time to explore the terms of that male projection, and in *Jimmy Dean* with an interesting result: Joe may have "mortgaged" his penis as the payment for his entrance into the symbolic, for his accession to phallic authority, but that payment is a rejection and the resulting figure of the law is a woman.

*The Laundromat,* Altman's hour-long adaptation of Marsha Norman's one-act play made for HBO in 1985, in many ways stands in paradigmatic relationship to the analyses of gender present throughout Altman's movies. Two women in the middle of the night encounter each other as they wash their clothes in a dingy laundromat. The older woman (Carol Burnett) is from a better part of town and has come finally to wash the clothes of her husband, who died six months before. The younger woman (Amy Madigan) washes her clothes so that she won't be there crying when her unfaithful husband returns home. Between a dead man and an unfaithful one, these two women reject the phallic suggestivity of a black man (Michael Wright) who momentarily enters what has become their space and subsequently achieve a temporary relationship of mother and daughter, of communication and communion. In one key scene, the older woman glances through a window into the office of the laundromat, where the male attendant sleeps through the entire story. The camera replicates her point of view and slowly pans the length of his reclining body as a country-western singer on the radio station intones, "A hundred years ago he was a hero."

Dead, asleep, vagrant, full of self-doubt, suicidal, homicidal, comically inept—masculine authority is in trouble. Altman has observed that "the death of Edgar in '3 Women' is the death of the [male] species, which is ok with me. . . . Our absence will not stop the universe. . . . The women in '3 Women' survive because they are taking care of each other.

And they do that because they are forced into it" (quoted in Demby 17). Set within divergent contexts of feminine powerlessness, these art films express contingencies coerced by patriarchical discourse. They are variously motivated to deflect the dominant stories that seek to organize our social structures. Their strategy as art cinema is frequently a refusal of the authority that resides even in narrative itself. They turn away from an ordered and ordering rhetoric of explanation and seek instead a form with its own power to interrogate the debilitations of masculinity. They develop a troubled and troubling portrait of engendered personality as heterogeneous and fluid, contradictory and distressed and open to change.

# Part III. Putting on the Show

# 7. Reflexive Show Business: Nashville and the Wild West

Narrative reflexivity hardly appears for the first time in fiction and drama during the twentieth century. Hamlet observes that "all the world's a stage" and then proceeds to stage a play within the play in which he plays to demonstrate the role of the fictional within the real. Similarly, a major characteristic of the international art cinema has been its experimentation and thus its reflexive referentiality about the materials, methods, and subjects of art. After making seven and a half films, Fellini makes a movie called *8½* about a director making a movie, which finally is the movie we're watching—a film thus doubly reflexive. Bergman points his camera at himself shooting a final scene in *Persona* and finally shoots a picture of the dying arc lamp in a movie projector. Godard's camera crane on the beach flies the red flags of revolution in *Sympathy for the Devil* (1968). Truffaut's director dreams of the young boy who steals the cinema poster advertising *Citizen Kane* in *Day for Night* (1973). The dispensations of twentieth-century art—with its fractures between history and value, between belief and action, between reality and perception, between perception and communication, between artist and medium—have forged a tradition of storytelling reflexivity, that "process by which texts, both literary and cinematic, foreground their own production, their authorship, their intertextual influences, their reception, or their enunciation" (Stam xiii). Patricia Waugh writes:

> Contemporary metafictional writing is both a response and a contribution to an even more thoroughgoing sense that reality or history are provisional: no longer a world of eternal verities but a series of constructions, artifices, impermanent structures. The materialist, positivist and empiricist world-view on which realistic fiction is premised no longer exists. It is hardly surprising, therefore, that more and more novelists have come to question and reject the forms that

> correspond to this ordered reality (the well-made plot, chronological sequence, the authoritative omniscient author, the rational connection between what characters "do" and what they "are," the causal connection between surface details and the "deep," "scientific laws" of existence). (6–7)

This reflexive, self-conscious, autoreferential mode in modern narrative and drama serves many functions. Reflexive narratives, or metanarratives, frequently address as their subject the relationship between real and fictional worlds. They point to the similarity between the artificiality of the world and its illusional representation. They reflect a doubleness in the "simultaneous joy in mystification and demystification, . . . between the will to create an illusion and the conscious decision to destroy that illusion. The lucidity of the illusionist, the puppeteer, or the filmmaker does battle with the desire to create a believable and lifelike image" (Stam 138). Reflexive storytellers simultaneously shatter illusion and comment on the reality so shattered. Bertolt Brecht's famous promotion of the "alienation effect" posits the importance of distanciation in the theater, where the audience recognizes processes of production rather than succumbs to illusions of reality. Reflexivity narratives critique the formulaic representations of popular narratives in their artificial ordering of disordered reality, and they challenge the ambiguous representations of aesthetic narratives in their disordering of orderly reality. They assert the significance of a subliminal reality that outruns narrative expression and containment. Moreover, they challenge the assumed "rules of reading." As they employ "various counter-techniques to undermine the authority of the omniscient author, of the closure of the 'final' ending, of the definitive interpretation" (Waugh 13), they urge an awareness of the plurality and multiplicity of meaning and describe for the viewer or reader an active, analytic, engaged rather than a passive, distanced position before the text.

This chapter and the next examine the reflexive terms of four films—*Nashville, Buffalo Bill and the Indians, The Player,* and *Prêt-à-Porter*—that take as their subjects different aspects of popular culture entertainment. These films represent the most consistent critique in Altman's films of the energy and the effects of the show business. They confront the audience with large casts of characters in minimal stories that intersect each other in inexplicable and complex ways. They confound the narrativity that reads films for clear causal progression and endings. They depict personal identity in bleak and pessimistic ways. But their understanding of life's disorder, disappointment, and debility emerges from an analysis of the values and the impact of the show business in American life. *Nashville* is a "battleground" of "hurtin' matches." *Buffalo Bill*'s stage western rewrites history and consumes personality. *The Player* commits murder for happy endings. *Prêt-à-Porter* encodes gender on the fashion floors of Paris. There is an exhilaration and excitement in all these films that mark their participation in the entertainments they critique, but their reflexive exploration of the negative costs of putting on the show make significant contributions to the self-portraits of art-cinema narration.

## Elements of Reflexivity

Michael Boyd develops a distinction between *elements* of reflexivity, reflexive techniques among different modes of narration, and *types* of reflexivity, where self-reference constitutes "the controlling compositional idea behind the entire work" (16). Altman's films demonstrate both kinds of narrative "bending back" on itself from *MASH* to *Dr. T & the Women.* In most of these films, reflexivity constitutes an element of the discourse, frequently with humorous effect, occasionally with metaphoric effect, regularly with philosophical effect. *MASH* concludes with the base loudspeaker, which has been such a salient part of the diegetic world of the film, announcing, "Tonight's movie has been *MASH.*" What has asked to be heard by the audience as part of the internal narration now asks to be heard as part of an external narration. Even as its reflexive nature participates in the anarchic humor of that film, this shift also reinforces the self-consciousness with which the array of stylistic features and structural principles of the film disrupt what was then the expected pattern of Hollywood narration.

The obscurities of the story in *Images* unmask the unreliability of the apparently objective narrative, so that to the very end the viewer struggles, as does Cathryn, to distinguish between subjective states and objective reality. The film's refusal to employ the traditional visual devices that distinguish subjective from objective shots recapitulates an art-cinema preoccupation with the crisis of objective self-awareness characteristic of schizophrenia. Repeated clues to the unaccountability of the rational surface are the recurrent images of cameras, binoculars, and glasses, self-reflexive images that call attention to the film's visual manipulation of reality. Reflexivity here works metaphorically to connote further the surrealistic possibilities of the film's seemingly realistic surface. Helene Keyssar explicitly compares *Images* to the art cinema:

With its play on a double meaning of "shooting" . . . *Images* recalls and provokes comparisons not only to *Persona* but also to another film made the same year (1966), Antonioni's *Blow-Up.* All three films exude filmic modernism; that is, they are self-conscious about their own processes and call into question the activities of shooting, of performance, and of projection. (208)

More humorous reflexivity occurs at the opening of *California Split.* At the end of the credit sequence, Charlie (Elliott Gould) turns on a teaching film for first-time patrons. The narration watches as he watches, and at the words "Poker has been around for a long time, but it isn't like this anymore," the teaching film shows a shot of miners sitting around a poker table from *McCabe & Mrs. Miller.* This quick quotation from the earlier Altman film hardly registers as the film continues to introduce the modern poker parlor to both the diegetic and the discursive audience: "Your pleasure is our business. We have prepared a short film to teach you the fundamentals of the game as we play it here. Service is our only commodity. This film is part of that service." Poker palaces, the game, movies—all here are part of the business of chance and entertainment, the movie, like poker, another place for the audience to gamble.

Humor also motivates the use of the song "Hooray for Hollywood" on the sound track of *The Long Goodbye* before the credit sequence begins and after the end of the story, especially given that the main effect of the film revises the Hollywood detective hero for the antiheroic mood of the American public at the end of the Vietnam War. But the more obvious play with the audience's sense of the constructedness of the story reality is the constant repetition of the "Long Goodbye Theme Song," composed by Johnny Mercer. It occurs intermittently on the sound track over the story action, and it occurs over and over at different times and places within the story: picked out by a musician in a piano bar where Marlowe receives his messages, heard as a door chime, played on the mobster's car radio while his girlfriend waits for him to finish business with Marlowe, played by the musicians as a dirge during the funeral that passes during Marlowe's first trip to Mexico, hummed by Mrs. Wade while Marlowe chases her through the streets of L.A. Like the Malibu gatekeeper whose imitations of Barbara Stanwyck, Jimmy Stewart, Gary Grant, and Walter Brennan a person must correctly identify to gain entrance, the music provides a running joke that recalls the presence of jokesters behind the narrative.

This same mood constantly shapes the ubiquitous presence of the radio as a sound setting in the story of *Thieves Like Us.* Here, however, the play of radio genres also provides an internal diegetic narrative presence that comments variously on the story action. The radio cop show *Gangbusters* plays during the first robbery scene. When Bowie and Keechie make love, the commentator for the "American School of the Air" dramatization of *Romeo and Juliet* melodramatically exclaims, "Thus did Romeo and Juliet consummate their first interview by falling in love with each other." "Consummate" here refers to sex, but the larger tragic trajectory of these star-crossed lovers is also signaled by the reference to Shakespeare's play. FDR's words, "Democratic government has the capacity to protect its people," sound as the gang stages their last bank robbery, and the radio sermon at the end of the film that urges it is "time to make America safe for democracy" comments ironically on the closure of Bowie's life. Such techniques work to employ elements from the surround of modern mass-media entertainment as part of the realistic space even as they also work reflexively as thematic commentary on the story whose action it accompanies.

One of the most aggressively self-conscious of Altman's early films is *Brewster McCloud.* Its mix of discourses play against each other—the story of Brewster's building his wings and the police efforts to solve the string of local murders stands over against the ornithology lecture delivered directly to the camera by the professor at the beginning, the end, and throughout the film, and all these stories contrast with the story about sex and flying. The experimental quality of the film, even after thirty years, calls attention to the artifice of its stories, its narration, and their constructions. Instead of the MGM lion's roar with that famous logo comes the voice of Jimmy Stewart saying, "I forgot the first lines." The voices of Houston radio stations, just as in *Thieves Like Us,* provide comic commentary on the story action. When Daphne Heap, played by actress Margaret Hamilton, who played the Wicked Witch of the West in *The Wizard of Oz,* dies in the film wearing Dorothy's red slippers, the film reflexively references another story about flight and multiple realities. During the credit sequence, she appears as a bad-tempered musician rehearsing the national anthem with an African American band. When she stops their out-of-tune playing and starts over, the whole film begins again, with the credit sequence itself starting over. This opening sequence suggests a metaphoric reading that contrasts different levels of representation. When Heap loses control of the band, the band members begin to play "Lift Every Voice and Sing," the "black national anthem." Beneath the rehearsals of national entertainment, Hollywood narration, and official representations lie other voices, other stories, subliminal realities. The same self-consciousness concludes the film. Following Brewster's death fall in the Astrodome, the end credits introduce all of the players, but now as members of a circus troupe: "The Greatest Show on Earth proudly presents the cast of *Brewster McCloud.*" The movie casts itself reflexively as a construct and at the same time characterizes that construction as an illusion, like a three-ring circus, whose multiple rings offer competing entertainments that are difficult to watch all at once and are impossible to sequentialize.

Brief moments of reflexivity abound elsewhere. *A Wedding* stages a rich farewell to the old star system and the old studio system when one of America's first movie sweethearts, Lillian Gish, dies and is comically comforted at her bedside by the former Hollywood contract director John Cromwell. Charlie Chaplin's daughter Geraldine, as the wedding coordinator, directs the wedding reception for a Desilu production in which Desi Arnaz Jr. plays the groom. The trick played on the audience with the automobile accident in *A Wedding* works superficially to introduce black humor, but at the same time it consciously quotes the absurd crash that concludes Godard's self-reflexive analysis of movies, moviemakers, art, tradition, and love in *Le Mépris* (1963). It satirically rereads the deception at work in the classical narrative's foreclosure of diegetic disorder. In *Health,* both Dick Cavett and Dinah Shore play themselves as television talk-show hosts. The film opens as a television show identified through the superimposed program card as "Cavett Sho/Health Conv./TAPE ROLL 1/C-22583/ST.PETE BCH.Fla." Reflexivity here reinforces the political message self-consciously and pompously delivered in the film: "The idea that you can merchandize a candidate for high office like breakfast cereal is the ultimate indignity of the democratic process. Nothing is to be gained by manipulating the minds of Americans by shows, slogans and the art of advertising." Before the credit sequence in *Popeye,* an old black-and-white cartoon begins, and Popeye exclaims, "Hey, what is this? One of Bluto's tricks? I'm in the wrong movie!" The film inverts the representation of cartoon reality by self-consciously creating a realistic cartoon. Later during the film when love blooms, Olive Oyl sings "He Needs Me" in perfect parody of the musical genre "I'm in Love with a Wonderful Guy." Reflexivity reinforces and mocks the romance of musical and the heroism of cartoon.

The international casts of characters employed in *A Wedding, Quintet,* and *Prêt-à-Porter* reflexively return the favor of the international art cinema, which frequently borrowed and paid homage to the images of classical Hollywood cinema. Brigitte Fossey worked with Zeffirelli; Bibi Andersson worked for Bergman; Fernando Rey worked for Buñuel; Vittorio Gassman worked with De Sica. Sophia Loren and Marcello Mastroianni in *Prêt-à-Porter* not only quote and reprise the strip scene from De Sica's *Yesterday, Today and Tomorrow* (1964); when Mastroianni whispers into Loren's ear, they also parody the monotone style of retrospective narration in the art-cinema classics *Last Year at Marienbad* and *L'Eclisse* (1962). Like so much of the New Wave cinema from Europe after World War II, Altman's films playfully reference other films, in ways that not only comment on thematic or story elements, but also produce cinematic in-jokes and puns linking films in a comic pastiche.

Director Robert Altman never literally appears in his films, but in *Tanner '88* his surrogate has a continuing role. The Deke Connors character initially appears as the campaign videographer whose first biography—that "neorealistic political film documentary"—of the candidate is a poorly received summary of the candidate's life with pious family appeals and political platitudes that evoke laughter from test audiences. During the first episode of the series, the Tanner character in a spontaneous, energetic, unguarded moment expresses his views and his values to his campaign workers. Sitting on the floor at the edge of the room, Deke, unnoticed by Tanner, captures the whole unrehearsed event in a low-angle shot through a glass coffee table. The resulting film catapults the faltering Tanner campaign into the forefront of the presidential primaries. Its slow zoom in on the refracted, multiple images of Tanner reflects a familiar style of the Altman films, complete with negative audience response: it causes a bar stool audience for the television campaign ad to look at each other and ask, "What the fuck was *that*?" Deke's balding head, stocky build, and Vandyke beard all suggest the Altman visage. And his unorthodox shooting—underwater shots through the legs of sexy women, overhead helicopter shots, mobile shots from wire-mounted cameras—constantly causes him to lose jobs and to seek new employment throughout the series. Get this shot, the ABC reporter yells at him, "or you can thrill cam your ass back to New York." Unorthodox, on the fringe, constantly seeking fresh financing, forever fascinated by new stories and new angles—Deke Connors satirizes the American art-film director.

Introduction of the persona of the director back into the text specifically occurs in *Vincent & Theo.* The narrative strategy of this film compares the life of Vincent van Gogh (Tim Roth) to that of his brother Theo (Paul Rhys) in the few years prior to their deaths in a variety of locations and a variety of interpersonal relationships as one tries to paint and the other tries to sell the paintings. The film pays little direct attention to the paintings themselves, although the narrative variously watches canvases being painted and puts the painter in scenes familiar from famous works by van Gogh; otherwise they pile up in the rooms and the galleries of the mise-en-scène. The film begins with a videotape of the contemporary sale at Christie's in London of a popular van Gogh painting of sunflowers for twenty-two and a half million pounds. The narrative cuts away from the auction when the price reaches fifteen million pounds to present an argument between the two brothers over art, life, religion, and money. The twentieth-century auction continues on the sound track simultaneously with the nineteenth-century sound track as the brothers argue. "I just can't make people buy what they don't want," says Theo. The key question of the film is, How can they support each other, one in the production, the other in the selling of iconoclastic art? The reflexivity here evokes the same question Altman's films have raised for more than thirty years: how to find financial backing to produce innovative art that is unpopular and misunderstood by the general public. Altman has explicitly explored the relationship between these brothers, his own experience, and a motivation for the film:

> I was not going to do a film about painting. I was going to do a film about a failed artist. . . . When you make art, you appear to be different from the people that you're showing it to, because that's why you're doing it. If you showed them everything they knew, they wouldn't be interested, and it wouldn't be art. So, you know, we're perceived as being mad, or eccentric, or crazy . . . the moment we get off the path that is a real, real general road. The minute anybody just stirs out a little bit, it's, there's, that person's crazy. ("Giggle")

## Compositional Reflexivity

*Vincent & Theo* dramatizes the tension between artists and the systems that support or disrupt their work and that distribute their work. Thus indirectly it represents the reflexivity that emerges in Altman's films as a type, rather than as an element of representation, in their arsenal of narrative techniques. Six of the Altman films in particular take as their subject reflexive analyses of the entertainment industry: *Come Back to the 5 & Dime, Jimmy Dean, Jimmy Dean*; *Nashville*; *Buffalo Bill and the Indians, or Sitting Bull's History Lesson*; *Prêt-à-Porter*; *The Player*; and *Kansas City*. These films display a reflexive stance toward the entertainment industry generally and the film industry in particular. They all present self-conscious indictments against show business as accessories to the violence and alienation of modern life. But the extent to which this reflexiveness works a critique on the Hollywood system has always been ambiguous. Early reactions to Altman's films expressed reservations about the politics of these films, and numerous critics of *The Player,* in the wake of its success, restated this skepticism about the integrity of Altman's vaunted experimentalism and independence. Steve Neale complained in 1976 that although "certain rhetorical strategies may to some extent mark the discourse as discourse, separate it from plot and diegesis in such a way that devices may appear unmotivated, 'self-conscious' or 'subjective' . . . this is not to say that the meta-discourse reveals its own operations . . . : There is no other discourse acknowledged *within the text* that can challenge its truth" ("New Hollywood" 121). Leonard Quart and Alissa Quart in 1992 charged that with *The Player,* "Altman has become a gifted, mainstream commercial director" (62), and Harvey Greenberg describes this suspicion as Altman's "seeking after a long fall from grace, to himself become a player in the industry establishment by the very act of debunking it" (30).

The critical situation here involves the debate about whether or not art-cinema products are "engaged" or "complicit" in their attitudes toward the entertainment industry. One level of this argument debates whether audiences are free to critique or be coerced by the ideology of the mass media, whether audiences are critical, active viewers and listeners rather than gullible voyeurs easily manipulated by the media. Another perspective assumes that because media reality is unreal, mediated, a simulacrum, always an ideological construct, politically engaged criticism and artistic practice will work to reveal the coercive and debilitating effects of mainstream discourse. Following the political concerns for Brechtian distanciation, this work "is meant as a critique of a narcotic, mystifying, politically demobilizing art which offers the public its own fantasies about how things are rather than a radical critique of those fantasies" (Stam 9–10). The deconstructive work of Altman's films, then, may be only partial, because it participates in the very reality it reveals as spectacle; it assumes a story reality, albeit more complex in its unspoken connections and meanings, without shattering the illusion to capture Altman and crew at work.

This debate demonstrates the ongoing vitality of a poetics that would substitute at the end of the century political critique for organic unity as an aesthetic yardstick employed for measuring "success" in a text. It nevertheless reveals particular aspects of the reflexive quality in the

Altman films. Thus critical interpretations can chart the extent to which these films manipulate "cinematic realism," the extent to which their practice variously displays a "radical surface" or fails to "destroy the image" or to alienate the popular audience. Meanwhile, Altman himself has said variously that the critics "don't get it" or "the audience is the enemy" or "I'm criticizing myself." Schatz argues that Altman's films work in two dimensions: they "come close to that synthesis of classical mythmaking and modernist demystification, creating films which can be read as popular storytelling even as they create a narrative subtext which, at least for those viewers responsive to their modernist impulses, call into question the nature of classical narration and the ideology that it reinforces" (*Old Hollywood* 244).

*The Player* suggests that "Robert Altman" after all constitutes the liberal, not the radical, text, the permitted—even necessary—subjectivity that interrogates the dominant discourse of the film industry as an "object of study" rather than an ideological practice to be exposed. The practice of the Altman films is not Godardian materialist cinema but Felliniesque art cinema. Bruce Kawin distinguishes among narrative reflexivity, authorial self-consciousness, and systematic self-consciousness (*Mind* 19–20). He calls attention to the levels of distinction among films that mirror themselves internally, films that examine the awareness of the artist's creative process, and films that explore the nature of textuality in their awareness of themselves (for instance, Bergman's light of projectors and the surfaces of screens in *Persona,* Truffaut's self-consciousness of directing in *Day for Night,* and the aggressive making of meaning by camera movement in *Wavelength,* 1967). Rather than a self-consciousness that reflects the movieness of the films themselves, Altman's films develop a reflexivity that critiques the world of mass media and the effects of "the show business." Their fictions comment on the entertainment-making business, the system of mass-media storytelling, their constructions of reality, and the effects of those constructions on social subjectivity. Reflexive stories want to examine the process of storytelling rather than tell other stories and may be considered criticism of the ideology of narrative teleology itself. Altman's reflexive films more particularly examine popular stories as commercial products that emerge from and shape cultural identity.

As a form of American art cinema, Altman's films clearly examine the expectations of classical narrative cinema, the nature of its stories and its storied worlds, and the terms of its readability. Their narrative discontinuities and stylistic lyricism as well as their broken forms of subjectivity critically call attention to the formal and thematic commitments of Hollywood to coherence and closure. Even though Altman's films rarely break the dramatic illusion sufficiently to indicate the ways that the audience, too, is manipulated, determined, troubled by the same economic forces of the show business that distort the lives of their characters and produce the cinematic illusion of their reality, the emotional instability of the characters in these reflexive films, their self-doubts, their double personalities, are intimately involved in their economic relationships with society, particularly their jobs as mass-media entertainers. Their difficulties of interpersonal communication and social action derive from the manipulation of writers, managers, and producers of mass-media entertainment. As Patricia Waugh describes the reflexive novel, "Metafiction thus converts what it sees as the negative values of outworn literary conventions into the basis of a potentially constructive social criticism" (11). Most of Altman's films construct subjects that convey a celebration of characters who must live within an isolating, threatening, or confusing world, and they experiment with film forms that could adequately contain that vision. The films consistently demonstrate a critical irreverence for traditional film genres and styles and thus appear self-consciously to reconstruct them with new designs. They clearly establish a self-conscious style of inverted stereotypes, improvisatory dialogue, graceful zooms and pans, vibrant and moody color, and unorthodox narrative structures.

## Entertainment as Metaphor

Altman has asserted that "the great film has never been made," because, he says,

> I don't think we've found a format for movies yet. I think we're still imitating literature and theater. I don't believe film should be limited to photographing people talking. Or walking from a car into a building, the kind of stuff we do. It can be more abstract, impressionistic, less linear. Music changes form all the time. I think if you can establish mood with a film, it might have more impact than anything we've done, just a mood. (quoted in Holdenfield 31)

The irreverence and self-consciousness about form in this theory and practice similarly appear in the films' thematic fascination with the conflicts between fantasy and practicality, dreamers and realists, independence and community, risk and belief, freedom and structure. Connie Bryne and William Lopez claim that "the acceptance of multilayered face value, the openness to unreasonable experience, the celebration of non-dialectical, non-motivational non-resolution comprise the essence of Altman's philosophical realism" (23). In this context, *Nashville* combines both a story and a narrative form that conveys again those paradoxes of contradictory and ambiguous personalities operating within a many-faceted reality whose significance and connections are forever subliminal. It energetically fuses the infectious sound, humor, and somber inevitability of the world of country-western music with a form as fluid as its music and as complex as the celebration and criticism that constitute its theme. Altman has described the city of Nashville as "the new Hollywood," by which he means it is the entertainment capital of a mass-media industry where "instant stars, instant music, and instant politicians" distill many of contemporary Americans' fears, desires, and values. Just as Nathanael West bleakly painted the "old" Hollywood of the 1930s in *Day of the Locust,* Altman has made "a metaphor for my personal view of society" (quoted in Gardner 26). And just as Preston Sturges used the role of a director to reflect ambiguously upon that earlier Hollywood in *Sullivan's Travels* (1942), Altman self-consciously uses the role of a television documentary maker to assess the creators of a modern mass media in *Nashville.*

Kermit Moyer argues that "Altman perceives a world in which imagination (linked to innocence and belief) and convention (linked to cynicism and doubt) perennially battle over the structure of reality" (12). This perspective permeates *Nashville.* The film portrays the lives of people involved in the business of artistic invention. It explores how the medium of country music expresses liberating acts of imagination, standing over against life's realities, and how that medium at the same

The movie as advertising for the record album *(Nashville).*

time imposes upon the artist-entertainer a set of conventions as rigorous and as threatening to the sufficiency of invention as any other. The film's digressive art-cinema narrative establishes a metaphor for this perception with two sets of oppositions—between the glittering public and the bleak private lives of the Nashville musicians, and between the insiders of the Nashville music scene and the outsiders, the audiences, who only watch that scene.

At the heart of these oppositions lies a central and informing aspect of the film's metaphor—death, as both a reality of life and an impetus to life's inventions. Altman asserts: "All my films deal with the same thing: striving, socially and culturally, to stay alive. And once any system succeeds, it becomes its own worse enemy" (quoted in Williamson 55). But the narrative gives one more turn of the screw to the tension between a necessary imagination and a threatening reality by also including the director's point of view as a mass-media entertainer within the frame of the reality-making camera. The narrative recounts the events of five days that culminate in the shooting of country music star Barbara Jean, but the media motif of the infranarrative, "in the sense of a visual plot unfolding concurrently with a verbal one" (Dick 124), is presented in such a way as to create a metanarrative that comments on both the kinds of sensibilities contained within the film and the kinds that produced the film. *Nashville* is an ominous film, as it depicts both invention and death as commodities of the media industry.

The narrative focuses this metaphor centrally on the distinction between the public and private worlds of nearly all the characters who make up the Nashville invention "system," and the distinction is seldom positive. Delbert (Ned Beatty), the "good old boy" who handles public relations for country music star Haven Hamilton (Henry Gibson), and his wife Linnea (Lily Tomlin), who sings gospel with the black choir from Fisk University, live together in a visually sterile upper-middle-class tract home, where Linnea communicates lovingly with their two deaf sons in the sign language that Delbert has never bothered to learn. The big star Hamilton, with his wife and son, is always onstage, always signing autographs, always conscious of the cameras—whether at the Grand Ole Opry, the airport, or the very public lawn of his home. Tom (Keith Carradine), Bill (Allan Nicholls), and Mary (Christina Raines), who make up a folk-rock trio that sings in the clubs in town, inhabit motel rooms whose clutter of clothes, equipment, food, and bottles characterizes the chaos of their personal relationships. Sueleen (Gwen Welles), the airport waitress whose lunch counter is her stage and its customers her audience, has a private world that consists only of a mirror in front of which she practices her impossibly bad singing. Albuquerque (Barbara Harris) finds a public stage wherever she can and privately runs from her husband and sleeps in abandoned cars. Barbara Jean (Ronee Blakley), the female star, and her husband-manager Barnett (Allen Garfield) are, like Haven, always on the stage or else alone in the public hospital that fills so much of the space in the movie.

The film establishes an opposition between the brilliant, fast-paced public world of Nashville entertainment at all levels—from Opry stage to airport cafe—and the private worlds that convey entrapment, homelessness, emptiness, chaos, insensitivity, and superficiality. The narrative's quick-cutting interspersal of these worlds conveys the sense of their mutual interchangeability and interdependence under the dominance of the music that constantly fills the sound track and comments on the lives of the performers. Barbara Jean laments, "How long must I pay these dues?" Tommy Brown (Timothy Brown) wonders, "If the bluebird flies then why can't I?" Linnea in one poignant moment teaches her deaf children to sing in sign. And throughout, the film echoes the theme song, which accepts the lack of freedom.

The other informing set of oppositions in the film's metaphor is that between insiders, characters actually involved in the business of invention, and outsiders, the strange heterogeneous cast of characters who constitute an audience for the insiders and whose presence defines the conflicting significance of the music world. Two of them, the Tricycle Man (Jeff Goldblum) and Opal (Geraldine Chaplin), the self-identified BBC reporter, particularly characterize the film's reflexivity. Among the others, Kelly (Scott Glenn), the Vietnam veteran, is the adoring Barbara Jean fan for whom the spell of her musical invention obliterates the memory of war such that he describes Vietnam simply as "kinda hot and wet." Sueleen's black friend Wade (Robert DoQui), on the other hand, speaks with the cynical clarity of jealousy and desire. He indicates how much he believes success has cost black singer Tommy Brown when he calls Brown an "Oreo cookie." And trying to convince her to go with him to Detroit, he tells Sueleen the painful truth about her singing after her strip at the political smoker: "They gonna tear your heart out. They gonna walk on your soul. They gonna use you!" Hal Phillip Walker's political advance man, Triplette (Michael Murphy), coldly manipulates the musicians by appealing to their desires and fears; he bribes Sueleen to finish her strip with the promise of a singing spot with Barbara Jean at the political rally. He promises Haven a gubernatorial endorsement for his participation. He turns Barbara Jean's collapse to his advantage and then threatens to destroy her reputation if she fails to take part in the rally. And at the same time, he calls their music "redneck crapola." To these outsiders Nashville's inventions represent musical escape, viciousness, or money.

The causal coherence of classical narrative realism succumbs to the subliminal coherence of a multifaceted reality. Art-cinema narration demands a reading strategy that mines unspoken depths for the motives, understandings, and events that connect surface representations. Here the usually romantic world of the musical (potentially the make-believe world of Nashville music) merges into the harshness of death and violence. The repeated references to weapons and killing and the continual depiction of guns throughout the film create a metaphoric, infranarrative structure that provides the context for the shooting that concludes the film. Haven Hamilton sings about the rightness of America, confirmed by its two hundredth birthday, and celebrates the national history of wars. Tom hostilely asks the uniformed Kelly, "Kill anybody today?" The Tennessee Twirlers greet Barbara Jean at the airport twirling white M-1 rifles instead of batons. A security guard calmly displays his service revolver to nurses in the hospital and talks about killing people in self-defense. The pistol-packing Lady Pearl (Barbara Baxley) drunkenly mourns the assassinated "Kennedy boys" and recalls the blood splattered on Jackie Kennedy's pink suit in Dallas. The narrative introduces most of its characters as they enter the airport at the beginning of the film behind a sign that reads reflexively, "All persons entering concourse are screened . . . for weapons." And Wade's assertion, "They gonna kill you in this town," reverberates across the film. The musicians flee from it, Mr. Green (Keenan Wynn) lives it, and Kenny (David Hayward) is increasingly bewildered and confused as he stumbles into the hostility, violence, and death of Nashville.

These two outsiders, Kenny and Mr. Green, convey the central aspect of the film's metaphor. Mr. Green's wife, Martha, lies dying through the whole film in a hospital room on the same floor where Barbara Jean is recuperating from her collapse. And Mr. Green, as he lives his wife's dying, stands at the furthest remove from the message of the music. For him the Nashville entertainment world, represented in its most bizarre fashion by his niece, the groupie L.A. Joan (Shelley Duvall), cruelly refuses to respect the reality of Martha's death.

Kenny, on the other hand, is attracted to the energy, the music, the stars of Nashville, and he is bewildered by them. Significantly, he seems to be the only character in town by accident. His car, pointing in the direction opposite the flow of traffic entering the city, breaks down in the big freeway scene that Opal sees as important for her documentary: "All these Americans smashing into each other." Kenny's contradictory assertion, then denial, of his desire to be a musician hints at his reasons for leaving town, and his violin case carries the major options of the film, a fiddle and a pistol. Opal asserts at one point that people like Lady Pearl who carry guns "stimulate the innocents who eventually pull the trigger." Her observation foreshadows Kenny's act but the narrative underlines the typical simplicity of her remark by the fact of "innocent" Kenny's pistol.

The music and the environment provide sufficient stimulation for him, however. Albuquerque, the first person he meets, is being chased by her husband, Star (Bert Remsen), who tells Kenny he looks like a dirty draft dodger. He is knocked down by the punch Wade throws at Tommy Brown in the Picking Parlor. The camera isolates him in the same frame with Hal Phillip Walker's sound truck proclaiming, "If there's any cleaning up to do, we're going to have to do it ourselves." As Connie White (Karen Black) sings lyrics that express inner darkness, the camera locks in a tight low-angle close-up on Kenny's face. After a tense, impatient telephone conversation with his overprotective and importunate mother (to whom he says "I love you" only after he breaks the connection), the camera watches him again in extreme low-angle close-up as he listens to Barbara Jean sing, "I want to walk away from this battleground." Seconds later, as she sings,

> You've got your own private world,
> I wouldn't have it no other way,
> But lately you've been hiding your blues,
> Pretending what you say,

the narrative again looks in close-up at Kenny's confused face. As the film approaches its climax, Kenny chases after the hysterical Mr. Green, who runs from his wife's burial to the rally in order to demand respect for the dead, and there Kenny shoots Barbara Jean. Deceit, violence, and finally death inform his relationship as an outsider to the world of Nashville.

Moreover, on the inside, Barbara Jean, with her white dress, jet-black hair, and scarlet lips, appears doomed from the beginning. "I'm tired of playing," she tells Barnett. "It's that careless disrespect I can't stand no more," she sings. The white flowers that Barnett believes to mean bad luck, to be "too funereal," and that constantly surround her become increasingly ominous symbols of death. The scene of her lying in the hospital room filled with flowers echoes fully the shot of Paul's dead wife in *Last Tango in Paris* (1972). Significantly, Faulkner's violent and death-filled novel *Light in August* lies open on her bed and *As I Lay Dying* lies on the bedside table as she begins to break down in the hospital, and the black clouds that ominously block the sun before her breakdown at Opryland foreshadow the clouds that darken the sky as she stands before a stark black-and-white background singing a song of escape and nostalgia about her parents and her youth just before she is shot.

Viewers conditioned to employ the reading strategies required for constructing meaning in classical narrative cinema fault the conclusion of this film because Barbara Jean's shooting seems unmotivated. But the narrative asks to be read more in terms of Altman's sense of subliminal reality, events connected not explicitly or causally, but by implication and suggestion. The shooting aptly summarizes the predominant characteristic, the mood, of *Nashville*'s metaphor. Death resides in the private relationships of these very public people, and death separates the lives of these insiders, the inventors and entertainers, from those outsiders who live with death, who recognize it, who cause it. Kenny shoots Barbara Jean to free her from a love affair that has become "this hurtin' match that ain't no good," or because she represents the "careless disrespect" that so destroys Mr. Green, or because Barbara Jean has touched the guilt and fears of his own life as she sings about loving her parents, or perhaps because she represents his own mother. Altman has said of the shooting:

> The reason we look for plots and collusions is that we are looking for a reason that computes. . . . We invented money, we invented values . . . we've invented this society, we've invented the buildings, we've invented the murders . . . , we've done the whole thing, and we demand logic, but it doesn't necessarily have to be there. (quoted in Bryne and Lopez 25)

The audience confronted not by real violence but by movie violence struggles to invent sense in an act that the movie and Altman insist is "senseless." The unmotivated action of the story parallels its lack of reason in the culture.

Similarly, the Nashville musicians indicate a need for meaning, and as they struggle to work out imaginative visions of themselves, their songs reflexively affirm the act of invention, and predominantly with lyrics composed by the actors themselves. Haven exhorts his audiences, in the hit song that made him famous, to rise above life's adversities and "keep a-goin'!" Barbara Jean's music constantly reveals the necessity of song:

> When I feel my life perishing like waves upon the sand
> With nothing to replace it but invention,
> So I make my rhymes and I sing my songs,
> Still they don't understand;
> To make them laugh was never my intention.

She sings explicitly, "Writing it down sorta makes me feel better, keeps me away from them blues." But her first song, the Protestant hymn "In the Garden," most clearly expresses the satisfaction of life's need through joyous song, and here the melody is inspired by the music of the voice of Jesus. This moment of peace in the hospital chapel is brief, but the words of the hymn suggest the importance of the musician's song. When she experiences times of distress, Jesus' voice sings to her. On stage, however, Barbara Jean cannot sing hymns, because her musical invention must entertain and sell.

Kurt Vonnegut Jr., in his review of *Nashville,* catches much of Altman's meaning, saying that our culture is a "pure and recent invention, inspired by money or power or fame. . . . And those who partake of that culture, especially the weak or simpleminded, feel compelled to invent personalities as novel and arbitrary and commercial as the inventions with which they hope to harmonize" (103). The narrative suggests that this danger lies in the nature of the mass media themselves. In a world where imaginative invention might exist only precariously in art, the exploitation, the hypocrisy, and the commerciality that constitute the vehicle, the industry, of mass art also constitute its necessity. *Nashville* conveys a world where art is made possible and necessitated and endangered by its own mode of existence.

But the film is yet more reflexive because, as Altman has pointed out, *Nashville* is "my view—my distorted view—of the culture" (quoted in Wicker, *Nashville* 1). Even as the narration significantly complicates the story structure in the film, it has framed that structure with viewpoints that are at once external to its subject as observers of it and internal to that subject by virtue of their impetus to observation. *Nashville* not only conveys structures of subliminal connectedness; it successfully realizes within the world of the film a self-referential point of view that is indige-

"This hurtin' match, it ain't no good" *(Nashville).*

nous both to the context of the *Nashville* metaphor and to the values it seems to ascribe to the contemporary world of mass-media entertainment. The outsiders serve not only to widen the parameters of insider/outsider oppositions in the film but also to characterize a media self-consciousness and to make the film more visible as a work of mass media.

What had hitherto been only rather cute self-conscious concerns to make the audience aware of the movieness in Altman's movies here seriously informs the entire film. One of the more striking visual moments of self-reference in *Nashville* is that warning sign at the airport, for the film does indeed screen its characters for weapons. The complex collage of twenty-four characters and the unique eight-track sound of the film work in themselves to render the medium visible. Additionally, the quasi-documentary quality of the film significantly emphasizes the societal metaphor Altman has described and calls attention to itself as media investigation. As Strother Purdy notes, "Most documentaries bring the act of filming, and the interviews that accompany it, right out into the open, and thus are highly visible films" (253).

In this film the narrative works more seriously to intertwine the story, its medium, and its maker. It is not only humorous to see Elliott Gould and Julie Christie enter the film playing themselves as stars (cuing perhaps within the documentary-story a contrast of "hippie" stars of Hollywood with the country-western stars of the "people"); their presence also evokes the play that is going on (Haven Hamilton is also Henry Gibson; Connie White is also Karen Black) and recalls earlier Altman movies in which they appeared (*MASH, McCabe & Mrs. Miller, The Long Goodbye,* and *California Split*). Indeed, when Haven remembers that Julie Christie once won an Academy Award, the audience may remember her award nomination for best actress as Mrs. Constance Miller. Gould even states that he is in Nashville to promote a movie, not to make one. The appearance of Christie and Gould further reminds us of Altman's tendency over the years to work, like Ingmar Bergman, with a repertory company of actors. Furthermore, the explicit reference to Bergman in the film connects with observations by Altman outside and with the character of the Tricycle Man inside the film. Altman has said he would "rather be Ingmar Bergman than George Roy Hill" (quoted in Holdenfield 31), and Opal observes in *Nashville* that Haven's party is "pure, unadulterated Bergman." But when she adds, "Of course the people are all wrong for Bergman," this narrative self-consciously evaluates its subject and one of its media auteurs.

The ubiquitous appearance of the Tricycle Man perhaps not too ingeniously suggests a reference to the director also in this strange, silent role. Bergman, in a famous passage, refers to himself as a magician:

> I remind myself with childish excitement that I am really a conjurer, since cinematography is based on deception of human eye. . . . When I show a film I am guilty of deceit. I use an apparatus which is constructed to take advantage of a certain human weakness, an apparatus with which I can sway my audience in a highly emotional manner—make them laugh, scream with fright, smile, believe in fairy stories, become indignant, feel shocked, charmed, deeply moved or perhaps yawn with boredom. Thus I am either an imposter or, when the audience is willing to be taken in, a conjurer. (*Screenplays* 15)

The Tricycle Man constantly performs sleight-of-hand magic in the film; moreover, he regularly serves as the bridge connecting one scene with another. He is also absolutely enthralled and delighted by the Nashville scene and looks around with an eagerness that characterizes both the adoration of a fan on pilgrimage to the country-western mecca and the narrative's frenetic editing and slow, enrapturing zooms on performing stars. The Tricycle Man's enthusiasm reflects, as does the soldier Kelly's, the emotional attraction to country music that Altman noted when he observed that Opryland is "run like a church" and that the film conveys in its positive depiction of the music and its singers. The childish delight of the conjurer motivates the visual energy and fun of the film.

But it also projects the imposter in the role of Opal, who more than any other character serves to tie scenes together and to reflect on the meaning of those scenes. She incisively comments on the nature of guns and violence in Nashville. She turns a striking visual contrast between

Nashville churches and a junk car lot into nonsense as she rhapsodizes over this "graveyard" against the sound of church bells. She callously interrupts Haven's son Buddy, whom she has enticed into singing his only musical composition, to fawn over Elliott Gould. And she literally reveals herself to be an imposter when she calls the BBC the "British Broadcasting Company" (rather like, as one reviewer noted, calling TWA Transworld Airplanes). She is enthralled by Nashville, like Kelly; she is perceptive and accurate about Nashville, like Wade; she is cruel and exploitative, like Triplette. And Altman makes the larger parallel explicit. Her role "was supposed to represent us . . . outsiders, full of bullshit. I don't know anything more about Nashville than she did" (quoted in Viertel and Walker 56). As the figure most troublesome to reviewers, Opal is an outsider, an English foreigner who provides significant insight into the violence and waste of American society, but the fact that she too is a media personality, a filmmaker, establishes her as a part of the culture that she observes and turns her pseudoliberal, intellectual theorizing into self-parody.

The director, like the Tricycle Man and Opal, is an outsider, but like both observer and observed, the subject and the object of this film. The narrative of the film reflects the sincere, often joyful, often empty lives of the Nashville entertainers; the metaphoric narrative structure of weapons and aggression characterizes those lives, but at another level that characterization is extended not just to those insiders Haven and Barbara Jean and Barnett and Delbert, but to the mass-media mode of their entertainment. *Nashville* is not Altman's *8½* or *Day for Night* or *Sullivan's Travels,* all films about directors and making movies, for the narrative calls attention to the moviemaker as a media-man shooting documentary-like entertainment, like Opal, as exploiter. The film at this level focuses on music and movies as part of the contemporary media environment.

Nashville is the recording capital of the world, where records are on sale even in the airport. The Goo-Goo Candy Company presents the Grand Ole Opry sequence in the film, complete with commercials and a television-style shot of the sponsor's logo. Radio and television call letters line the walls of the auto race track. A television commentator announces Barbara Jean's arrival at the beginning of the film and speaks directly to the viewer as television audience. People commonly communicate by loudspeakers, radio, and telephones. Microphones and photographers are everywhere, and the viewer as audience is frequently photographed by cameramen in the background. Communication by these devices often provides scene-to-scene transition: the narrative cuts back and forth between Connie White's Opry performance and the hospital room where Barbara Jean and Barnett listen to that performance on radio. The telephone conversation between Triplette and the bartender setting up the smoker establishes the editing link between Delbert's home and the bar where Sueleen is auditioning. And the recorded voice of Hal Phillip Walker broadcast through a roving sound truck conveys the viewer's only perception of the presidential candidate. Opal even carries her tape recorder to bed. Tom seduces women with his songs and makes love to them against the background tape recordings of his own music. In one ultimately media-laden shot, he gets out of bed as the tape ends and telephones another woman while *The Electric Company* plays on television.

The mass media are everywhere as pervasive in *Nashville* as the motif of guns and violence. Bryne and Lopez have described the film as "a media event about media events and mediated non-events. *Nashville* is about our Total Media Surround in which ideas are produced and disseminated at such a high rate that a superstructure of mass consciousness is created which transcends interpersonal or personally assimilable communications" (23). The film depicts the values of religion, politics, and art within the context of entertainment, and entertainment is subsumed under the manipulative conventions of the media. The credit scenes of the movie introduce us to a presidential candidate who is a sound truck, to an ominous Haven Hamilton with red-and-white hair and blue headphones who sings patriotism into a dark sound booth, and to a choir shouting they believe in Jesus to a large microphone inside a glass-walled studio. The narrative center of the film celebrates a belief in Jesus, the idealism of politics and patriotism, and the importance of artistic invention at the same time that it criticizes the media that communicate and potentially replace those values. Lady Pearl sadly recalls her enthusiasm and dedicated work for the Kennedys while Triplette, with bribes and threats, lines up musicians for his candidate Hal Phillip Walker, presidential nominee of the Replacement Party.

Less obvious than the sense of eroded political values is the treatment of religion. The five-day structure of *Nashville* ironically centers on Sunday, which seems ostensibly to represent a climax of peace and hope, or even the still center around which swirl the politics, entertainment, and death in the film. The camera picks out major characters humbly singing hymns with the choirs or congregations of various Nashville churches. And in the simple white hospital chapel, Barbara Jean sings her first and most moving song, "In the Garden," a moment that represents her greatest freedom from the pressures of the music business. But this moment is fleeting; the narrative satirically juxtaposes the close-up profile of the superstud Tom on Saturday night with a brilliant stained-glass Jesus to open the sequence that finally concludes with the sound of a siren and the sound truck candidate talking about the untaxed multimillion-dollar income of American churches. Connie White's lyrics reflect the significance of this Nashville world as they express a desire for salvation and a loss of faith. The choir whose members begin the film affirming their belief in Jesus close the film singing the cynical popular hit that laments the loss of freedom and asserts indifference to that loss.

This kind of value displacement characterizes the film's metaphor, which begins with the words "And now after years in the making, Robert Altman presents Nashville." In its opening moment the film critiques the developing synergies among entertainment products in the mass media. What follows is a very loud television commercial, not for the movie, but literally for the movie's sound-track album. The movie itself, then, is introduced merely as the background and promotional motivation for the album, which significantly omits all of the religious music in the film. Although this opening sequence captures the energy and excitement so infectious in the film, this media consciousness has become serious and questioning by the concluding sequence. The backdrop for the rally is Nashville's Parthenon, a typical bit of American pseudoculture, tightly flanked on both sides by the huge equipment vans of WSM-TV, WNGE-TV, and WEND-TV. Overhead, the Goodyear blimp flashes ads for Hal Phillip Walker. On the grass a television set shows ABC television newsman Howard K. Smith as himself doing a news commentary on Walker, and boxing the whole square is the narrative's camera-crane vantage point. Keyssar points out that "throughout the final sequence of *Nashville,* Altman remarks the peculiar transparency of our recent history by filming someone photographing each sordid gesture. . . . Our memories of John Kennedy's assassination, of the Vietnam war, of the Watergate hearings, are inseparable from our recollections of seeing photographs, of watching televised projections of these events" (167).

The constant repetition of cameras shooting at everything in sight throughout the film climaxes with a long zoom in from the crane position through the columns of the Parthenon on the car carrying Walker, a sighting of the telescope on the candidate, and the stage is set for a big media event: the choir, the politicians, the musicians, and a shooting.

Two of the most telling shots about the film's media attitude follow the shooting of Barbara Jean: a shot of Opal pushing her way through the crowd yelling, "Can you please tell me what happened?" and a shot of the crowd and a man standing in the foreground with a movie camera mounted on his shoulder, a bored cameraman who has shot it all waiting for further action to shoot.

In his review of *Nashville,* Kurt Vonnegut Jr. writes that for him at one time "all cultures seemed riddled with absurdities when viewed by outsiders seeking easy laughs or reasons for condemnations. This left me in poor condition to criticize any culture, including my own. And I criticize my own now because it has become so dangerous" (103). His review links his personal vision about contemporary society, expressed just prior to the film in his novel *Breakfast of Champions,* with Altman's film. The film, too, has linked *Nashville* to Vonnegut, whom Altman calls his favorite author. In the film, the country-western musician Merle Kilgore plays himself but under the name of Trout, and the linking of his real and movie names—Kilgore and Trout—creates the name of Vonnegut's favorite novelist, the central character in *Breakfast of Champions.* This punning allusion to the novel—which at one time Altman considered adapting for the screen—is significant, for there the self-conscious novelist includes himself in his indictment of the danger in contemporary society:

> People were doing their best to live like people invented in story books. This was the reason Americans shot each other so often: it was a convenient literary device for ending short stories and books. . . . Once I understood what was making America such a dangerous, unhappy nation of people who had nothing to do with real life, I resolved to shun storytelling. (209–10)

While Vonnegut discovers this disturbing relationship between the actions of people and the shape of traditional fiction, *Nashville* discovers a disturbing relationship between a deathwardness in the culture and the tendency of the mass media to promote death through their conventionalizing and exploitation of life. The movie studies both the necessity of invention and the trap it becomes. The sympathy it projects for characters like Barbara Jean is sympathy for entertainers, but the hostility it projects for outsiders like Opal is also directed at the exploitative image makers of the media. The fractured art-cinema narration of *Nashville* both reflects a sense of the disconnectedness of contemporary life and implicates the entertainment industry in that alienation.

Since *MASH,* Altman's films have conveyed both the insecurity of their central, generally male, characters and a reflexivity whose defiant experimentalism parallels their reaction against classical discourse. Altman says about *The Player* that, as with *MASH,* its "structure is like a snail; it turns back into itself like a fantail shrimp; it reflects itself" (Keogh 13). Both films represent the emptiness of moral values in the contemporary culture but in particular the culture of the moviemaking industry. Altman says of *The Player*: "Amorality is what we're talking about, certainly in Hollywood. . . . Whatever makes money, turns a profit in a short period of time is all they are interested in, and they seem to be free of any guilt in connection with that. . . . The amorality of it is something indigenous to it; it's what it's about" *(The Player).* The experimental reflexivity of these films also recounts the anxieties of masculinity. They set arrogant, powerful men like Triplette in *Nashville* against the abusive insecurity of Barnett, the murderous self-confidence of the mining company against the ineffectual gambler in *McCabe,* the figure of the law against its unscrupulous, unfaithful, and clownish subversion by the motorcycle cop in *Short Cuts.* "A woman's not going to think very much of a man if she goes into business with him," says McCabe, revealing the extent to which a sense of the masculine motivates behavior that seeks to control the image of women.

This trajectory of reflexivity links troubled masculinity, problematic representations of women, and reflexive play with the rules of classical narrative. *Come Back to the 5 & Dime, Jimmy Dean, Jimmy Dean,* for instance, explicitly interrogates the relationship among the representation of women as objects of desire, the representation of insecure masculinity, and the representation of Hollywood as the purveyor of disabling images of gender roles. The film, like so many of Altman's movies, examines the false fronts that abound in this personal identity: Juanita's religious blindness, Sissy's rubber breasts, Joe's masculinity, the replica Mona has built as a shrine to the false front of the set of the film *Giant,* and indeed the front half of the film's set design. Like *Nashville, Buffalo Bill and the Indians, The Player, Prêt-à-Porter,* and *Kansas City, Jimmy Dean* depicts the impact of the entertainment media upon the lives of the producers, the stars, and their audiences. The phallocentric culture has defined places of individuality before the ideal image of James Dean as alienating images constructed in the cinematic mirror, as "just a front . . . , a false front." "It *is* real, just deceiving to the eye, that's all. . . . That's the way they do things in Hollywood." *Jimmy Dean* attacks the false facades of the movies and the illusory self-images they engender.

Hostility toward the relationship between entertainment and illusion motivated the very first Altman film, a 1957 documentary on the image of James Dean, and thematically structures the later reflexive work—in Altman's words, "to undo this God thing, to find out the truth. I don't like the idea of superstars—they're an excuse for the masses not to think about their own problem" (quoted in Allen 28). In these films, deception, illusion, and idolatry reflexively characterize the impact of the media upon the self.

## Show Business History

*Buffalo Bill and the Indians* even more closely examines the concept of stars in relation to a sense of self, of social identity, and the entertainment industry. The film's story projects a rich density of fact and fiction, of history, legend, and personal vision. Its recounting of Buffalo Bill remythologizes the legendary figure whose life by the age of forty had already been transmuted into the pages of western hagiography and inaugurated the reign of the cowboy hero. The film describes William F. Cody at a time when his legend was beginning to precede and determine his reality and when, no longer just the dime-novel hero, he was rapidly becoming a show business star. Cody's biographers reveal a man incredibly enmeshed in a confusion of staged personalities and frontier realities. During the Sioux Wars of 1876, for instance, Buffalo Bill (while wearing the stage costume for his role back in Chicago in the play *Scouts of the Plains*) killed and scalped Chief Yellow Hand within the month following Custer's death at the Little Big Horn. The film shows a man caught between a weak sense of his personal identity and the demands of an increasingly successful and rigid media personality.

Where *Nashville* portrays the bleak symbiosis between the private personalities of Nashville entertainers and modern mass-media production systems, *Buffalo Bill* depicts the western hero in the service of that same mass-media reality and again describes the loss of human spirit that accompanies the business of packaging stars for sale to an audience. The film enlarges Henry Nash Smith's understanding of Buffalo Bill: "The persona created by the writers of popular fiction was so accurate an expression of the demands of the popular imagination that it proved powerful enough to shape an actual man in its own image" (114). The film posits Buffalo Bill as an amalgam of Cody himself, the dime-novel writers, and the show business producers and publicists as well. Its subject is as much these image makers as it is William F. Cody, and as it retells episodes in the life of this hero, the film's self-reflexive framing of the tale makes clear the extent to which the shapers of this persona now include Paul Newman, Robert Altman, and Dino De Laurentiis.

The film once again employs the episodic format of art-cinema narration and structures this vision through a metaphoric pattern of parallel and mutually reinforcing conflicts. It sets these conflicts in 1885, when Cody was thirty-nine, a heavily coded age of transition in our culture, and a time of literal transition for the Cody of history and the development of Buffalo Bill's Wild West. By 1869, when Cody was only twenty-three, he had earned a small part in history as a scout for the Fifth Cavalry in the decisive battle against the Cheyenne in the Battle of Summit Springs. More significantly, perhaps, Ned Buntline (Edward Zane Carroll Judson) began in 1869 the legendary enshrinement of Cody with his serial publication in the *New York Weekly* of *Buffalo Bill, King of the Border Men,* wherein he publicized Cody's name but based his story on the older dime-novel tradition of Daniel Boone and Kit Carson. And in 1885, the last year of his life, Buntline published his last of only four Buffalo Bill dime novels, his small inauguration of a series ultimately to comprise more than seventeen hundred original and reprinted titles. In 1885, Prentiss Ingraham began to produce an average of two Buffalo Bill dime novels a year. He would eventually produce more than two hundred titles in the process of making Buffalo Bill the greatest hero of the dime-novel industry.

Cody had spent the ten years between 1872 and 1883 playing himself on eastern stages and fighting Indians on the western plains. He had attempted a traveling western show for one disastrous season in 1883 and in 1884 entered into partnership with the masterful producer Nate Salsbury, who, aided by the public relations know-how of an old Cody retainer and admirer, "Arizona John" Burke, began to build "The Wild West or Life among the Red Men and the Road Agents of the Plains and Prairies—a Equine Dramatic Exposition on Grass or under Canvas of the Adventures of Frontiersmen and Cowboys" into the prototype of the movie western. In 1885 Annie Oakley, the famous markswoman, joined the show, as did for a few months Chief Sitting Bull, against whom the army had fought at the Little Big Horn in 1876 and who would be killed in the events culminating in the massacre at Wounded Knee in 1890. This irresistible combination of "talent" made 1885 the first successful season for Buffalo Bill's Wild West show; within five months it "had been seen by a million persons for a profit of $100,000" (D. Russell 318).

As an "interrogative" work "particularly in the absence of a single

Western history becomes show business *(Buffalo Bill and the Indians).* Wisconsin Center for Film and Theater Research.

privileged discourse which contains and places all the others" (Belsey 92), *Buffalo Bill* develops a complex of three conflicting relationships among these historical characters: (1) between Buffalo Bill (Paul Newman), "the Star," and Sitting Bull (Frank Kaquitts), "the Indian"; (2) between Ned Buntline (Burt Lancaster), whom Altman calls the "Legend Maker," and Nate Salsbury (Joel Grey), "the Producer," and John Burke (Kevin McCarthy), "the Publicist," and Prentiss Ingraham (Allan Nicholls), "the journalist"; and (3) between Buffalo Bill and William Cody. Within the role created for him as showman, Buffalo Bill experiences conflict with another showman, Sitting Bull, about whom Ingraham says pompously, "If he wasn't in the show business, he would never have become chief." Sitting Bull challenges Buffalo Bill's sense of showmanship because he inadequately plays his role as stage Indian, because he understands the sham of Cody's role, and, most important perhaps, because he has the better sense of reality. Buffalo Bill, whose life is always performance and deception, complains when the chief arrives from the reservation under military guard, "He didn't even dress up!" Moreover, he mistakes Halsey (Will Sampson), the "tall impressive Indian in the red blanket," for the chief, who is really a "small weary old man." When

Sitting Bull first enters the Wild West arena, he discovers with great amusement that Cody's pistols are loaded not with single bullets, but with buckshot. The narrative's staging of Sitting Bull's debut in the show reflects historical accounts. One study of the show business image of the Indian states: "The fickle public, always looking for new heroes, found Sitting Bull. They came to jeer and, as if by magic, the bloodthirsty savage turned into a noble one before their very eyes" (Friar and Friar 63). Contrary to Buffalo Bill's certainty that the chief would be humiliated in front of the crowd because he refused to play a role in a phony dramatization of Custer's death, the story's crowd, like the crowds of history, applaud Sitting Bull. And when the chief performs his only act, making the gray horse dance at the sound of a pistol shot, and does so successfully before President Cleveland, Buffalo Bill can only mutter "that damn Indian ain't professional."

More than Cody's jealousy motivates his defensiveness about Sitting Bull's showmanship. The struggle involves the senses of reality that are displayed in the visual contrast between the simply dressed Sitting Bull with a single feather in his hair and the show's huge advertising image of "the Killer of Custer" that looms over the chief in the arena, an Indian in gaudy, fringed costume with a large, feathered warbonnet. A central aspect of the film is the dichotomy between two separate realities, two attitudes toward history: the show business version and the Indian version, both of which reflect subliminal reality. The show business version represses history beneath its classical narrative causality of conflict between stereotypical cowboys and Indians. The Native American reality posits a spiritual realm beyond the knowledge of white men. Sitting Bull refuses to perform the reenactment of the death of Custer, not because it reveals the Indians in a bad light and ends with Buffalo Bill riding in finally to chase away the Indians, but because "Sitting Bull says it did not happen that way." When Cody welcomes Sitting Bull to Codyland, he ironically claims, "It ain't that much different than real life." But the meaning of the film's subtitle, *Sitting Bull's History Lesson,* marks the great distance that has developed between a Native American and a commercial white reality. Cody refuses to create an act that depicts Sitting Bull's sense of truth, that "the cowardly white man" fights only against women, old people, children, and dogs, because, as he says, "I got a *better* sense of history than that." For Sitting Bull that sense of history "is nothing more than disrespect for the dead." Significantly, both men perform their own differing praises in verse. Cody recites a poem about himself:

Nature's proud she made this man—
This man, Buffalo Bill.
For it's always been his plan
To save others from the kill. (Rudolph and Altman 40)

Sitting Bull declaims:

My Father has given me this land.
In protecting it I have had a hard time.
The rivers flow with the blood of my people.
The winds blow the echoes of lies.
The white man has stolen the truth.
My desire is to love all nature.
My desire is to be loved by all that
is pure and good. (Rudolph and Altman 91–92)

History and biography become the stuff of popular entertainment, which acquires the facts of reality and repackages them as show business. The subliminal reality of the "actual" West lies outside the Fort Ruth headquarters of the Wild West show, the show already a fictionalizing of the place and an "imaging" of frontiersmen like Cody. In the entertainment business's descriptions, the "real" dies to a fictive history.

Just as in *Nashville, Buffalo Bill* uses the reality of death to comment on the unreality of the show business world. During the opening scene of the film, a rehearsal of an Indian attack on a settler's cabin, one of the Indians is accidentally hurt. "That's the real thing," one onlooker exclaims. The viewer's first meeting of Buffalo Bill comes between this Indian's dying and his burial. Juxtaposed to the operatic singing of Buffalo Bill's mistress is the chant of the Indian deathwatch, an event the script calls "strictly real." Buffalo Bill's first heroic appearance in the ring is followed by a long telephoto shot of the show's Indian camp. Perspective is flattened; the tepees appear to float in a haze, and the slow beat of a tom-tom now accentuates the burial chant of the mourning Indians. The visual montage of the bustling Wild West show with the Indian camp from a distance, the aural montage of Buffalo Bill's brassy theme song or the opera music of his mistresses with the eerie death chants of the Indians run throughout the film as a metaphoric depiction of the gap separating the thriving show business and a dying race. All that producer Salsbury hears in this chant is a new idea for the show: "If properly handled a singing Indian could be an act of inspirationment." "Arizona John" Burke declares near the end of the film, as Buffalo Bill vanquishes the Sioux chief played now by his former interpreter in the gaudy costume of Wild West advertising: "Sitting Bull's not dead. Not as long as Buffalo Bill's alive to kill him in every show" (Rudolph and Altman 149).

The complexity of these representations shifts the film out of the classical narrative register into the domain of art-cinema essay. Where producer De Laurentiis wanted an action picture, Altman produced a history lecture. Its significant conflicts among the Buffalo Bill image makers over possession of William Cody mirror the conflicting assertions of historians. One scholar has claimed that dime novelist Buntline "knew more about what the public wanted than he did about what Cody had actually done. On this basis he made Buffalo Bill a literary hero. . . . He laid the foundation of an American legend, and with his inherent sense of popular taste made it a formidable thing" (Fishwick 122). Another asserts this role for Cody's publicity man, Burke: "While the authors of dime-novels spun their mirages on pulp and the range cowboys captured the popular imagination with their rugged and hearty tournaments and contests of riding and roping, John Burke created for the public the lasting heroic image of a Westerner" (Westermeir 278). Don Russell, in his life of Cody, singles out Prentiss Ingraham as "the writer who was to make Buffalo Bill known throughout the world" (263). But most historians agree that under Salsbury's firm hand "the format of the Wild West Show was brought to theatrical perfection and its business affairs were conducted with an equal efficiency. Salsbury made all the difference; the enterprise had lacked only a show-wise administer to make it paramount" (Burke 154–55).

Throughout the film, Buntline appears as a chorus remarking on the differences between his dime-novel image of Buffalo Bill and the emerging show business image: "Profit is all that counts, creative thinking is gone forever" (Rudolph and Altman 72), he says to his authorial successor Ingraham. John Burke, on the other hand, proclaims to Buntline, "We've turned the page you were written on" (71). Salsbury's apologia that "we're involved in living American drama, . . . so you can't have anything that isn't authentic, genuine, and real" (8) is also grounded in his own authorial concerns as the master semiotician: "All I care about is the Wild West. I'm going to Codyfy the world" (36).

The film depicts this conflict between the writers early in the film when Ingraham goes to Buntline for interpretation of the puzzling motto about the Buffalo Bill-Sitting Bull relationship, "Foes in '76, Friends in '85," and Buntline sarcastically calls him "the Shakespeare of the half-dimes." The conflict between the novelist Buntline and producer Salsbury comes to a head when Salsbury, in response to Buntline's sarcastic description of Salsbury's star (as opposed to Buntline's old hero) as a man who "never gets in trouble, never looks bad in public," orders Buntline to leave the camp because "we're simply not in the yesterday business." The conflict between Salsbury and Burke, the PR man, appears in the exchange between the two when Cody rides out with ruffles and flourishes to meet Sitting Bull. Salsbury proudly exclaims, "That's my star!" And Burke points out, "He belongs to all of us, Nate." "*Our* star," responds Salsbury. Then they turn to watch Cody and assert with sanctimonious pride, "America's star!" The art cinema engages in social critique and exposes its own participation in the predominant values of the culture. In *Buffalo Bill,* the film, its makers, and its audience share in the broad culpabilities of mass-media entertainment. The show business has appropriated history for patriotism and profit.

The film characterizes Buntline as the man who began the image of Buffalo Bill as dime-novel hero, but it also accepts Salsbury's own claim to have exploited the power of the dime-novel image in the process of converting William Cody into "America's national entertainer" and the Wild West show into a national institution that lasted for thirty-five years (Salsbury 205). In the film, Salsbury asserts, "I'm in the stage picture business," and the narrative asserts the show as a forerunner to twentieth-century entertainment. In particular, the film asks reflexively to be read in its parallel to the stars, manager, writers, and producers of the Hollywood show business. Altman has stated that "Buffalo Bill was the first movie star, in one sense, the first totally manufactured American hero" (quoted in Williamson 54).

If the real Chief Sitting Bull must die in the narrative in order that a showman portray him in the ring, so the real William F. Cody is dying throughout the film to the media hero Buffalo Bill. The demands of the latter ultimately require the capitulation of the former. The narrative here accepts what historian Don Russell calls the "myth that Cody was 'just another scout' who would never have been heard of had not Ned Buntline written novels about him, and who . . . ever after lived in a thick fog of wonder, honestly incapable of discriminating between what happened in his life and what Ned Buntline swore had happened" (152–53). The film makes Buntline a one-man chorus who chronicles this conflict between real-life hero and show business figure and examines the loss of personal identity in the face of media-constructed subjectivity.

The sequence of events at the end of the film reveals the increasing isolation of Cody and the dominance of Buffalo Bill. Alone after a successful command performance before President Cleveland, Buffalo Bill confronts his maker, Ned Buntline, in one of the dramatic highlights of the film. The camera looks at the reflected image of Buffalo Bill in the mirror as Buntline tells him that he is "way past livin'" because "a hundred years from now they'll still be shoutin' your name." But when he says, "You ain't changed," Buffalo Bill's response expresses his entrapment: "I ain't supposed to. That's why people pay to see me." Buntline drinks a farewell toast to his creation—"It's been the thrill of my life to have invented you"—and rides off, jumping his horse over a fence into a pitch blackness that fades into an additional show business depiction of the western hero on a Punch and Judy puppet stage.

The penultimate scene of the film occurs five years later. Buffalo Bill is now a star, the Wild West show a success. Cody, metaphorically, and Sitting Bull, literally, are dead as active subjects, but they live on as the subjects enacted by the narrative relationship of cowboy and Indian. In this scene, the narrative cuts to a future time that reveals a highly successful business operation in motion. His staff now looking more like businessmen are handling a system that grosses more than two million dollars a year promoting Buffalo Bill's Wild West. Almost ignored, an aging William Cody sits alone in a chair talking nostalgically to his makeup man. And moments later, when word arrives that Sitting Bull has been killed, no one tells Cody because he is playing the role of Buffalo Bill in the arena.

In the last scene of the film, when "Buffalo Bill" kills "Sitting Bull," both men of history have passed away, and their roles are filled by actors. The film's art-cinema essay on the Buffalo Bill story not only conveys the loss of identity that accompanies the transmutation of individual personality into entertainment star, its recreation of the western hero indicates that this transition in identity inevitably results in a concomitant distortion, or displacement, of an antecedent reality. It furthermore characterizes the evolution of mythical heroes as representatives for the writers and producers who articulate that identity. The viewer at once watches a minor frontier hero named William Cody becoming a show business deity manufactured and manipulated by Ned Buntline, John Burke, Nate Salsbury, and Prentiss Ingraham and also watches the process of manufacturing as the film enlarges the camera perspective to include this film as part of the manipulation that constantly reinterprets history. Just as Salsbury presents the Buntline-Ingraham creation of Buffalo Bill's Wild West starring William F. Cody, so "Dino De Laurentiis presents

Robert Altman's ABSOLUTELY ORIGINAL AND HEROIC ENTERPRISE OF INIMITABLE LUSTER, *Buffalo Bill and the Indians,* starring Paul Newman."

The film reflexively freezes the traveling Wild West show of history into the fixed set location of the film. The opening scene of the film appears to be an Indian attack on a settler's cabin, with a movie voice-over introducing it, but then a voice cries out, "Cease the action," and the camera pulls back to reveal the space as a set. The narrative now depicts the scene as a rehearsal for something that a second earlier stood for reality and reflexively describes at the same time the illusion-making aspects of the movie itself. Dreams serve the same function. Prior to the president's visit to the Wild West show, an event predicted by Sitting Bull's dream, Buntline asserts that Cody never dreams, that he's "just a sleeper." But that night after the show and the departure forever of Buntline, his "first" author, Cody finally dreams, and the dream involves a sublimation of William F. Cody to the image function of show business. The dream at once represents the subject as a relation and the identification process involved in his role as a show business star as a subject for another signifier: "I got people with . . . no lives . . . livin' *through me*!" (Rudolph and Altman 40). Finally, the only resolution for his conflict with the Indians and with himself is through a sense of the immortality of his show business reality: "In one hundred years . . . in other people's shows . . . I'm still *Buffalo Bill* . . . star! You're still . . . the *Injun*!"(141).

Earlier in the film when he returns from his unsuccessful attempt to track Sitting Bull in the mountains, Cody stares dispiritedly at the heroic portrait of himself on his wall, and the camera, looking at Cody in close-up and then at the painting in close-up, marks the distance developing between the man and his image. In the dream scene the narrative severs the relationship between the two completely when it purposefully shatters the dramatic illusion of the film. The scene is prefaced by the announcement of Sitting Bull's death. He appears wearing the show costume of a chief and does a strange dance in Cody's head. Then William Cody, the dreamer, addresses the painted image of Buffalo Bill—astride his white horse, resplendent in beaded buckskins, golden hair streaming down—and exclaims, "My god, he's riding that horse right," but it is also, then, Paul Newman, actor, who turns and looks directly into the camera—in the most aggressive disruption of the narrative illusion in Altman's films—and says, "or if he ain't, how come all y'all took him for a king?"

The moment at once asserts the splitting of the ego and the displacement of the unstable historical subject into the symbolic system of the show business, of entertainment, of Hollywood. The reflexive movement here particularly uncovers the ideological function of popular entertainment to establish a unified, coherent subject position. Buntline earlier had asserted that "Injuns gear their lives to dreams" and compared Sitting Bull's dreaming to Cody's actions: "Now, I ain't an expert on the subject, but what Bull does is sure a hell of a lot cheaper than mounting a Wild West show, which is just dreamin' out loud" (Rudolph and Altman 123). The show business, the dream, the western narrative are forms of the symbolic order that work to control the essential discontinuities, the inherent instability of the ego. Here the film reveals the conditions of subjectivity as the purchase of meaning, of unity, and of heroic action at the expense of the heterogeneous, the unconscious, the psychologically unsaid. From the opening moment in the film to the breaking of illusion when Newman addresses the camera, the narrative constantly reinforces the hero's struggle against the forces of the show business that threaten his identity by aligning himself with those forces.

Politically, the film bares this ideological formulation, but it does not in the process restore any sense of individual authenticity. Rather, "Robert Altman" becomes another author function in the fictive reconstruction of historic personality. As the image of Buffalo Bill is situated within an intertextual space designated by "the western," the tension William F. Cody/Buffalo Bill is further compounded by the narrative's authorial manipulation of the taken-for-granted aspects of three generic western patterns. The mythological founding of a new civilization that authorized Buffalo Bill in films like *The Plainsman* (1936) is strikingly conveyed in the iconography of a fort with flag flying at the edge of a lovely Rocky Mountain valley. But Fort Ruth, here, is a circus headquarters. The ideological expression of manifest destiny implicit in *Pony Express* (1953) is conveyed here as racist superiority. Cody tells Sitting Bull in his dream that "the difference 'tween a white man and a Injun in *all* situations is . . . a Injun is red!" (Rudolph and Altman 141). And the ritualistic resolution of the conflict between the individual and society in William Wellman's film *Buffalo Bill* (1944), and so many other westerns, is here completely displaced by the multiplication of conflicting individualities in Cody. As in nearly every other depiction of Buffalo Bill or Wild Bill Hickok or Wyatt Earp—the gallery of historic individuals that fills America's western stories—the film reflexively authors the heroic personality under the contradictory influence of competing cultural values.

At the self-reflexive level of the discourse as well as the dramatic level of the story, William F. Cody is a subject situated by the authorial voices of the mass media. The film's retelling of the Buffalo Bill story not only conveys the loss of identity that accompanies the transmutation of individual personality into entertainment star; this re-creation of the western hero indicates that this transition in identity, with its concomitant distortion, or displacement, of an antecedent reality, inevitably characterizes the evolution of mythical heroes, who are always representatives of the writers and producers who articulate that identity. If the western hero at one time "confirmed Americans in the traditional belief that obstacles were to be overcome by the courageous, virile, and determined stand of the individual as an individual" (Curtie 765), *Buffalo Bill and the Indians* deflates this image. Its hero confirms no traditional heroic values but rather confirms an uncertainty about the identity of our heroes because of their construction by mass-media image makers who shape reality to fit their own image. Altman's art cinema reflects upon itself as a mediated, expressive construction of reality, complicit in the forces of modernity that destabilize social identity, action, and communication.

# 8. Fiction's Fashion: Paris Originals and Hollywood Imitations

Since *MASH,* Altman has demonstrated an antipathy toward the authority of the Hollywood production system. His genre films rewrite the conventions of classical story patterns. His stylistic play with zoom lens, panning shots, and sound tracks routinely confuses the narrative eyes and ears of audiences. His eccentric casting of both male and female characters challenges the popular representation of the body. The privileging of creativity by actors establishes improvisatory moods. Narrative causality is disconnected and disorienting. As they catalog the aggressive signatures of one of Hollywood's most transgressive directors, Altman's reflexive films convey a critical hostility toward the values of the entertainment industry. Two of these films made in the 1990s once again focus specifically on the terms of production and consumption of popular culture entertainment. *Prêt-à-Porter* examines the glamour, seductions, and politics of the fashion industry and its influence on the social nature of gender roles. And perhaps *The Player* is Altman's most overt satire and cynical critique of the film business. Both films deploy large casts to represent major characters, and their consequent expansion of story gaps reinforces the experience of subliminal reality. As major segments of popular culture, films and fashion engage audiences' common knowledge to fill the discontinuities in story and discourse. Like the depiction of country music and Wild West shows in *Nashville* and *Buffalo Bill,* these films are big, high-energy productions. They revel in the allure of the show business, even as they reflexively and obliquely construct art-cinema narratives that examine the unspoken desires, anxieties, and estrangements that motivate the values of the contemporary entertainment world.

## Reflexive Hollywood

*The Player* is the most cinematically reflexive of Altman's films. It tells the story of Griffin Mill (Tim Robbins) a Hollywood producer who unintentionally kills a writer he thinks is threatening him, successfully evades being charged with murder, happily marries his victim's girlfriend, and successfully maneuvers his way to the top of the studio power structure by supplying a formulaic happy ending to a film not unlike those directed by Altman himself. The film depicts the producer as someone who gets away with the murder of writers on one hand and who authorizes narrative trash on the other. Moreover, the film characterizes both crimes as gestures with roots in the same impulses that generate the power of the masculine gaze in the classical cinema. The cause-effect logic of the film's untypically linear stories suggests a trajectory of desire that begins in masculine anxiety about personal authority and power and ends in a fantasy of legal and sexual control. The representation of that anxiety derives from the literal threat to Mill's life by an unidentified writer and from the implied threat to his job by the sudden appearance in the studio offices of a rival script producer. It finds release in the voyeuristic image of the sexy blond whose desirability motivates in post hoc fashion the producer's inexplicable murder of her writer boyfriend. At story's end, this desire needs finally to have conquered the multiple anxieties that derive from economic, emotional, and legal transgressions. The narrative thus examines the distribution of male power in terms of the representation of women in popular culture. In the process, the film aggressively totals up a bill of particulars against the Hollywood system and its players who "get away with it" in their hypocritical and callous treatment of colleagues, in their sexist regard of women, in their cynical and materialistic development of story product, in their drive for industrial power.

In the best of Altman's films about women—*Nashville, 3 Women, Jimmy Dean, Kansas City,* and *Cookie's Fortune*—the mix of narrative reflexivity and the debilitation of women fully implicate the narrator in the films' critique of social practice. *The Player* develops the critique more explicitly than does any other Altman film. Its politics are far away from *MASH*; indeed, it explains the structures of that film as well as those of the classical cinema. The anxieties of male competition and insecurity here play out in the Hollywood studio, and the characteristic male response to those fears in the subjugation of women is analyzed as the inevitable narrative trajectory of Hollywood cinema, which works to establish a hierarchy of male superiority and female dependency.

The media reviews of *The Player* variously charted its "scathing deconstruction of contemporary Hollywood" (Greenberg 29)—the ruthless assistant producer, the constant stream of selling, the callousness of the production system, the five dozen actors who play themselves, and so on. For many, the film worked as a roman à clef whose fictional characters ask to be read in terms of the real players they represent. What grounds the film's reflexive analysis of the filmmaking world, however, is its structure of four interlocking stories all woven together throughout the narrative. In a familiar use of the classical narrative code, the resolution of one story determines the outcome of another, but the film embeds these stories in complex ways that inform and comment on each other. They work like Chinese boxes whose opening requires the audience to read though the ambiguities of multiple associations for the metaphoric design and meanings of art-cinema narration.

At the innermost level of this structure lies the central film within the film, the *Habeas Corpus* story, whose selling, development, and production runs through most of *The Player.* This story, in which a zealous district attorney prosecutes the woman he loves for a murder she did not commit and sends her to the gas chamber, details the conflict between classical happy endings and art-cinema bleakness. The second story, the studio story, which most immediately contains *Habeas Corpus,* recounts the competition between production chief Griffin Mill and his new rival Larry Levy (Peter Gallagher) for production control in the studio and exposes the insecurities of masculine authority that underlie Hollywood storytelling. Their competition for successful concepts, scripts, and stars is generally conveyed as a parody of "high-concept" story ideas and is most specifically dramatized in the buying and producing of *Habeas Corpus.* The third story, the murder story, centers on the tension between Mill and the never-identified writer who is threatening Mill's life because of his indifferent rejection of a concept the writer pitched to Mill sometime in the past. Mill kills writer David Kahane (Vincent D'Onofrio), who he mistakenly thinks to be the author of these threats, in an act that posits murder as an effect of the entertainment industry and motivates the final conflict in this story between Mill and the Pasadena police, who ineffectually try to solve the mystery of Kahane's death. The fourth story, the love story, focuses on implied competition between Bonnie Sherow (Cynthia Stevenson), Mill's initial girlfriend and studio assistant, and June Gudmundsdottir (Greta Scacchi), initially Kahane's girlfriend and ultimately Mill's wife. Mill's callous dismissal of the one and his appropriation or acquisition of the other both motivate and explain key action in the other stories and simultaneously characterize the values that underlie the movie business.

Usually in classical narrative the innermost story shapes and informs the resolution of the dominant story. In a telling reversal of the conventional narrative chain of plot resolutions, the resolutions of these four stories occur in order from the most prominent conflict to the most minor. First of all, in the murder story of "Who shot the writer?" Mill defeats the police, whose chief detectives are Whoopi Goldberg, an assistant named Willow (a parodic imitation of Jodie Foster's FBI agent in *The Silence of the Lambs,* 1991), and a creepy and silent Lyle Lovett, who is ultimately picked out of a lineup as the killer. Then, in the studio tale of "who controls the studio," Mill not only defeats Levy for the position of producer, he becomes chief executive officer of the studio. And in the *Habeas Corpus* story, the district attorney learns at the last minute of the innocence of his true love and rescues her just in time from death in the gas chamber.

Each of these stories centers on a conflict with the law. The studio story and the murder story depict the intense play of anxiety and insecurity that lies beneath the frenzied surface of pitches, deals, and interpersonal associations in Hollywood. Both pit the central character against the power of some authority. During the first scene of the film—an eight-minute traveling shot that self-consciously references the opening of Welles's *Touch of Evil* and Bernardo Bertolucci's "great tracking shot with Winger in *The Sheltering Sky*" (1990), the narrative marks the threats to both Mill's job and his life. The Boston bank that controls the studio worries about profits, and three suits talk about the facts that "heads will roll" and that they are "looking to replace Griffin." During the second scene, Mill implores the administrative secretary to tell him the situation: "Should I be looking for a job?" That evening at a party he asks his lawyer, played by the movie director Sydney Pollack, "What's going on with my job? . . . Am I out?" Many of the early scenes in the narrative appear motivated to focus not only on Mill's paranoia but on the accuracy of his fears about the rivalry from Levy as his new "roommate" in script procurement for the studio. In Hollywood, the real law is the least powerful and significant. The final authority is the happy ending of narrative fantasy and the producers who provide this product.

The threats to Mill's life lead him to the writer David Kahane, but his murder of Kahane results less from his fear of the writer than from his anger caused by the writer's taunts. When Mill urges the writer to contact him at the studio, Kahane replies, "Who will I ask for? Larry Levy?" Mill is immediately defensive: "What's Levy got to do with this?" Kahane taunts:

Script producer suspected of murder *(The Player).*

> Don't you read the trades? The *New York Times* business section? He's moving in; you're moving out. You can't make a deal. That's what they say. Yesterday's news. . . . I can't wait to tell the world that when Griffin Mill can't cut the pressure at work, he drives out to Pasadena to pick fights with writers. . . . You're in over your head. That's why you're losing your job. Then what are you going to do? I can write! What can you do?

In part, the producer kills the writer in response to this evocation of incompetence: "Keep it to yourself!" Mills yells repeatedly as he smashes Kahane's head against the concrete.

The murder story is the dominant story by virtue of its violent transgression of the law, but it is also the first of the stories to be resolved in the film. Goldberg leads the comic team of investigating detectives, who, the film suggests, are on the surface humorously incompetent but in reality secretly knowledgeable. The detectives, the studio security chief, Mill, and the audience all know Mill did it, but he gets away with his crime by chance. One of the key scenes in the film occurs when Mill beats the law, defended by a lawyer in a wheelchair (echoing Raymond Burr's television lawyer Perry Mason, by way of his later role as a wheelchair-bound detective in *Ironside*) and confronted by an eyewitness who mistakenly and ironically identifies one of the detectives as the culprit, despite the pointed efforts of the law to direct her gaze to the real murderer. Mill walks out of suspicion, out of prosecution, out of the police station into a diegetic ellipsis of a year's time and into his victory over studio competition. Here his success against the law seems literally to motivate his success at the studio, although the cause-effect arrangement of events in the narrative is subliminal rather than direct.

The Hollywood producer gets away with murder, and that victory precedes, if not motivates, Mill's successful defeat of another law. In the studio story, Mill outwits his opponent by urging that Levy supervise the production of *Habeas Corpus* as a film with no stars and an unhappy ending—the kind of movie Altman asserts "would have been my kind of movie. But that picture doesn't sell any tickets" (quoted in Keogh 13). In a reaction that Altman no doubt recalls from his thirty-year resistance to studio types, Mill calls it "a completely fucked-up idea with no second act," a "piece-of-shit idea." But it offers him a way to power. The scenes of studio combat are interestingly repressed from the discourse, but the implication is that Mill triumphs over his rival by rescuing the studio from making a Robert Altman art film. His concept of stars and happy endings, as opposed to the art-cinema concept he planted with Levy at the start, not only masters his rival but more significantly displaces the head of the studio himself and earns Mill the position of studio chief, the boss, the law. In his new position at the end of the film, all anxiety overcome, he holds the power to complete *Habeas Corpus* the way he desires and the way he knows will sell. Success in Hollywood ultimately demands the rejection of art-cinema narration.

The narrative strategy of that revised film-within-the-film is revealing. It works by situating the heroine in a position of false guilt that then doubly motivates her rescue by the hero, the law's man, the district attorney. Played by Bruce Willis and Julia Roberts, the two actors play themselves as actors playing the roles of hero and heroine in the *Habeas Corpus* story. Willis and Roberts carry the multiple signification of masculine power and police authority on one hand (Bruce Willis from *Die Hard,* 1988, and *Die Hard 2,* 1990) and female dependency on the other (Julia Roberts from *Pretty Woman*). *Habeas Corpus,* as a Hollywood studio fiction, seeks to generate audience anxiety about the outcome of the wrongly condemned woman—will the hero arrive at the gas chamber in time to save her life? There are several audiences here: the witnesses gathered to watch the execution in the "*Habeas Corpus* story," the studio production team gathered to watch the final cut of *Habeas Corpus* in the studio story, and the actual audience of *The Player.*

The happy ending that every level of audience desires and expects, and the one they all get, situates the woman falsely, and thus sympathetically, as guilty of murder in order that the male rescue her. Thus the narrative trajectory of this story works at once to pronounce justice (truth wins in the end), to celebrate successful romance (the hero rescues his love), and to establish the dependency of the female on the male (Willis carries the barely conscious Roberts off in his arms to a state of hierarchically structured wedded bliss). Thus too then in the project of the film's outer narrative, Mill's rescue from the arms of the female law in the Pasadena police station motivates his rescue of the studio from the error of making a transgressive Altman film. His studio success is motivated by the production of a classical Hollywood story in which the male asserts his superiority by at once winning and subduing the female.

The fourth narrative—the love story involving Mill, his girlfriend and story editor Bonnie, and the writer Kahane's girlfriend June—focuses the energies of all these interwoven stories. The narrative offers no particular reason for Mill to assume that Kahane, among the hundreds of writers listed in his computer and address files, is the author of the threatening postcards he has received. But his visit to Kahane's apartment establishes an inevitable if ambiguous link between Mill's fear from the threats and his murder of the writer. If it is uncertain why Mill goes to Kahane's apartment, editing and cinematography sharply focus a purpose in his departure. The film presents the first encounter between June and Griffin as an exercise in cinematic voyeurism and male desire. Griffin reaches June on a portable telephone and stands outside her window watching her as they converse. The whole conversation occurs as a play of shot/reverse-shot cinematography that establishes her as the object of visual desire, the object of Griffin's desire whom he will possess after he dispenses his anxiety in the murder of her boyfriend.

The insecurities that underlie the confrontations with authority throughout *The Player* are at once crystallized and suspended in this moment when the hero takes possession of the woman with his eyes. Part of this effect emerges in the verbal wit: Kahane calls June, ostensibly a citizen of Iceland, the "ice queen," and the play of "icy" and "I see" mirrors the visual movement between the camera's seeing and Mill's seeing June in the silvery blue light of her apartment. The space in its luminescence suggests both a silver screen and, in its window-barred rectangles, a prison. Altman has spoken explicitly about the motivation of this moment:

> The shots through the windows through all this [scene] go into what films are generally, which is voyeurism, that you're looking into an

> area that you're not supposed to be seeing. So we're taking you into privileged territory, and it just sets up that theme generally. . . . It's intrigue, mystery. . . . We're really doing a little flirtation scene here; we're trying to set up the sense of some sexual tension between these two. *(The Player)*

Jean Lepine, the cinematographer, explains this scene even more explicitly: "We were able to play with reflection, with reality, with the dream and the poetry of the dialogue. . . . It's the scene of the voyeur, and I am the voyeur. . . . All that play, that subtlety works very good with the camera" (in Altman, *The Player*). June as the object of Mill's gaze reflects both his desire and his distance from that desire. The shot/reverse-shot editing of this dramatic moment in the film at once offers his gaze to the audience for their subjective identification and critically, reflexively examines the looking.

Furthermore, June's dialogue as well as her image hints at the causal links between this scene and Mill's confrontation with Kahane. She claims that the misleading names of Greenland and Iceland were a ploy of the natives to "thwart Viking kings who wanted to steal their women." Thus the film suggests another motive for Mill's murder aside from his fear of Kahane and his angry reaction to Kahane's taunts. Altman has said that "those scenes were the hardest to direct in the whole picture. The hardest to direct, to act, to write. Because it's very dangerous: you're breaking all the emotional rules. It's primitive stuff. You kill a guy and then you take his woman. . . . It could be a motive . . . : He had seen her,

Woman as object of the gaze *(The Player).*

and he went to find the guy after that. . . . He could now have another reason for the killing" (quoted in Smith and Jameson 26). The last shot of the scene silently captures Mills in medium close shot from inside the apartment with only part of his body and face visible. He has put down the phone and stares intently into the space, his face awash in the silvery glow of its light. The next shot begins the murder sequence: muted and dark colors, tracking ground-level shot of expensively shod feet walking briskly, traditional Hollywood thriller music on the sound track—Mill strides purposefully toward his meeting with the ice queen's boyfriend, the threat to his life, a representative of all those writers who daily offer him the wares whose purchase can make or break his power. The crime at the center of this film results from the pressures of anxiety and desire in the show business.

Another level of metaphoric motivation is at work in this sequence as well, however. The film reflexively calls attention to the fact that the woman is not real but a figment of the man's imagination. She hardly reacts to Kahane's death. She loses one lover and acquires another. Her responses, like her paintings, are never finished. Altman says about her:

> I realized that if I show him watching her and she doesn't know she's being observed, he can create a fantasy about her. . . . I felt that to make this woman so interesting to him, I'd let him create her. I took the position that June Gudmundsdottir too doesn't exist. . . . I felt that we should make her a movie character. I tried to explain it to Greta [Scacchi]: you're not a real person. You're acting in a movie; you don't have to find out the truth in this woman, because she doesn't really exist . . . like a blank movie screen on which you can project your desires. (quoted in Keogh 12–13)

Thus June's existence is a projection of masculine competition, of insecurity, of longing.

The second encounter between June and Griffin reflects what Altman calls Griffin's "creating her right down the line." She reveals that she likes words and letters, but "I'm not crazy about complete sentences." The two of them take pictures of each other as they talk. Altman notes: "The polaroids are just another reminder of what I'm doing, that I've got a camera on these people as they're taking pictures of each other. Pictures are important. Voyeurism is important." June says to Griffin that "knowing that you've committed a crime is suffering enough. . . . Maybe it wasn't a crime after all. Anyway, what difference does it make? It has nothing to do with how things really are." Says

Altman: "It's almost like he's writing her as he goes along. And so again we have another movie inside of a movie. . . . This whole scene is . . . excusing him. She in a way is saying to him everything he wants to hear . . . , and what she's saying is that none of this is real, including her, especially her" *(The Player).*

The third scene between the two is equally significant because it follows upon Griffin's realization that he has killed the wrong man and that the source of the threats to his life now has the power of knowing his guilt in the murder of the writer. Narrowly surviving an attempt on his life with a rattlesnake, the shaken Griffin goes to June's apartment, where he intends to confess, but where instead he declares that the closeness of death has revealed to him that he loves her. As clearly marked in the sensuous but extremely expressionistic sex scene between June and Griffin in the Hot Springs resort later, Hollywood perception equates confession with possession. Again in a play of shot/reverse-shot editing, the woman is displayed as the passive object of Griffin's desiring gaze. The scene progresses from his paranoia and anxiety through her distance before his gaze to the revelation that she has been at work on the integration of fragments of Mill's photographic images into her artwork. Her paintings weave his fractured image in with snakelike paintings that recall Willie's drawings in *3 Women.* The scene simultaneously constitutes her as the object of desire and the subject of dismemberment. As the other stories in the film then work to contain masculine fears, they parallel the logic of this fourth story, which seeks to possess and control the image of Gretta Scacchi.

Altman self-consciously reflects on the audience manipulation involved in refusing to show Scacchi's breasts. Scacchi brought to *The Player* a professional persona of nudity from playing nude scenes in her prior films. But Altman retells with enthusiasm the story of Paul Newman's explaining *The Player* to him: "It's about getting to see the tits of the girl whose tits you don't care about seeing, and not getting to see the tits of the girl whose tits you want to see" (quoted in Breskin 75). Altman's understanding of this character receives much attention in his extensive commentary about the film; it reflects what he pointedly considers a major difference between the screenwriter and his own concept of the narrative: "She doesn't even exist. She's a hallucination. She's the character a guy like Griffin would dream up for the hero of his movie to get involved with. Somebody who had nothing to do with the movies—except that she is the ultimate movie character. She's the movies" (quoted in Smith and Jameson 26).

Thus this central figure is an empty place, the movies, yet elicits responses both as good man's daughter and as threatening object of desire who dismembers, splinters, and reconstitutes the masculine image. Altman's understanding of this desire motivates his development of the Scacchi role. It explains the central logic of the film's essay, that the Hollywood narrative develops out of masculine dread/apprehension/vulnerability and circulates around the image of the woman as the object of desire, the possession of which brings power, potency, success, defiance of the law. The reflexive dimension of looking courses throughout the film, most noticeably in scenes about watching movies. In the art theater just before he kills Kahane, Mill tellingly watches the tragic humiliation of father and son in the debilitating final scene of *The Bicycle Thief* (1948). And finally in front of three separate audiences—the witnesses gathered to watch the execution in *Habeas Corpus,* the management production crew gathered to screen the final cut of *Habeas Corpus,* and the actual audience of *The Player*—the hero uses a shotgun to smash the screens that separate him from his desire, snatches his beloved from the arms of death, and, under the beneficent gaze of the law and the applause of at least two audiences, carries the heroine into the freeze frame of a happy ending.

Griffin Mill performs three telling acts at the end of *The Player.* He fires Bonnie—the woman with the undesirable breasts, the honest colleague who represents the all-too-real call to integrity, the film executive screenwriter Michael Tolkin calls "the film's conscience" (in Altman, *The Player*)—because she defends the Altmanesque version of *Habeas Corpus.* Mill acquiesces to blackmail to make the movie we have just seen, thus reflecting the power of the movies to contain the fears and insecurities of their makers. And Mill goes home to the pregnant June in an idyllic setting full of thousands of flowers, an American flag, and a happy ending of colorful sunny intensity. Hollywood guilt motivates a fantasy, authored by an invisible writer, in which he substitutes the real Bonnie for the imaginary June. The fantasy closes on Griffin, protective husband, potent father, successful studio head—and master of all he surveys.

Mill's firing of Bonnie summed up for many reviewers the moral bankruptcy of Hollywood chronicled by *The Player*—the "mortification of those who are subservient" to Hollywood's power, their powerlessness, their shame (Clements 128). Altman sees it differently, calling this very reflexive film "a little bit of a fairy tale. . . . it's a film about film, it's of film, and I used Hollywood as a metaphor for what I see as the biggest malady of our civilization right now, which is greed" *(The Player).* The film's happy ending, however, reflects more than just this problematic morality. Like *Nashville,* like *Buffalo Bill, The Player* constitutes a remarkable gloss on the venalities of the entertainment industry—greed and deceit certainly, but also indifference, insecurity, and hostility toward women. These films parade a gallery of arrogant and unlikable male images across their crowded canvases, and women are constantly at the mercy of these men—economically, emotionally, professionally. Two scenes are particularly revealing of the reflexive mix of desire and hostility that marks the entertainment's representation of women in these films. In her final performance in *Nashville,* country star Barbara Jean is depicted in a low-angle slow zoom in on her face as she sings a song of painful reminiscence. The angle, the lens movement, and her song of desire all classically mark her as the object of desire. And immediately upon completing her song, she is shot by the out-of-work male fiddle player who is unable to compete on the Nashville scene. At the end of *The Player,* Griffin Mill refuses to talk to Bonnie as he leaves the studio for home. Bonnie, who has literally associated studio behavior with the phallus and who in this scene has literally fallen in the studio street, establishes one of the images that conveys an understanding of problematic male power in the entertainment industry simultaneously manipulating women as objects of desire and control.

Paul Ricoeur writes that "reflexion is the act of turning back upon itself by which a subject grasps in a moment of intellectual clarity and moral responsibility, the unifying principle of the operations among which it is dispersed and forgets itself as a subject" (quoted in Stam xiv). The subject here, the player, is the moviemaker and the audience. Altman says, "We're admiring all the wrong things. And this film to me is just an essay, just a reminder. *The Player* is a horror film about our society. Unless we stop being players, we're all going to come to the same terrible happy ending that he did, which means he's soulless" *(The Player).* The film not only chronicles the greed of the entertainment industry; it more profoundly and self-consciously finds the roots of classical Hollywood discourse in the anxiety of a phallocentric culture that seeks solace and release in the objectification and control of the desirable female. Its reflexive awareness of these issues reprises the representations of masculine insecurities, the depictions of feminine dependency and debilitation, and the refusals of narrative authority that course throughout Altman's films, that constitute the expressive ambiguities, that motivate the unspoken realities, the faint clues and indirections of Altman's art cinema.

## Women's Clothes Make the Man

The entertainment industry, its setting, its players, and its audiences are constituted by different roles in *Prêt-à-Porter,* but the film nevertheless examines these players in the interplay of social forms and cultural values. Sold as a "*Nashville* for a new generation," its vehicle for analyzing the nature of the show business in the 1990s is the international fashion industry, and, like *Nashville,* it juxtaposes productions and artists, insiders and outsiders, players and audiences. As in *Nashville,* no central story focuses the narrative energies of the film. Rather, its many stories are presented as brief vignettes that recur around the annual spring designer shows in Paris. The film's cacophony of stories and characters demands the familiar reading strategies for constructing meaning in Altman's films. The narrative links events, situations, and people in confusing ways that force the viewer to read between the lines. Narrative kernels are minimally developed and are apparently connected only by the proximity to fashion and the randomness of narrative. The gaps and silences that constitute causality urge a metaphoric understanding of the unspoken dimensions of the story.

The major structural signature of this film, like that of *Nashville* and *The Player,* is the play of fictional characters around the margins of the colossal entertainment machines of popular culture. The film invites the viewer to enjoy the game of stargazing, looking for the "real" performers who play "themselves," including the actual models and designers. The fiction reflects upon, derives from, illustrates, examines, critiques, and ultimately is fascinated by the power of the show. Altman went reluctantly to his first fashion show in 1984; about that event, he has said: "The minute that the show started, the music hit, I just thought, Wow! This is the circus! This is great. It even brought tears to my eyes. I thought, I've got to make a film about this" (quoted in Leitch 14). *Prêt-à-Porter* is "not about what to wear" but about what we "want and need from fashion," about what we want and need from entertainment. The world of producers, designers, models, merchandisers, and reporters emerges under the critical gaze of outsiders. The entertainment business encompasses competition for power and gendered insecurity that reveals the motivations of its products at once as a critique and as an embrace of its energies.

Early in the film, two important fashion editors, just arrived to cover the new fashion presentations, complain about their erroneous room assignments at the Grand Hotel in Paris. Their fight over the "Salomé Suite" and the "Faust Suite" explicitly references two cultural tales, two mythic paradigms, whose generic force identifies key ideological issues in the film. On one hand, the Faustian exchange of one's soul for knowledge reflects a sense of identity as a power transaction that involves short-term gain and long-term loss. On the other hand, the feminine dance of multilayered fashion and sensuality aims to procure the head and silence the voice of male prophecy. These stories metaphorically suggest a critical social economy that shapes a particular art-cinema reading strategy in this film. *Prêt-à-Porter* develops an exuberant, multifaceted set of fictions that seem marginally related to each other in this documentary-like representation of the 1994 Paris fashion scene, all asking to be read as a lyrical description and metaphoric analysis of fashion's contradictory role in the construction of social subjectivity. It reflexively examines the entertainment industry again, and its depiction of the contemporary fashion scene emerges as a fantasy of masculine anxiety and feminine security within a system of discourse that at once constructs and contains the feminine. The film's representation of the fashionable and fashioned body recalls Foucault's observation that "the body is . . . directly involved in a political field; power relations have an immediate hold upon it; they invest it, mark it, train it, torture it, force it to carry out tasks, to perform ceremonies, to emit signs" (quoted in O'Sickey 25). The film examines a series of gendered relationships of power and authority in which varying images of masculine weakness, vulnerability, and insecurity motivate clothing and displaying the female body. The film at once celebrates the beautifully clothed female body and announces the need to contain and control its authority.

Leslie Rabine provides another important perspective for a critical understanding of the work in this film. She describes two bodies in fashion magazines of the past thirty years—one body that is liberated and "seductive to women" and another body that is enfranchised by, situated in, articulated through the language of fashion that primarily contains feminine subjectivity as a work of the patriarchy (59). Thus, even as women are engendered as a community, they are also at the same time defined by a common semiological system of presentation. Codes of fashion in the dominant ideology simultaneously empower, subvert, and constrain the feminine. In *Prêt-à-Porter* the fictional television fashion reporter Kitty Potter (Kim Basinger) delineates the two bodies defined by Rabine when she challenges the real designer Thierry Mugler to explain why the "overt, extreme, sexual subtext" of his clothes "is squarely at odds with the image of women as capable and independent of men."

Rabine's perspective generates a critical paradigm that posits two key tensions apparent in the fashion entertainment business—between masculine impotence and feminine dominance on one hand, and between masculine fear and control of the feminine on the other. *Prêt-à-Porter* engages these tensions primarily in its juxtaposition of fictional characters with the actual world of Paris fashions during the showing of the prêt-à-porter collections of spring 1994. Much of the journalistic criticism of the film at the time of its release dismissed Altman's characters and made-up scenarios as farcical, flimsy, ineffective parody of the fashion scene. But the force of the film lies in this very contrast between its phony, silly, even adolescent fictions and the slick, self-confident, professional power of the "real thing." Indeed, the film's awkwardly double title *Ready to Wear (Prêt-à-Porter)* signifies its textual duality. As in *Nashville, Tanner '88,* and *The Player,* the narrative aggressively mixes fictional and documentary reality. Its insertion of fictional characters—like Zelig and Forrest Gump—into historical moments achieves a cinematic point of view that comments reflexively on that real-world actuality. Analysts of postmodern culture frequently note that the distinction between real life and fictional forms frequently blurs. The audience in this film must recognize the play of different documentary and story realities as a causal relationship with a dependent interconnectedness among them. The real world of fashion in the film—like the real world in *Nashville, Buffalo Bill, The Player,* and *Kansas City*—is the phenomenon that motivates the fiction, the invention, the entertainment that in turn occasions the designers, promoters, consumers, and critics of that real. Fantasy constructs the reality even as the fiction exposes the illicitness, the deficiency, the pettiness, the masquerade, the meanness of actual desire.

Rabine asserts that "the pleasure of looking at the photographic images forms one part of a continuum with the pleasure of recreating the body and the pleasure of masquerade. The continuum turns inside out the commonly accepted opposition between fantasy as internal, unreal, private and reality as external" (63). As the fashion reporter for FAD-TV warns at the beginning of the film, the viewer will witness two phenomena: there will be "great lapses in taste, but there will also be dazzling moments of rare beauty." Altman's sense of subliminal reality links the two in myriad directions. The fashion shows, and the cinematic representation of them, actualize a rich, entertaining plenitude, while the fictional tales of competition, exploitation, and sexuality embody desire and duplicity, need and insecurity. The fiction's fashion photographer, Milo, pointedly describes his work as "taking advantage of other people's anxieties." Similarly, the stories emerge from and reflect the need to control and the insecurity of that control. Dismissed critically as fluff, these fictions all display a trajectory of masculine impotence, against which, because of which, the reality of the fashion world appears as powerful fantasy.

During the credit sequence in the film, an Italian tailor named Sergio (Marcello Mastroianni) purchases two identical neckties at the Christian Dior shop in the Kremlin and mails one to the lord of Paris fashion, Olivier de la Fontaine (Jean-Pierre Cassel). The ties become the sign by which, like two spies, the men later meet in the Paris airport. Nothing in the story explains their relationship except that Sergio is the long-ago lover of de la Fontaine's wife, Isabella (Sophia Loren). The accidental death of the fashion designer as the two men drive from the airport sets up a misguided criminal investigation by Inspector Tantpis (Jean Rochefort) in a reiteration of Blake Edwards's spoof of masculine detective archetypes in Inspector Clouseau. The investigation aimlessly searches for Sergio, who wanders through other episodes of the film, a fugitive from the law stealing clothes to use for disguise.

De la Fontaine's death has two significant consequences. On one hand, it rejuvenates the social career of his wife, who has "not been on the social circuit for twenty-five years." Kitty Potter reports that Isabella de la Fontaine "rocked the fashion world by taking her husband's symbolically vacant seat on the front row" of the collection shows. The sixty-year-old Sophia Loren simultaneously rejuvenates the famous voluptuous body type of the 1960s and a fashion style of dress and hat that consternates everyone in the contemporary Paris fashion scene. Thus the initial major fictional story in *Prêt-à-Porter* sends one man to his death and the other into hiding and ends in the assertion of retro feminine fashion. Loren's role represents the displacement of the male, the disruption of contemporary fashion, and the rejection of current fashion's prescribed body. She wears exactly the vintage clothing that Kaja Silverman describes as "a sartorial strategy that works to denaturalize its wearer's specular identity, and one that is fundamentally irreconcilable with fashion" ("Fragments" 194).

On the other hand, the death of the husband occasions the former lover Sergio's return to the arms of his beloved Isabella. Their bedroom scene reprises Loren's famous striptease for Mastroianni thirty years before in the De Sica film *Yesterday, Today and Tomorrow.* The scene moves from Mastroianni howling like a wolf in sexual anticipation and ends very pointedly with his falling asleep at the climactic moment of her disrobing. Isabella dresses again and leaves after placing a note on the sleeping lover's chest that reads "two husbands—two deaths." The economic power of fashion and the power of romance belong to dead and impotent old men, and the commanding feminine is repeatedly characterized in the film as Sophia Loren striding through public adulation with out-of-fashion assertion, self-assurance, and authority.

The point and significance of the film resides not in any logical rhetoric of explanation, as in classical narrative cinema, but in the juxtaposition of separate little stories, none complete in itself and none clearly connected to any other. The Sergio-Isabella-Olivier nexus provides one paradigm; the fictional-factional distinction offers another metaphoric pattern by which the film asserts its understanding of the role played by fashion in contemporary mass culture. Meaning in the film emerges from a reading of the multiple associations and parallels established by the narrative. The art cinema of Robert Altman presents a motion painting of diverse and chaotic performance and display, tableaux whose purpose appears first as the recognition of similarity and then as a construction of connections implied but not spoken in the discourse. Interpretation notices that half a dozen other fictional stories in the film repeat the correlation of gendered insecurity and the role of fashion.

In these fictions the producers, the designers, the models, the distributors, and the promoters of fashion represent a swirl of diversely gendered sexuality that characterizes both the audience and the system of fashion. For instance, in the fiction of fashion editors, the three women editors of the magazines *Harper's Bazaar, British Vogue,* and *Elle* pursue the commercially hot fashion photographer Milo, who is described as "having a lock on how women should look in the nineties." Played by Stephen Rea, the Milo character ironically carries into the film the popular association of gender confusion that circulates around Rea's role as an IRA gunman in *The Crying Game* (1992). The linkage of his power to his camera takes on specifically phallic dimensions in the scenes where each of the editors tries to seduce him in order to procure his popular photography for her magazine. His response is to refuse sex, to humiliate each of the women sexually, and then to take pictures of each with his tiny pocket camera. Peter Lehman asserts that "there is a virtual epidemic of shortness of every kind in Altman's films" (*Running* 121), reflecting masculine anxiety. The transition that Lehman traces in *McCabe & Mrs. Miller* from the literal small penis of the cowboy who does not know how to use a gun to the symbolic derringer of McCabe is dramatically refigured in Milo's tiny camera.

Although the three editors display a catty competitiveness among themselves and the international magazines they represent, they share a sexual victimage before Milo's camera. One of the women in revenge steals Milo's negatives from an important fashion shoot, another of the fictions that significantly recounts the humiliation of powerful French woman designer Simone Lowenthal (Anouk Aimée) by a Texas cattleman's purchase of her company. The three editors then join forces to confront Milo in an obviously self-satisfied and symbolic act of castration. He calls their meeting "a scene from Macbeth" when the three triumphant "witches" retrieve the images of their exposure by negotiating to exchange his strutting and arrogant dominance for the return of his film. The photographic production, reproduction, and promotion of fashion here emerge as competitive sexual arrogance and control.

Another paradigmatic story depicts Tim Robbins, as a *Washington Post* sports reporter out of his league in reporting on fashion, and Julia Roberts, as a fashion editor from the *Houston Chronicle,* who are by chance and competition lodged in the same hotel room and who are metaphorically locked together through the loss of their suitcases and their wardrobes. Having nothing but white hotel bathrobes to wear, the two watch the showings of the prêt-à-porter collections on their hotel room television set and make love repeatedly under a completely enshrouding bedsheet. Robbins and Roberts play different halves of unreal but romantically and satirically successful couples in *The Player,* and their relationship here ironically recalls the equally romantic and fashionable couple of Roberts and Richard Gere, who similarly spend most of their time in a hotel room in *Pretty Woman.* This sex, however, occurs out of reach of fashion and the camera's desiring eye. Undressed and hostile to each other, the two develop a relationship of unbridled sexual desire. The absence of their clothes—his "classic sports journalist's separates" (Bruzzi 31) and her power suit—occasions the loss of social buffers. Stella Bruzzi writes, "Bereft of clothes (and hence social status), the two are relieved of the burden of conformity" (32). Both apparently married, with families back home, they engage in continuous sexual intercourse throughout the film, punctuated by distant scenes of the fashion shows on their television set. The connections between these fictions and fashion's realities are everywhere unstated in the film and leave the viewer to construe the subliminal relationships.

The film seems to employ this story for a variety of effects that relate to the way the characters fulfill their roles as arrogantly masculine sports reporter and sexily feminine fashion reporter. Significantly, it also concludes on the joking representation of diminished male power. At the end of the film, after they recover their clothes, two separate shots display the now clothed couple to each other and to the audience. When the very tall Robbins in a high-level medium shot puts on his dress sport clothes, he discovers the trousers and jacket have been drastically altered in order to fit the much shorter Mastroianni, who had stolen and altered them earlier. Thus standing in clothes dramatically too short for him and looking clownishly like an adolescent, he exclaims to Roberts, "I feel like I've grown since I've known you." She, on the other hand, is depicted in a slow pan from her feet up to show her in a low-angle shot wearing a power suit that signifies high fashion and seduction as well as Julia Roberts's own star power. The story ends in another image of a strong woman who strides out of the fictional space of sexual abandon into the working world dressed in confidence and authority.

The fictions in *Prêt-à-Porter,* however, display a broader range of gendered personalities as motivations of the fashion world than this simple duality of heterosexual male and female. The photographer and the editors display the impetus of sexual domination. Robbins's and Roberts's characters depict heterosexual heat underlying professional fashion. Loren's character represents contented self-sufficiency in rebellious retrograde fashion. But one of the more interesting figures in the fiction, the fashion merchandiser Major Hamilton (Danny Aiello) from Marshall Fields in Chicago, is transvestite. Early in the film, one character observes that "women make clothes for themselves or for other women, but men make clothes for the woman they want to be with or the woman they want to be." The narrative conceals the merchandiser's cross-dressing from the audience until late in the film, so that his sexuality appears in terms of secrecy, anxiety, and paranoia. As the most explicit representative of the consumer in the film, this midwestern buyer is routinely configured as uninteresting to the fashion world, whether designers, models, or reporters, but his personal insecurity is deflected by the masquerade afforded him by fashion. His wife (Teri Garr) happily powershops throughout the film and plays out the image of woman as mindless fashion shopper. The final act, however, reveals that she shops out of love and chooses the clothing to meet his needs for sexual identification. In the conclusion of this story the narrative marks the transvestite's insecurity, caught between love on one hand and the fear of social exposure on the other, by sending him in chase after the fashion reporter for the *New York Times,* who has taken his picture in a restaurant full of other cross-dressing men. Her camera threatens to expose the insecure sexual personality that romance and fashion permit him to engage and to own. Her power in this scene is marked as an unknowing theft of his identity.

Thus the fictional stories played by actors largely reflect similar structural resolutions in one way or another—the fashion photographer reduced to shooting children against a billboard of another photographer's work at the end of the film, Tim Robbins's character dressed in clothes that have become too small, Mastroianni's character asleep on the bed of sexual reunion, the fashion buyer driven in panic to catch the reporter who has photographed him in his cross-dressed finery. At the same time, the film mixes three fictional designer shows into the actual prêt-à-porter collections, and reading between the lines in these stories discovers again a recurring relationship between fashion design and sexual subjectivity. One of the fictional fashion designers is black and gay, another is bisexual, and the third is the seduced and abandoned mistress of de la Fontaine. The fashions of both Cort Romney (Richard E. Grant) and Cy Bianco (Forest Whitaker) are marked by their gaudy and flamboyant qualities. The men's homosexual romance is clandestine, but their clothing designs permit an expression of the sexy, warm, lush, extravagant personalities unavailable to them socially as lovers. Humorous desperation frequently characterizes their personal behavior in the fiction, but the clothes displayed in their openings constitute a resistance to socially sexual intransigence by their reality. Indeed, these clothes are the creations of actual designers—Bianco's designed by Xuly Bet and Romney's by Vivienne Westwood—actually on display in the film with the same spectacular dimensionality as in the Paris showrooms.

The story of the third designer consumes the largest amount of the fictional space in the film and recounts the efforts of a Texas financier (Lyle Lovett) to purchase the clothing line of designer Simone Lo (Lowenthal). She has been the mistress of fashion lord de la Fontaine, whose death at the beginning of the film establishes her loss as opposed to the liberation evident for his wife, Isabella. Bereaved by the loss of her lover and horrified by the necessity of selling her failing line of clothing, Lo recalls the abject artists Cathryn in *Images* and Willie in *3 Women.* The slimy financier, who the dialogue and the mise-en-scène associate with reptiles, pays her a compliment that in fact reflects her humiliation when he tells her that in Texas she is held in the same esteem as a cow. The narrative explicitly foregrounds her abjection, both emotional and financial, through most of the middle section of the film as her son sells off her clothing line. The appearance of her logo on the designer cowboy boots ludicrously worn by beautiful models in a shoot orchestrated magisterially by Milo dramatically marks the masculine American ownership of production.

Somehow connecting these three narratives is the thin thread of a story about fictional character Albertine (Ute Lemper), a model who is very visibly pregnant by some unknown but routinely remarked-upon father (implied to be de la Fontaine). Her pregnancy is pointedly displayed by the revealing clothes she wears and by the serial rejection of her presence in the shows of other designers. Designer Romney says in disgust, "Pregnancy is not my silhouette this year." Her story concludes dramatically with that of Simone Lo, who, despondently preparing to open her collection with cowboy boots, is inspired by the figure of Abertine's eminent motherhood—the boots and the pregnancy both dramatic signs of the absent male. Jane Gaines, in discussing fashion designers in classical Hollywood, describes how the "requirement of continuity met the most resistance from the actresses' bodies . . . in the case of pregnancy, when the designer worked against time to produce a perfectly proportioned denial of the most fully elaborated signs of femaleness" (20).

Lo's inspiration works in the opposite direction. In the widely described and discussed final sequence of the film, she sends her models down the fashion runway completely naked and concludes her show with Albertine wearing nothing but a bridal veil and carrying a wedding bouquet. Altman underlines the effect of the event by playing it together with the music of alternative Irish rock group the Cranberries singing "You're So Pretty the Way You Are." This scene has been widely associated by critics with the fairy tale of the emperor's new clothes and asserted to be the key to Altman's parody of the fashion world: "Altman's gesture is . . . confronting the fragility (as he perceives it) of our reliance on clothing for identity and safety" (Bruzzi 33). Few have appreciated that the scene is simultaneously a celebration and resistance that embraces rather than rejects the energy of the Paris fashion world. The scene represents the ultimate femaleness, the double display, the triumph of women over both ownership and abandonment; the joissance not of clothing but of show, of showing, of presentation, of display; the female body not as an object but as a form of assertion, of fashion itself.

Among the many fictional and actual stories of the film's diegesis, the dominant internal narrative suggests a meaningful focus in the Kim Basinger role. Kitty Potter is the fashion reporter for FAD television, who, like the phony BBC reporter Opal in *Nashville,* functions as the narrative device that reflexively stitches together the divergent scenes and stories that constitute the film. The role mirrors the real-life work of CNN's fashion coordinator in 1994, Elsa Klensch, who at one point Kitty interviews "as herself." Basinger's stereotypical star looks also suggest the fashion reporting of model Cindy Crawford for *House of Style* on MTV. She too is a major persona of the entertainment industry, which wears many costumes in this film. Within the context of stories whose male characters suffer defeat or diminishment in the face of the women characters, the Kitty Potter role is complex and reflects the multiple determinations of meaning in the art-cinema text. It models the psychological and ideological work of the film that represents the display of male insecurity as entwined with the display and control of the feminine, which is simultaneously a resistance to and a recuperation of that control. Kim Basinger plays the role as something of a southern blond lightweight who only knows what she reads on the prompt cards scripted by her assistant. She hardly understands the many foreign languages that she repeatedly attempts and butchers in this international setting. She consistently seems to be another example of the film's fiction that fails to measure up to the power of fashion's "real." Thus the film simultaneously puts on display the desirable, sexy female and seeks to contain her energy.

The ultimate look in fashion *(Prêt-à-Porter).*

The image of Kitty Potter emerges contradictorily between her silly incompetence in reporting the scene she covers and the obvious authority of her televisual position of power. Her voice, her image, and her large omnipresent microphone appear on television in practically all the significant—and many insignificant—scenes in the film. The narrative locates her as the interpretative voice of the Paris collections, both within the story and within the discourse. Whether pretending or not to the presence, sophistication, knowledge, and focus she represents in the film, the character is both an object of desire and an image of feminine authority. And the end of her story occurs with the end of the Simone Lo and Albertine stories. As the nude models gather for a curtain call with the designer, she strides from the show room to tell her television audience about the importance of what she has seen. Her refusal to report condemns the sham she believes she has witnessed. Even then as she is ejected from the story, she asserts an authority over its infatuations.

Curiously, many of the film reviewers who read the Basinger role as a joke nevertheless accepted and repeated her interpretation of the Lo show as phony. She exclaims, "What the hell am I talking about? . . . Is that fashion . . . out there? I've been forever trying to find out what this bullshit is all about, and you know what? I've had it!" Kitty Potter puts down her microphone and stalks off the set, out of the frame, and out of the film, and the text apparently exerts its ultimate control over Kim Basinger as she voices this critique. But the art-cinema narration suggests a confluence of resistance here: Lo resists her loss of financial independence; Albertine resists the necessity of a husband in her putative marriage to the designer; the nude models resist Fashion; and the Cranberries' lyrics assert self-confidence in personal beauty. Even as the text asserts control over Kitty's resistance, her intelligent and knowledgeable assistant, the writer behind the scenes, takes up the mike and the new Kitty Potter exuberantly describes the significance of Lo's triumph: she has made "a celebration of fashion in the profoundest sense of the word . . . , and most of all she has spoken to women the world over, telling them not about what to wear, but how to think about what they want and need from fashion."

Altman's art films chronicle a variety of ways in which women are positioned culturally by weak, insecure, consciously or unconsciously ineffective males, and this positioning occurs especially within the media industry. Many of the formal experiments worked by Altman's films on the codes of classical Hollywood cinema reflect a rhetoric of refusal and derive from an anxiety about the authority of narrative order and closure. Once again in *Prêt-à-Porter,* Altman builds multiple, minimal, incoherent narratives that nevertheless stand in contrast to the force of the show business. Roland Barthes in *The Fashion System* contrasts much of fashion's appeal, what he calls the "euphoria of Fashion," with "dramatic, even catastrophic" narratives and happy endings in "a struggle between good and evil": Fashion's "narrative is fragmentary, limited to citations of decor, situation, and character, and deprived of what could be called organic maturation of the anecdote; in short, Fashion would derive its euphoria from the fact that it produces a rudimentary, formless novel without temporality" (261–62). Like the jazz in *Kansas City,* it shapes a space of safety against the temporal orders controlled and directed by the patriarchy. Fashion is like the Altman narrative itself, not the novelistic but the poetic spectacle, pure performance, the dailies rather than the final cut, underneath which runs a masculine insecurity and anxiety of power.

Stella Bruzzi interprets these images and lyrical stanzas: "The intention behind his topsy-turvy, multi-narrative film is thus to prove fashion's inadequacy. . . . The repetitive parade of catwalk shows are served up as lavish, empty farces, a succession of ephemeral, frothy gestures, simply vying with each other to be the most spectacular and thus, under the film's rules, the silliest" (32). But the sheer number and energy of these moments suggests another significance. The narrative punctuates the last two-thirds of *Prêt-à-Porter* (beginning with Isabella de la Fontaine's assuming the seat of her dead husband) with ten different fashion shows—three by fictional designers whose clothes nonetheless are the professional work of real designers Vivienne Westwood, Lamine Kouyate, and Nino Cerruti. They take their place in line with the actual shows of Christian Lacroix, Issey Miyake, Jean Paul Gaultier, Sonia Rykiel, and Christian Dior. Despite the fact that Kitty Potter seems unable to sum up the significance of the fashions, the film seems to celebrate the power of the showings. The kinesthetic mix of editing, moving cameras, shifting angles and framing; of loud, hypnotic musical rhythms (whose origin, whether in the diegetic or discursive space, is impossible to distinguish); and the constant, graceful motion of female bodies in an unending swirl of exotic clothing make the fashion scenes in *Prêt-à-Porter* among the most vibrant and energetic and assertive images in all of Altman's work. If the fictional stories work as parody, the real runways work as celebration. Leslie Rabine articulates part of the appeal in the visual representation of fashion in the media: "The endless repetition of similar images, most of which are inimitable to the point of irreality, invites a look that drifts rapidly through them in a semihallucinatory state" (63). Like the country music in *Nashville,* like the murals in *3 Women,* like the Wild West show in *Buffalo Bill,* like the jazz in *Kansas City,* like *Salomé* in *Cookie's Fortune,* like nursery tales in *Images* and *The Gingerbread Man,* the fashion shows are defensive, and they generate jouissance.

When Potter attempts to interview Sonia Rykiel in the film, Rykiel's shaky English prompts Potter to exclaim, "We need a translator here!" One translator who analyzes the effects of Rykiel's fashions also captures the appeal of their representation as fantasy in the fashion media. Hélène Cixous asserts that "Sonia Rykiel fabricates the dream of the body: to freely be of a body with the legs, the belly, the thighs, the arms, with the air of the sea, with space." And she locates this fantasy in "the most intimate part of myself, the ancient restless and tranquil site, where the body felt itself take its first steps. This garment is native; its model: the body's internal sensation of itself, the secret of the body. Sonia Rykiel designs this sensation" (95). The clothing, the power in its presentation, the hypnosis of its allure, its potential for ultimate identification—all recall for Rabine an "infantile 'mythical moment' of disjunction between the pacification of need . . . and the fulfillment of desire . . . , between the object that satisfies and its sign which describes both the object and its desire" (64). The conjunction of wearing fashion, celebrating the female body, and putting on the show constitutes at once an expressive analysis and critique of the show business—its power, its coercive influence, and its hypnotic beauty.

Barthes argues that fashion's "illusion of a quasi-infinite richness of the person" is a function of diverse and conflicting "psychological essences" that "have a nostalgic value: they give evidence of a dream of wholeness according to which the human being would be everything at once" (*Fashion* 254, 255). Barthes postulates the attraction of fashion to reside in "a double dream, which the rhetoric of Fashion places within a woman's reach . . . dreaming of being at once herself and another" (255–56). The effect of the fictional tales in the film is to chronicle and confront masculine insecurity in the face of forceful, effective women who stride forth purposefully, self-confidently, and authoritatively. The effect of the fashion shows, then, is at once enjoyment in the liberation of the feminine and participation in fashion's containment of that freedom. The significance of Simone Lo's nude fashions represents an assertive acceptance even as it puts on display violation and loss. Barthes argues that the "reassuring function" of such "vestimentary play" is that fashion exorcises the insecurity: "The game of clothing is here no longer the game of being, the agonizing question of the tragic universe; it is simply . . . the final luxury of a personality rich enough to be multiplied, stable enough never to be lost" (257).

Art-cinema strategies of signification ask us to recognize the contrasting cognitive patterns. They suggest that *Prêt-à-Porter* thus participates in the representation of the play between, on one hand, the masculine need reflected in the fictions of insecurity and, on the other, the feminine need reflected in the resistance of Lo's naked models, in Potter's disavowal of the phallus, and in the liminal, rhapsodic display of fetishistic plenitude and completeness. In the film, Gianfranco Ferré, "Italian designer resident at the venerable old French house of Christian Dior," articulates this awareness when he says that the impetus behind his designs is "the energy that the woman needs in these times. . . . I like to make fantasies with them . . . so she can make her own tradition with the freedom she needs." The process, then, of dressing, of what Rabine calls

> the process of enacting the fantasies of fashion . . . upon the body . . . along with any erotically charged daydream it might include, also entails on the symbolic level a ritualized reenactment of a "mythical moment" itself, covering not the separation between biology and sign but between two signs, that of the unclothed, un-made-up body as sign of unmastered biology and of the clothed body symbolizing a self-produced coherent subject. (64)

The significance of these representations is nevertheless contradictory. Both in narrative complexity and in expressive realism the film reflects the ambiguities of the art cinema. Cixous distinguishes between the clothes and the moments that are for shelter and for peace and "shield-clothes, mirror-clothes, shimmering, dazzling clothes, clothes which both attract and repel the gaze, clothes of the armor species, clothes which remold the body to a precise measure, to perfect composure, clothes which adorn. I have had some. Few. I never liked them. I donned them to go to war" (97). The film's fictions put on display threatening women whose power in part derives from their fashioned assertiveness. The three mavens of fashion from *Elle, British Vogue,* and *Harper's Bazaar* go to war. They resist the photographic humiliation of their exposed bodies, as much in their own stylistic processional down a metaphoric runway into Milo's hotel room as in their possession of his film. Isabella strides assertively along another symbolic runway, to the cemetery for her husband's funeral, in a huge scarlet hat that signs her liberation from the dead lord of fashion. When Julia Roberts appears in her power suit, she is transformed from the sloppy, wine-addicted nymphomaniac into the assertive, self-confident woman whose power is reflected in her assertion of her name, Eisenhower, "like the general," as a signifier of the law. And Lo's naked models embrace the fashion of the body itself as the ultimate sign of both resistance and self-sufficiency.

Barthes, however, suggests how the subliminal reality of the body confronts fashion with "a well-known discontinuity" between language and speech, and observes that whether the model's body, the fashionable body, or the transformed body, in all cases "the body is taken 'in charge' by the intelligible system of signs, and sentience is dissolved in the signifier." Nudity itself, he asserts, "is nothing more in Fashion than the sign of the dressy" (*Fashion* 260). The female nude in art has always revealed the temporarily fashionable form dictated by social norms. As Anne Hollander observes in *Seeing through Clothes*:

> The placement, size, and shape of the breast, the set of the neck and shoulders, the relative girth and length of the rib cage, the exact disposition of its fleshy upholstery, front and back—all these, along with styles of posture both seated and upright, are continually shifting according to the way clothes have been variously designed in history to help the female body look beautiful (and natural) on their terms. (190)

Even unclothed, the body types that glide down Simone Lo's runway are recognizable. Tall, thin, small-breasted, flat-bellied—these bodies reflect the interposition of Twiggy between the voluptuousness of Sophia Loren's fashionable body from the late-1950s and the anorexic dictation of contemporary fashion in the mid-1990s. Although Lo's show of naked resistance concludes the film's fictional stories, the discourse continues during the credits and replays the dominance of the fashion show's "real." The metaphoric images in this sequence foreground the curtain calls of the various designers with their models clustered around them as they appear at the ends of their shows to receive the accolades of the audiences. Not the clothes, not the models, but the creators are celebrated here, just as the film also credits its production staff. Salient among these final images is additional footage of the Dior show that prominently displays a female model shrouded in a black, head-to-toe garment with wide side panels that are stretched out like the wings of a butterfly. These panels are held by the only male models in the film, who manipulate the wings to fling the woman forward and then to pull her back. This gesture perfectly symbolizes the reflexive, analytic energy of the film, liberating and controlling the feminine.

One year after the release of this film, when the fashion documentary *Unzipped* (1995) appeared, critics repeatedly compared it to *Prêt-à-Porter.* Gene Siskel, for instance, in the *Chicago Tribune* described it as "a marvelous documentary about the fashion industry that accomplishes everything Robert Altman's 'Ready to Wear' failed to achieve" (7B). *Unzipped* is a better film as a work of criticism only if the viewer adapts the perspective of Sonia Rykiel when she writes:

> Lean closer to hear the rustle of fabric, the words of the artist, his passion for dress. Lean even nearer to see that he is not destroying but having new thoughts, repositioning, reworking, reshaping the same form on which he has already thought, positioned, worked, shaped, everything being drawn from the depths of the eternal and essential memory he has of the object already conceived long ago. (104).

*Unzipped,* directed by its subject's lover, treats designer Isaac Mizrahi as an object glamorized by the entertainment world like the models and fashions are themselves. Fashion is serious business in the capitalist social economy, and a seamless connection runs through the axis fashion-model-designer-reviewer-filmmaker-movie-critic-consumer. The fashion reviewers and the film reviewers positively appreciated *Unzipped* because stylistically it is reverent. Model Lauren Hutton exulted that "Mizrahi loves company," that *Unzipped* "is real insider stuff" (73). The film portrays its designer at once as creator and star, and the reviews adoringly reflect what Siskel unself-consciously described as "the coziness between designers and the trade press" (7B).

*Prêt-à-Porter,* on the other hand, must fail from this point of view because it is irreverent in the disconcertingly self-conscious play of fictional farce and documentary show that subverts seriousness. Two little moments convey the ideological and psychological contexts within which the film works and in many ways disavows. After the editor of *British Vogue* facetiously answers a frivolous question from a *New York Times* reporter, she asks, "Doesn't anyone ask anything serious every now and then?" The reporter quickly responds, "Okay, how do you feel that fifty percent of the world's pollution is caused by the textiles industry?" The question draws only shocked silence.

In another moment, when Sophia Loren pronounces her would-be lover, Mastroianni, to be as dead as her husband and leaves him asleep on the hotel bed, the camera pans to a dark adjacent room where a television set conveys a strange picture, almost in black and white, of men dressed like sheep bending over in a line and playing leapfrog. The sheep costumes have short stiff tails that stick out with a phallic suggestivity as the men play a kids' game in sheep's clothing. On one hand, the Altman fictions reflect only an abstract insecurity in the face of the economic system that produces these marvelous vestimentary fantasies through the labor of women in North and South American and Asian sweatshops. On the other hand, Altman's oblique imagery suggests a psychic energy that displaces male anxiety about sexual subjectivity into the pleasurable decoration and display of the female body.

Robert Hilferty, in his review of *Prêt-à-Porter,* claims that "what Altman envisions here is women's revolt, Trojan Women for postmodern times" (37), but even as the film offers a subjectivity for women that transcends the control fashion ultimately works on the female consumer, it demonstrates the power of the entertainment machine (like the Altman movie itself) to reinvoke that control. When fictional Kitty Potter asks real designer Thierry Mugler to reconcile the sexy and the independent energy his clothes evoke, he replies lasciviously, "It's about getting a good fuck, baby." And Christian Lacroix explicitly describes the ideological function of his designs. He wants "people to be a little bit disturbed" because they "don't know where was the reality." *Prêt-à-Porter* reiterates Leslie Rabine's observation that "in the logic of fashion, it is not resistance that is contained, but the conflict itself between freedom and dominance. In this conflict . . . the dominant term is doubled, acting as both one pole of the conflict and as the enclosure that contains the conflict" (63). Simone Lo's nudes celebrate resistance to the codes of fashion, and Christian Dior's shroud puts the woman on display as a subject that fashion liberates and then recaptures. *Prêt-à-Porter* conveys those two bodies—one that is authoritative, free, and sexually confident; the other a sociopolitical body positioned by the web of power relations that still dominates women economically, politically, sexually, and physically through systems of objectification like the show business. Whence, then, says Roland Barthes, fashion's "ambiguous status: it signifies the world and signifies itself, it constructs itself here as a program of behavior, and there as a luxurious spectacle" (*Fashion* 291). Like the art cinema, the film and fashion lyrically reflect the contemporary social world of alienated and insecure individuals who are simultaneously liberated and constructed by the economies of popular entertainment.

# 9. Worlds Elsewhere: *Short Cuts*

Few directors have remained so canonical within the critical world and so pervasively unpopular with the viewing public as Robert Altman. After a decade of small-budget theatrical films and industrial invisibility, Altman crafted the disruptive narrative strategies of *Nashville* and *A Wedding* into *The Player,* a popular, ironic, reflexive critique of people who get away with murder in the movie industry. *The Player*'s entertaining mix of strong voices and coherent intrigue marked the return of the art-cinema director for some critics, but for others it represented an art director who had sold out the unpopular but artistic inventiveness and integrity of films like *Nashville.* However, just as the enormous box-office success of *MASH* in 1970 financed risky and unpopular films such as *Thieves Like Us* and *California Split, The Player* purchased Altman the freedom to make another critically popular and financially unsuccessful film. *Short Cuts* was acclaimed along with *The Piano* and *Schindler's List* as one of the best films of 1993, but unlike those other two, *Short Cuts* failed to make it into the list of the top twenty financial "hits" of the year. Nevertheless, 1992's financial success allowed Altman to come around in 1993 and, as he says, "jump off the cliff again" with another film resistant in its art-cinema complexities to audience appreciation.

*The Player* develops a big narrative on the showy lives of the image makers in the entertainment industry. *Short Cuts* stops down its focus to convey a fragmentary record of the lives of people at the edges of power, of emotion, of energy, of communication, and examines again the meaningfulness of marginality. Twenty-two characters constitute nine different but overlapping family situations that—pulled apart—might be read as separate, if spare, narratives. None of these situations is shaped by any clearly delineated conflict that is begun, intensified, and resolved during the three hours of the film. Here are represented a range of people little noticed in society who are nevertheless recognizable as constructed by its values and conveyed in a manner quite deliberately designed as contrastive/comparative analyses of social identity. *Short Cuts* thus returns to an art-cinema weaving of twenty-two characters into a modernist tapestry that confounds the visual literacy of popular entertainment. Its requisite reading strategy involves the identification of some metaphoric similarity under which to arrange all of the dissimilar situations, qualities, styles, and behaviors that address us from the work. This process amounts to aligning our cultural and generic repertoires with those of the film, an adaptation process like the symbiosis of fiction and film that reflects signs from the social milieu shared between work and audience. It also affords a dramatic illustration of the complexity that characterizes the narrative process of Altman's art cinema. At the beginning of this book, *Kansas City* served to illustrate the categories of form, social identity, and reflexivity that I understand to characterize the art cinema of Robert Altman. Here in the end, *Short Cuts* summarizes the imaginative reach, the aesthetic implication, and the interactive demand of subliminal reality as an organizing concept of this cinema.

In particular, the distinctions between classical and art-cinema narratives and between realist and discursive reading procedures help to situate this process. Readerly texts depend upon conventions of empirical commonsense realism, of coherent plots constructed around cause-effect logic, of psychological desires located in central characters, and of quests and conflicts concluded with emotional and logical clarity. Writerly texts put the intelligibility of all these conventional orders at risk. They question social, psychological, and narrative stability. They portray reality as constructed rather than discovered, and they demand active participation from the viewer who would construct meaning from the fragments of narrative.

Classical narratives posit a real world of social identification, no matter how stylized their representation. Characters may be ideal figures, but the audience grounds their luminary presence on the screen in the reality of the star system and comprehends their actions in a commonsense psychology of human behavior. Some characters are major (strong, knowing, active, productive) and others are minor (weak, uncertain, hesitant). Actions prompt reactions and have efficacious consequences; they develop along sequential, logical paths of causes and effects that presuppose and reify hierarchies of value, authority, and responsibility. These narratives naturalize personal history with beginnings, middles, and ends. They assume an integrity of identity and behavior between fictional characters and between text and viewer that can be recognized and interpreted like the events of the "natural world." Conventional reading schemata of the classical text decode their signs as plausible representations of the real even as the novelistic, beginning with Henry Fielding and continuing with contemporary television soap opera, constitutes a structured substitution for the real.

A central quality of art-cinema narration, on the other hand, is its claim to represent a truer reality: its human figures are "people," not "characters"; their physiognomy is ordinary rather than idealized. The behavior of these people frequently seems motivated by unseen events and unknown causes and suggests the necessity of psychoanalysis for comprehension. Actions may prompt reactions, but not in any logical or sequential way. Narrative order disappears. Narrative lines multiply. People assume major roles in some stories and minor roles in others. These textual qualities engage a conventional reading strategy that discovers meaning through a correlation with everyday reality.

At the same time these modernist narratives seek to deliver a greater verisimilitude of empirical experience than that of classical realism, their deconstruction of classical narrative structures such as the linear development of conflicts also demands a discursive reading strategy that recognizes the textual rhetoric of engagement. In texts where the social subject is unstable and fragmented, where story and plot time are fractured, where story reflects on its telling, where cause and effect are subliminal, the narrative gaps require active reading from the viewer to produce coherent identities and actions. The absence of narrative logic engages the viewers' active participation in the explanation of behavior and demonstrates social realism and personal identity to be constructed rather than given. Thus the the art cinema frequently invites a reading of character and identity, action and plot as textual devices communicating values implicit in the discourses and ideologies that intersect to produce them. Its narrative qualities urge reading as a discursive activity that foregrounds the interrelationships among cultural value, social position, and public discourse.

Altman's films require a variety of reading strategies, but the distinction between a realist and a discursive strategy focuses two central perspectives that are particularly relevant to *Short Cuts,* Altman's adaptation of Raymond Carver's short stories, and generally relevant to all Altman's films. Constructing meaning in these disconnected stories requires attention not to a narrative but to a poetic order, in which, as Roman Jakobson taught in his famous definition of the poetic, the syntagmatic relationships are constructed on the paradigmatic axis. The audience must read metaphorically rather than metonymically. The audience must also read discursively—that is, semiotically—aware of the fact that the paradigms juxtaposed by the narrative constitute an exploration of the divergence of similar signs, the slippage of signification under those signs, the inevitable but fluid construction of social identity by conflicting ideologies. *Short Cuts* epitomizes the subliminal reality of Altman's films. Its refusal to specify connections, to rationalize behavior, to explain significance forces the viewer to import patterns of personality, relationship, and motivation to the movie.

Adaptations focus the possibilities and potential of constructing more than the explicit meanings of a film by activating an awareness of the complex terms of readability in which meaning always derives from a multiplicity of external cultural and generic codes. Informed, critical reading of adaptations like *Short Cuts* involves an intertextual recognition of the fact that present artifacts, events, and people relate symbiotically to absent but informing contexts. Dudley Andrew analyzes the intertextual significance represented by adaptation: "Its distinctive feature, the matching of the cinematic sign system to prior achievement in some other system, can be shown to be distinctive of all representational cinema" because "every cinematic rendering will exist in relation to some prior whole lodged unquestioned in the personal or public system of experience. . . . Adaptation delimits representation by insisting on the cultural status of the model, on its existence in the mode of the text or the already textualized" (*Concepts* 96–97). Adaptations, like Altman's films, always posit their meanings in reference to other work, other experience, other codes of encryption and communication.

Barbara Johnson begins her collection of essays titled *The Critical Difference* by describing the contrary operation of rereading. She calls the realistic act of reading an encounter with the already read: "What we can see in a text the first time is already in us, not in it; in us insofar as we ourselves are a stereotype, an already-read text; and in the text only to the extent that the already-read is that aspect of a text that it must have in common with its reader in order for it to be readable at all." The act of rereading, on the other hand, is discursive and involves the "text's difference," "the text's way of differing from itself. . . . Far from constituting the text's unique identity, it is that which subverts the very idea of identity, infinitely deferring the possibility of adding up the sum of a text's parts or meanings and reaching a totalized, integrated whole" (3–4). Adaptations as rereadings thus, like subliminal reality in Altman's films, engage viewers in an interactive process that activates the potential of the "writerly" text, ourselves writing, rather than the already-read play of meanings that classical narrative assumes.

*Short Cuts,* Carver's fiction, and Altman's concept of subliminal reality all resist the closure of thematic meaning, structural unity, and authorial vision. They especially make us aware of the terms and contexts of meaning rather than the flow of events in a story. Jay Bolter, discussing the nature of hypertextual discourse in digital communication, writes that "what we have traditionally called the structure of the text is the relationship between the linear experience of reading and the network of allusions among elements that are separated in the physical space of the book" (53). The adaptation relationship itself as well as the relationship between story and reality in Altman's films model a concept of texts as nodes of meaning situated by the intersection of numberless textual strands that cohere momentarily in the present commingling of reading or viewing subject and discourse. They posit conceptual systems that replace "ideas of center, margin, hierarchy, and linearity" with "multiple linearity, nodes, links, and networks" (Landow 2). At the technical level of sound recording this same effect is discernible, as Rick Altman describes:

> In the face of cinema's apparent willingness to adhere to the printed word's single-channel aesthetic, Altman not only chose to use traditional technology in a new manner, but he also developed a new sound technology, specifically dedicated to a non-hierarchical multichannel soundscape. The characteristic Altman approach to sound may thus be read as an overt attempt to break out of cinema's heretofore literary model, to fight the tendency to reduce sound to its meaning, to replace the single-channel linearity of written discourse by a three-dimensional multiplicity calling for a radically different level and type of spectator—and especially auditor—activity. ("24-Track" 8)

Readers, viewers, and auditors, then, navigate their own subjectivity, composed of a similar weave of references to other webs of texts, into the labyrinth of sociological, psychological, historical, aesthetic allusions, quotations, and referentiality that constitute the narrative. The meanings they construct from this encounter emerge from the possibilities offered by the story and the possibilities of their own experience. Indeed, the story offers a galaxy of choices through which they make a path by their reading.

Subliminal reality shapes narratives that are not linear and hierarchical sequences of signs constructed on an interior framework of meaning but are themselves networks of intersecting discourses that reference numerous meaning-making structures along many divergent pathways. Stories have no center but open onto plural centers that always lie elsewhere. The very process of reading a film, or interpreting it, or critiquing it constitutes the importation of other texts to give meaning, a center, wholeness to that text. Absence, gaps, silences in the text always reference some other text, some other name, some other place. When a filmmaker attempts to adapt a narrative from print to film, a common assumption posits this act as an interpretation whose value will consist in its illumination of some originary nucleus, discoverable, translatable. Both texts, however, not only approach but recede from each other in myriad directions. Joy Gould Boyum describes this multitextual symbiosis in reader-response terms:

> If we indeed resymbolize a text in the process of reading and consequently make it our own, and if we do the same in watching a film, consider the complexity of the process involved in watching a film of a book we have read—in other words, of crystallizing a new film experience out of the stuff of memory (which here includes the book on which that film is based) and thus interpreting on the basis of a prior interpretation the actual cinematic interpretation laid before us. (50)

Adaptation poses a constantly open, constantly interrogative textuality. Cinematic adaptations of fiction never adapt merely the "prior whole" of the literary text but a wide array of other cultural texts as well—formal, cultural, ideological, psychological.

Robert Scholes writes that "we are never outside the whole web of textuality in which we hold our cultural being and in which every text awakens echoes and harmonies." He defines two kinds of reading—the centripetal and the centrifugal. *Centripetal* reading tends "to seek original truth or original intent as the master protocol of readings that will be as positive and unchanging as they can be." It "conceives of a text in terms of an original intention located at the center of that text." On the other hand, *centrifugal* reading insists on "the freedom and creativity of the reader along with the mutability of meanings in general." It "sees the life of a text as occurring along its circumference, which is constantly expanding, encompassing new possibilities of meaning" (*Protocols* 7–8).

This conceptualization of reading defines the dialectical tension that both subliminal reality and the multiple textuality of adaptations engage in the process of making meaning. Viewers are always "connecting one time to another, one place to another, one text to another through the figures of memory, which are the same as the figures of speech . . . by connecting signs and weaving texts, using the figures of resemblance, contiguity, and causality to accomplish this work" (*Protocols* 18). Although part of the resemblance construes a plottedness to our lives, a pattern of beginnings, middles, and ends that implies in its teleology some purpose, some conclusion, thus some intention, some meaning, "something in us" also resists this running down toward the end, works against a "textual fundamentalism" that believes "texts always say just what they mean"(*Protocols* 52) and understands, even asserts, that the book and the world are both unknowable and disappointing in their endless plurality. Reading centrifugally in this context "requires us to connect what is represented in the text with what we see in the world" (*Protocols* 154), requires us to seek a balance between textual fundamentalism and "hermeneutic nihilism."

Two different kinds of adaptation texts motivate centrifugal reading strategies within an intertextual frame of reference. Popular adaptations, mainstream criticism, and conventional audience expectations routinely assume some intended cinematic fidelity to some originary literary text. The intertextual adaptation of multiple other texts is tacit, the other texts assumed, taken for granted, naturalized. One must discover their textual promiscuity by reading against the grain of their silences. For instance, adaptations contemporaneous with *Short Cuts* in the 1990s, such as *Little Women* (1994), *The Age of Innocence* (1993), *Ethan Frome* (1993), *Pride and Prejudice* (1995), *The Last of the Mohicans* (1992), *The Wings of the Dove* (1997), and *Wuthering Heights* (1992), undertake to treat faithfully texts that ostensibly ask to be read in their own right as classical novels—marked, that is, by a formal intentionality of beginning-middle-end, structured around cause-effect logic and the psychological, goal-oriented behavior of central characters (despite the fact that these novels may variously inflect romantic, realistic or modernist sensibilities). Each of these adaptations makes sense in terms of its intended fidelity to some prior text whose earlier adaptation of the human order is taken to be naturalistic and representational.

Other adaptations, however, take for granted an intertextual web of meaning, both formally and philosophically. Their fidelity is pledged to a multiplicity of social meaning, and their narrative practice seeks to liberate rather than constrain that plurality. Virginia Woolf in *Orlando* "employs a panoply of mockery, allusion, selfconsciousness and parody as her subject collides with the conventions of the last three-and-a-half centuries, in order to undermine the idea that male and female are separate and fixed opposites" (Ouditt 149). Sally Potter's film adaptation of *Orlando* (1992) "alludes to so many forms—literature, obviously, but also painting, choreography and music" and produces a film that "is polysemic in a way that resists absolutes" (Ouditt 153–54). James Joyce's "The Dead" and John Huston's film adaptation (1987) both start with a Twelfth Night dinner party in turn-of-the-century Dublin to portray cultural paralysis that opens on unspeakable relations of class and gender and three hundred years of English-Irish relationships. *Dr. T & the Women* simultaneously adapts the myth of Hestia, the Book of Job, *Sullivan's Travels,* and *The Wizard of Oz.* Such films demand an intertextual reading strategy—that is, they activate a network of references, presuppositions, allusions, sources, and derivations in both story and discourse that identifies subliminal reality. Raymond Carver's fiction in six volumes during the 1970s and 1980s and Altman's thirty-three films reflect both narrative strategies and philosophical perspectives that dramatize the inevitability of an intertextual repertoire in interpretation. In particular, Altman's initial reading of Carver appears as an edited collection of nine stories and one poem titled *Short Cuts,* and then his adaptation of that collection into the film displays a rich yet cryptic referentiality that turns meaning down unexpected corridors, into other streets, other texts, centers elsewhere. Efforts to measure the fidelity of one to the other encounter only the infinite regress of plural texts. These works recapitulate and compound the intertextual referentiality foregrounded by the art cinema in their themes, narrative structures, and rhetorical devices.

David Bordwell, in his book *Making Meaning,* analyzes the different schemata critics employ to map semantic fields onto literary and cinematic texts. Critical discourse on Carver's work illustrates the full range of these various topological, template, and procedural patterns that organize the meanings to which a "faithful" film adaptation might aspire. Some literary critics employ procedural categories that map the meanings of Carver's stories to his biography and his indebtedness to "hardscrabble working-class" origins. Others employ stylistic schemata to map the echoes of Joyce, Chekhov, James, Hemingway, Kafka, and O'Connor (Campbell 4; A. Meyer 25). One writes, "Quick cuts, elliptical dialogue, blunt ironies, and plain surfaces as narrative devices originate in a tradition of short story writing that . . . is a reflection of the fragmentary and alienated condition of the twentieth-century self" (Facknitz in Campbell 130). Other critics use realistic schemata to construe in Carver's work the "dark side of Reaganism" (Nesset 102). They employ template schemata to discover the patterns of "catastrophic failure" and dis-ease in modern life (A. Meyer 22) or the "way people wrest salvation from adversity" (Campbell 167). Depending on the collection, other critics see the stories reflecting either the "existential chronicle of Hopelessville" or the "secret of deep human sympathy" (Nesset 62). Through artistic schemata, critics argue, his stories refuse the kind of totalizing fiction that organizes plot, story, and character into a coherent view of social reality. Or, in the words of John Barth, they convey the realism of "post-Vietnam, post-literary, postmodernist blue collar neo-early-Hemingwayism" (quoted in Runyon 3).

Even though *Short Cuts* was nominated for a Golden Globe award for best adaptation, many fans of Raymond Carver faulted the film as faithless work. If "fidelity" or "faithfulness" must always be measured against an array of a priori texts from other sign systems, then the question, What's adaptable in Carver? becomes the question of what's readable in his minimalist stories. In Bordwell's terms, what semantic fields reside in the critical arsenal for constructing meaning in the Carver texts? Indeed, several of Carver's most famous stories, including "A Small Good Thing" and "So Much Water So Close to Home"—both of which Altman adapts—exist in various versions. Which should claim the greatest fidelity? The Carver critical establishment offers a wide array of answers and presuppositions. Adam Meyer notes that Carver's stories are often "referred to as being 'open' or 'ambivalent' or 'indeterminate,' and this condition does place something of a burden on the reader. The open ending invites collaboration between author and reader, but many readers have complained about being left 'holding the bag'" (23). That quality itself, however, changes across the different stages of his work, so that Ewing Campbell distinguishes between the "essential Carveresque" and the "new fiction" of Carver's last two collections of stories (49).

The minimalism of Carver's stories means that less is more, or rather that less generates more. As short stories laid out linearly they provoke questions about sequentiality: Why does that story follow this story? Randolph Paul Runyon, in his book *Reading Raymond Carver,* pursues the thesis that Carver's collections ask us to read the "interstices between the stories" (1). We read centripetally for connectedness across and within the stories. Runyon says: "We will not, then, find a single buried narrative from beginning to end in the short story sequences. . . . But we will find other stories, meta-stories in which the stories themselves, together with their constituent motifs, images, and turns of phrase, are part of the plot" (8). Yet he also recognizes that even as "their appearance together between the covers of a single volume and the very order of their appearance" seems to "give the reader enough clues to begin to reconstruct what seems to be missing," he also points out that "there is no guarantee that what is missing will be found" (83). In other words, even as we read centripetally for relatedness, for causality, for motivation, the stories force us centrifugally out of the texts. Carver's strategy frustrates our narrativity. His range of associations, almost poetic in their condensation, activates a density of causal assumptions, and his silences energize our sensitivity to the intertextual outside because of the sparseness of the inside and force us to look for centers of meaning on the periphery of his stories.

## Carver's Stories

The male character has a meaningless job at the hospital. His wife successfully sells vitamins door-to-door. She manages a crew of other saleswomen, and "there was no end to the girls." Sheila is a lesbian who loves the wife and leaves for Portland. Donna feels bad for having to quit working for the wife. The man cheats on his wife with Donna and takes her to a bar, where a black Vietnam veteran propositions her with money and shows them his war trophy of a severed Vietnamese ear. Donna moves to Portland. What is the meaning of all these events? What chain of associations does this chain of associations unleash?

Three men on a fishing trip find the nude body of a woman in the river where they leave her for three days until the end of their planned stay, when they notify authorities. The wife of one of the men is upset by their action. She hates him and pities him. She takes their child to his mother, who has the same name she does. Her mother-in-law is always judging her. She recollects that her marriage began in seduction. She goes to the dead girl's funeral. What is the meaning of this story, of the cultural references opened by its cryptic signs?

Mr. Slater is "out of work." He's home alone waiting for the mail. Aubrey Bell, a traveling vacuum cleaner salesman, arrives to give him a free demonstration. Mr. Slater thinks he is losing his mind. He watches as Aubrey Bell vacuums up "little bits" of his life. He watches as the salesman leaves with the letter just left by the postman. What is the meaning of this?

The Carver critical establishment tells us that these stories evoke a sense of self, the nature of selfhood in the contemporary world, a vision of the self, personal survival in the face of defeat (Nesset 13; Saltzman

22; Campbell 17). Campbell tells us that the Carver stories are meaningful when read through semantic fields of sentimentality, cultural myth, and "a therapeutics of passion" (52). On one page alone, for instance, he references Jane Tompkins, Jesus Christ, Little Eva, Michel Foucault, and Ernest Hemingway as the broad range of a priori texts "lodged unquestioned in the personal or public system of perception" that the Carver texts adapt and through which they in turn become meaningful (53–54).

The subliminal reality of these writerly stories demands readers' construction of causality, their search through the web of references and events rearranged to make these stories meaningful, their clearing a path through all the possible connections that the text enables and that enable it. And their own critical and ideological repertoire engages these cryptic indirections. The characters in "Neighbors" feel that "they alone had been passed by somehow," and "being passed by" connects these characters with the characters of all the other stories in the *Short Cuts* collection. But part of that emotion also derives from anxiety about jobs, about relationships, about self-confidence in another half of these stories; it motivates violence in three of them; it relates to sexual insecurity in another five stories, and infidelity in yet another three. All the stories may also reveal the "strangeness behind banality." Moreover, guilt, noncommunication, alienation, and isolation reference other conceptual frames in this network of connections; the moods of social paranoia, sexual dysfunction, interpersonal inadequacy, and lack and desire also emerge and proliferate from the intertext. Claire Kane in the story "So Much Water So Close to Home" believes: "There is a connection to be made of these things, these events, these faces, if I can find it. My head aches with the effort to find it" (Carver 89).

This intertextual multiplicity of the Carver stories invites the reader to write a path through their web of references, and critics adapt a wide number of divergent texts that enfranchise their adducing sufficient data from the stories to produce a reading of them. To what then must any cinematic adaptation of Carver be faithful? When Kirk Nesset asserts that Carver's stories "are faithful to his world" (49), he recognizes a procedure of intertextuality that locates meaning in some authorial text. Thus the Altman film *Short Cuts* may adapt in the first place the "Altmanesque." No other American filmmaker has more consistently asked the audience to adapt an interrogative stance toward narrative cinematic discourse—its subjects and modes, its structure, its representation of culture, its required reading strategies. Altman's films embrace the drive for a heightened realism characteristic of the international modernist cinema. These films indeed document a physical, tangible world of an everyday reality, but at the same time they explore that reality as shifting, deceptive, incoherent, contradictory, ephemeral. They seek to convey Altman's sense of subliminal reality:

> I'm not so much interested in a good yarn as I am atmosphere, of people's behavior and having a feeling out of this . . . something that can be put on the screen that an audience will watch and will come away . . . not being able to articulate what they think about it. I am more interested in the subliminal reality. I'm more interested in touching people on an unconscious basis to where they sense something rather than intellectually know or agree to something. *(The Player)*

Thus the cinematographer for *Short Cuts,* Walt Lloyd, remarks that "we sought a natural look for this film . . . about people's innermost feelings" (in Kaplan and Dorr). Practically all of Altman's films look at the destabilized subject, the self as a construct of contradictory and frequently debilitating social forces. The fidelity of *Short Cuts* to this "world" then establishes some sort of homologous relationship to the fidelity of Carver's stories to the Carveresque.

## Altman's Film

Discovering what's readable is just as complex a process in *Short Cuts* as it is in Carver's fiction. The centrifugal energies are dense and bewildering. Their requisite reading strategy involves the identification of some metaphoric similarity under which to arrange all of the like situations, qualities, styles, behaviors that address the viewer from the works. Altman suggests that he has discovered something in Carver to adapt when he says that Carver "wrote one big story." He may be referencing that one big story when he further observes, "You have a lot of things in your head at once, but you always end by saying this one thing" (in Kaplan and Dorr). But he may also be referencing the fact that when "you write just one thing, you're always writing about all those unsaid things as well." Thus the question about relatedness in the sequentiality of the published short stories takes on greater significance when we read a book titled *Short Cuts: Selected Stories* by Raymond Carver, with an "introduction by Robert Altman." What intertextual glue has Altman found that links these stories? The order in this volume suggests a reading, a path that Altman has cleared through the web of interconnectedness of Carver's fiction. The adaptation of that set of stories in his film suggests even further that he has a reading of the Carver work to which his film would be faithful. But the Altman collection *Short Cuts* and the movie of the same name constitute very different rewritings of Carver's minimal stories and represent differing interpretations of Carver as well as the cultural intertext.

Comparing the film stories to Carver's seems to support a conservative, centripetal approach to adaptations. Carver wrote one story; Altman is saying one thing. Our reading then can be motivated to see the fidelity between these two works. "We've taken liberties with Carver's work," says Altman (in Kaplan and Dorr), but those liberties may be read as his efforts to show the causal links between action and reaction missing from Carver's stories, missing links that send us out into the intertext for the social or psychological texts that explain character behavior and narrative structure. Carver tells the story of Jack and his dog in "Jerry, Molly, and Sam" with minimal representation of location, characterization, and situation. Altman's adaptation of the story represents Jack as a motorcycle cop named Gene (Tim Robbins) in the suburbs of Los Angeles who's cheating on his wife, Sherri (Madeleine Stowe), and who gets rid of his dog as one of the things in his life that fray his nerves. His secret sexual partner is the Mrs. Slater absent from Carver's "Collectors," and the wife's sister is the wife in Carver's story "Will You Please Be Quiet, Please?" These liberties seem to understand and partially to explain the stories. Altman's cowriter on *Short Cuts,* Frank Barhydt, conveys the same impression: the adaptation process is "a matter of taking the stories into your mind and throwing the book away. What you remember is the essence of it . . . , and the rest you improvise. We're faithful to the spirit of Carver" (in Kaplan and Dorr). And that fidelity amounts to jazz variations on Carver's fiction.

But faithful as understood by Dudley Andrew means adapting a wide range of a priori texts, and these rewritings by *Short Cuts* evidence this process. Like Faulkner's efforts to clarify the stories of the Compsons in *The Sound and the Fury,* Altman's explanations only tell more stories, each in their own right as cryptic as the earlier ones, an expansion of sequentiality rather than an explanation of any of them. Altman has been faithful not to some reading of the Carver texts but to the intertextual effect of those stories, their representation of the tacit dimensions of human understanding, their enactment of the gaps in motivation between word and action, between action and reaction, between thought and word. There are many ways to navigate this web, many links to pursue in multiple directions, many cues for constructing divergent meanings. Altman's film is faithful to the narrative effect that demands centrifugal reading, that process Scholes identifies as seeing "the life of a text as occurring along its circumference, which is constantly expanding, encompassing new possibilities of meaning" (*Protocols* 8). What Carver really did, says Altman, "was capture the wonderful idiosyncrasies of human behavior, the idiosyncrasies that exist amid the randomness of life's experiences. And human behavior, filled with all its mystery and inspiration, has always fascinated me" ("Introduction" 7).

Bordwell describes a dominant strategy for making meaning in narrative texts as the procedural schema that uses realism to follow the textual cues. Thus we seek to comprehend, motivate, internalize the relationships of twenty-two people in nine families with common names and ordinary jobs. But the sheer number of characters makes the names meaningless and blurs the boundaries of family relations. We are forced then to read these lives through the procedural schemata Bordwell designates as compositional motivation. Significance lies not in the social reality of these individuals but in the rhetoric that activates the play of differences among the textual signs. The set of oppositions between guilt and confession, distrust and acceptance, infidelity and faithfulness, destruction and construction, apathy and responsibility, life and death together define subjectivity. Their readability depends upon our familiarity with discursive codes, generic and cultural, and our familiarity with the ideological repertoire that structures social and textual identities.

Like Carver's stories, any one of the narratives focused by a set of characters puzzles and delights in the rich web of psychological, sociological, aesthetic relationships they subsume. The man who fishes for three days is married to a clown who entertains kids next door to the house where a little boy has been hospitalized because he's been hit by a car driven by a waitress whose daughter is the friend of a telephone sex salesgirl whose husband services the pool of the cello player who lives next door to the dying boy. This reconstruction matches a round of connections not clearly apparent in the narrative's complex editorial mixing of stories. Not only does this process open a whole range of cultural understandings for a reading concerned with connections, it also suggests the random, reversible, interchangeable, obscure, and yet obvious paths, the shortcuts, any reading can follow—rather, that any reading selects through the proliferating networks of human interactions.

Intertextual complexities abound everywhere. One sequence is illustrative. In the middle of the film there is a series of shots (within part of the movie's adaptation of "So Much Water So Close to Home") of the three men fishing: a medium shot that zooms in slightly on Vern (Huey Lewis) standing in a rushing river and working to land a large fish (he yells "Yahoo!") cut to a still medium shot of Stuart (Fred Ward) holding up a netted fish (he shouts, "Looka here. It's about three or four pounds!") cut to a medium shot that zooms in slightly on Gordon (Buck Henry) struggling with a hooked fish (he shouts, "Hey, did I tell you? It's Moby fucking Dick up here! Looka this!") cut to a still medium shot of the refracted nude body of the murdered girl tethered under shallow water at the edge of the river. The narrative frames this series of shots with a medium shot of Honey (Lili Taylor, part of the story "Neighbors") that looks at her through a screen-filling tropical fish tank at which she hypnotically stares from the other side of the tank. The New Age electronic music of Mark Isham rises on the sound track as the scene shifts to the men fishing and continues across this scene. With the shot of the nude body in the water, the sound track also carries Gordon's voice-over, "Come on, baby, come to Poppa!" as the sound of Isham's music cuts abruptly to the sounds of cello music, before the narrative cuts to a medium close-up of the stocking feet of Zoe (Lori Singer) on either side of her cello; the camera tilts up from her feet to convey a medium close shot of the cellist, eyes closed, practicing the dirgelike Cello Suite in C Minor by Johann Sebastian Bach. How does the narrative ask the viewer to read this thirty-second segment of the three-hour film?

The fishing men resonate to other stories and situations both within and of course outside of the film. Their assertive macho style and whiskey drinking in other moments contrast with the ultramodern apartment that Honey and her husband, Bill (Robert Downey Jr.), are watching for their neighbors. The camera zooms in slightly and focuses on a gray fish tinged in yellow that swims back and forth in refraction through prism-shaped forms across the foreground as Honey, now out of focus in the background, is left behind by the editing for the Hemingwayesque world of men in the wild, L. L. Bean catalogs, and the boys' weekend out. They have retreated to the romantic, Wild West and live off the land. But Hemingway also evokes a paradigm of sexual wounds, and the fishing resonates with Christian metaphors about salvation. Concepts of masculine domesticity, coarseness, and dishonesty stream through their weekend. This is no place for women, but their biggest fish describes the feminine as nameless, naked, silent, violently dead. Gordon's shouted remark recalls Melville's great American novel, violent sex acts, and off-color jokes as paradigms that register the significance of the fishing.

Shaping this scene by the perspectives on two living women, the narrative depicts the feminine trapped in a meditation on exotic sensuality, like the fish and the dead body, both broken images seen under water. Middle-class upward mobility, unspoken sexual desire, and gendered social roles all offer schemata for reading this shot. Zoe's music abruptly replaces the values of New Age reverie with the solemn tone of the funereal classic. Playing a dirge, she also may be read as accompanying the deathward movement of other women in the film, such as Stuart's wife, Claire (Anne Archer), or foreshadowing her own suicide, or reflecting the roles of women in this contemporary culture. These complexities of association and potential meanings resonate and multiply across the film and beyond it to other texts, and they reflect the complexity of reading the film.

Reviews of *Short Cuts* further reveal this process of the social construction at work in the production of cultural meanings generally and the ways in which Altman's films particularly push interpretation out into active quests for meaningful paradigms. One critic organizes the film around the concept of "missed connections." Another finds an organization of the film's meaning in "desperate inchoate yearning." For another, *Short Cuts* treats "moral quandary." Others isolate "poisonous domestic relationships" or "dysfunctional America" or "failure to communicate" as reading rubrics that naturalize these realities and trace their signs through the film's complex depiction of a contemporary Los Angeles. Terrence Rafferty locates an "anxious, unsettled mood" as "the only unifying principle of the disparate narratives" (98). The productive strategies of interpretation similarly isolate different motifs that may be said to organize the structure of the film. Bob Spitz, for instance, identifies "a rupture of male spleen" as the defining metaphor around which "each oddball episode is seamlessly interwoven" (68). What Spitz finds at once "utterly pleasurable" and "deeply disturbing" in this film becomes the material for a popular culture reification; its organizing principle is constructed as the battle of the sexes. He quotes one of the actors in the film, who calls it "the battle that defines us all." Tess Gallagher, Carver's widow, asserts that both authors write about the "erosion of trust," about "who do you trust and how do you trust them" (in Kaplan and Dorr). Altman himself, who here is just another reader of his own text in terms of Carver's stories, claims that the opposition "luck or fate" is "the idea of the chain of events" in the film (in Kaplan and Dorr).

Thus the film poetically lays bare a social structure, quoting it in ways that recirculate through this repetition of voices that participate in the cultural construction of shared identities. As what he calls a collaborator with Carver in the adaptation of his stories to film, Robert Altman asserts that he sees "all of Carver's work as just one story." And that story makes sense not syntagmatically but paradigmatically. Altman asserts, "Raymond Carver made poetry out of the prosaic." For Altman indeed the informing perspective for his work in the adaptation is not to be found within the nine stories but rather in the poetic story "Lemonade." The poem is "the basis of the whole picture for me" (in Kaplan and Dorr). In *Short Cuts* the collaboration between artists on the one story they share produces a cinematic poem whose readability may reside in yet another poem where, as he confronts the death of his son, a man "would like nothing more now than to just die" (Carver 157). More important, however, is the nature of subliminal reality. Altman says:

> The Lemonade story is really a perfect example of what all the film is about, . . . what all the stories are about. They're about those little crossroads that we constantly meet in our lives . . . and to try to figure out which one of those road branches got us to where the dilemma is, it's almost impossible. (in Kaplan and Dorr)

A larger paradigmatic dichotomy employed in the film engages both realistic and discursive readings. Death is a real-life occurrence structuring a great number of Altman's films. In the 1970s, every Altman film from *That Cold Day in the Park* to *A Perfect Couple* contains death as a central event in the story. Several deaths occur in *Short Cuts,* and the death of a little boy after being hit by a car is particularly illuminating in light of other films. The boy is struck early in the film and then lies dying in the hospital through most of the stanzas in the middle of the film. *Nashville, A Wedding, 3 Women,* and *McCabe & Mrs. Miller* all employ a similar device of a character's dying as a measure and commentary on the actions simultaneous with that dying. In *Vincent & Theo, The Player,* and *Kansas City,* the imminent death of a central character similarly shapes the viewer's reading of events. Death is not just a realistic event but a metaphor for many of the interpersonal relationships suggested in *Short Cuts.* More important, however, it establishes an oppositional structure—life and/or/versus death—to inform viewers' attention to the codes and values that constitute social identity and that conventional reading naturalizes as real.

Death is a force institutionalized through a number of parameters to shape individual subjectivity and behavior. It takes many forms in the film, and each of these representations posits a way of living. As the boy, Casey, lies in a coma, his grandfather (Jack Lemmon), in a scene created in the screenplay, is moved by guilt over an infidelity that broke up his family and, in the face of his grandson's death, he makes an anguished confession to his son (Bruce Davison). He can't remember Casey's name; he has not seen his son in years, and even now at the hospital he ignores the parents' fear as they wait at Casey's bedside, but he seeks the understanding of his son for his long-ago failures, his death as a father. Death here is constructed through a paradigm of guilt, confession, and forgiveness. That paradigm shapes the way we conceptualize the Jack Lemmon role as a real character, and discursively we recognize the work of the film as a social construction of reality, seeking ways to conceptualize the short cuts of everyday experience.

In the fiction of a doctor (Matthew Modine) and his artist wife (Julianne Moore), death takes the form of distrust. The doctor is obsessed over a minor sexual encounter that took place between his wife and another man some years earlier, and his obsession drives a wedge between him and his wife. Like many other vignettes in the film, this one has an unresolved conflict, and whether our reading produces a longing for resolution in any particular way or not, the representation of this couple's tensions and unhappiness posits acceptance as the absence in this relationship. Death in relationships especially seems to focus the experiences of wives in all the couples of the film.

In the fiction of Betty (Frances McDormand) and Stormy (Peter Gallagher), who have gone through a divorce with a battle over custody of their child, the central phenomenon consists of the methodical dividing up of their property by Stormy. With a chain saw, he cuts everything in the house into small pieces during a weekend when Betty is out of town with another of her serial boyfriends. Death here is destruction, and its missing opposite is the construction of furniture, the building of a relationship, the crafting of a family.

Three stories appear central from the construction of meaning motivated by the life/death motif. In one, Lois (Jennifer Jason Leigh) is a mother of three who works as a voice in the telephone sex trade. Jerry (Chris Penn) is a swimming pool maintenance man who regularly overhears his wife's uninvolved voicing of physical sex acts while tending the children and the house. Death here is construed as the abstraction of sex for sale merely as empty words. The absence of meaningful sexual fulfillment from the husband's perspective motivates one of the most gruesome moments in the film: Jerry's frustrated desire for what is missing not just in his wife's giving of her voice to strangers on the phone but in their own bed explodes in his violent murder of a young girl in the city park who resists his advances. This death emerges from the absence of life as the satisfaction of sexual desire.

One of the most haunting of Carver's stories, "So Much Water So Close to Home," is also Altman's account of the three men's journey into the back country to fish, their discovery of the young woman in the river near their camp, their ignoring her for three days while they enjoy their camping trip, and then their reporting her death to police upon their return. The life/death dichotomy here runs like a major fault line between one of the men, Stuart, and his wife, Claire, who is horrified by the men's behavior in ways neither she nor the story can articulate. The fiction sparked interesting reactions from the actors in this sequence. The men enjoy their fishing trip because what else could they do? asks actor and writer Buck Henry. That "what else" marks the central absence—"feelings that weren't in our repertoire" according to Huey Lewis—aggressively pursued by the wife: responsibility to the dead and the living.

Only one fiction in the film implies a kind of traditional trajectory from conflict to resolution and evokes some sense of this responsibility. Death in the family of Gene, the motorcycle cop, and his wife, Sherri, is again represented as a family matter—by his sexual infidelity, his dishonesty, his abandonment of the family dog in another neighborhood. Before the film ends, Gene comes to his senses: he returns to his wife's bed, he recovers the children's dog, and, emblematic of his newfound responsibility, he takes up a megaphone to broadcast warnings to the neighborhood during the earthquake that ends the film. The tone of this sequence is comical, and our realistic reading of Gene's behavior cautions us not to take his new behavior seriously. Nevertheless, discursively we read in this episode two sides of the life/death dichotomy that elsewhere the film figures as the presence of death and the absence of its opposite.

The one story in *Short Cuts* not adapted from Raymond Carver narrates the relationship between jazz singer Tess (Annie Ross) and her daughter, Zoe, a classical cellist. Tess's songs, with titles such as "I Don't Want to Cry Anymore," "To Hell with Love," and "Prisoner of Life," metaphorically replicate the suffering contingent upon the absences of honesty, of respect, of attention, of caring, of love construed by all the other vignettes in the film. And the cello music of Zoe runs like a mournful dirge throughout the film to the point of her suicide. Death for her is a response to a life where its opposite—communication, contact, meaningfulness—is always absent. In some ways the music, its performance, and the lives of the mother and daughter reflect the same paradigm developed in *Images, 3 Women, Jimmy Dean,* and *Cookie's Fortune,* of women alienated and alone, contemplating death, committing suicide—or murder—and using art as a defense against the debilities of their relationships with men.

Part of what *Short Cuts* finds readable in the stories of Carver is their minimalist representation of the real world of marginal people, a kind of art-cinema silent majority in the usual realm of Hollywood storytelling. They are strange and ordinary, unlovable and compelling, living at the margins of our attention in situations that are tragic, comic, and inconsequential. Carver's stories give the reader disquieting glimpses into the shabby lives of people whose voices are seldom heard and whose pains echo long after their brief words are overheard. Carver's widow, Tess Gallagher, describes them as "caricature-like abrasions of the real" (in Kaplan and Dorr). And the craft of these works lies in their coercion of our reading as a process of filling in the gaps of explanation. Says Altman, "The audience carries the characters with it through the whole picture, which means that the audience is doing the work, the writing, the creating" (in Kaplan and Dorr). What all this work produces for a realistic reading of film, of fiction, of life's meaning is perhaps that vague sense that Hemingway calls "the end of something." Or what Emily Dickinson describes as "the feeling of zero at the bone." But those meanings hover centrifugally at the margins of these lives, these texts, our readings of them.

Altman thus admires a subliminal reality in Carver stories for the reading strategy they motivate. "They're more about what you don't know rather than what you do know, and the reader fills in the gaps, while recognizing the undercurrents" ("Introduction" 7). The art cinema generally and *Short Cuts* specifically model the process of adaptation that forever marks the fissures, the transitory, the fractured nature of vision, knowledge, appropriation. We have to recognize the undercurrents. And the irony of this centrifugal reading is also, perhaps paradoxically, a centripetal desire for connectedness even though it seeks centers of meaning out there in the intertext, rather than here in the text. Our writing produces a reading; we make the writerly text readable. Altman himself reveals the drive to respond to the question, What does all this mean? What connects these stories? What links one node in the web to another? The shortcuts that take us from word to word, story to story are an "erosion of trust," the "strangeness behind the banality," "the arbitrary nature of luck in the scheme of things." What may explain everything is the Carver poem with which Altman concludes his short story collection. What may explain everything is the long monologue on infidelity delivered by the Jack Lemmon character, written for the movie. What may explain everything is the mother-daughter relationship between the jazz singer and her daughter's suicide, also written for the movie. Or what explains everything may be the significance of art and performance and the jazz and classical music performed by these two women.

Yet in the end these stories only expand our understanding of these lives; they do not explain them, or close them down on any center of intended or intentional meaning. They also tell us about the way Altman's art films are readable. He says: "I'm trying to use a form here of telling these stories, of showing them in such a way that the audience is making up the stories actually. . . . They have to fill in the gaps . . . , and if I can get the audience to actively do that . . . , millions of people making up their own story about what happened in these gaps, . . . it might be a whole new way of allowing the audience participation, the sense of participation." Altman recalls Fellini telling him that "the best film is all the dailies"(in Kaplan and Dorr). Trying to figure what random branches in the hypertextual web of subliminal reality get us to any particular place carries us to many locations. What then do they or the process mean? Maybe, in Altman's words, "a little alchoholism, infidelity, and self-doubt," or maybe just the ubiquity of ketchup on everybody's kitchen table, is "the common denominator . . . of these American people" (in Kaplan and Dorr).

The title of the film is punning, playful, and informing. Short cuts are the equivalent to that literary mode of modernist realism called a "slice of life." They also represent the brief editorial fragments that cascade over the viewer for three hours in this film. And the shortcuts are routes that takes us from here to there in geographic space more quickly than other routes (although of course they may take us a longer way around as well). Trailers for the film layered a dissolve of images from the film's different stories under an image of street maps. *Short Cuts,* says Altman, involves the movement between names and places on such maps, "a kind of sign language," he says, that has nothing to do with causes and effects, but faithful to an understanding of subliminal reality, "it's the only thing you can trace" (in Kaplan and Dorr).

Maps are always characterized by selection and absence—selections among the places shown on them and always the absence of the physical, actual, geographic places designated by the play of shapes, lines, and colors. *Short Cuts* draws a map whose surface is a signifier of presence and absence charting a terrain of social values. That terrain delineates identity in white, middle-class family relationships, and it ignores other parts of the city: the slums of the poor, the ghettos of the gay, the invisibility of blackness, the Latino/a majority, the unmelted ethnic diversity of America's second city, the power of the entertainment industry, the fantasy of Disneyland. It never abandons reference to some real world, but it forces us to read that world and its maps in terms of what they exclude.

Carver's minimal stories and Altman's art films model a hypertextual reality in which the process of reading, of making meaning, is one of freedom and choice—freedom centrifugally to choose divergent, intersecting, multidirectional pathways, contradictory pathways through a web of many options. But those options are also already always lodged out there in the intertext of our experience. Thus centripetally these stories offer us centers of connection, no matter how multiple or diverse. They reconfirm and reconstitute our narrativity. They require us, in the words of Robert Scholes, "to connect what is represented in the text with what we see in the world" (*Protocols* 154). The Carver-Altman texts model adaptation's multiple textuality as a process in which "we must keep on reading, keep on rewriting the texts that we read in the texts of our lives, and keep on rewriting our lives in the light of those texts" (155). Any study of Altman's films, like the study of adaptations, designates a discursive space among the films it privileges. It locates textuality as a process, and it activates a multiple subjectivity in play against the closure of thematic meaning, structural unity, and authorial vision.

# Conclusion: The Alternative Gaze

A number of debates circulate in contemporary film history and criticism: whether or not the blockbuster, high-concept mentality of mainstream filmmaking has supplanted the traditional mode of classical narrative storytelling; whether mainstream cinema represents a postclassical Hollywood; whether current Hollywood films maintain a commitment to classical norms. Some film historians argue that a brief moment in the late 1960s and early 1970s gave birth to an American art cinema, but others dispute not only the fact of such a phenomenon but the existence of an art cinema at all. However it is read, the postmodern mode of the Hollywood industry seems to represent the commodification of production, distribution, and consumption of the movies—prepackaged, presold, predigested. Going to the multiplex today, like going to the supermarket or the mall, means shopping for the stories or the produce or the clothing designed, wrapped, and promoted by merchandising and advertising to meet the desires already shaped by the same commodity machines. Altman observed about the success of *The Player*:

> That's what Hollywood's like. . . . So many people have responded to it . . . because they see that that's the same as in the museum business or the magazine business or the journalism business, in the political business or in the lawyer business or . . . in the savings and loan business. It's all the same thing. (quoted in Smith and Jameson 27)

In the midst of this environment circulate the films of Robert Altman. Idiosyncratic, pessimistic, ironic, oblique, exuberant, experimental—the films constitute a modernist narrative cinema that refuses commodification. These films illustrate the vicissitudes and the possibilities of an American art cinema. They define its formal practice and thematic commitments. They illustrate its longevity in a Hollywood described by *The Player*'s empty phrase, "Movies, Now More Than Ever!" The films and

Altman's career amount to a defiance of the mainstream values of the entertainment industry. Following the success and critical acclaim of *MASH* which propelled him initially into that mainstream, Altman turned around and made the chaotic and puzzling box-office failures *Brewster McCloud* and *Images.* Following his first popular success in fifteen years with *The Player,* Altman adapted the stern fictions of Raymond Carver into *Short Cuts,* a three-hour movie that few understood or appreciated. Thus, says Altman, "Admire me, not for how I succeed and not for how 'good' the films are, but for the fact that I keep going back and jumping off the cliff" (quoted in McGilligan 1). The cliff is conventional Hollywood moviemaking.

The value system of classical Hollywood cinema appears in its commitment to the stability and homogeneity of personality, of social interchange, even of narrative voice, all maintained by the structure and closure of plot. It carries a debt to classical literary realism in "its concern for coherence and causality in narrative structure, for the autonomy of the individual self in the presentation of character, for a readable homogeneity and urbanity of style" (Lodge 26). It energizes but then systematically holds in check political, psychological, and sociological forces that threaten and define a predominant ideology. The art cinema, on the other hand, reflexively seeks to estrange viewers from the illusion of reality in order to make them critically self-conscious of the values narrative logic would posit as "natural" and absolutely given. It takes as its very subject matter those instabilities that constitute the "limit texts" of the classical narrative. It foregrounds troubled personal identity, troubled economic relationships, and troubled communication. It dramatizes the powerlessness, the traumas, the effects of social alienation and estrangement and critiques the corporate or institutional forces, including the cinema itself, that contribute to those traumas.

"Jumping off the cliff" for Altman means making films like *Nashville, A Wedding, Short Cuts,* and *Prêt-à-Porter,* which instead of a single unified story construct open-ended, causally muddled narratives with many characters in numerous minor stories that strikingly recall the multiple depiction of private and public realities in modernist literary narratives. They capture the flux and essence of life situations by describing an emotional and subjective circle around them through the viewpoints of major and minor characters. They develop a broad range of knowledge through the limited perspectives of many divergent characters. The viewer's sense of that field significantly exceeds that of any single character, yet the awareness nevertheless remains limited, tacit, subliminal.

Experience is forever greater than the sum of its witnesses and participants. These works impose formal order on the disconnections of experience through metaphor and lyric rather than narrative logic.

Classical narrative cinema assumes a contractual relationship with its audience that cues the viewer to construct an intelligible, coherent story world. Whether in the representation of story character or in the representation of narrative figure, the art cinema positions the viewer before the contradictory world of expressive reality that asks to be read in its ambiguity. Altman's art films take the Hollywood cinema for granted and demonstrate a traditional understanding of the symbiotic relationship of popular art forms to the resolution of social conflict and anxiety and for the communication of cultural order and value. They regularly reflect a commitment to a representable world full of recognizably individual characters performing socially inscribed actions. Yet the multiple, unfocused, and unclosed stories of these films turn narrative conventions against themselves. All reflect disavowal of the ordered rationality of formulaic beginnings, middles, and happy ends. They suggest an impetus to disorder as well as the drive for resolution and characterological unity. As modernist films they include a vision of contemporary life that cannot easily be contained by the narrative certainty of popular Hollywood discourse.

The craft of the traditional narrative, of classical realist fiction, maintains a paradigmatic tension between the basic human need for order and peace, for security from the confusions of life, for a familiar and predictable world, and the contrary need for anxiety, confusion, and jeopardy, for novelty, mystery, and danger. John Cawelti argues about the familiar qualities of popular adventure, mystery, and romance that "the essence of the experience of escape and the source of its ability to relax and please us is . . . that it temporarily synthesizes these two needs and resolves these tensions" (*Adventure* 53). In the twentieth century, the popular dramatic modes of film and television ironically assumed the effort of the traditional novel to create an ordered, coherent world with credible and realistic characters. Numerous scholars have noted the extent to which the technical possibilities of the new film medium at the beginning of the twentieth century informed many of the experimental energies of literary modernism. Indeed, it is routine in this regard to remember that James Joyce opened and managed the Volta, Dublin's first movie house, in 1906. At the same time, however, the cinema began very early to employ the craft of fiction from classical realism, not to enhance the formal possibilities demonstrated by Sergei Eisenstein, but to further the conservative storytelling practice that became the classical Hollywood cinema. Robert Stam points out that

> the classical fiction film has maintained, on the whole, an aesthetic corresponding to that of the nineteenth-century mimetic novel. The cinema also took on the novel's social function as a school for life, an initiatory source of models for behavior. In its dominant mode, it became a receptacle for the mimetic aspirations abandoned by the more advanced practitioners of the other arts . . . in painting, . . . in the theatre, . . . in the novel. (10)

A counter tradition in narrative has historically inclined toward disorder, ambiguity, and uncertainty. One of the most pervasive experiments of the modernist movement in twentieth-century narrative art shifted attention away from the story told with transparency and certainty about the hierarchies of the social world to the stream of consciousness of narration, to the philosophical and psychological insecurity of narrators. Linear sequentiality and coherent perspectival point of view gave way to multiple perspectives on the simultaneity of spatial and temporal constructions. The "single, separate person" of nineteenth-century romanticism mutated into the contradictory multitudes of mass culture. The self became a subject—to the state, to the sentence, to the sensibility of popular taste, subject to ratification. The modernist dispensation described social identity no longer as discrete, essential, possible, but rather as a construction of external forces that Louis Althusser described as the "ideological state apparatus" (160)—religion, government, education, business, law, family. Discussing Faulkner's *As I Lay Dying,* Silvio Gaggi asserts, "The 'I' that is dying is the self itself, at least the understanding of the self as a coherent, unified, separate, and self-sufficient entity" (*From Text* 50). Similarly, the subjectivity of modernist narrative emerges as an amalgam of a physical reality that is ephemeral under the pressures of history, race, and class; of a social reality shaped by the absent past; and of a personal experience of unity with a mysterious and unspeakable other. Gaggi argues, "That interaction produces a subject in flux, a symbolic subject that perpetually adjusts and redefines itself in response to ungovernable energies that always lie beyond it" (150).

Art-cinema narration rejects the dramatic certainty of traditional discourse as inadequate to confront the radical discontinuities of modern existence, as they were first posited by the aesthetic modernists in the first quarter of the century and as they were resubscribed by the postmodernist disillusionment, cynicism, and play of the "counterculture" movement in the 1960s. Nearly all of Altman's films explore interrelationships among the demands of life—always associated with images of death, from *That Cold Day in the Park* to *Cookie's Fortune*—and the necessary structures and inventions for survival evolved by vulnerable, insecure characters whose innate weaknesses these films convey with irony and sympathy, compassion and exaggeration. Especially in *California Split, Brewster McCloud, Images, 3 Women, Vincent & Theo, The Player, Short Cuts, Prêt-à-Porter, Kansas City,* and *Cookie's Fortune,* the stories reveal the characters' creation of formal designs whose efficacy against the apprehensions of life consists not in resolving but in displacing anxieties, fears, insecurities. They mirror this defensive creativity in the characters by simultaneous efforts in the narration, in the discourse, to reconstruct the various conventions of narrative order so that they doubly convey the discords of content.

Where the homogeneity of the classical narrative seeks to establish the self "in positions of coherence and responsibility for his actions so that he is able to act" (Coward and Ellis 75), Altman's films reveal the contradictory, powerless, isolated, and fragmented ego. Their stories seldom provide the context for significant, heroic action; rather, they reveal spaces that enclose and forces that act upon a multiplicity of selves. The self in sexual exchange and the crisis of the self in romantic relationships represent the substantial core in most of these films, but especially in *McCabe & Mrs. Miller, A Wedding, Short Cuts, Prêt-à-Porter, Kansas City,* and *Dr. T & the Women.* Brewster McCloud, Philip Marlowe, Buffalo Bill, Griffin Mill, and Seldom Seen are avatars of the single, separate person, a major correlative paradigm to more negative images of "a perfect couple." When these films code the social subject as situated within a larger community—in *MASH,* in *Health,* in *Secret Honor,* in *The Player*—the individual exists as a dependency of group need or is subsumed by the energy and pressures of others. The economic subject of these films is produced and trapped by larger systems of political, cultural, and historic necessity.

Peripheral certainly to the high-concept film or the new classicism, Altman's films disorient in their quirkiness, confuse in their narrative structure, challenge in the complexity of their stories, and depress in the cynicism of their vision. They interrogate, as Robert Kolker notes, "the patriarchal structures of cinematic narrative," "the distortions of personality caused by patriarchy," and "manufactured images that are accepted as historical realities" (380). They also evoke reading schemata generated by the kind of productive vision described by postmodern architect Robert Venturi:

> I like elements which are hybrid rather than "pure," compromising rather than "clean," distorted rather than "straightforward," ambiguous rather than "articulated," perverse as well as impersonal, boring as well as "interesting," conventional rather than "designed," accommodating rather than excluding, redundant rather than simple, vestigial as well as innovating, inconsistent and equivocal rather than direct and clear. I am for messy vitality over obvious unity. I include the non sequitur and proclaim the duality. (53)

Part of the "messy vitality" in Altman's films rests on the contemporary cultural ephemera of modern life and suggests what Philip Stevick calls "those qualities of disconnection and the absence of significance by making a fiction out of pop images, free floating, without context, a set of images that allows, in some marvelous equipoise, the coexistence of an appalling view of the meaninglessness of the world along with a sense of wit and play which makes that meaningless quality bearable and often very funny" (141). Altman's films brim over with the artifacts of contemporary culture: war movies in *MASH*; the Tennessee Twirlers in *Nashville*; a souped-up Gremlin in *Brewster McCloud*; Wheaties and beer for breakfast in *California Split*; *Ladies' Home Journal,* tuna melts, and the Creature from the Black Lagoon in *3 Women*; the all-night supermarket in *The Long Goodbye*; the dating service in *A Perfect Couple*; the desert motel in *Fool for Love*; the entire Hollywood surround of *The Player*; contemporary fashions in *Prêt-à-Porter*; hurricane reports on the television weather news in *The Gingerbread Man*; the Dallas Cowboys cheerleaders in *Dr. T*; and Coca-Cola everywhere.

Ihab Hassan discerns the continuing presence of the modernist practice and vision in contemporary discourse as the discovery of the aesthetic in the popular, the location of the comic in the serious, the constant mix of modes of representation that constitutes a joyous interrogation, a deadly play that disorients the contemporary audience. He defines this practice as indeterminacy, a "complex referent which these diverse concepts help to delineate: ambiguity, discontinuity, heterodoxy, pluralism, randomness, revolt, perversion, deformation . . . a vast will to unmaking affecting the body politic, the body cognitive, the erotic body, the individual psyche" (*Dismemberment* 269). Yet the recirculation of contemporary surfaces, its reduplication that comically transcends its cultural banality, owes its existence in Altman's films not just to the director's comment on their presence. Indeed, such commentary is mockingly dismissed in the opening voice-over lines of the MGM lion of *Brewster McCloud,* "I forgot the first line," and again when Opal absurdly ponders the significance of yellow school buses in a Nashville junkyard. The fashion reporter's running commentary about fashion in *Prêt-à-Porter* at once critiques the industry and hides it under the inevitability of television commentary itself. Such elements also exist as functions of their participation in the cultural milieu, and they represent authorial silence. Appropriated haphazardly, nonjudgmentally along with the good, the bad, and the ugly, they reflect in part the feigned masculine silence that unleashes paranoia and violent schizophrenia in *That Cold Day in the Park,* but more profoundly they emerge from a refusal of authority that undercuts the traditional legislative role for the Artist.

The authorial voice in these films is self-consciously disconnected from the discourse in a number of ways—from the ironic play of loudspeakers in *MASH* to the seemingly randomized point of view in *Nashville,* to the human voice abandoned for its cartoon alternative at the end of *Popeye,* to the happy crowds leaving the fashion show at the end of *Prêt-à-Porter.* Even though the characters murdered in *Brewster McCloud* are unsympathetic, the killing itself is presented in an emotionally flat and distanced way. The silence of authority most aggressively appears in the weakening of narrative order and structure, in the multiple randomness of point of view, in the mix of divergent voices within the texts, in the negative depiction of male heroes. Even the most enthusiastic critics of Altman's films frequently find fault with their disruptive heterogeneity or their refusal to authorize emotional if not logical coherence. Virginia Wright Wexman pointedly asserts, "These motifs ridicule the director's role as a creator of profound truths by insisting that what we are witnessing is merely a work of 'popular' art, and, as such, not to be taken too seriously" ("Critical" 17).

Altman's movies also reflect sensitivity to a middle-class American malaise at the end of the twentieth century. Subliminal in their fragmentary depiction of what he calls "infidelity, alcoholism, and self-doubt" (in Kaplan and Dorr), the films nevertheless depict an American reality. *Short Cuts* epitomally turns its gaze on television newsmen, motorcycle policemen, waitresses, telephone sex saleswomen, chauffeurs, nightclub singers, pool service men, clowns for hire, and bakers. Marginal, disconnected, powerless, living lives that hardly admit of narrative purpose, these unheroic characters stream through Altman's movies, and none perhaps so revealingly as his African American figures. For thirty years the alterity of Altman's movies associate their view of contemporary culture with the alternative gaze of African Americans at the margins of that culture. At the end of *Nashville,* the presidential candidate's motorcade drives to the Parthenon, where the political rally for the Replacement Party will end the film in imagery that evokes the still-unhealed wounds of the Vietnam War and political assassinations. The African American character Wade drives against the stately flow of this motorcade and shouts out his window: "All y'all goin' the wrong way!" Wade's words of judgment echo across the film. They represent within the diegetic world the stance that motivates the narrative strategies and energy of the film—a critical view of callousness, greed, and cynicism in the entertainment politics of America, shaped by and shaping fragmented lives in fragmented stories.

Throughout Altman's films African American characters play relatively small roles that provide the viewer with an internal gaze and voice of negative evaluation—on the family lives, the entertainment, the wars, the politics, and the history of dominant white personalities, values, and actions. They mark from spaces within the diegesis the kinds of critical perspectives measured by Robert Kolker as "Altman's explorations and revelations of hypocrisy, duplicity, manipulation, and humiliation" (378). In short, they stand as surrogates simultaneously for the narrative strategies of the film and the thematic energies that seem to motivate them.

In *Kansas City,* for instance, the jazz originating powerfully from the black ghetto provides, through the representation of the racial other, a telling angle of vision on the efforts of the white characters in the dominant story. That commentary has become more aggressive than in any other Altman film, although no less difficult to understand. As music it asks to be read metaphorically against the rhetorical turns of story. Krin Gabbard has demonstrated that the musical cutting contest between the Lester Young and Coleman Hawkins characters plays against the killing of Blue for his collaboration with a white man in attempted robbery of his own people, that the "jockeying for power and masculine superiority among musicians parallels the game played out between Johnny and Seldom" ("Kansas City" 148). He argues indeed that the force and flow of the music contrasts dramatically with the lack of connection and continuity in the story of white politicians and their petty associates.

As early as 1975, Robin Wood analyzed the narrative indirections of

Altman's films as "merely his defence against a too intense involvement in the fiction, the Smart-ass shrugging off of the responsibilities of engagement" ("Smart-Ass" 160). More recently, in his biography of Altman, Patrick McGilligan argues that the unfocused narrative discourse and obscure style of Altman's movies develop as "the better defense against failure" (163), as "a strength born of a weakness" (434), "born of his own inadequacies" (437). But Gabbard has suggested a more provocative source for the thirty-year production of eccentric narratives. He explicitly asserts a psychological and aesthetic identification between the two young men from Kansas City, the biographical Altman and the figure of young Charlie Parker, the fourteen-year-old African American who constantly reiterates throughout *Kansas City* the image of the diegetic racial gaze. But the Parker figure watches and explicitly evaluates the world of African American jazz rather than the world of white male inadequacy. Parker grows up as a major iconoclast and innovator into mature jazz greatness. Gabbard writes, "Like Parker, Altman is an artist who assimilated a body of material that few regarded as art and then went on to create his own brilliant but eccentric brand of that art" ("Kansas City" 153). He thus suggests a link between the narrative form of the Altman films on one hand and what on the other hand is the racial other that authorizes perspectives within the diegesis of these films. The alternative gaze inside the film parallels the innovative construction of story.

Future jazz greatness—the alternative gaze *(Kansas City).*

Describing black ways of watching Hollywood film, bell hooks writes:

> Black looks, as they were constituted in the context of social movements for racial uplift, were interrogating gazes. We laughed at television shows like *Our Gang* and *Amos 'n' Andy*, at these white representations of blackness, but we also looked at them critically. Before racial integration, black reviewers of movies and television experienced visual pleasure in a context where looking was also about contestation and confrontation. (199)

The minor African American characters like Charlie Parker in Altman's films are all avatars of what hooks calls the "oppositional gaze" in the kind of art films that for her "demystified 'whiteness,' since the lives they depicted seem less rooted in fantasies of escape" (209). They represent figures within the story who designate an alternative gaze on the diegetic world that in turn echoes the alternative gaze that constructs the narrative discourse in the first place—marginal, defensive, threatening, seeing.

Such perspectives deflect attention and speak subliminally. The concept of the subliminal derived much of its power from romanticism, which saw heaven and eternity in wildflowers and grains of sand. It heard the natural world speak ineffably beyond its surfaces, and symbolic expression became a methodology for conveying this other realm that stretched transcendentally beyond the five senses. But naturalism, modernism, and the harsh realities of two world wars intervene between the romantic and the contemporary imagination. The modernist recognizes the sublime as well, but the war neuroses of the twentieth century coerce the silence of veterans. Personal powerlessness seeks expression in objective correlatives of experience, because some things are better left unsaid. Some things indeed are unspeakable. The more things matter, the more difficult they are to convey. Representation becomes sublimation, but significance bleeds into the text everywhere. Like modernism, the stories, the characters, and the vision of art-cinema narration share a perspective distrustful of conventional public order and process. They remain insecure about the importance, the meaning, indeed the possibility of communication. They employ a method of indirection, of fragmentation, of randomness and multiplicity.

Discussing *Short Cuts,* Altman has indicated that he was looking for a new way to tell stories. But his subliminal representation of the reality of American lives at the end of the century is not new. Its methodology is poetic, its style is lyrical, its vision is interrogative. The music and stanzas of his films, their images and their rhythms, their impressionistic metaphors and associations, their negative tableaux of social alienation, their personal essays on the culture industry, ask to be read as strategies of an American art cinema. It has been my purpose in this volume to trace the diffuse and open stories, the insecurity of social identification, and the reflexive examination of the show business as contributions of Altman's films toward a definition of this cinema. Interpreting their perplexing discourse becomes an activity of deciphering texts to discover the codes by which meaning is encrypted. The subliminal reality of Altman's movies motivates the kinds of interpretations and understandings that arise from reading between the lines, excavating the silences, puzzling over the gaps and indirections of their telling. It results in cinematic short cuts whose lyrical piling of story onto story, of associational leaps across chasms of causality and relation reveal meanings unspoken, half glimpsed, suppressed, intuited. And the process at once develops a way of reading Altman's movies as well as a way of understanding the art cinema as a mode of film practice.

The political and social crosscurrents in the United States from the late 1960s to the early 2000s display all the energies that make reality a strong competitor of fiction in the contemporary world: the Vietnam War and the antiwar movement, the drug culture and counterculture of hippies and yippies, Nixon and Watergate, the oil shortage and gas lines, the Bicentennial celebration, Jimmy Carter and the Ayatollah Khomeini, Ronald Reagan and yuppies, the collapse of the Soviet Union, the Middle Eastern Gulf War, the Clinton presidency from the Fleetwood Mac campaign song to "zippergate," and the Florida vote counts in the 2000 presidential election. Altman's films during these decades reveal a remarkable range of experimental competition with traditional Hollywood fiction. The resistance movements of the sixties enfranchised Altman's experimental narrative style, and the financial success of *MASH* permitted him to explore and rewrite classical form throughout the seventies. But the synergies of story, craft, and merchandising of high-concept Hollywood at the beginning of the eighties banished his mode of filmmaking to theater and cable television. The visibility of *Tanner '88* at the end of the Reagan presidency gave new life to a career shaped by opposition to values that would make a movie star president, and *The Player* launched yet another comeback in Hollywood. Altman's movies of the 1990s, especially *Vincent & Theo, Short Cuts, Prêt-à-Porter, Kansas City,* and *Cookie's Fortune,* constitute the most dramatic illustration of art-cinema narration in all of his films. Their disruptions of form not only articulate but emerge from socially ineffective identities of gender and occasion attacks on the culpability of the media in their putting on display story and subjectivity itself.

A producer who worked with Altman on *Kraft Suspense Theater* in the early 1960s recalled his disagreement with the director: "I represented what he hated most in television, and that is the very commercial, highly plotted story, and he hated commercial storytelling with a vengeance" (quoted in McGilligan 218). Altman's films generate the vastly unpopular and uncommercial cinema of subliminal reality. As Altman has said:

> What I'm really talking about is taking the linear references out of film and having something happen that works on the individuals in the audience so that the information they get from the film suddenly invades all the information they have accumulated in their lifetime. . . . It's making something spherical rather than linear. The more and more of this I do, the more I want it to be like you're in a universe, you're inside a sphere. There isn't any end and beginning to it. (quoted in Fuller 81)

These films are peripheral to the industrial concern for high-concept movies, "cinematic products with a narrative that could be boiled down to a single sentence and then marketed visually through print advertising and especially commercials" (Wyatt, "Roadshowing" 79). They are marginal to the "contemporary classical cinema" that continues to demonstrate the "glory of the Hollywood system," its ability "to weave an intricate web of character, event, time and space that can seem transparently obvious" (Thompson 11, 49). About Hollywood filmmakers, Altman says, "They didn't learn anything from Einstein: They know the train's moving, but they don't know the station's moving too" (quoted in Smith and Jameson 29). In the face of a contingent and absurd world, Altman's films exuberantly play with the dimensions of form and the features of cinematic craft and develop a powerful interrogation of the interactions among actions, beliefs, and systems of entertainment in contemporary culture. A hostility to endings, an oppositional gaze on the values of American life, and a censure of the entertainment industry—these constitute the central elements of Robert Altman's thirty-year film career and the major ingredients of an American art cinema.

# Acknowledgments

This book began with *Nashville* in 1975 and, like all projects of such age, had a great many assistants along the way to whom I owe special thanks. Haven Hamilton's song from that film, "Keep A-Goin'," was the theme song for a group of us who watched the idealism of the 1960s dissolve into the "me generation" of the 1980s. Lynne Waldeland, who has been my friend and close colleague in film studies in the English Department at Northern Illinois University through all my career, has been a continuing fan of Altman's movies and a great supporter of this work. Jeff Chown has been less a fan of Altman but a valued friend and NIU colleague in film and auteur studies. The FSU group—Bob Eberwein, Krin Gabbard, Bill Luhr, Peter Lehman, Fred Silva, Peter Stowell, and Hans and Bonnie Braendlin—have listened to my analyses of Altman's films since 1977 and have critiqued and encouraged my insights.

A key development in my orientation to Altman's films occurred in summer 1978, when I participated in David Bordwell's National Endowment for the Humanities seminar on film theory and criticism at the University of Wisconsin. As we worked on the model of the art cinema, the critical background and direction of my understanding of Altman's work took crucial shape. A number of graduate students have shared my interests in these films over the years, but Ted Clontz, Phyllis Gooden, Michelle Johnson, Allyson Vaulx, Kelli Keltz, Stephanie Kummerer, Lynn Nelson, Heather Macintosh, Kerry Schindl, and Brock Silvey in my doctoral seminar on Altman's films in 1998 gave special impetus to the final shaping of this book. Fred Kitterle, dean of the College of Liberal Arts and Sciences at NIU, supported this project with three grants in the Undergraduate Research Apprentice Program: Catherine Doederlein and Nancy McVittie made valuable contributions to my understanding of *Cookie's Fortune* and *Dr. T & the Women.* Terry F. Robinson worked closely and collaboratively with me to develop the analysis of *The Gingerbread Man.* Mary Beth Koos gave me important assistance in reading the painterly dimensions of Altman's films. Mark Waters and Steve Roman helped me collect and correct bibliographic details at the end of this work. During a period when I had substantial administrative duties in English graduate studies and first-year composition, Ellen Franklin, Jan Vander Meer, Bonnie Anderson Caswell, and Theresa Kinniry were vital in helping me balance administration, teaching, and research. In the final stages of this book's development, I owe a large debt to the critical guidance of Bob Kolker, Justin Wyatt, and Jennifer Moore. Gordon Means and Dale Thurman in Media Services at NIU helped with image reproductions, and finally, Judy Selhorst, Carolyn Law, Stacey Provan, and Sara Erickson brought the project through copyediting, proofreading, and indexing.

My daughter, Sarah, grew up watching Altman and the Tarheels with me, and watching her mature as this book has grown has been one of the great joys of my life. Finally and foremost, the reason for everything is my wife, Lois.

## Robert Altman Filmography

*Countdown* (1968)
*That Cold Day in the Park* (1969)
*MASH* (1970)
*Brewster McCloud* (1970)
*McCabe & Mrs. Miller* (1971)
*Images* (1972)
*The Long Goodbye* (1973)
*Thieves Like Us* (1974)
*California Split* (1974)
*Nashville* (1975)
*Buffalo Bill and the Indians, or Sitting Bull's History Lesson* (1976)
*3 Women* (1977)
*A Wedding* (1978)
*Quintet* (1979)
*A Perfect Couple* (1979)
*Health* (1979)
*Popeye* (1980)
*Come Back to the 5 & Dime, Jimmy Dean, Jimmy Dean* (1982)
*Streamers* (1983)
*Secret Honor* (1984)
*O.C. & Stiggs* (1985)
*Fool for Love* (1985)
*Aria* (1987)
*Beyond Therapy* (1987)
*Vincent & Theo* (1990)
*The Player* (1992)
*Short Cuts* (1993)
*Prêt-à-Porter* (1994)
*Kansas City* (1996)

*Robert Altman's Jazz '34* (1996)
*The Gingerbread Man* (1998)
*Cookie's Fortune* (1999)
*Dr. T & the Women* (2000)
*Gosford Park* (2001)

**Television Productions**

*Two by South (Rattlesnake in a Cooler/Precious Blood)* (1982)
*The Laundromat* (1985)
*The Dumb Waiter* (1987)
*The Room* (1987)
*The Caine Mutiny Court Martial* (1988)
*Tanner '88* (1988)
*Gun* (1997)

# Bibliography

Allen, Jennifer. "Cher and Altman on Broadway." *New York Magazine,* 1 February 1982, 26–31.

Allen, Robert C., and Douglas Gomery. *Film History: Theory and Practice.* New York: Alfred A. Knopf, 1985.

Althusser, Louis. *Lenin and Philosophy and Other Essays.* Trans. Ben Brewster. London: New Left, 1971.

Altieri, Charles. "The Hermeneutics of Literary Indeterminacy: A Dissent from the New Orthodoxy." *New Literary History* 10 (autumn 1978): 75–90.

Altman, Charles F. "Psychoanalysis and Cinema: The Imaginary Discourse." *Quarterly Review of Film Studies* 2 (August 1977): 257–72.

Altman, Rick. "Introduction: Film Sound." *Yale French Studies* 60, no. 1 (1980): 3–15.

———. "Moving Lips: Cinema as Ventriloquism." *Yale French Studies* 60, no. 1 (1980): 67–79.

———. *The American Film Musical.* Bloomington: Indiana University Press, 1989.

———. ed. *Sound Theory, Sound Practice.* London: Routledge, 1992.

———. *Film/Genre.* London: British Film Institute, 1999.

———. "24-Track Narrative? Robert Altman's *Nashville.*" *Cinémas: Journal of Film Studies* 1, no. 3 (24 November 2000). On-line at http://www.revue-cinemas.umontreal.ca/cinemas/vol001no03/08–altman.htm

Altman, Robert. "Giggle and Give In: An Interview." *Vincent & Theo.* Perf. Tim Roth, Paul Rhys. 1990. Videodisc. Los Angeles: Hemdale Home Video, 1991.

———, director. Scene commentary. *The Player.* Perf. Tim Robbins, Greta Scacchi, Fred Ward, Whoopi Goldberg, Peter Gallagher, Cynthia Stevenson, Vincent D'Onofrio, Richard E. Grant. 1992. Videodisc. Santa Monica, Calif.: Voyager, 1992.

———. "Introduction." In Raymond Carver, *Short Cuts: Selected Stories.* Ed. Robert Altman. New York: Vintage, 1993. 7–10.
———, director. Scene commentary. *Short Cuts.* Perf. Tim Robbins, Jennifer Jason Leigh, Andie MacDowell, Julianne Moore, Fred Ward, Anne Archer, Jack Lemmon. 1993. Videodisc. Voyager, 1994.
———, director. Scene commentary. *Thieves Like Us.* Perf. Keith Carradine, Shelley Duvall, John Schuck, Bert Remsen. 1973. Videodisc. Los Angeles: MGM Home Entertainment, 1997.
———, director. Scene commentary. *The Gingerbread Man.* Perf. Kenneth Branagh, Embeth Davidtz, Robert Downey Jr., Daryl Hannah. 1997. Videodisc. New York: PolyGram, 1998.
———, director. Scene commentary. *Cookie's Fortune.* Perf. Glenn Close, Julianne Moore, Liv Tyler, Chris O'Donnell, Charles S. Dutton, Patricia Neal. 1999. Digital videodisc. New York: USA Home Entertainment, 1999.
———, director. Scene commentary. *Nashville.* Perf. Karen Black, Ronee Blakley, Keith Carradine, Shelley Duvall, Henry Gibson, Michael Murphy, Lily Tomlin. 1975. Digital videodisc. Hollywood, Calif.: Paramount Home Video, 2000.
Altman, Robert, and Frank Barhydt. *Short Cuts: The Screenplay.* Santa Barbara, Calif.: Capra, 1993.
Altman, Robert, Barbara Shulgasser, and Brian D. Leitch, eds. *Robert Altman's Prêt-à-Porter.* New York: Hyperion, 1994.
American Film Institute. "Interview with Laszlo Kovacs and Vilmos Zsigmond." *Dialogue on Film* 3 (1974): 1–28.
———. "Robert Altman Seminar." *Dialogue on Film* 4 (1975): 2–26.
Ames, Christopher. *Movies about Movies: Hollywood Reflected.* Lexington: University of Kentucky Press, 1997.
Andersen, Kurt. "A Player Once Again." *Time,* 20 April 1992, 78–80.
Andrew, Dudley. *Concepts in Film Theory.* New York: Oxford University Press, 1984.
———. "The Unauthorized *Auteur* Today." In *Film Theory Goes to the Movies.* Ed. Jim Collins, Hilary Radner, and Ava Preacher Collins. New York: Routledge, 1993. 77–85.
Anobile, Richard, ed. *Popeye: The Movie Novel.* New York: Avon, 1980.
Ansen, David. "Come Back to the 5 & Dime Jimmy Dean, Jimmy Dean." *Newsweek,* 20 December 1982, 90.
———. "The Neo-noir '90s." *Newsweek,* 27 October 1997, 68–70.
Armes, Roy. *The Ambiguous Image: Narrative Style in Modern European Cinema.* Bloomington: Indiana University Press, 1976.

Ascher-Walsh, Rebecca. "Tough Cookie: Robert Altman Raged, John Grisham Jumped, and *The Gingerbread Man* Nearly Crumbled." *Entertainment Weekly*, 30 January 1998, 16–17.

Aufderheide, Patricia. "Secret Honor: Interviews with Donald Freed and Robert Altman." *Cineaste* 14, no. 2 (1985): 13–14.

AuWerter, Robert. "Robert Altman." In *Directors in Action*. Ed. Bob Thomas. Indianapolis: Bobbs-Merrill, 1973. 60–65.

Bachmann, Gregg. "*McCabe & Mrs. Miller*: Altman's Showdown with the Western." *Creative Screenwriting* 4 (fall 1997): 97–111.

Baker, Charles A. "The Theme of Structure in the Films of Robert Altman." *Journal of Popular Film* 2, no. 3 (1973): 243–61.

———. "Illusion and Reality in *Nashville*." *Studies in the Humanities* 10, no. 2 (1983): 93–98.

Barthes, Roland. *S/Z: An Essay*. Trans. Richard Miller. New York: Hill & Wang, 1974.

———. *The Pleasure of the Text*. Trans. Richard Miller. New York: Hill & Wang, 1975.

———. "The Third Meaning." In *Image–Music–Text*. Ed. and trans. Stephen Heath. New York: Hill & Wang, 1977. 52–68.

———. "The Death of the Author." In *Theories of Authorship*. Ed. John Caughie. London: Routledge & Kegan Paul, 1981. 208–13.

———. *The Fashion System*. Trans. Matthew Ward and Richard Howard. New York: Hill & Wang, 1983.

Baudry, Jean-Louis. "Author and Analyzable Subjects." In *Apparatus*. Ed. Therese Hak Kyungcha. New York: Tanam, 1980.

Beaver, Frank. "An Interview with Robert Altman." *Michigan Quarterly Review* 22 (winter 1983): 45–55.

Bellour, Raymond. "The Obvious and the Code." *Screen* 15 (1974): 12–20.

Belsey, Catherine. *Critical Practice*. London: Methuen, 1980.

Belton, John. "Technology and Aesthetics of Film Sound." In *Film Sound: Theory and Practice*. Ed. Elisabeth Weis and John Belton. New York: Columbia University Press, 1985. 63–72.

Belton, John, and Lyle Tector. "The Bionic Eye: The Aesthetics of the Zoom." *Film Comment* 16 (September/October 1980): 11–17.

Benstock, Shari, and Suzanne Ferriss. "Introduction." In *On Fashion*. Ed. Shari Benstock and Suzanne Ferriss. New Brunswick, N.J.: Rutgers University Press, 1994. 1–20.

Benthall, Jonathan, and Ted Polhemus, eds. *The Body as Medium of Expression*. New York: Dutton, 1975.

Berger, John. *Ways of Seeing*. New York: Dutton, 1972.

Berger, Thomas. *Little Big Man.* Greenwich, Conn.: Fawcett, 1964.

Bergman, Ingmar. *Ingmar Bergman: Four Screenplays.* Trans. Lara Malmstrom and David Kushner. New York: Simon & Schuster, 1960.

———. "Bergman Discusses Film-Making." *Film and/as Literature.* Ed. John Harrington. Englewood Cliffs, N.J.: Prentice Hall, 1977. 224–28.

Bergstrom, Janet. "An Interrogation of the Cinematic Sign: Woman as Sexual Signifier in Jackie Reynal's *Deux Fois.*" *Camera Obscura* 1 (fall 1976): 11–26.

Bernardoni, James. *The New Hollywood: What the Movies Did with the New Freedom of the Seventies.* Jefferson, N.C.: McFarland, 1991.

Bernstein, Mathew. "Robert Altman's *Buffalo Bill and the Indians; or Sitting Bull's History Lesson*: A Self-Portrait in Celluloid." *Journal of Popular Culture* 13 (summer 1979): 17–25.

Bettelheim, Bruno. *The Uses of Enchantment.* New York: Alfred A. Knopf, 1975.

Billman, Carol W. "Illusions of Grandeur: Altman, Kopit, and the Legends of the Wild West." *Literature/Film Quarterly* 6 (summer 1978): 253–61.

Biskind, Peter. *Easy Riders, Raging Bulls: How the Sex-Drugs-and-Rock 'n' Roll Generation Saved Hollywood.* New York: Simon & Schuster, 1998.

Bloom, Allan. *The Closing of the American Mind.* New York: Simon & Schuster, 1987.

Boggs, Joseph M. *The Art of Watching Films,* 2d ed. Palo Alto, Calif.: Mayfield, 1985.

Bogle, Donald. *Toms, Coons, Mulattoes, Mammies, and Bucks: An Interpretive History of Blacks in Film.* New York: Viking, 1973.

Bohn, Thomas, and Richard Stromgren. *Light and Shadows: A History of the Motion Picture.* Port Washington, N.Y.: Alfred, 1975.

Bolcom, William. *McTeague: Opera in Two Acts.* Libretto by Arnold Weinstein and Robert Altman. Chicago: Edward B. Marks Music, 1992.

Bolter, Jay. *Writing Space: The Computer, Hypertext, and the History of Writing.* Hillsdale, N.J.: Lawrence Erlbaum, 1991.

Bordwell, David. "The Art Cinema as a Mode of Film Practice." *Film Criticism* 4, no. 1 (1979): 56–64.

———. *Narration in the Fiction Film.* Madison: University of Wisconsin Press, 1985.

———. "Classical Hollywood Cinema: Narrational Principles and Procedures." In *Narrative, Apparatus, Ideology.* Ed. Philip Rosen. New York: Columbia University Press, 1986. 17–34.

———. *Making Meaning: Inference and Rhetoric in the Interpretation of Cinema.* Cambridge: Harvard University Press, 1989.

Bordwell, David, and Kristin Thompson. *Film Art: An Introduction,* 2d ed. New York: Alfred A. Knopf, 1986.

Bordwell, David, Kristin Thompson, and Janet Steiger. *The Classical Hollywood Cinema: Film Style and Mode of Production to 1960.* New York: Columbia University Press, 1985.

Bourget, Jean-Loup. *Robert Altman.* Paris: Éditions Ramsay, 1981.

Bourne, Michael. "Altman Stages Kansas City Jam Session." *Down Beat* 62 (August 1995): 12.

———. "Goin' to Kansas City and Robert Altman Takes You There." *Down Beat* 63 (March 1996): 22–27.

Bowles, Stephen E. "*Cabaret* and *Nashville*: The Musical as Social Comment." *Journal of Popular Culture* 12 (winter 1978): 550–56.

Boyd, Michael. *The Reflexive Novel: Fiction as Critique.* Lewisburg, Penn.: Bucknell University Press, 1983.

Boyum, Joy Gould. *Double Exposure: Fiction into Film.* New York: New American Library, 1985.

Bradbury, Malcolm, and James McFarlane, eds. *Modernism: 1890–1930.* New York: Penguin, 1976.

Branigan, Edward. *Point of View in the Cinema: A Theory of Narration and Subjectivity in Classical Film.* Berlin: Mouton, 1984.

———. *Narrative Comprehension and Film.* London: Routledge, 1992.

Braudy, Leo. *The World in a Frame: What We See in Film.* Garden City, N.Y.: Anchor, 1976.

Braudy, Leo, and Robert Kolker. "Robert Altman: An Interview, Part I." *Post Script* 1 (fall 1981): 2–7.

———. "Robert Altman: An Interview, Part II." *Post Script* 1 (winter 1982): 2–14.

Breskin, David. "'I Try to Debunk Myself as Much as Anybody Else': Interview with Robert Altman." *Rolling Stone,* 16 April 1992, 74–77, 86, 94–95.

Brod, Harry, ed. *The Making of Masculinities: The New Men's Studies.* Boston: Allen & Unwin, 1987.

Brodie, Fawn. *Richard Nixon: The Shaping of His Character.* New York: W. W. Norton, 1981.

Bromell, Henry. "Solving Problems." *Atlantic,* January 1981, 82–84.

Brooks, Cleanth, and Robert Penn Warren. *Understanding Fiction,* 2d ed. New York: Appleton-Century-Crofts, 1959.

Brown, Royal S. "Film Music: The Good, the Bad, and the Ugly." *Cineaste* 21, nos. 1–2 (1995): 62–67.

Browne, Nick. "The Spectator-in-the-Text: The Rhetoric of *Stagecoach.*" In *Movies and Methods,* vol. 2. Ed. Bill Nichols. Berkeley: University of California Press, 1985. 458–75.

———. "American Narrative Studies of Film: Between Formalism and Postmodernism." *Quarterly Review of Film Studies* 10 (1989): 341–46.

Bruce, Bryan. "Madness, Pleasure, and Transgression: *Looking for Mr. Goodbar.*" *CineAction!* 2 (fall 1985): 7–13.

Bruzzi, Stella. "Cinema and Haute Couture: *Sabrina* to *Pretty Woman, Trop Belle Pour Toi, Prêt-à-Porter.*" In *Undressing Cinema: Clothing and Identity in the Movies.* New York: Routledge, 1997.

Bryne, Connie, and William Lopez. "*Nashville* (an Interview 'Documentary')." *Film Quarterly* 29 (winter 1975–76): 13–25.

Budd, Mike, Robert M. Entman, and Clay Steinem. "The Affirmative Character of U.S. Cultural Studies." *Critical Studies in Mass Communication* 7, no. 2 (1990): 169–84.

Burch, Noël. *Theory of Film Practice.* London: Secker & Warburg, 1973.

———. "Porter or Ambivalence." *Screen* 19 (winter 1978–79): 91–105.

———. "Film's Institutional Mode of Representation and the Soviet Response." *October* 11 (winter 1979): 77–96.

Burke, John. *Buffalo Bill, the Noblest Whiteskin.* New York: Putnam, 1973.

Cadbury, William, and Leland Poague. *Film Criticism: A Counter Theory.* Ames: Iowa State University Press, 1982.

Callens, Johan. "Through the Windows of Perception: Shepard's *Fool for Love* on the Screen." In *American Literature and the Arts.* Brussels: Vubpress, 1991. 83–112.

Campbell, Ewing. *Raymond Carver: A Study of the Short Fiction.* New York: Twayne, 1992.

Canaday, John. *Mainstreams of Modern Art, David to Picasso.* New York: Simon & Schuster, 1962.

Canby, Vincent. "Film View: A Satire, a Melodrama, a Celebration." *New York Times,* 15 June 1975, 2.1, 2.17.

———. "Robert Altman's Gallery of American Portraits." *New York Times,* 4 July 1976, 2.1.

Caramello, Charles. *Silverless Mirrors: Book, Self, and Postmodern American Fiction.* Tallahassee: University Press of Florida, 1973.

Cardullo, Robert J. "The Space in the Distance: A Study of Altman's *Nashville.*" *Literature/Film Quarterly* 4, no. 4 (1976): 313–24.

Carroll, Noël. "The Future of Allusion: Hollywood in the Seventies (and Beyond)." *October* 20 (1982): 51–78.

Carver, Raymond. *Short Cuts: Selected Stories.* Ed. Robert Altman. New York: Vintage, 1993.

Caughie, John. "Fiction of the Author/Author of the Fiction." In *Theories of Authorship: A Reader.* Ed. John Caughie. London: Routledge & Kegan Paul, 1981. 197–207.

Cavell, Stanley. *Pursuits of Happiness: The Hollywood Comedy of Remarriage.* Cambridge: Harvard University Press, 1981.

Cawelti, John C. *The Six-Gun Mystique.* Bowling Green, OH: Bowling Green University Popular Press, 1970.

———. *Adventure, Mystery, and Romance: Formula Stories as Art and Popular Culture.* Chicago: University of Chicago Press, 1976.

Chatman, Seymour. *Story and Discourse: Narrative Structure in Fiction and Film.* Ithaca, N.Y.: Cornell University Press, 1978.

———. *Coming to Terms: The Rhetoric of Narrative in Fiction and Film.* Ithaca, N.Y.: Cornell University Press, 1990.

Chesire, Godfrey. "Against the Odds: An Interview with Robert Altman." *Spectator Magazine,* 17–23 March 1983, 507–8.

Chodorow, Nancy. *The Reproduction of Mothering: Psychoanalysis and the Sociology of Gender.* Berkeley: University of California Press, 1978.

Cixous, Hélène. "Sonia Rykiel in Translation." In *On Fashion.* Ed. Shari Benstock and Suzanne Ferriss. New Brunswick, N.J.: Rutgers University Press, 1994. 95–99.

Clarke, Arthur C. *Childhood's End.* New York: Ballantine, 1953.

Clements, Marcelle. "Altman's 'The Player': More Smug Revenge." *Premiere,* June 1992, 128.

Cohen, Steven, and Ina Rae Hark, eds. *Screening the Male: Exploring Masculinities in the Hollywood Cinema.* New York: Routledge, 1993.

Cole, Michael, and Helen Keyssar. "The Concept of Literacy in Print and Film." In *Literacy, Language and Learning: The Nature and Consequences of Reading and Writing.* Ed. David R. Olson, Nancy Torrance, and Angela Hildyard. Cambridge: Cambridge University Press, 1985. 50–72.

Coles, Robert. "Compassion from Carver, Male Swagger from Altman." *New York Times,* 17 October 1993, H1, H25.

Collins, Amy Fine. "Ready to Wear." *Harper's Bazaar,* December 1994, 50.

Collins, Jim, Hilary Radner, and Ava Preacher Collins, eds. *Film Theory Goes to the Movies.* New York: Routledge, 1993.

Combs, Richard. "Playing the Game; or Robert Altman and the Indians." *Sight and Sound* 48, no. 3 (1979): 136–42.

———. "Kansas City, Kansas City," *Film Comment* 23 (March/April 1997): 68–71.

Conley, Tom. "Noir in the Red and the Nineties in the Black." In *Film*

*Genre 2000: New Critical Essays.* Ed. Wheeler Winston Dixon. Albany: State University of New York Press, 2000. 193–210.

Cook, David. *A History of Narrative Film.* New York: W. W. Norton, 1981.

———. "Auteur Cinema and the 'Film Generation' in 1970s Hollywood." In *The New American Cinema.* Ed. Jon Lewis. Durham, N.C.: Duke University Press, 1998. 11–37.

Cook, Pam, and Mieke Bernink, eds. *The Cinema Book,* 2d ed. London: British Film Institute, 1999.

Corliss, Richard. "Keith Carridine and Shelley Duvall of *Thieves Like Us.*" *Film Comment* 10 (May 1974): 14–15.

———. "Bisoncentennial Celebration." *New York Times,* 23 July 1976, 67–70.

———. "Streamers." *Time,* 17 October 1983, 89.

———. "Beyond Therapy." *Time,* 2 March 1987, 74–75.

Corrigan, Timothy. *A Cinema without Walls: Movies and Culture after Vietnam.* New Brunswick, N.J.: Rutgers University Press, 1991.

———. "Auteurs and the New Hollywood." In *The New American Cinema.* Ed. Jon Lewis. Durham, N.C.: Duke University Press, 1998. 38–63.

Costello, William. *The Facts about Nixon.* New York: Viking, 1960.

Coward, Rosalind, and John Ellis. *Language and Materialism: Developments in Semiology and the Theory of the Subject.* London: Routledge & Kegan Paul, 1977.

Cowie, Elizabeth. "Storytelling: Classical Hollywood Cinema and Classical Narrative." In *Contemporary Hollywood Cinema.* Ed. Steve Neale and Murray Smith. London: Routledge, 1998. 178–90.

Coyne, Michael. "Legends Revisited, Legends Revised in 'Bicentennial Westerns': *Buffalo Bill and the Indians, The Outlaw Josey Wales,* and *The Shootist.*" In *The Crowded Prairie: American National Identity in the Hollywood Western.* London: Tauris, 1998. 166–83.

Crawley, Tony. "Altman's Playground." *Photoplay,* August 1986, 40–43.

Cripps, Thomas. *Slow Fade to Black: The Negro in American Film, 1900–1942.* New York: Oxford University Press, 1977.

Crist, Judith. "Altman Returns to the Labyrinth." *Saturday Review,* April 1977, 51–52.

Crofts, Stephen. "Authorship and Hollywood." *Wide Angle* 5, no. 3 (1983): 16–22.

Crotta, Carol A. "The Caine Mutiny Court-Martial." *TV Guide,* 7 May 1988, 43–44.

———. "Everyone Here Is a Bit Tilted." *TV Guide,* 7 May 1988, 43–44.

Culler, Jonathan. "Literary History, Allegory, and Semiology." *New Literary History* 7 (1976): 259–70.

———. *Structuralist Poetics.* Ithaca, N.Y.: Cornell University Press, 1976.

———. *The Pursuit of Signs: Semiotics, Literature, Deconstruction.* Ithaca, N.Y.: Cornell University Press, 1981.

Cunningham, John M. "The Tin Star." In *The Western Story: Fact, Fiction, and Myth.* Ed. Philip Durham and Everett Jones. New York: Harcourt Brace Jovanovich, 1975. 209–22.

Currie, Gregory. "*The Long Goodbye*: The Imaginary Language of Film." *British Journal of Aesthetics* 33, no. 3 (1993): 207–19.

Curtie, Merle. "Dime Novels and the American Tradition." *Yale Review* 26 (June 1937): 761–68.

Cutts, John. "M.A.S.H., McCloud and McCabe: An Interview with Robert Altman." *Films and Filming* 18 (November 1971): 40–44.

Dannzinger, Marie. "Basic Instinct: Grappling for Post-Modern Mind Control." *Literature/Film Quarterly* 22, no. 1 (1994): 7–10.

Danto, Arthur C. *Analytical Philosophy of History.* London: Cambridge University Press, 1968.

Davis, Peter G. "Booty and the Beast: *McTeague*'s Score Is Crammed with Goodies." *New York,* 16 November 1992, 99–100.

Dawson, Jan. "Robert Altman Speaking." *Film Comment* 10 (March 1974): 40–41.

deCordova, Richard. *Picture Personalities: The Emergence of the Star System in America.* Champaign: University of Illinois Press, 1990.

Deemer, Charles. "*Short Cuts*: The Los Angelesation of Raymond Carver." *Creative Screenwriting* 4 (fall 1997): 11–17.

Demby, Barbara Jeffries. "Robert Altman Talks about His Life and His Art." *New York Times,* 19 June 1977, sec. 2, pp. 1, 17.

Dempsey, Michael. "Altman, the Empty Staircase and the Chinese Princess." *Film Comment* 10 (September 1974): 10–17.

Denby, David. "Private Picture." *New York,* 29 December 1980, 47–48.

———. "Come Back to the 5 & Dime Jimmy Dean, Jimmy Dean." *New York,* 1 February 1982, 86–87.

———. "Ready to Wear." *New York,* 2 January 1995, 67.

Derrida, Jacques. *Of Grammatology.* Trans. Gayatri Chakravorty Spivak. Baltimore: Johns Hopkins University Press, 1976.

Diawara, Manthia, ed. *Black American Cinema.* New York: Routledge, 1993.

———. "Black Spectatorship: Problems of Identification and Resistance." In *Film Theory and Criticism: Introductory Readings,* 5th ed. Ed. Leo

Braudy and Marshall Cohen. New York: Oxford University Press, 1999. 845–53.

Dick, Bernard F. "Narrative and Infra-Narrative in Film." *Literature/Film Quarterly* 3 (1975): 124–30.

Diffley, Kathleen. "Reconstructing the American Canon: E Pluribus Unum?" *Journal of the Midwest Modern Language Association* 21 (fall 1988): 1–15.

DiPiero, W. S. "Wish and Power: Recent Altman." *Chicago Review* 30 (summer 1978): 34–51.

Doane, Mary Ann. "The Voice in the Cinema: The Articulation of Body and Space." *Yale French Studies* 60, no. 1 (1980): 33–50.

———. "Ideology and the Practice of Sound Editing and Mixing." In *Film Sound: Theory and Practice*. Ed. Elisabeth Weis and John Belton. New York: Columbia University Press, 1985. 54–62.

———. *The Desire to Desire: The Woman's Film of the 1940s*. Bloomington: Indiana University Press, 1987.

———. *Femmes Fatales: Feminism, Film Theory, Psychoanalysis*. New York: Routledge, 1991.

Doane, Mary Ann, Patricia Mellencamp, and Linda Williams. "Introduction." In *Re-Vision: Essays in Feminist Film Criticism*, Ed. Mary Ann Doane, Patricia Mellencamp, and Linda Williams. Frederick, Md.: University Publications of America, 1984. 1–17.

Dowd, Maureen. "'Eighty-Eightsomething.'" *New Republic*, 1 August 1988, 37–40.

Dunning, J. "The Man Who Painted Robert Altman's *3 Women*." *New York Times*, 24 April 1977, sec. 2, p. 19.

Durgnat, Raymond "The Man with No Genre." In Norman Kagan, *American Skeptic: Robert Altman's Genre-Commentary Films*. Ann Arbor, Mich.: Pierian, 1982. xi–xvii.

Duynslaegher, Patrick. "I Am the Window You Are Looking Through." *Films Illustrated* 7 (September 1977): 20–23.

Dyer, Richard. *Heavenly Bodies: Film Stars and Society*. New York: St. Martin's, 1986.

———. "Resistance through Charisma: Rita Hayworth and *Gilda*." In *Women in Film Noir*, exp. ed. Ed. E. Ann Kaplan. London: British Film Institute, 1998. 115–22.

Ebert, Roger. "Show Biz Bill Cody." *Chicago Sun-Times*, 2 July 1976, 49.

———. "Beyond Narrative: The Future of the Feature Film." In *The Great Ideas Today*. Ed. Mortimer J. Adler. Chicago: Encyclopedia Britannica, 1978. 176–215.

———. "Shelley Duvall Is Cookin' in Olive Oyl Role." *Chicago Sun-Times,* 14 December 1980, sec. 3, pp. 1–2.

———. "Dr. T & the Women." *Chicago Sun-Times,* 13 October 2000. On-line at http://www.suntimes.com/ebert/ebert_reviews/2000/10/101303.html

Eberwein, Robert T. "Spectator-Viewer." *Wide Angle* 2, no. 2 (1978): 8–9.

———. *Film and the Dream Screen: A Sleep and a Forgetting.* Princeton, N.J.: Princeton University Press, 1984.

Elder, Sean. "Dark Victory (Robert Altman's *Short Cuts* and His Leading Ladies)." *Vogue,* October 1993, 218–19.

Ellis, Jack. *A History of Film.* Englewood Cliffs, N.J.: Prentice Hall, 1979.

Ellis, Joan. "Forget the Plot and the People; Just Soak Up the Feel of Robert Altman's Depression-Era Kansas City." *Nebbadoon.com,* February 1996. On-line at http://ellis.nebbadoon.com/docs/joined_reviewfiles/kansas_city.html

Elsaesser, Thomas. "The Pathos of Failure: American Films in the 70s—Notes on the Unmotivated Hero." *Monogram* 6 (1975): 13–19.

———. "On finit le spectacle? (à propos de *Nashville*)." *Positif* 197 (September 1977): 21–27.

———. "*Nashville*: Putting on the Show." *Persistence of Vision* 1 (1984): 35–43.

———. "Specularity and Engulfment: Francis Ford Coppola and *Bram Stoker's Dracula.*" In *Contemporary Hollywood Cinema.* Ed. Steve Neale and Murray Smith. London: Routledge, 1998. 191–208.

Emery, Robert J. *Robert Altman.* Documentary film. American Film Institute series "The Directors." New York: Media Entertainment, 1999.

Engle, Gary. *"McCabe and Mrs. Miller." Journal of Popular Film* 1 (fall 1972): 268–87.

Farber, Steve. "Let Us Now Praise—Not Overpraise—Robert Altman." *New York Times,* 29 September 1974, sec. 2, p. 1.

Faust, M. "Vincent and Theo." *Video* 15 (1991): 74.

Feineman, Neil. *Persistence of Vision: The Films of Robert Altman.* New York: Arno, 1976.

Ferncase, Richard K. "Robert Altman's *The Long Goodbye*: Marlowe in the Me Decade." *Journal of Popular Culture* 25, no. 2 (1991): 87–90.

Fetterley, Judith. *The Resisting Reader: A Feminist Approach to American Fiction.* Bloomington: Indiana University Press, 1978.

Feuer, Jane. "*Nashville,* Altman's Open Surface." *Jump Cut* 10/11 (1976): 31–32.

———. *The Hollywood Musical.* Bloomington: Indiana University Press, 1982.

Fiedler, Leslie. *The Return of the Vanishing American.* New York: Stein & Day, 1968.

Fine Line Features. "The Production." *Kansas City* Web site. On-line at http://www.flf.com/kc/index.html

Fishwick, Marshall William. *The Hero, American Style.* New York: McKay, 1967.

Fiske, John. *Television Culture.* London: Methuen, 1987.

Fokkema, Douwe W. *Literary History, Modernism, and Postmodernism.* Philadelphia: John Benjamins, 1984.

Folsom, James K. *The American Western Novel.* New Haven, Conn.: College & University Press, 1966.

Foucault, Michel. "What Is an Author?" In *Theories of Authorship: A Reader.* Ed. John Caughie. London: Routledge & Kegan Paul, 1981. 282–91.

Fox, Terry Curtis. "*Nashville* Chats." *Chicago Reader,* 4 July 1976, 1–20.

Frank, Philip. "Satirizing Hollywood: The Self-Referentiality of Robert Altman's *The Player.*" In *Proceedings of the Conference on Film and American Culture.* Ed. Joel Schwartz. Williamsburg, VA: College of William and Mary, 1994.

Friar, Ralph, and Natasha Friar. *The Only Good Indian . . . The Hollywood Gospel.* New York: Drama Book Specialists, 1972.

Friesen, Eldon. "A Deconstruction of Hollywood." *24 Frames per Second,* February 1998. On-line at http://www.24framespersecond.com/offcamera/writings/altman.html

Frye, Northrop. *The Anatomy of Criticism.* Princeton, N.J.: Princeton University Press, 1957.

Fuller, Graham. "Altman on Altman." In *Projections 2.* Ed. John Boorman and Walter Donohue. London: Faber & Faber, 1993. 149–81.

Gabbard, Krin. "Altman's *3 Women*: Sanctuary in the Dream World." *Literature/Film Quarterly* 8, no. 4 (1980): 258–64.

———. *Jammin' at the Margins: Jazz and the American Cinema.* Chicago: University of Chicago Press, 1996.

———. "Kansas City Dreamin': Robert Altman's Jazz History Lesson." In *Music and Cinema.* Ed. James Buhler, Caryl Flinn, and David Neumeyer. Hanover, N.H.: Wesleyan University Press, 2000. 142–57.

Gabler, Neal. "Robert Altman Mediaized." *Cinegram* 2, no. 1 (1977): 2–5.

Gaggi, Silvio. *Modern/Postmodern: A Study in Twentieth-Century Arts and Ideas.* Philadelphia: University of Pennsylvania Press, 1989.

———. *From Text to Hypertext: Decentering the Subject in Fiction, Film, the Visual Arts, and Electronic Media.* Philadelphia: University of Pennsylvania Press, 1997.

Gaines, Janet. "Introduction: Fabricating the Female Body." In *Fabrications: Costume and the Female Body.* Ed. Janet Gaines and Charlotte Herzog. New York: Routledge, 1990. 1–27.

Gallagher, Tag. "Shoot-Out at the Genre Corral: Problems in the 'Evolution' of the Western." In *Film Genre Reader II.* Ed. Barry Keith Grant. Austin: University of Texas Press, 1995. 202–16.

Gallagher, Tess. "Kindred Spirits." *Harper's Bazaar,* September 1993, 200–201.

Gans, Herbert J. "*Nashville*: The Film as a Statement about Society." *Social Policy* 6 (November/December 1975): 57–58.

Gardner, Paul. "Altman Surveys Nashville and Sees 'Instant America.'" *New York Times,* 13 June 1975, 26.

Gass, William H. *Willie Masters' Lonesome Wife.* New York: Alfred A. Knopf, 1971.

Geduld, Harry M. "The Gospel According to *Popeye.*" *Humanist,* March/April 1981, 55–56.

Geertz, Clifford. "Deep Play: Notes on the Balinese Cockfight." *Daedelus* 101 (winter 1972): 20–57.

Gehr, Richard. "O.C. and Stiggs." *Video* 11 (1988): 67.

Gelmis, Joseph. *The Film Director as Superstar.* Garden City, N.Y.: Doubleday, 1970.

Genette, Gerard. *Narrative Discourse: An Essay in Method.* Ithaca, N.Y.: Cornell University Press, 1980.

Geng, Veronica. "Between the Devil and the Deep Blue Sea." *New York Review,* 18 November 1993, 66–68.

Gentry, Ric. "Negotiating New Cinematic Avenues via *Short Cuts.*" *American Cinematographer* 74 (November 1993): 32–38.

Giannetti, Louis. *Masters of the American Cinema.* Englewood Cliffs, N.J.: Prentice Hall, 1981.

Giddens, Gary. "Altman's Back." *Village Voice,* 6 November 1990, 65–72.

Giles, Paul. "The Cinema of Catholicism: John Ford and Robert Altman." In *Unspeakable Images: Ethnicity and the American Cinema.* Ed. Lester D. Friedman. Urbana: University of Illinois Press, 1991. 140–66.

Gledhill, Christine, ed. *Home Is Where the Heart Is: Studies in Melodrama and the Woman's Film.* London: British Film Institute, 1987.

———. "Image and Voice: Approaches to Marxist-Feminist Film Criticism." In *Multiple Voices in Feminist Film Criticism.* Ed. Diane Carson,

Linda Dittmar, and Janice Welsch. Minneapolis: University of Minnesota Press, 1994. 109–23.

———. "*Klute* 1: A Contemporary Film Noir and Feminist Film Criticism." In *Women in Film Noir,* exp. ed. Ed. E. Ann Kaplan. London: British Film Institute, 1998. 20–34.

Goffman, Erving. *The Presentation of Self in Everyday Life.* Garden City, N.Y.: Doubleday, 1959.

Goldberg, Ron. "The Long Goodbye." *Video* 16 (1992): 67.

Golden, Mike. "A Robert Altman Film? A Fiction." *Creative Screenwriting* 4 (fall 1997): 5–10.

Goldstein, Patrick. "Rebel's Return." *Vogue,* May 1992, 254–57.

Gomery, Douglas. "The American Film Industry of the 1970s: Stasis in the 'New Hollywood.'" *Wide Angle* 5, no. 4 (1984): 52–59.

———. *The Hollywood Studio System.* New York: St. Martin's, 1986.

Gorbman, Claudia. "Teaching the Soundtrack." *Quarterly Review of Film Studies* 1 (1976): 446–52.

———. "Narrative Film Music." *Yale French Studies* 60, no. 1 (1980): 183–203.

———. *Unheard Melodies: Narrative Film Music.* Bloomington: Indiana University Press, 1987.

Graczyk, Ed. *Come Back to the 5 & Dime, Jimmy Dean, Jimmy Dean: A Comedy-Drama.* New York: Samuel French, 1982.

Graff, Gerald. *Literature against Itself.* Chicago: University of Chicago Press, 1979.

———. *Professing Literature: An Institutional History.* Chicago: University of Chicago Press, 1987.

Grandee, Charles. "Ready to Wear." *Vogue,* January 1995, 72–73.

Grant, Barry Keith, ed. *Film Genre Reader II.* Austin: University of Texas Press, 1995.

Greenberg, Harvey Roy. "Hearts of Time." *Psychiatric Times,* July 1992, 29–30.

Greenspun, Roger. "Floating: *Three Women.*" *Film Comment* 13 (July/August 1977): 55–57.

Gregory, Charles T. "Knight without Meaning? Altman's *Long Goodbye.*" *Sight and Sound* 42, no. 2 (1973): 85–89.

Gross, Larry. "An Interview with Robert Altman on the Set of *Nashville.*" *Millimeter* 3 (February 1975): 24–29.

Hall, Billy, executive producer. *Altman on His Own Terms.* Documentary film. Los Angeles: Fox Movie Channel, 2000.

Hall, Stuart. "Encoding/Decoding." In *Culture, Media, Language.* Ed.

Stuart Hall, Dorothy Hobson, Andrew Lowe, and Paul Willis. London: University of Birmingham Press, 1980.

Harmetz, Aljean. "The 15th Man Who Was Asked to Direct *MASH* (and Did) Makes a Peculiar Western." *New York Times Magazine,* 20 June 1971, 10–11, 46–47, 49, 52–54.

Hasbrang, Richard. "*Saturday Night Fever* and *Nashville*: Exploring the Comic Mythos." *Journal of Popular Culture* 12 (winter 1978): 557–71.

Hassan, Ihab. *Paracriticisms: Seven Speculations of the Times.* Urbana: University of Illinois Press, 1975.

———. *The Dismemberment of Orpheus: Toward a Postmodern Literature,* 2d ed. Madison: University of Wisconsin Press, 1982.

Hearty, Kitty Bowe. "Bob and Ray." *Premiere,* November 1993, 59–61.

Heath, Stephen. "Film/Cinetext/Text." *Screen* 14 (spring/summer 1973): 102–27.

———. "Film and System: Terms of Analysis, Part I." *Screen* 16 (spring 1975): 7–77.

———. "Film and System: Terms of Analysis, Part II." *Screen* 16 (summer 1975): 91–113.

———. "Comments on 'The Idea of Authorship.'" In *Theories of Authorship: A Reader.* Ed. John Caughie. London: Routledge & Kegan Paul, 1981. 214–20.

———. *Questions of Cinema.* Bloomington: Indiana University Press, 1981.

Heller, Zoe. "Hollywood's Last Angry Man." *Vanity Fair,* October 1993, 170–74.

Henry, Buck. "Back Road to *Short Cuts* (Working for Robert Altman)." *Film Comment* 29 (September/October 1993): 34–35, 37–38.

Hershey, Gerri. "Ready to Wear." *Gentlemen's Quarterly,* December 1994, 89–90.

Hey, Kenneth R. Review of *Fool for Love. USA Today,* 7 March 1986, 94–95.

Hilferty, Robert. "Film Review: *Ready to Wear (Prêt-à-Porter).*" *Film Quarterly* 48 (1995): 35–38.

Hill, Jim. *The American West from Fiction (1823) into Film (1909–1986).* Jefferson, N.C.: McFarland, 1990.

Hillier, Jim. *The New Hollywood.* New York: Continuum, 1994.

Hoberman, J. "1975–1985: Ten Years That Shook the World. " *American Film* 10 (June 1985): 34–60.

———. "Rerunning for President." *Village Voice* 37 (1992): 57.

Holdenfield, Chris. "Zoom Lens Voyeur: A Few Minutes with *Nashville*'s Bob Altman." *Rolling Stone,* 17 July 1975, 28–31.

Holland, Norman H. *The Dynamics of Literary Response.* New York: W. W. Norton, 1975.

———. "Unity Identity Text Self." In *Reader Response Criticism: From Formalism to Post-structuralism.* Ed. Jane P. Tompkins. Baltimore: Johns Hopkins University Press, 1980. 118–33.

Hollander, Anne. *Seeing through Clothes.* New York: Avon, 1978.

Hooker, Richard. *M*A*S*H.* New York: Pocket Books, 1969.

hooks, bell. *Reel to Real: Race, Sex and Class at the Movies.* Bloomington: Indiana University Press, 1996.

Horan, Patrick. *The Importance of Being Paradoxical: Maternal Presence in the Works of Oscar Wilde.* Madison, N.J.: Fairleigh Dickinson University Press, 1977.

Houpt, Simon. "Robert Altman Refuses to Blink." *New York Globe and Mail,* 3 April 1999, C1–C2.

Hutcheon, Linda. *Narcissistic Narrative: The Metafictional Paradox.* Waterloo, Ont.: Wilfred Laurier University Press, 1980.

Hutton, Lauren. "Mizrahi Loves Company." *Entertainment Weekly,* 11 August 1995, 73.

Huyssen, Andreas. *After the Great Divide: Modernism, Mass Culture, Postmodernism.* Bloomington: Indiana University Press, 1986.

Iser, Wolfgang. *The Act of Reading: A Theory of Aesthetic Response.* Baltimore: Johns Hopkins University Press, 1978.

Jacobs, Diane. "Robert Altman." In *Hollywood Renaissance.* Cranbury, N.J.: A. S. Barnes, 1977. 63–96.

Jameson, Fredric. *The Political Unconscious: Narrative as Socially Symbolic Act.* Ithaca, N.Y.: Cornell University Press, 1981.

———. *Postmodernism; or, The Cultural Logic of Late Capitalism.* Durham, N.C.: Duke University Press, 1991.

Jameson, Richard T. "Film Noir Today: Son of Noir." *Film Comment* 10 (November/December 1974): 30–33.

———. "*Nashville*: Writin' It Down Kinda Makes Me Feel Better." *Movietone News,* 4 September 1975, 1–24.

———. "Tanner '88." *Film Comment* 24 (May/June 1988): 73–75.

———. "Robert Altman on 'The Player.'" *Film Comment* 28 (May/June 1992): 20–21.

Jameson, Richard T., and Kathleen Murphy. "'. . . They Take on Their Own Life . . .': Robert Altman." *Movietone News,* 16 September 1977, 2–13.

Jeffords, Susan. *The Remasculinization of America: Gender and the Vietnam War.* Bloomington: Indiana University Press, 1989.

———. *Hard Bodies: Hollywood Masculinity in the Reagan Era.* New Brunswick, N.J.: Rutgers University Press, 1994.

Jenks, Tom. "*Short Cuts*: Robert Altman Shoots the Stories of Raymond Carver." *Esquire,* September 1993, 102–9.

Johnson, Barbara. *The Critical Difference: Essays in Contemporary Rhetoric of Reading.* Baltimore: Johns Hopkins University Press, 1980.

Johnson, Brian D. "Vincent and Theo." *Maclean's,* 26 November 1990, 74.

Johnson, Steve. "High Caliber Talent: Robert Altman's Prints Are All over *Gun.*" *Chicago Tribune,* 11 April 1997, 5.3.

Joost, Nicholas, and Franklin E. Court. "*Salomé,* the Moon, and Oscar Wilde's Aesthetics: A Reading of the Play." *Papers on Language and Literature* 8 (1972): 96–111.

Kael, Pauline. "Forty-Eight Characters in Search of a Director." In *When the Lights Go Down.* New York: Holt, Rinehart & Winston, 1980.

———. "Come Back to the 5 & Dime Jimmy Dean, Jimmy Dean." *New Yorker,* 15 November 1982, 177–78.

———. "Fool for Love." *New Yorker,* 27 January 1986, 84–87.

———. "Vincent and Theo." *New Yorker,* 19 November 1990, 130–33.

———. Interview with Robert Altman. In *Short Cuts* videodisc. Santa Monica, Calif.: Voyager, 1994.

Kagan, Norman. *American Skeptic: Robert Altman's Genre-Commentary Films.* Ann Arbor, Mich.: Pierian, 1982.

Kaplan, E. Ann. *Women and Film: Both Sides of the Camera.* New York: Methuen, 1983.

———. "Introduction to 1978 Edition." In *Women in Film Noir,* exp. ed. Ed. E. Ann Kaplan. London: British Film Institute, 1998.

Kaplan, Mike, and John Dorr, directors. *Luck, Trust, and Ketchup: Robert Altman in Carver Country.* In *Short Cuts* videodisc. Santa Monica, Calif.: Voyager, 1994.

Karolides, Nicholas. *The Pioneer in the American Novel.* Norman: University of Oklahoma Press, 1967.

Karp, Alan. *The Films of Robert Altman.* Metuchen, N.J.: Scarecrow, 1981.

Kasindorf, Jeanie. "Home Movie: Robert Altman, the Aging Bad Boy of Film." *New York,* 16 March 1992, 50–55.

Kass, Judith M. *Robert Altman: American Innovator.* New York: Popular Library, 1978.

Kasson, Joy S. *Buffalo Bill's Wild West: Celebrity, Memory, and Popular Culture.* New York: Hill & Wang, 2000.

Kauffmann, Stanley. "Three from the Theatre." *New Republic,* 23 March 1987, 24–25.

Kawin, Bruce F. *Mindscreen: Bergman, Godard and First-Person Film.* Princeton, N.J.: Princeton University Press, 1978.

———. *The Mind of the Novel: Reflexive Fiction and the Ineffable.* Princeton, N.J.: Princeton University Press, 1982.

Keller, Julia. "Robert Altman Brings 'Dr. T' to the Pig, er Big, Screen." *Chicago Tribune,* 23 October 2000, 5.1.

Keller, Julia, and Michael Wilmington. "Where the Boys Are." *Chicago Tribune,* 3 November 2000, 5.1.

Kempley, Rita. "'Dr. T': Take with Two Aspirin." *Washington Post,* 13 October 2000, C1.

Keogh, Peter. "Death and Hollywood." *Sight and Sound* 2 (June 1992): 12–13.

Keyser, Les, and Barbara Keyser. *Hollywood and the Catholic Church: The Image of Roman Catholicism in American Movies.* Chicago: Loyola University Press, 1984.

Keyssar, Helene. *Robert Altman's America.* New York: Oxford University Press, 1991.

Kinder, Marsha. "The Return of the Outlaw Couple." *Film Quarterly* 27, no. 4 (1974): 2–10.

———. "The Art of Dreaming in *Three Women* and *Providence*: Structures of the Self." *Film Quarterly* 31, no. 1 (1977): 10–18.

Kitses, Jim. *Horizon's West: Studies in Authorship in the Western Film.* Bloomington: Indiana University Press, 1970.

Klawans, Stuart. "Vincent and Theo." *The Nation* 251 (1990): 743.

Klein, Michael. "Nashville and the American Dream." *Jump Cut* 9 (1975): 6–7.

Klinkowitz, Jerome. *Literary Disruptions: The Making of a Post-contemporary American Fiction.* Urbana: University of Illinois Press, 1975.

Kloman, Harry, Lloyd Michaels, and Virginia Wright Wexman. "'A Foolish Optimist': Interview with Robert Altman." *Film Criticism* 7, no. 3 (1983): 20–28.

Kolker, Robert. *A Cinema of Loneliness; Penn, Kubrick, Scorsese, Spielberg, Altman,* 3rd ed. New York: Oxford University Press, 2000.

Kopit, Arthur. *Indians.* New York: Bantam, 1971.

Kornblau, Gary. "On the Logic of the Candidate Tanner." In *Tanner '88* videodisc, vol. 2. Santa Monica, Calif.: Voyager, 1992.

Kornitzer, Bela. *The Real Nixon.* Chicago: Rand McNally, 1960.

Kozloff, Sarah. *Invisible Storytellers: Voice-Over Narration in American Fiction Film.* Berkeley: University of California Press, 1988.

Kramer, Peter. "Post-classical Hollywood Film: Concepts and Debates."

In *The Oxford Guide to Film Studies.* Ed. John Gibson and Pamela Church Gibson. Oxford: Oxford University Press, 1998.

Kroll, Jack. "Review of *Quintet.*" *Newsweek,* 12 February 1979, 88.

———. "Review of *Streamers.*" *Newsweek,* 7 November 1983, 131.

———. "Robert Altman Gives Something Back." *Esquire,* May 1992, 86–92.

———. "The Player Returns." *Newsweek,* 26 April 1993, 62–63.

Krutnik, Frank. *In a Lonely Street: Film Noir, Genre, Masculinity.* London: Routledge, 1991.

Landow, George P. *Hypertext 2.0: The Convergence of Contemporary Critical Theory and Technology.* Baltimore: Johns Hopkins University Press, 1997.

Langbaum, Robert. *The Mysteries of Identity: A Theme in Modern Literature.* New York: Oxford University Press, 1977.

Larner, Jeremy. "Dukakis . . . Jackson . . . Tanner?" *TV Guide,* 4 June 1988, 10–11.

Leach, Edmund. *Culture and Communication: Logic by Which Symbols Are Connected.* London: Cambridge University Press, 1976.

Leff, Leonard. "Quilts, Radios, and Baseball Gloves: The Accessible World of *Thieves Like Us.*" *Film Heritage* 12 (winter 1976–77): 31–39.

Lehman, Peter, ed. *Close Viewings: Understanding Film.* Gainesville: University Press of Florida, 1990.

———. *Running Scared: Masculinity and the Representation of the Male Body.* Philadelphia: Temple University Press, 1993.

Lehman, Peter, and William Luhr. *Authorship and Narrative in the Cinema.* New York: G. P. Putnam's Sons, 1977.

Leitch, Brian D. "The Interview." In *Robert Altman's Prêt-à-Porter.* Ed. Robert Altman, Barbara Shulgasser, and Brian D. Leitch. New York: Hyperion, 1994. 8–39.

Lemons, Stephen. "Robert Altman." *Salon.com,* 15 August 2000. On-line at http://www.salon.com/people/bc/2000/08/15/altman/index.html

Levin, Lear. "Robert Altman's Innovative Sound Techniques." *American Cinematographer* 61 (1980): 336–84.

Levin, Sid. "The Art of the Editor: *Nashville.*" *Filmmakers Newsletter* 8 (August 1974–75): 29–33.

Levine, Robert. "Robert Altman and Company." *Film Comment* 13 (January/February 1977): 4–13.

Lévi-Strauss, Claude. "The Science of the Concrete." In *Ritual, Play, and Performance.* Ed. Richard Schechner and Mady Schuman. New York: Seabury, 1976. 428–44.

———. "The Structural Study of Myth." In *The Critical Tradition: Classic Texts and Contemporary Trends,* 2d. ed. Ed. David H. Richter. Boston: Bedford, 1998. 836–43.

Lewis, Jon. "Money Matters: Hollywood in the Corporate Era." In *The New American Cinema.* Ed. Jon Lewis. Durham, N.C.: Duke University Press, 1998. 87–121.

Lewis, R. W. B. *The American Adam.* Chicago: University of Chicago Press, 1955.

Leyda, Jay, ed. *Film Makers Speak: Voices of Experience.* New York: Da Capo, 1977.

Lightman, Herb, and Michael Duvall. "Altman Shoots Super-16." *American Cinematographer* 63 (September 1982): 889–91.

Limerick, Patricia Nelson. *A Legacy of Conquest: The Unbroken Past of the American West.* New York: W. W. Norton, 1988.

Linderman, Lawrence. "Penthouse Interview: Robert Altman." *Penthouse,* January 1981, 79–86, 122.

Lipnick, Edward. "Creative Post-Flashing Technique for *The Long Goodbye.*" *American Cinematographer* 54 (March 1973): 278–81.

Lippy, Tod. "Writing *Nashville*: A Talk with Joan Tewkesbury." *Scenario* 1 (winter 1995): 105–9, 205.

Lodge, David. *After Bakhtin: Essays on Fiction and Criticism.* London: Routledge, 1990.

Lucci, Sebastiano, ed. "Una Bibliografia su Robert Altman." *Cinema Studio* 1, no. 5 (27 August 1999). On-line at http://www.cinemastudio.com/archivio/numero005/universita/bibliografiaaltman.htm

Luhr, William. *Raymond Chandler and Film.* New York: F. Ungar, 1982.

Lyons, Donald. "Flaws in the Iris: The Private Eye in the Seventies." *Film Comment* 29 (July/August 1993): 44–53.

Lyotard, Jean-François. *The Postmodern Condition: A Report on Knowledge.* Trans. Geoff Bennington and Brian Massumi. Minneapolis: University of Minnesota Press, 1984.

Macklin, Anthony F. "Nashville: America's Voices." *Film Heritage* 11, no. 1 (1975): 6–10.

———. "Welcome to Lions Gate: Interviews with Director Alan Rudolph and Composer Richard Baskin." *Film Heritage* 12, no. 1 (1976): 1–17.

———. "The Artist and the Multitude Are Natural Enemies: An Interview with Director Robert Altman." *Film Heritage* 12 (winter 1976–77): 1–23.

———. "Vincent and Theo." *Film Comment* 29 (September/October 1993): 42–43.

Malmgren, Carl Darryl. *Fictional Space in Modernist and Postmodernist Fiction.* Lewisburg, Penn.: Bucknell University Press, 1985.

Maltby, Richard. "'Nobody Knows Anything': Post-classical Historiography and Consolidated Entertainment." In *Contemporary Hollywood Cinema.* Ed. Steven Neale and Murray Smith. London: Routledge, 1998. 21–44.

Maltin, Leonard. "Images Lost and Found." *Entertainment @ Home* 1, no. 1 (1996): 24–29.

Man, Glenn. *Radical Visions: American Film Renaissance, 1967–1976.* Westport, Conn.: Greenwood, 1994.

Mandel, Howard. "Cutting It." *Sight and Sound* 4 (March 1994): 11.

Maritain, Jacques. *Creative Intuition in Art and Poetry.* New York: Meridian, 1955.

Martin, Wallace. "Postmodernism: Ultima Thule or Seim Anew." In *Romanticism, Modernism, Postmodernism.* Ed. Harry R. Garvin. Lewisburg, Penn.: Bucknell University Press, 1980.

Marx, Leo. *The Machine in the Garden.* New York: Oxford University Press, 1964.

Maslin, Janet. "From Altman, a Salome Story with Southern Sugar and Spite." *New York Times,* 2 April 1999, B13.

Mast, Gerald. *The Comic Mind: Comedy and the Movies.* Indianapolis: Bobbs-Merrill, 1973.

Mast, Gerald, and Marshall Cohen, eds. *Film Theory and Criticism: Introductory Readings,* 3d. ed. New York: Oxford University Press, 1985.

Mast, Gerald, and Bruce Kawin. *A Short History of the Movies,* 7th ed. Boston: Allyn & Bacon, 2000.

McClelland, C. Kirk. *On Making a Movie: Brewster McCloud.* New York: New American Library, 1971.

McConnell, Frank D. *The Spoken Seen: Film and the Romantic Imagination.* Baltimore: Johns Hopkins University Press, 1975.

McGilligan, Patrick. *Robert Altman: Jumping Off the Cliff, a Biography of the Great American Director.* New York: St. Martin's, 1989.

McLean, Albert. *American Vaudeville as Myth.* Lexington: University of Kentucky Press, 1965.

McMurtry, Larry. "McMurtry on the Movies: Woody Allen, Keith Carradine, Lily Tomlin, and the Disappearance of Grace." In *Film Flam: Essays on Hollywood.* New York: Simon & Schuster, 1987. 95–100.

Merrill, Robert. "Altman's *McCabe and Mrs. Miller* as a Classic Western." *New Orleans Review* 17, no. 2 (1990): 79–86.

Metz, Christian. "Aural Objects." *Yale French Studies* 60, no. 1 (1980): 24–32.

———. *The Imaginary Signifier: Psychoanalysis and the Cinema.* Trans. Celia Britton et al. Bloomington: Indiana University Press, 1982.

Meyer, Adam. *Raymond Carver.* New York: Twayne, 1995.

Meyer, Michele. "Ready to Wear." *Glamour,* January 1995, 116.

Michener, Charles. Interview with Robert Altman. *Film Comment* 14, no. 5 (1978): 15–18.

Miles, Margaret Ruth. "Fashioning the Self." *Christian Century,* 8 March 1995, 273–75.

Miles, Richard. *That Cold Day in the Park.* New York: Delacorte, 1965.

Milne, Tom. "Robert Altman: Backgammon and Spinach." *Sight and Sound* 50 (summer 1981): 182–86.

———. "Robert Altman Talking." *Sight and Sound* 50 (Summer 1981): 184–86.

———. "Health." *Sight and Sound* 50 (summer 1981): 186–87.

Mitchell, Harmen. "Altman Muses on Music and . . ." *Ann Arbor News,* 18 January 1984, E4.

Mitchell, Lee Clark. *Westerns: Making the Man in Fiction and Film.* Chicago: University of Chicago Press, 1996.

Modleski, Tania, ed. *Studies in Entertainment: Critical Approaches to Mass Culture.* Bloomington: Indiana University Press, 1986.

Monaco, James. "Welcome to Palm Springs and Welcome to L.A." *Literature/Film Quarterly* 6, no. 2 (1978): 171–74.

———. "Robert Altman and the Myth of Character." In *American Film Now.* New York: Oxford University Press, 1979. 312–27.

Morgenstein, Joe. "A Small Town Murder Makes for Great Comedy in 'Cookie's Fortune.'" *Wall Street Journal,* 2 April 1999, W1, W6.

Moyer, Kermit. "'Did You Ever See an Elephant Fly?' Style and Substance in the Films of Robert Altman." *Film Heritage* 11, no. 1 (1975): 11–16.

Murphy, Mary. "Crisis of a Cult Figure (Profile of Film Director Robert Altman)." *New West* 2 (May 1977): 36–37.

Naremore, James. "Authorship and the Cultural Politics of Film Criticism." *Film Quarterly* 44, no. 1 (1990): 14–22.

———. *More Than Night: Film Noir in Its Contexts.* Berkeley: University of California Press, 1998.

Nayman, Ira. "The Adaptable Altman." *Creative Screenwriting* 4 (fall 1997): 84–96.

Neale, Steve. "'New Hollywood Cinema.'" *Screen* 17 (1976): 117–22.

———. *Genre*. London: British Film Institute, 1980.

———. "Art Cinema as Institution." *Screen* 22 (1981): 11–39.

———. "Questions of Genre." *Screen* 31 (1990): 45–66.

———. *Genre and Hollywood.* London: Routledge, 2000.

Ness, Richard. *Alan Rudolph: Romance and a Crazed World.* New York: Twayne, 1996.

Nesset, Kirk. *The Stories of Raymond Carver: A Critical Study.* Athens: Ohio University Press, 1995.

Newman, Charles. *The Postmodern Aura: The Act of Fiction in an Age of Inflation.* Evanston, Ill.: Northwestern University Press, 1985.

Nichols, Bill. *Ideology and the Image: Social Representation in the Cinema and Other Media.* Bloomington: Indiana University Press, 1981.

———, ed. *Movies and Methods.* Berkeley: University of California Press, 1985.

Nobile, Richard J., ed. *Popeye, the Movie Novel.* New York: Avon, 1980.

Novak, Ralph. "Vincent and Theo." *People Weekly,* 19 November 1990, 21–22.

Nowell-Smith, Geoffrey. "A Note on 'History/Discourse.'" In *Theories of Authorship: A Reader.* Ed. John Caughie. London: Routledge & Kegan Paul, 1981. 232–41.

———. "Art Cinema." In *The Oxford History of World Cinema.* Ed. Geoffrey Nowell-Smith. New York: Oxford University Press, 1996. 567–75.

O'Brien, Daniel. *Robert Altman, Hollywood Survivor.* London: Batsford, 1995.

O'Brien, Tom. "Beyond Therapy." *Commonweal* 114 (1987): 183–84.

Oliver, Bill. "The Long Goodbye and Chinatown: Debunking the Private Eye Tradition." *Literature/Film Quarterly* 3 (summer 1975): 240–48.

O'Neill, Edward R. "Robert Altman." In *The Oxford History of World Cinema.* Ed. Geoffrey Nowell-Smith. New York: Oxford University Press, 1996. 470–71.

O'Sickey, Ingeborg Majer. "Barbie Magazine and the Aesthetic Commodification." In *On Fashion.* Ed. Shari Benstock and Suzanne Ferriss. New Brunswick, N.J.: Rutgers University Press, 1994. 21–40.

O'Toole, Lawrence. "Streamers." *Maclean's,* 28 November 1983, 70.

———. "Beyond Therapy." *Maclean's,* 9 March 1987, 57.

Ouditt, Sharon. "*Orlando*: Coming across the Divide." In *Adaptations: From Text to Screen, Screen to Text.* Ed. Deborah Cartmell and Imelda Whelehan. London: Routledge, 1999. 146–56.

Palmer, R. Barton. *Hollywood's Dark Cinema: American Film Noir.* New York: Twayne, 1994.

Parrinder, Patrick. *Science Fiction: Its Criticism and Its Teaching.* London: Methuen, 1980.

Pechter, William S. "Altman, Chabrol, and Ray." *Commentary* 62 (October 1976): 75–78.

Penley, Constance, and Sharon Willis, eds. *Male Trouble (Camera Obscura).* Minneapolis: University of Minnesota Press, 1993.

Percheron, Daniel. "Sound in Cinema and Its Relationship to Image and Diegesis." *Yale French Studies* 60, no. 1 (1980): 16–23.

Perry, Bridget. *The Popeye Book.* New York: Dell, 1980.

Phipps, Keith. "Robert Altman." *The Onion A.V. Club,* August 2000. Online at http://avclub.theonion.com/avclub3626/avfeature_3626.html

Pittman, Bruce. "Tracking Altman's Movies." *Take One* 5, no. 3 (1976): 39–40.

Place, Janey. "*Buffalo Bill and the Indians*: Welcome to Show Business." *Jump Cut* 23 (October 1980): 21–22.

———. "Women in Film Noir." In *Women in Film Noir,* exp. ed. Ed. E. Ann Kaplan. London: British Film Institute, 1998. 47–68.

Plecki, Gerald. *Robert Altman.* Boston: Twayne, 1985.

Potter, Christopher. " . . . His Latest Film's Reception." *Ann Arbor News,* 18 January 1984, E4.

Pribram, E. Diedre, ed. *Female Spectators: Looking at Film and Television.* New York: Verso, 1988.

Pudovkin, V. I. "Asynchronism as a Principle of Sound Film." In *Film Sound: Theory and Practice.* Ed. Elisabeth Weis and John Belton. New York: Columbia University Press, 1985. 86–91.

Purdy, Strother. "Can the Novel and the Film Disappear?" *Literature/Film Quarterly* 2 (1974): 237–55.

Pye, Michael, and Lynda Myles. *The Movie Brats: How the Film Generation Took Over Hollywood.* New York: Holt, Rinehart & Winston, 1979.

Quart, Leonard. "On Altman: Image as Essence." *Marxist Perspectives* 1 (spring 1978): 118–25.

Quart, Leonard, and Alissa Quart. "Film Reviews: The Player." *Cineaste* 19, nos. 2–3 (1992): 60, 62.

Rabine, Leslie W. "A Woman's Two Bodies: Fashion Magazines, Consumerism, and Feminism." In *On Fashion.* Ed. Shari Benstock and Suzanne Ferriss. New Brunswick, N.J.: Rutgers University Press, 1994. 59–75.

Rabinowitz, Peter J. *Before Reading: Narrative Conventions and the Politics of Interpretation.* Ithaca, N.Y.: Cornell University Press, 1987.

Rafferty, Terrence. "The Player." *New Yorker,* 20 April 1992, 81–82.

———. "Carverville." *New Yorker,* 27 September 1993, 98–100.

Ray, Robert. *A Certain Tendency in the Hollywood Cinema, 1930–1980.* Princeton, N.J.: Princeton University Press, 1985.

Reich, Howard. "Altman Hits All the Wrong Notes." *Chicago Tribune,* 15 August 1996, 5.1, 5.3.

Reid, Max. "The Making of *California Split*: An Interview with Robert Altman." *Filmmakers Newsletter* 7 (October 1974): 24–27.

Richolson, Janice. "The Player: An Interview with Robert Altman." *Cineaste* 19, nos. 2–3 (1992): 61.

Rickey, Carrie. "Tarnishing the Gilded Age: Robert Altman Directs *McTeague.*" *Opera News* 57 (November 1992): 12–23.

Rodowick, David N. *The Difficulty of Difference: Psychoanalysis, Sexual Difference, and Film Theory.* New York: Routledge, 1990.

Rollin, Roger B. "Robert Altman's 'Nashville': Popular Film and the American Character." *South Atlantic Bulletin* 42 (November 1977): 41–50.

Romney, Jonathan. "In the Time of Earthquakes." *Sight and Sound* 4 (March 1994): 8–11.

Ronald, Paul. "The Stormy Saga of *Popeye*; or, How an Unlikely Crew Guided a Musical to Port." *American Film* 7 (December 1980): 30–36, 73–74.

Rose, Mark. *Alien Encounters: Anatomy of Science Fiction.* Cambridge: Harvard University Press, 1981.

Rosen, Philip, ed. *Narrative, Apparatus, Ideology.* New York: Columbia University Press, 1986.

Rosenbaum, Jonathan. "Improvisation and Interactions in Altmanville." *Sight and Sound* 44, no. 2 (1975): 90–95.

———. "An Altman Album." *Film Comment* 14 (September 1978): 12–14.

Rubenstein, Roberta. *"Brewster McCloud." Film Quarterly* 25 (winter 1971): 44–49.

Rudolph, Alan, and Robert Altman. *Buffalo Bill and the Indians.* New York: Bantam, 1976.

Runyon, Randolph Paul. *Reading Raymond Carver.* Syracuse, N.Y.: Syracuse University Press, 1992.

Russell, Catherine. "*Nashville*: The Show Must Explode." In *Narrative*

*Mortality: Death, Closure, and New Wave Cinemas.* Minneapolis: University of Minnesota Press, 1995. 192–208.

Russell, Don. *The Lives and Legends of Buffalo Bill.* Norman: University of Oklahoma Press, 1960.

Ryan, Michael, and Douglas Kellner. *Camera Politica: The Politics and Ideology of Contemporary American Cinema.* Bloomington: Indiana University Press, 1988.

Rykiel, Sonia. "From Celebration." In *On Fashion.* Ed. Shari Benstock and Suzanne Ferriss. New Brunswick, N.J.: Rutgers University Press, 1994. 100–110.

Sack, Chuck. "Joan Tewkesbury on Screenwriting: An Interview." *Literature/Film Quarterly* 6 (winter 1978): 2–25.

Salsbury, Nate. "The Origins of the Wild West Show." *Colorado Magazine* 32 (July 1955): 205–8.

Salt, Barry. *Film Style and Technology: History and Analysis.* London: Starword, 1983.

Saltzman, Arthur M. *Understanding Raymond Carver.* Columbia: University of South Carolina Press, 1988.

Sanjeck, David. "The Case for Robert Altman." *Literature/Film Quarterly* 19, no. 1 (1991): 66–68.

———. "It Could Have Been Worse: Robert Altman's *O.C. and Stiggs.*" *Post Script* 13, no. 3 (1994): 39–53.

Sarris, Andrew. Review of *McCabe & Mrs. Miller.* In *Film 71/72: An Anthology by the National Film Commission.* Ed. David Denby. New York: Simon & Schuster, 1972. 119–28.

———. "Robert Altman Dreams a Movie." *Village Voice,* 22 April 1977, 40–41.

Sawhill, Ray. "Vincent and Theo." *Newsweek,* 26 November 1990, 78.

———. "The Player." *Film Quarterly* 46 (1992–93): 47–50.

———. "A Movie Called 'Nashville.'" *Salon.com,* 27 June 2000. On-line at http://www.salon.com/ent/movies/feature/2000/06/27/nashville/index.html

Schatz, Thomas. "The Structural Influence: New Directions in Film Genre Study." *Quarterly Review of Film Studies* 2 (August 1977): 302–12.

———. *Hollywood Genres: Formulas, Filmmaking, and the Studio System.* New York: Random House, 1981.

———. *Old Hollywood/New Hollywood: Ritual, Art, and Industry.* Ann Arbor: UMI Research Press, 1983.

———. "The New Hollywood." In *Film Theory Goes to the Movies.* Ed.

Jim Collins, Hilary Radner, and Ava Preacher Collins. New York: Routledge, 1993. 8–36.

Scheldahl, Peter. "*McCabe & Mrs. Miller*, a Sneaky Great Movie." *New York Times,* 24 July 1971, 11.

Schine, Cathleen. "Tanner '88." *Vogue,* July 1988, 48.

Scholes, Robert. *Fabulation and Metafiction.* Urbana: University of Illinois Press, 1979.

———. *Textual Power: Literary Theory and the Teaching of English.* New Haven, Conn.: Yale University Press, 1985.

———. *Protocols of Reading.* New Haven, Conn.: Yale University Press, 1989.

Schrader, Paul. "Notes on Film Noir." In *Film Genre Reader II.* Ed. Barry Keith Grant. Austin: University of Texas Press, 1995. 213–26.

Schreger, Charles. "Altman, Dolby, and the Second Sound Revolution." In *Film Sound: Theory and Practice.* Ed. Elisabeth Weis and John Belton. New York: Columbia University Press, 1985. 348–55.

Schroder, Alan. "*Thieves Like Us*: Altman and Tewkesbury's Faulkner." *Creative Screenwriting* 4 (fall 1997): 24–32.

Scott, A. O. "'Dr. T and the Women': Such Fascinating Creatures." *New York Times,* 13 October 2000. On-line at http://www.nytimes.com/2000/10/13/arts/13wome.html

Scott, Nathan A. *The Broken Center: Studies in the Theological Horizon of Modern Literature.* New Haven, Conn.: Yale University Press, 1966.

Searles, Hank. *The Pilgrim Project.* New York: Pocket Books, 1964.

Segal, Naomi. *The Unintended Reader: Feminism and Manon Lescault.* London: Cambridge University Press, 1986.

Seidenberg, Robert. "Vincent and Theo." *American Film* 15 (1990): 62–63.

Seidler, Victor J. *Rediscovering Masculinity: Reason, Language, and Sexuality.* New York: Routledge, 1989.

Self, Robert T. "Author, Text, and Self in *Buffalo Bill and the Indians.*" In *Ambiguities in Literature and Film.* Ed. Hans P. Braendlin. Gainesville: University Press of Florida, 1989. 104–16.

Shepard, Sam. *Fool for Love and Other Plays.* New York: Bantam, 1984.

Shulgasser, Barbara. "House of Altman (Making of *Ready to Wear*)." *Vanity Fair,* November 1994, 174–75.

Siegel, Sol Louis. "Secret Honor." *Video* 17 (1993): 57–58.

Silverman, Kaja. *The Subject of Semiotics.* New York: Oxford University Press, 1983.

———. *The Acoustic Mirror.* Bloomington: Indiana University Press, 1988.

———. *Male Subjectivity at the Margins.* New York: Routledge, 1992.

———. "Fragments of a Fashionable Discourse." In *On Fashion.* Ed. Shari Benstock and Suzanne Ferriss. New Brunswick, N.J.: Rutgers University Press, 1994. 183–96.

Simon, William G., and Louise Spence. "Cowboy Wonderland, History, and Myth: 'It Ain't All That Different Than Real Life.'" *Journal of Film and Video* 47 (spring-fall 1995): 67–80.

Siskel, Gene. "First Rate Fairy Tale for Adults." *Chicago Tribune,* 14 December 1980, 2.3.

———. "Altman Targets Hollywood in Masterful 'Player.'" *Chicago Tribune,* 24 April 1993, 7C.

———. "*Unzipped* Gives Open-Window View of Fashion Industry." *Chicago Tribune,* 18 August 1995, 7B.

Sklar, Robert. *Movie-Made America: A Cultural History of American Movies.* New York: Random House, 1975.

Smith, Gavin. "Faultlines of a Daydream Nation." *Film Comment* 29 (November 1993): 36–37.

Smith, Gavin, and Richard T. Jameson. "'The Movie You Saw Is the Movie We're Going to Make.'" *Film Comment* 28 (May/June 1992): 20–30.

Smith, Henry Nash. *Virgin Land: The American West as Symbol and Myth.* New York: Vintage, 1950.

Smith, Murray. "Theses on the Philosophy of Hollywood History." In *Contemporary Hollywood Cinema.* Ed. Steven Neale and Murray Smith. London: Routledge, 1998. 3–20.

Sobchack, Thomas. "Genre Film: A Classical Experience." *Literature/Film Quarterly* 3 (1975): 196–204.

Sobchack, Vivian. *Screening Space: The American Science Fiction Film, 1950–75.* South Brunswick, N.J.: A. S. Barnes, 1990.

Sorapure, Madeleine. "Being in the Midst: Italo Calvino's *If on a Winter's Night a Traveler.*" *Modern Fiction Studies* 31 (winter 1985): 702–9.

Spitz, Bob. "Rough Waters: Robert Altman's Best Film Has a Dark Undertow of Male Rage." *Mirabella,* September 1993, 68–71.

Sragow, Michael. "The Sad and Hilarious Tale of Dr. T and Big D." *Salon.com,* 12 October 2000. On-line at http://www.salon.com/ent/col/srag/2000/10/12/altman/index.html

Staiger, Janet. "The Politics of Film Canons." *Cinema Journal* 24 (spring 1985): 4–23.

———. "With the Compliments of the Auteur: Art Cinema and the Complexities of Its Reading Strategies." In *Interpreting Films: Studies in the Historical Reception of American Cinema.* Princeton, N.J.: Princeton University Press, 1992. 178–95.

Stam, Robert. *Reflexivity in Film and Literature: From Don Quixote to Jean-Luc Godard.* Ann Arbor: UMI Research Press, 1983.

Staples, Kate. "The Postmodern Always Rings Twice: Constructing the *Femme Fatale* in 90s Cinema." In *Women in Film Noir,* exp. ed. Ed. E. Ann Kaplan. London: British Film Institute, 1998. 164–82.

Stein, E. "The 21st New York Film Festival: Forbidden Revelations." *Film Comment* 19, no. 6 (1983): 74.

Sterritt, David. "Robert Altman." In *American Directors,* vol. 3. Ed. Jean Pierre Coureodon. New York: McGraw-Hill, 1983. 27–38.

———, ed. *Robert Altman Interviews.* Jackson: University Press of Mississippi, 2000.

Stevick, Philip. *Alternative Pleasures: Postrealist Fiction and the Tradition.* Urbana: University of Illinois Press, 1981.

Stewart, Garrett. "'The Long Goodbye' from 'Chinatown.'" *Film Quarterly* 29, no. 1 (1975): 25–32.

Stewart, James G. "The Evolution of Cinematic Sound: A Personal Report." In *Sound and the Cinema: The Coming of Sound to American Film.* Ed. Evan William Cameron. New York: Redgrave, 1980. 38–68.

Stewart, Robert. "Reimagining Raymond Carver on Film: A Talk with Robert Altman and Tess Gallagher." *New York Times Book Review,* 12 September 1993, 41–42.

Stull, William L. "Raymond Carver." In *Dictionary of Literary Biography Yearbook: 1988.* Ed. J. M. Brook. Detroit: Gale, 1989.

Sugg, Richard P. "The Role of the Writer in *The Player.*" *Literature/Film Quarterly* 22, no. 1 (1994): 11–15.

Suleiman, Susan. "Introduction: Varieties of Audience-Oriented Criticism." In *The Reader in the Text: Essays on Audience and Interpretation.* Ed. Susan Suleiman and Inge Grosman Suleiman. Princeton, N.J.: Princeton University Press, 1980. 3–45.

Summers, Anthony. *The Arrogance of Power: The Secret World of Richard Nixon.* New York: Viking, 2000.

Tarantino, Michael. "Movement as Metaphor: *The Long Goodbye.*" *Sight and Sound* 44 (spring 1975): 98–102.

Telotte, J. P. *Voices in the Dark: The Narrative Patterns of Film Noir.* Urbana: University of Illinois Press, 1989.

Terry, Bridget. *The Popeye Story.* New York: Dell, 1980.

Tewkesbury, Joan. *Nashville: An Original Screenplay.* New York: Bantam, 1976.

Thomas, Kevin. "Altman's Cast Fits to a T in 'Dr. T & the Women.'" *Los Angeles Times,* 13 October 2000. On-line at http://www.calendarlive.com/top/1,1419,L-LATimes-Movies-X!ArticleDetail-6985,00.html

Thompson, Kristin. *Storytelling and the New Hollywood: Understanding Classical Narrative Techniques.* Cambridge: Harvard University Press, 1999.

Thompson, Kristin, and David Bordwell. *Film History: An Introduction.* New York: McGraw-Hill, 1994.

Thomson, David. "Altman's Astonishing Decade." *New York Times,* 11 June 2000. On-line at http://www.nytimes.com/library/film/061100altman-films.html

Tibbetts, John. C. "Robert Altman: After 35 Years, Still the 'Action Painter' of American Cinema." *Literature/Film Quarterly* 20, no. 1 (1992): 36–42.

Tolkin, Michael. *The Player, The Rapture, The New Age: Three Screenplays.* New York: Grove, 1995.

Tompkins, Jane P. *Reader Response Criticism: From Formalism to Post-structuralism.* Baltimore: Johns Hopkins University Press, 1980.

Travers, Peter. "Vincent and Theo." *Rolling Stone,* 15 November 1990, 162–63.

———. "Robert Altman's *MASH.*" *Rolling Stone,* 14 October 1993, 125–27.

Tuska, John. *The Filming of the West.* Garden City, N.Y.: Doubleday, 1976.

Twain, Mark. *Roughing It.* Hartford, Conn.: American Publishing, 1880.

Tyderman, William, and Steven Price. *Wilde Salome.* Cambridge: Cambridge University Press, 1996.

Venturi, Robert. *Complexity and Contradiction in Architecture,* 2d ed. New York: Museum of Modern Art, 1977.

Venturi, Robert, Denise Scott Brown, and Steven Izenour. *Learning from Las Vegas: The Forgotten Symbolism of Architectural Form.* Cambridge: MIT Press, 1986.

Viertel, Jack, and David Walker. "The Long Road to Nashville." *New York Times,* 13 June 1975, 52–58.

Volpicelli, Lou. *Arts Visits with Robert Altman.* Documentary film. New York: ABC Video Enterprises, 1982.

Von Rhein, John. "The Lyric Goes Prospecting for Gold: Will *McTeague*

Prove There's Life in American Opera?" *Chicago Tribune,* 25 October 1992, 13.4–13.5.

———. "Golden Opera: Bolcom and Team Craft a Brilliant *McTeague* in World Premiere at Lyric." *Chicago Tribune,* 2 November 1992, 5.1, 5.3.

Von Ziegesar, Peter. "Robert Altman's Journey Home." *New York Times,* 27 August 1995, 2.9–2.10.

Vonnegut, Kurt Jr. *Breakfast of Champions.* New York: Dell, 1973.

———. "Nashville—A Shadow Play of What We Have Become and Where We Might Look for Wisdom." *Vogue,* June 1975, 103.

Wallace, Mike. Interview with Robert Altman. *60 Minutes,* CBS Television, 22 January 1978.

Warshow, Robert. *The Immediate Experience: Movies, Comics, Theatre, and Other Aspects of Popular Culture.* Garden City, N.Y.: Anchor-Doubleday, 1964.

Waters, Harry F. "Tanner '88." *Newsweek,* 15 February 1988, 82.

Watrous, Peter. "The Movies Miss Another . . . ." *New York Times,* 11 August 1996, 2.26.

Waugh, Patricia. *Metafiction: The Theory and Practice of Self-Conscious Fiction.* New York: Methuen, 1984.

Weinraub, Bernard. "Hollywood Captivated by an Altman Film about How Awful It Is." *New York Times,* 18 February 1992, C13, C18.

Weis, Elisabeth, and John Belton, eds. *Film Sound: Theory and Practice.* New York: Columbia University Press, 1985.

Westermeir, Clifford. "Buffalo Bill's Cowboys Abroad." *Colorado Magazine* 52 (fall 1975): 277–89.

Wexman, Virginia Wright. "Critical Survey." In Virginia Wright Wexman and Gretchen Bisplinghoff, *Robert Altman: A Guide to References and Resources.* Boston: C. K. Hall, 1984. 9–27.

———. *Creating the Couple: Love, Marriage, and Hollywood Performance.* Princeton, N.J.: Princeton University Press, 1993.

White, Hayden. *Tropics of Discourse: Essays in Cultural Criticism.* Baltimore: Johns Hopkins University Press, 1978.

Wicker, Tom. "*Nashville*: Dark Perceptions in a Country Music Comedy." *New York Times,* 15 June 1975, 2.1, 2.17.

———. *One of Us: Richard Nixon and the American Dream.* New York: Random House, 1991.

Wilde, Alan. *Horizons of Assent: Modernism, Postmodernism, and the Ironic Imagination.* Baltimore: Johns Hopkins University Press, 1981.

Wilde, Oscar. *Salomé.* In *The Complete Works: Stories, Plays, Poems and Essays.* New York: Harper & Row, 1989.

Wilden, Anthony. *The Language of the Self.* Baltimore: Johns Hopkins University Press, 1968.

———. *System and Structure: Essays in Communications and Exchange.* London: Tavistock, 1980.

Williams, Alan. "Is Sound Recording Like a Language?" *Yale French Studies* 60, no. 1 (1980): 51–66.

———. "Is a Radical Genre Criticism Possible?" *Quarterly Review of Film Studies* 9, no. 2 (1984): 121–25.

Williamson, Bruce. "Playboy Interview: Robert Altman." *Playboy,* August 1976, 53–68, 160.

Willis, Sharon. *High Contrast: Race and Gender in Contemporary Hollywood Film.* Durham, N.C.: Duke University Press, 1997.

Wills, Gary. *Nixon Agonistes: The Crisis of the Self-Made Man.* Boston: Houghton Mifflin, 1970.

Wilmington, Michael. "Laughing and Killing: Robert Altman and *The Player.*" *Sight and Sound* 61, no. 2 (1992): 10–15.

———. "Robert Altman's Best, for Real." In *Tanner '88* videodisc, vol. 1. Santa Monica, Calif.: Voyager, 1992.

———. "Short Cuts." In *Short Cuts* videodisc. Santa Monica, Calif.: Voyager, 1994.

———. "Altman Riffs on the Town That Inspired 'Kansas City.'" *Chicago Tribune,* 21 August 1996, 5.1, 5.5.

———. "Well Practiced: Altman's 'Dr. T & the Women.'" *Chicago Tribune,* 13 October 2000, 7.1.

Wimsatt, W. K. *The Verbal Icon: Studies in the Meaning of Poetry.* New York: Noonday, 1958.

Witcover, Jules. *The Resurrection of Richard Nixon.* New York: Putnam, 1970.

Wolfe, Naomi. *The Beauty Myth: How Images of Women Are Used against Women.* New York: William Morrow, 1991.

Wollen, Peter. *Signs and Meanings in the Cinema.* Bloomington: Indiana University Press, 1981.

———. "Godard and Counter Cinema: *Vent d'Est.*" In *Film Theory and Criticism: Introductory Readings,* 5th ed. Ed. Leo Braudy and Marshall Cohen. New York: Oxford University Press, 1999. 499–507.

Wolpin, Stewart. "M*A*S*H." *Video* 16 (1992): 67–68.

Wood, Michael. *America in the Movies: or, Santa Maria, It Had Slipped My Mind.* New York: Basic Books, 1975.

———. "Nashville Revisited: 2 Altmans." *Antioch Review* 24 (April 1976): 102–10.

Wood, Robin. "Smart-Ass and Cutie-Pie: Notes toward an Evaluation of Robert Altman." *Movie* 21 (autumn 1975): 1–17.

———. "Mad Smile of a Hollow Civilization: Robin Wood on *Buffalo Bill and the Indians.*" *Times Education Supplement,* 6 August 1976, 42.

———. *Hollywood from Vietnam to Reagan.* New York: Columbia University Press, 1986.

Wright, Will. *Sixguns and Society: A Structural Study of the Western.* Berkeley: University of California Press, 1975.

Wyatt, Justin. *High Concept: Movies and Marketing in Hollywood.* Austin: University of Texas Press, 1994.

———. "Economic Constraints/Economic Opportunities: Robert Altman as Auteur." *Velvet Light Trap* 38 (fall 1996): 52–67.

———. "The Formation of the 'Major Independent': Miramax, New Line and the New Hollywood." In *Contemporary Hollywood Cinema.* Ed. Steven Neale and Murray Smith. London: Routledge, 1998. 74–90.

———. "From Roadshowing to Saturation Release: Majors, Independents, and Marketing/Distribution Innovations." In *The New American Cinema.* Ed. Jon Lewis. Durham, N.C.: Duke University Press, 1998. 64–86.

Yacowar, Maurice. "Actors as Conventions in the Films of Robert Altman." *Cinema Journal* 20 (fall 1980): 14–28.

Yates, John. "Smart Man's Burden: *Nashville, A Face in the Crowd* and Popular Culture." *Journal of Popular Film* 5, no. 1 (1976): 19–28.

York, Susannah. *In Search of Unicorns.* London: Hodder & Stoughton, 1973.

Zacharek, Stephanie. "Dr. T & the Women." *Salon.com,* 13 October 2000. On-line at http://www.salon.com/ent/movies/review/2000/10/13/dr_t/index.html

Zatlin, Linda Gertner. *Aubrey Beardsley and Victorian Sexual Politics.* Oxford: Oxford University Press, 1990.

Zwonitzer, Mark. "Tanner '88." *Rolling Stone,* 5 May 1988, 30–32.

# Permissions

The University of Minnesota Press gratefully acknowledges permission to reprint the following previously published material in this book.

Portions of the introduction are revised from "Robert Altman and the Theory of Authorship," *Cinema Journal* 25, no. 1 (fall 1985): 3–11; copyright 1985 by the University of Texas Press.

Portions of chapter 2 are revised from "The Sound of *MASH,*" which originally appeared in *Close Viewings: Understanding Film,* edited by Peter Lehman (Gainesville: University Press of Florida, 1990), 141–57; copyright 1990. Reprinted with the permission of the University Press of Florida.

Portions of chapter 3 are revised from "Systems of Ambiguity in the Art Cinema," *Film Criticism* 4 (fall 1979): 74–80 (reprinted by permission of *Film Criticism*) and "The Art Cinema and Robert Altman," *Velvet Light Trap* 19 (winter 1982): 30–34 (copyright 1982 by the University of Texas Press).

Portions of chapter 4 are revised from "The Perfect Couple: 'Two Is Half of One' in the Films of Robert Altman," *Wide Angle* 5, no. 4 (1983): 30–37, copyright Ohio University, Athens Center for Film and Video. Reprinted with permission of Johns Hopkins University Press.

Portions of chapter 5 are revised from Robert T. Self and Terry F. Robinson, "Troubled Masculinity and Abusive Fathers: Duality and Duplicity in *The Gingerbread Man,*" *Journal of Film and Video* 52 (2000): 41–56. Reprinted with permission of *Journal of Film and Video.*

Portions of chapter 7 are revised from "Invention and Death: Commodities of Media in Robert Altman's *Nashville,*" *Journal of Popular Film* 5 (winter 1976): 273–88 (copyright 1976; published by Heldref

Publications, 1319 18th Street NW, Washington, D.C., 20036-1802, and reprinted with permission of the Helen Dwight Reid Educational Foundation) and "Author, Text, and Self in Robert Altman's *Buffalo Bill and the Indians,*" which originally appeared in *Ambiguities in Literature and Film,* edited by Hans Braendlin (Gainesville: University Press of Florida, 1989), 104–16 (copyright 1989; reprinted with the permission of the University Press of Florida).

Poetry from *Buffalo Bill and the Indians,* by Alan Rudolph and Robert Altman, copyright 1976 by Dino De Laurentiis Corporation. Used by permission of Bantam Books, a division of Random House, Inc.

Song lyrics from *One I Love You,* words and music by Ronee Blakley and Robert Altman, copyright 1975 Universal MCA Music Publishing, Inc., a division of Universal Studios, Inc. (ASCAP). International copyright secured. All rights reserved.

Song lyrics from *Dues,* words and music by Robert Altman, copyright 1975 Universal MCA Music Publishing, Inc., a division of Universal Studios, Inc. (ASCAP). International copyright secured. All rights reserved.

# Index

**Robert T. Self** is professor of English at Northern Illinois University. He is the author of *Barrett Wendell* and editor of *Literature, Society, and Politics: The Collected Essays of Barrett Wendell.* His articles have appeared in *New England Quarterly, Journal of Popular Film, Velvet Light Trap, Literature/Film Quarterly, Journal of Film and Video, Film Criticism,* and *Cinema Journal.*